ERIC E. WILLIAMS SPEAKS

OTHER BOOKS BY SELWYN R. CUDJOE

Resistance and Caribbean Literature
Movement of the People
A Just and Moral Society
V. S. Naipaul: A Materialist Reading
Caribbean Women Writers (edited collection)

Eric E. Williams SPEAKS

ESSAYS ON COLONIALISM AND INDEPENDENCE

Edited by Selwyn R. Cudjoe

Calaloux Publications • *Wellesley, Massachusetts*
Distributed by the University of Massachusetts Press • *Amherst*

Copyright © 1993 by Calaloux Publications
All rights reserved. Except for brief quotations in a review, this book or parts thereof, must not be reproduced in any form without permission in writing from the publisher. For information write: Calaloux Publications, P.O. Box 812028, Wellesley, Massachusetts 02181.

Distributed by the University of Massachusetts Press, Box 429, Amherst, Massachusetts 01004.

First published 1993 by Calaloux Publications.

International Standard Book Number (cloth) 0-87023-887-6
International Standard Book Number (paper) 0-87023-888-4
Library of Congress Catalog Card Number 93-17851

Printed in the United States of America

Library of Congress Cataloging-in-Publication Data
Williams, Eric Eustace, 1911–
    Eric E. Williams speaks / edited by Selwyn R. Cudjoe; additional essays by C. L. R. James, Erica Williams-Connell, and Selwyn R. Cudjoe.
        p. cm.
    Includes bibliographical references.
    ISBN 0-87023-887-6 (cloth)—ISBN 0-87023-888-4 (paper).
    1. Trinidad and Tobago—Politics and government.   2. Williams, Eric Eustace, 1911– .   I. Cudjoe, Selwyn Reginald.   II. Title.
F2121.W517 1993   93-17851
972.98304—dc20   CIP

The paper used in this publication meets the minimum requirements of the American National Standard for Permanence of Paper for Printed Library Materials Z39.48–1984.

*For Diane
and
Nello Mitchell, a PNM stalwart*

The beauty of the tropical night has assumed a new meaning for the thousands who storm the gates of the University [of Woodford Square]. The record of the past year [June 1955–June 1956] proves that the P.N.M. made no idle boast when, adopting the phraseology of unemployed seamen, it took as its motto: "The P.N.M. stands for Knowledgeism."

—PNM Weekly, June 1956

CONTENTS

Acknowledgments		vii
Introduction	Selwyn R. Cudjoe	1
Eric E. Williams and the Politics of Language	Selwyn R. Cudjoe	35
My Relations with the Caribbean Commission, 1943–1955	Eric E. Williams	111
The Case for Party Politics in Trinidad and Tobago	Eric E. Williams	167
Perspectives for Our Party	Eric E. Williams	207
Massa Day Done	Eric E. Williams	237
Independence Day Address	Eric E. Williams	265
The Chaguaramas Declaration	Eric E. Williams	271
Trinidad and the Revolution in Political Intelligence	George Lamming	317
A Convention Appraisal	C. L. R. James	327
Address to the PNM Women's League	Erica Williams-Connell	353
Bournes Road Address	Erica Williams-Connell	369
Appendix: The PNM and the University of Woodford Square: A Historical Record		397
Selected Bibliography		407
Contributors		417
Index		421

ACKNOWLEDGMENTS

A few persons read this book and encouraged me in seeing it through. Chief among them are Nello Mitchell, Jonathan Culler, Mario Cesareo, Anthony County, Roy Thomas, and Clement London. I thank them all for their assistance. I thank Erica Williams-Connell for her encouragement and the many photographs that she allowed us to use in this text. I would also like to thank Tricia Caesar for typing George Lamming's essay and the historical chronology of Williams's speeches from its original source. Thanks are also in order for Trudie Calvert, whose efficiency and insightfulness in her corrections are appreciated always, and Dennis F. Kulis, who carefully shepherded this project from infancy to maturity. I also thank the anonymous millions who made the PNM what it is and who thereby gave to the society a potent social and political organization. Without them this book would not have been possible.

NOTE ON TEXTS

All of Eric Williams's, C. L. R. James's, and George Lamming's essays have been taken from the original sources. Obvious typographical errors have been corrected, but capitalization and punctuation are retained as in the original. All other essays are published here for the first time.

INTRODUCTION
by Selwyn R. Cudjoe

Eric Williams addresses a political crowd at Woodford Square in 1956.

INTRODUCTION TO ERIC E. WILLIAMS SPEAKS
by Selwyn R. Cudjoe

> The party is conceived of as a vast educational agency equipped with an important research department, the data being presented in simple language and an attractive manner to the people to encourage them to form their own opinions. This will involve a party newspaper, party information leaflets and newsletters, party pamphlets, to serve as the basis of discussion groups within the party. The party recognises that to educate is to emancipate.
> —Eric Williams, *The Case for Party Politics in Trinidad and Tobago*

Even though I had thought of republishing Eric Williams's most important essays on colonialism for quite some years, the task of such a publication did not seem as urgent until I visited Trinidad during the last two weeks of May 1992.[1] Four events that seemed to reflect a retrogression in the political discourse of the national life demanded that these addresses be republished. I have always believed that 1955–62 was one the most important periods in the life of the society, a time when the People's National Movement, as the vanguard political organization of our society, embodied the aspirations of its people. Although I am not inclined to attribute the total significance of that period to any one individual (I believe that the important collective efforts of the People's Education Movement under De Wilton Rogers and John Donaldson, Sr., have not been properly appreciated)[2] I believe that Eric Williams's articulation of the colonial problematic and his understanding of the sociopolitical needs of the society dur-

---

[1] Eric Williams, leader of the People's National Movement (Trinidad and Tobago), became the first premier (1956–62) and Prime Minister (1962–81) of the society.

[2] See De Wilton Rogers, *The Rise of the People's National Movement*, Vol. 1 (Port of Spain: De Wilton Rogers, n.d.), for a discussion of the work of the People's Education Movement and the work that led up to the formation of the PNM.

Introduction

ing that period are yet to be surpassed by any contemporary politician or political organization. To this author, his theorizing of our social and political conditions is even more relevant when contrasted with the confused articulation of the present political directorate and the confused intellectual emanations that are being presented via our local media.[3]

The first event that reflected the political decline into which the society has descended was reflected in an article by Morgan Job that was published in the *Bomb* on May 15, 1992. Speaking in the aftermath of the Los Angeles rebellion in the United States, Job made the following comment:

> The problem in LA [Los Angeles], as in those areas of T&T [Trinidad and Tobago] with a similar culture is how to make those people abandon a culture [presumably, self-imposed] which is destructive—how to make those people more productive. THERE IS NO WAY KNOWN TO MAN TO SAVE a people who do not want to save themselves, and to save illiterate, amoral, savage, ghetto blacks, wherever they are, from their rampage of murder, looting, raping, and breeding all the little girls they can, demands HONESTY. In fact every urban ghetto must solve the same problems. IT'S NOT A PROBLEM CONFINED TO THE BLACK PEOPLE.[4]

When I first read those words I was taken aback. The confused jumbling of his prose was one thing, but the vulgarity of the sentiments contained therein was another. I was not sure if Job was serious or whether I was witnessing a spoof, a parodic takeoff on a recent incident. After reading this article about three times,

---

[3] One needs to point out the important work that is being done by Selwyn Ryan, Maxie Cuffie, Lloyd Best, Merle Hodge, Raffique Shah, and others and the vigorous debate that takes place in the local newspaper on questions of race, ethnicity, and such matters.

[4] "We Must Face the Facts, Change the Culture," p. 7.

it occurred to me that Job was in dead earnest and meant everything he said. On May 22 Maxie Cuffie offered a rather intelligent response in which he pointed out the folly of Job's proposition. In a telling introduction Cuffie observed that "Michael Jackson permed his hair, straightened his nose, lifted his cheeks, cleft his chin, bleached his skin, then looked at the man in the mirror and sang: 'It doesn't matter if you're Black or White. Yeah, yeah, yeah.' Dr. Morgan Job has abandoned the cosmetics but seems of like mind."[5] Yet the enormous amount of vulgarity contained in Job's prose pointed to the diminished sense of national purpose that seemed to be reflected in those activities. Indeed, the crude national political debate had assumed a life of its own and my intervention did not seem likely to change things very much. I had promised not to respond to Job if only because I felt repulsed by the vulgarity of his article and his cunningly depraved ideological move of beginning the article by condemning "those people" in one sentence and, by the end of the following sentence, collapsing "those people" into "a people," thereby condemning an entire racial group for what seemed to be a necessary and indispensable human response to oppression: the recourse to rebellion. In fact, they would have acted in a manner less than human if they allowed the barbarities that were and are committed against them daily to continue unabated. It would be of no importance to Job that the Irish rebellion that took place in New York in 1863 possessed very much the same ingredients as that which occurred in Los Angeles in 1992.[6] But these Irish people were considered neither animals nor savages. They merely responded to real and/or perceived injustices against them and thus gained a nation's respect as a people.

---

[5] "Having Patience with Job," *Trinidad Guardian,* May 22, 1992. It is important that in an unsigned position in the *Express,* the Trinidad and Tobago Chamber of Industry and Commerce felt it necessary to respond to Cuffie's article of the above date (see "Money Not the Answer," *Express,* June 4, 1992). The seriousness with which Job is taken was reflected in a column by another reporter who praised Job for his honesty and fearlessness (see Kamal Persad, "This Prophet Deserves Honour," *Sunday Express,* June 28, 1992).

[6] See *New York Times,* May 29, 1992 (Letter to the editor).

Introduction

Another striking aspect of the overall frame of the article was its attempt to condemn and defame the contributions that Williams made to national life, a continuing preoccupation of Job as I have been made to understand.[7] For example, Job begins his article by accusing Williams of "lying again for the benefit of humouring hungry and ignorant black people" when Williams brought to the attention of "cheering black people in Woodford Square" that "the blackest thing in slavery was not the black man." Job does not complete the other part of Williams's thought but goes on to invoke Selwyn Ryan, an important Trinidadian thinker, to argue that through his remarks on slavery Williams was "managing the politics of the community." The excerpt of *Massa Day Done*, from which the above quote is taken, was made to appease his white audience rather than "the hungry and ignorant black people" and read in part, "If Massa was generally white, not all whites were Massa, at the same time . . . whilst massa remained, his complexion became darker."[8] Apart from not examining what Williams said or meant, Job is comfortable enough to pose the almost irrelevant, childlike, and defamatory statement, not about Eric Williams, who is his main target of rebuke and ridicule, but at Erica Williams-Connell, Williams's daughter, which would seem to be the cheapest of the cheapest shots, but then again vulgarity knows no limits when it is on the rampage. He asks: "Did Erica Williams ever date any black man from Laventille, or Troumacaque or Beetham Flats? Do you hold that against her if she did not, or the fact that she is now married to a white man." Of what relevance is such diatribe and what purpose does it serve in public discourse? Isn't Erica Williams-Connell's choice of a mate her own private business and should it be the subject of public debate when she does not even live in the island?

Within that same week, *Think Again*, Job's book of essays, was launched at the Trinidad Country Club, "the first book-launching

---

[7] See, for example, his continuing diatribe against Williams in *Think Again* (El Socorro, San Juan: Alkebu Industries, 1991).

[8] See *Massa Day Done* in this volume.

there within living memory."⁹ According to Anthony Milne, who covered the event, "The only invited speaker who didn't show, whose presence would have completed a major media coup, was U.S. ambassador, Sally Cowal. Instead, she sent Dr. Norman Antokol to talk, at length and without notes, on security."[10] To my mind, such a powerful coincidence of events was not arbitrary. It spoke of an unusual alliance that was being formed to denigrate black people in the society. Indeed, Kamal Persad's description of Job as "a modern version of an Old Testament Judaic prophet" who "has a very disturbing effect on a lot of people, especially Africans," and who is concerned about "black advancement," should make many leery and put every politically conscious citizen on his or her guard.[11] Anyone who condemns "an entire generation of Afro-Caribbean intellectuals [George Lamming, Eric Williams, C.L.R. James, Walter Rodney, George Beckford]" and is lauded for so doing is neither prophet nor scribe: he has simply sold his birthright for a mess of pottage and thirty pieces of silver.[12]

It is easy to conclude that Job's sentiments about black people, despite the disclaimer in bold type that the behavior exhibited in Los Angeles is "NOT A PROBLEM CONFINED TO THE BLACK PEOPLE," is negative in that it is only black people that Job feels emboldened to attack. The white elite at the Trinidad Country Club (both as sponsors and those who supported this effort by attending) felt emboldened enough to honor the ideas of a person whose sole function is to denigrate African people, whose only purpose is to act the role of an intellectual dilettante, and to assume the charlatan's prose and pose in the process.

---

[9] "Counterblast to the 'Fabian Consensus,'" *Express*, May 25, 1992.

[10] Ibid.

[11] Kamal Persad, "This Prophet Deserves Honour." See also Kim Johnson, "Inside Job's Treasure Trove," *Sunday Express*, June 21, 1992.

[12] Persad, "This Prophet Deserves Honour."

Introduction

The second striking incident that assaulted my sensibilities has to do with the sentiments expressed by Patrick Manning, prime minister of Trinidad and Tobago, and, by virtue of his being the leader of the People's National Movement (PNM), the heir of Williams's political legacy. In an address to the PNM's St. Ann's East Constituency, Manning declared, as though it were self-evident, that the days of fighting "'the old colonial masters,' transnational corporations and the private sector are over."[13] Drawing on the sentiments of the old Negro spiritual, he sounded almost as Poor Ole Joe himself when he noted:

> The enemies of the PNM are hunger, starvation, poverty and unemployment, not the private sector.... In order to have employees you must have employers. There is no point in getting into any confrontational mode with employers....
>
> Gone are the days where we are fighting colonial masters, we won that battle long ago. Gone are the days where we have to continually view transnational corporations with suspicion, today we are much more experienced and much more confident in our ability to deal on an even basis with these organisations.[14]

Coming from the leader of a political party whose most significant achievement was its ability to bring a considerable amount of the economic activity of the society under the arm of the state, it is extremely puzzling to hear such a statement especially when the electorate of Trinidad and Tobago voted in large numbers to remove a party that was committed to the "privatisation" of the economy. Coupled with his government's program of "liberalisation," which essentially opens up the economy to all and sundry, the outlook of the "new PNM" seems frighteningly

---

[13] "Days of Fighting 'Colonial Masters' Are Over, Says PM," *Express*, May 25, 1992.

[14] Ibid.

close to that of the National Alliance for Reconstruction (NAR) government. Indeed, a close adviser in the inner sanctum of the Manning inner circle declared to this author that the "PNM was merely the NAR with a human face." She considered this a compliment to Manning, but given his desire to continue as the former government had done she did not seem too far off course.

That wasn't all. On his return from meetings with the IMF and the World Bank, if the reports of the *Trinidad Guardian* are to be believed, Manning promised "to divest some of its [the government's] assets in order to pay off debts to international agencies." Such divestment, he noted "would begin in the petrochemical sector with ammonia, methanol and urea."[15] Within three weeks of that announcement, members of the International Finance Corporation (IFC), a subsidiary of the World Bank, were in Trinidad to advise the government on the best course of divestment. As Ken Valley, the acting finance minister, noted, "Cabinet had agreed to invite the team to talk with Government to develop proposals for assisting Government in its divestment undertakings." The IFC team met with officials of Fertrin, the methanol plant, Trinidad and Tobago Oil Company (Trintoc), Trinidad and Tobago Petroleum Company Limited (Trinitopec), and other related companies. Although Mr. Manning and his government have not spelled out their plans, it has become evident that his government intends to dismantle everything that Williams had sought to do: that is, to build a petrochemical base upon which a small economy could at least begin to talk about its economic and political autonomy. Such a course of independent development does not seem to resonate well with Manning, who seems to be intent on continuing the job of dismantling the state sector which the NAR government began. Although George Harvey might have written in jest or jaded irony, he seemed to have captured the essence of the new PNM when he shouted "Free at last! Free at

---

[15] John Babb, "Money from Divestment to Pay off Debts," *Trinidad Guardian*, May 19, 1992.

Introduction

last! I almost shouted the salutations on behalf of the born-again People's National Movement (PNM) last week." [16] He continued:

> I grew up in a PNM-created atmosphere in which business operations were viewed with suspicions and all businessmen as not wholly honest or nice people.
>
> It was a period too when the PNM felt that the only way to fuel sustainable economic growth was to funnel billions of petro-dollars in State-operated schemes. Private sector was only intended to play a complementary role to the monetary adventures of Government.
>
> So when new Prime Minister Manning brought the economic and business policy into sharper focus *it was a recanting of the operations of the old PNM.*[17]

While I do not think that the economic position postulated by Harvey is quite correct, the point seems to be made with a clarity that I could not have offered: the new PNM, under Mr Manning, recants the economic policy of the old PNM, under Eric Williams. According to Harvey, the new watchwords are: "trade liberalisation and open market economy."[18]

As benign and as salutary as such positions may sound, placed side by side with the rise of this new "savage class" of "animals," as Job calls the scrunting masses of Laventille and other such areas, it is very clear that black (read African masses) are under attack from the dominant class. Yet we remain under the illusion that all is well, that the effects of colonialism are behind us, that the outlines of a new social order have been forged and all we have to do is to open up the society to all and sundry under the guise of liberalization. Despite the Alien Land Holding

---

[16] "PNM in a Business Suit," *Sunday Guardian,* May 24, 1992.

[17] Ibid. Emphasis added.

[18] Ibid.

Act that was designed to keep the lands of our country in the hands of nationals, land is being bought up by non-Trinidadians in a way that suggests that most of the best lands will be out of local hands if progressive and positive action is not taken soon to stop such a situation.[19] Tobago remains a place where the worse excesses are taking place. Colonialism, we are told, is no longer a factor in the equation. On his part, Job continues to maintain that "no amount of rubbish about slavery, racism and colonialism will save black people from self-inflicted degradation and destruction," which, at least on this issue, puts Manning on the same side with Morgan Job and the Trinidad and Tobago Chamber of Industry and Commerce.

There is a further consideration entangled with the doctrine of "trade liberalisation" and an "open market economy." There is evidence aplenty that such approaches to economic development in a period of adjustment do not necessarily work in the best interest of the country, as the present tug-of-war between Japan and the United States suggests. But there is an example closer at home. In an insightful article, "Perspectives on Adjustment-Type Programmes and Economic Development in the Third World with Special Reference to the Caribbean," Kari Levitt recognized the difficult choices that we, as a small economy, have to make during the present period of adjustment and notes our vulnerability to what she calls "the balance of payments disequilibria" brought to the fore by the difficult issue of "how the burden [of adjustment] is to be distributed between classes and sectors of society" and most critically "who decides, by what process are policies determined, [and] whose interests are served [by the policies of adjustment?]"[20] Drawing on the Jamaican example of 1985 in which the debt/GNP ratio reached 195 percent, and debt/

---

[19] The Alien Land Holding Act was repealed in 1990 and replaced by The Foreign Investment Act that allowed non-citizens to buy lands without even applying for a license.

[20] A feature address delivered at A Regional Public Policy Symposium, hosted by MCT and Associates Ltd., Port of Spain, Trinidad, May 1992. All other quotes by Levitt are taken from this article.

Introduction

export ratio reached 273 percent, one of the highest in the world, Levitt noted that Jamaica had found itself in a "TOTAL DEBT TRAP ... forced to accept *every imaginable liberalization conditionality which could possibly have been required of any country.*"

In layman's terms what Levitt means is that Jamaica's debt is almost twice as much as the value of goods and services the society produces or close to three times Jamaica's exports. The Trinidad and Tobago case is not as bad as the Jamaican situation, but it is very clear that the liberalization of Jamaica's economy and the opening up of the island's market to foreigners did not lead to the salvation of the society or dynamic economic growth. It simply led to the weakening of the Jamaican economy and left it more firmly in the hands of foreigners and with a debt it would never be able to repay. Despite the liberalization of trade policies, the people of the country grew more impovished seeking to rival the people of Haiti and Guyana. In this context, Levitt's warning is important. She says:

> Under pressure from the local private sector, and as a *conditionality* required by the Inter American Development Bank—now an important U.S., policy instrument—and again as a *conditionality* required by the Enterprise of the Americas Initiative (EAI) for debt forgiveness Jamaica liberalized the exchange rate regime in September 1991. Jamaica was advised that this would result in the return flow of dollars parked in foreign accounts. Well, the pundits were wrong; a speculative attack on the Jamaican currency brought the country to the brink of political and social breakdown by early April 1992, as the [Jamaican] dollar broke through the 30 to one barrier.
>
> Under the tutelage of the IFIs and USAID, Jamaica has now made adjustments that have transformed the socioeconomic model of the postcolonial era to privilege speculators and traders and has impovished the mass of the people, including its middle classes. The government

is now unable to provide the most basic social services, including education and health. That was the situation before the most recent budget, which will reduce the public service by 8,000 persons and further cut budgetary allocations for social expenditures. Jamaica has adjusted to achieve an overall public sector deficit of about 1 percent GNP, composed of a *surplus* of some 3 percent GNP on central government and public enterprises, to offset Bank of Jamaica losses of some 6 percent due to the operation of monetary policy. The public sector is now programmed for *negative* domestic borrowing matched by continuing external grants and loans.

Jamaica is bound hand and foot to the Washington-based agencies, with no prospect of an end in sight. The government is emasculated. Patronage in the ghettos is increasingly dispensed by the dons. With financial and exchange rate liberalization, the stability of the currency now depends on whether the major private sector exporters will join Butch Stewart in undertaking responsibility for holding the exchange rate at some predetermined level. Jamaica has reached the zenith of liberalization and privatization. The exchange rate now depends on the patriotism of the large-scale private sector and the commercial banks, which made a pile of money in currency trading in the speculation against the Jamaican dollar. Is this to be the model for Trinidad and Tobago? I most sincerely hope not.

Levitt notes further that the people of the Caribbean have experienced a decade and a half in which scores of countries have gone through what has been called structural adjustment. In light of those experiences, she warns that we do not "sell out our patrimony—our physical assets and our heritage of pride in our country and independence of spirit which has been the contribution of former generations of political leaders who sought to take these countries from political to economic independence." Obviously, the reference here is to the leaders who pioneered the independence of the society and whose major emphasis has been the desire of Trinidadians and Tobagonians to undertake as autonomous a path to development as possible. It certainly does not mean selling out national assets to private corporations, both national and international.

I have quoted Levitt at length if only to demonstrate that Manning, Job, and the Trinidad and Tobago Chamber of Industry and Commerce are really in the same boat. Their design, both explicitly and implicitly, is to lead the country down the wrong path, back to an age of slavery as Erol McCloud, president of the Oilfield Workers Trade Union (OWTU), has warned; back into an era when private enterprise reigned supreme and black men and women were hewers of wood and drawers of water. Given this scenario, the only future we can hope for is one in which African people are made into homeless vagabonds, vagrants, and scrunters in a land that their mothers and fathers made, living in a state of animality and savagery which Job considers the true vocation of African people in the Caribbean. And if one has any notion that the middle classes are to be exempt from such prognostications one only has to recognize that in Jamaica, as Levitt noted, even the middle classes became impoverished victims of the IMF and the World Bank.

The third incident has to with two columns that appeared in the *Express* in which the attempt was made to reduce Walter Rodney, one of the most important sons of the Caribbean, to a "failed Marxist," whatever that means, in its story "Rodney No Role Model." The article argues that *How Europe Underdeveloped Africa*, one of Rodney's most polemical works, "offers no original ideas. It is an expansion of the Marxist theme, that European wealth was accumulated through the plunder of the peoples of the New World and the profit of plantations based on slave

---

[21] *Express*, April 23, 1992.

labour. The accuracy or otherwise of this Marxist analysis is still in dispute."[21] To the Chamber of Commerce it does not matter that W. E. B Du Bois's *Black Reconstruction in America* (1935), Eric Williams's *Capitalism and Slavery* (1942), C. L. R. James's *The Black Jacobins* (1938), Robin Blackburn's *Overthrow of Colonial Slavery, 1776–1848* (1988), with a certain degree of congruence, have all demonstrated that capitalism was built on the backs of slaves in the sugarcane and cotton plantations of the New World. It takes an unsigned column by the Trinidad and Tobago Chamber of Industry and Commerce, those apostles of private enterprise, to tell us that all of the wisdom that was acquired from 1956 through 1992 was really a belief in false doctrines and that two of the pioneers of the ideological doctrines of contemporary Trinidad and the Caribbean, Williams and James, were wrong all along. What they wish to tell us is that the members of the Chamber of Commerce and Industry are our champions and always have had our best interest at heart. Today, like Moses of old, they have arisen to save "the hapless people of the Caribbean."[22]

In a second article entitled "We Need New Heroes," the Chamber of Commerce and Industry goes on to tell us that Rodney's political philosophy of the 1960s was irrelevant "to the problems posed for Caribbean survival in the decades of the nineties.... A memorial of Walter Rodney would be a memorial to failure and the evocation of a dead cause. It is not capitalism or white people but the ideas of Walter Rodney and those who think like him that have kept the Caribbean floundering in the backwater of progress, blindly striking out at imagined enemies."[23] Could anyone in his or her right mind believe that it is the ideas of Walter Rodney "and those like him" who have kept the Caribbean in the backwater of progress? And since Rodney is a spiritual descendant of Toussaint L'Ouverture, Paul Bogle, Marcus Garvey, José Marti, Arthur Cipriani, Cola Rienzi, Eric Williams, Albizu Cam-

---

[22] Ibid.

[23] *Express*, May 21, 1992.

Introduction

pos, and other such heroes, are we now to be told that it was the ideas of these great patriots that have "kept the Caribbean floundering in the backwater of progress"? Are we now to be told that slavery and colonialism were not so bad after all and that, indeed, all along white people had all these goodies in store for us? That, indeed, in the dawning of this neocapitalist age, under the tutelage of the Chamber of Industry and Commerce, that all would be well. Are we to believe that the treadmill, the cat-o-nine tails, and the brutality practiced against black people didn't exist? Are we to disregard the eyewitness accounts of Mary Prince of Bermuda, Ashton Warner of St. Vincent and James Williams of Jamaica, accounts of brutality during slavery, all written during the early part of the nineteenth century?[24] In 1993, are we to believe that these things never happened and the accounts of brutality against Caribbean peoples contained in Bartoleme de Las Casas's *Devastation of the Indies,* Theodore Weld's *American Slavery as It Is,* or James's *The Black Jacobins* never occurred? For the sake of accuracy, let the record show three examples of the brutality that were practiced against our ancestors, and I dare the Chamber of Industry and Commerce and Job to demonstrate that these instances of brutality had nothing to do with the social, spiritual, and cultural development of Caribbean peoples. In the process, I wish to ask the members of the Chamber of Commerce and Industry if Walter Rodney and his kind were responsible for the following brutal acts against the nonwhite people of the Caribbean.

Our first account of such brutality is given by Bartoleme de las Casas, a Spanish bishop who accompanied Columbus to the Caribbean:

> Some of the secular Spaniards who have been here for many years say that the goodness of the Indians is unde-

---

[24] See *The History of Mary Prince, A West Indian Slave* (London: F. Westley and A. H. Davis, 1831), *Negro Slavery Described by a Negro, Being the Narrative of Ashton Warner, a Native of St. Vincent's* (London: Samuel Maunder, 1831), and James Williams, *A Narrative of Events, since the First of August, 1834* (London: J. Rider, 1838).

niable and that if this gifted people could be brought to know the one true God they would be the most fortunate people in the world.

Yet into this sheepfold, into this land of meek outcasts there came some Spaniards who immediately behaved like ravening wild beasts, wolves, tigers, or lions that had been starved for many days. And Spaniards have behaved in no other way during the past forty years [1511–51], down to the present time, for they are still acting like ravening beasts, killing terrorizing, afflicting, torturing, and destroying the native peoples, doing all this with the strangest and most varied new methods of cruelty, never seen or heard before, and to such a degree that this Island of Hispaniola, once so populous (having a population that I estimated to be more than three millions), has now a population of barely two hundred persons....

The reason for killing and destroying such an infinite number of souls is that the Christians have an ultimate aim, which is to acquire gold, and to swell themselves with riches in a very brief time and thus rise to a high estate disproportionate to their merits. It should be kept in mind that their insatiable greed and ambition, the greatest ever seen in the world, is the cause of their villainies. And also, those lands are so rich and felicitous, the native peoples so meek and patient, so easy to subject, that our Spaniards have no more consideration for them than beasts. And I say this from my own knowledge of the acts I witnessed. But I should not say "than beasts" for, thanks be to God, they have treated beasts with some respect; I should say instead like excrement on the public square.[25]

---

[25] Bartoleme de Las Casas, *The Devastation of the Indies,* trans. Bill M. Donovan (Baltimore: Johns Hopkins Press, 1992), pp. 29–32.

Introduction

The second account is offered by James, the "armchair socialist," as the Chamber of Commerce called him:

> There was no ingenuity that fear or a depraved imagination could devise which was not employed to break their spirit [the spirit of the slaves] and satisfy the lusts and resentment of their owners and guardians—irons on the hands and feet, blocks of wood that the slaves had to drag behind them wherever they went, the tin-plate mask designed to prevent the slaves from eating the sugarcane, the iron collar. Whipping was interrupted in order to pass a piece of hot wood on the buttocks of the victim; salt, pepper, citron, cinders, aloes, and hot ashes were poured on the bleeding wounds. Mutilations were common, limbs, ears and sometimes the private parts, to deprive them of the pleasures which they could indulge in without expense. Their masters poured burning wax on their arms and hands and shoulders, emptied the boiling cane sugar over their heads, burned them alive, roasted them on slow fires, filled them with gunpowder and blew them up with a match; buried them up to the neck and smeared their heads with sugar that the flies might devour them; fastened them to nests of ants and wasps; made them eat their excrement, drink their urine, and lick the saliva of other slaves. One colonialist was known in moments of anger to throw himself on his slaves and stick his teeth into their flesh.[26]

The third account, observed by Sarah M. Grimké, a daughter of Judge Grimké, a member of the supreme court of South Carolina, speaks to the contradictory impulses of slavery and the specific brutality practiced against our women:

---

[26] C. L. R. James, *The Black Jacobins* (New York: Vintage, 1989), pp. 12–13.

A handsome mulatto woman, about 18 or 20 years of age, whose independent spirit could not brook the degradation of slavery, was in the habit of running away: for this offence she had been repeatedly sent by her master and mistress to be whipped by the keeper of the Charleston work-house. This had been done with such inhuman severity, as to lacerate her back in a most shocking manner; a finger could not be laid between the cuts. But the love of liberty was too strong to be annihilated by torture; and, as a last resort, she was whipped at several different times, and kept a close prisoner. A heavy iron collar, with three long prongs projecting from it, was placed round her neck, and a strong and sound front tooth was extracted, to serve as a mark to describe her, in case of escape. Her sufferings at this time was agonizing; she could lie in no position but on her back, which was sore from scourgings, as I can testify, from personal inspection, and her only place of rest was the floor, on a blanket. These outrages were committed in a family where the mistress daily read the scriptures, and assembled her children for family worship. She was accounted, and was really, so far as alms-giving was concerned, a charitable woman, and tender hearted to the poor; and yet this suffering slave, who was the seamstress of the family, was continually in her presence, sitting in her chamber to sew, or engage in her other household work, with lacerated and bleeding back, her mutilated mouth, and heavy iron collar, without, so far as appeared, exciting any feelings of compassion.[27]

Against these accounts, the Chamber of Commerce and others would still like us to believe that black people have been living in a world of make-believe when they say that white people,

---

[27] "Narrative and Testimony of Sarah M. Grimké," in *American Slavery as It Is: Testimony of a Thousand Witnesses* (New York: American Anti-Slavery Society, 1839, rpt. 1968), p. 22.

Introduction

slavery, and colonial-capitalism were unkind to them. After all, these forms of social organization always had the best interest of Afro- and Indo-Caribbean peoples at heart and now we merely carry on this delusionary behavior in religiocultural practices such as Shango, Rastafarism, and Myalism. Williams, James, Norman Manley, T. A. Marryshow, A. R. F. Webber, C. D. Rawle and others were liars. Today, more than ever, if we wish to be free, all we need to do is to embrace the economic policies of the Chambers of Commerce and Industry, the transnational corporations, the IFCs, and the private enterprise firms. Only their know-how can set us free. All we have to do is to believe in their moral prescriptions and the purity of their intent and all would be well with us.

Such an assault on our intelligence would not be so bad if we knew that the political party that was elected to govern our affairs was of a different persuasion and was pursuing a different ideological line. But we open the newspapers and are told by the leader of the PNM very much what the Chambers of Industry and Commerce are saying: colonialism is no longer the problem (those days are over), the enemy of the PNM is not private enterprise (so workers and employers must unite); the salvation of the people does not lie in their hands but in the private sector and its leaders, the very group that defames and ridicules the persons who brought us out of the house of bondage and the lion's den. That the Chamber of Industry and Commerce defends Morgan Job so assiduously and the Trinidad Country Club finds his rehashed daily columns so erudite and elevating in their scholarly content must mean that Job, the personification of hard and honest thinking, must be seen as one of our new intellectual role models. At any rate, that is the conclusion the Chamber of Industry and Commerce would like us to draw.

In this present stage of our social and political development, it is very clear that no black revolutionary symbol is free from the contempt of the reactionaries who roam in our midst. They will not be satisfied until their defamation of our people is complete and our most sacred political symbols are desecrated. I suspect the next target will be C. L. R. James, followed in short order by Eric Williams. Already, Job has begun to desecrate the memory of Williams. When the luminance from the stars of Williams, Rodney, and James begin to fade who will stand in the wings to replace them? Who, then, would designate who our heroes should be? Would it be the members of the Chambers of Industry and Commerce or the revolutionary parties created by our people, in their wisdom, to articulate and serve our best interest?

Such rewriting of history is a very interesting phenomenon. It reminds me of a recent biographical sketch of William Burnley, the largest slaveholder of Trinidad and Tobago, in which the latter was described as "an entrepreneur." V. S. Naipaul, a Trinidadian writer who makes no claim to progressive extremism, describes Burnley's early beginnings in Trinidad in the following manner:

> It was also noted, after laughter at the discomfiture of the plunderers of widows and orphans, that fortunes were beginning to disappear. All property in dispute and all dead men's estates and moneys had been passing into the hands of an official called the depositario. In a year property worth £180,000 had so passed, and only £4,000 had been heard of again. The depositario was a 'young Virginian gentleman, William Burnley; he was laying the foundations of the biggest and most enduring Trinidad fortune. He became so rich so quickly that he was soon being called in to advise the government about this and that; in racial matters he even became liberal. Smith said that moneys taken in by the depositario went to a receiver in London and were invested in government securities; estates in Trinidad were managed by the depositario. "Managed": it was the word that frightened local men of property, some of whom had started as managers.[28]

---

[28] V. S. Naipaul, *The Loss of El Dorado* (London: Andre Deutsch, 1969), p. 287.

Introduction

In *Movement of the People,* I demonstrated how both before and after slavery Burnley made thousands of pounds from his estates, his having received almost £50,000 pounds from the £20 million pounds Britain gave to the owners of slaves in the British Caribbean.[29] Yet we are to infer from the logic of the Chamber of Commerce that it was Walter Rodney and his kind, rather than U.S.-born William Burnley, who ripped us off for millions, who are the enemies of the people of the Caribbean.

Thus, in contemporary Trinidad and Tobago, we are finding a curious twist to our history: our heroes become villains and the villains become heroes. In the age of liberalization our prime minister does not stand unequivocally behind the progressive nationalism for which the PNM stood in 1955 when they supported the aims and aspirations of the Bandung Conference. Instead, he is accused of plagiarizing speeches about Williams rather than composing his own. It would seem that he cannot even speak spontaneously about the aspirations of which the founder of his own party stood.

Such a chaotic state of affairs brings me to the fourth incident that dramatized the importance of reprinting Williams's early essays, James's comments about Williams and Erica Williams-Connell's striking comments about her father's legacy. It has everything to do with the publication of *Magnum,* a three-page spread that appears in the *Trinidad Guardian* every two weeks or so. "The official organ of the People's National Movement," this newsspread is supposed to present/expose the point of view of the PNM to the nation. I have never spoken at length with Eric Williams, but I shudder to imagine what he or James would have thought of having the views of the PNM disseminated via the pages of the *Trinidad Guardian.*

---

[29] See Selwyn R. Cudjoe, *Movement of the People* (Tacarigua: Calaloux Publications, 1983), especially "Slavery, Colonialism Independence, 'the Same Khaki Pants': The Exploitation of the Working People Continues," pp. 97–120.

To put this travesty in perspective one must read two essential documents that are associated with the PNM: Williams's "Perspectives for Our Party" (1958) and James's *PNM Go Forth* (1960), later amended to read *Party Politics in the West Indies*. Since the former was prepared at a time when Williams and James enjoyed a very special friendship, these ideas must be seen as coming out of the special intellectual/theoretical alliances at one of the most advanced stages of the progressive nationalist movement in Trinidad and Tobago. Such a travesty becomes even greater when one tries to understand the manner in which the PNM was conceived and what a progressive nationalist party is supposed to stand for. It was always understood by the PNM faithful that not only was the party separate from the government but the party had a distinct function to play vis-à-vis the education of its members and the society, that the task of the party—being the most advanced consciousness of the society—was to mold the consciousness of its members and ultimately to lead the society in the direction it ought to go. Such a task could be accomplished in only one way: through the active and intensive propagandizing of the party's views through the publication of a party newspaper whereby the views of the party could be argued over, shaped, and subsequently advanced by the larger community. Without such an organ a party does not have the right to call itself a party. As my brother Giles would say, "it just doesn't qualify" for such a name. Without an organ that actively advances the ideas, goals, and objectives of a party, a party is not worthy of existing. In other words, the presence of a party newspaper distinguishes a *fly-by-night* organization from a *national movement*, which the PNM claims to be. Even though there might have been degeneracy all around the party, within the society and without, even though there were reactionary positions presented by the Jobs and the Chambers of Industry and Commerce, the party newspaper always existed to promulgate values that spoke to the dignity of a people in struggle, the need for interracial unity, the imperative to oppose the IMF, the obligation to rally the party

Introduction

faithful around ideas that matter to the society and to be thinking constantly about how best to serve the interest of the party and subsequently the nation. That is the function of a party newspaper. Anything less is "stuff and nonsense."

Instead, what do we have? Take the absurdity that we find in *Magnum* of April 17 (Vol. 3, No. 1), 1992. Dialogue, they say in their editorial, is necessary for national progress. What, you may ask, is the importance of dialogue, our editorial responds: "The record will show that the tradition of consultation has been established in this country by governments of the PNM which led Trinidad and Tobago between the period 1956 and 1986.

"The PNM has always seen consultation as a mechanism for achieving the participatory democracy to which it is irrevocably committed because we believe that it is through the process of consultation that our national perspectives are enriched."

One is not too sure how consultation leads to the achievement of participatory democracy because consultation merely means that you consult with a population to find out what the population thinks. Yet inherent in this consultation is the notion that somebody has the answers to the problems posed and the people are used merely as a sounding board to find out if those ideas are correct or feasible. In the process, the society or the party does not collectively discuss ideas and through such a discussion arrive at the best course of action to take. In this context consultation represents a process in which one group (Prime Minister Manning and his colleagues) has the answers and merely thrusts those ideas upon an expectant party and public for their approval rather than for their considered discussion and judgment. The worst such example occurred after the last general elections when PNM's successful candidates merely sat at home and waited until they got *the* call from on high to tell them the posts (cabinet and parliamentarian) to which they were appointed. For example, Marilyn Gordon, one of the political leaders of the PNM, was never consulted on any of these decisions by the ruling group. Such a conception is confirmed when the editorial lists what it considers the major achievement of consultation:

> Some people may consider the third advantage [of consultation] the most important. It is the psychological bonus which can lead to the mobilization of the energies of the peoples. It is a fact that when people can express their views, when they can feel they are heard, when they are given an opportunity to participate they find renewed spiritual commitment to their community and nation.
>
> There is no doubt that this condition must be the foundation for taking a nation out of any crisis, and the PNM cherishes this aspect of the genuine course of consultation upon which it has embarked.

This is the crux of the matter: consultation is designed only to make people feel good, to achieve what they call "renewed spiritual commitment" toward their community and the nation. When such consultation replaces the genuine discussion of issues, democracy within the party is effectively murdered, and such violence cannot be too far behind for the *society*. There can be no effective democracy within the society if there is no democracy within the *party* under the tutelage of some father who thinks he knows best. Very quickly things begin to fall apart, and this, I argue in "Eric E. Williams and the Politics of Language" was one of Williams's failings during his tenure in office.

Of worse vintage is an article called "Poly-Tricks vs Politics" by Hal Greaves. His position is to let the party faithful know "that the conduct of an election and the administration of a republic are two totally different things." One would have thought that after having noted in its editorial that the party has been in power for thirty years, the party faithful would have been aware of this fact. But one could let this pass. In the second paragraph he gets to the meat of his argument when he notes that "this article is a warning to all members of the PNM that to heed the sentiments expressed by the Prime Minister when he said no jobs for the

Introduction

boys. If we live PNM first, Trinidadians after, Tobagonians will be considered if they toe the line, it will not only doom the PNM but the nation."

These sentiments come from the "official voice" of the party. No jobs, I presume for "the boys and girls" who ensured that the bigger boys and girls got jobs and were also able to give jobs to other boys and girls who were not even responsible for the victory of the party. Greaves goes on: "Politics is a call to serve, service to the nation not special interest groups. . . .The government must be careful and never surround itself with advisors who having their own private agendas will whisper only the counsel they chose. No party must place itself above the interest of the nation. Being a member of the PNM should mean that we are here to serve, not to get. Still people feel as though something is owed to them and maybe it is."

Such a statement needs to be addressed sentence by sentence to understand its nonsensical content.

"Politics is a call to serve, service to the nation not special interest groups."

First, to get back to basics. The *American College Dictionary* defines politics as "the science or art of political government" or "the practice or profession of conducting political affairs." As would be noted, neither of these definitions talks about service either to a nation or to special interest groups. It talks about the art of conducting political affairs. In the case of the party, politics must mean the art of promoting the ideas or ideology of the party, which would seem to suggest that it is the boys or girls who are committed to the ideals of the party who are best equipped to carry out these ideas and ideals. In fact, if pushed further I would argue that politics has everything to do with the promotion and promulgation of the ideas a group sets for itself and the ways of achieving those ideas, which would seem to suggest that the success of a political party (private/special/self-interested) demands that the boys of the party be placed in positions where they can carry out the ideas of that self-interested group.

"The government must be careful and never surround itself with advisors who having their own private agendas will whisper only the counsel and compliments that they chose."

What to make of this statement? Strictly speaking, the present government of Trinidad and Tobago (that is, the authoritative body of the body politic) consists of three parties that possess members in the House of Representatives and the Senate with some independent members being nominated in the latter. I suspect, however, that Mr. Poly-Tricks is speaking about the party that commands the majority votes to lead or, in popular parlance, "to form the government." In this case it is not possible for the winning party to surround itself with persons having their own private agendas. Indeed, although they may have private concerns as we all do, their function is to promote the agenda of the party. This would seem to suggest that the members of a party, for example a Marilyn Gordon or a Nello Mitchell, general secretary of the party are much more likely to promote the party's agenda than someone such as Occah Seepaul, Speaker of the Legislative Council, or a Kusha Haracksingh, chairman of Caroni Ltd. Both are latecomers to the Party. The logic of Mr. Greaves or Mr. Manning that a Seepaul or a Haracksingh is more likely to carry forward the agenda of the PNM defies both logic and common sense. It is a fantasy of the worse kind.

"No party must place itself above the interest of the nation." Even though this is a clumsy formulation of a position, I will try to respond. As I noted, a political party, particularly the PNM, must reflect the most advanced political awareness of the nation. If it is not and does not so consider itself, it ought not to be in power. As such, it possesses (or should possess) the most politically advanced cadres of the nation. This, at least, is the only reason why someone is asked to vote for the PNM rather than NAR or the United National Congress (UNC). As a party, we argue that we are more informed, more conscious, more aware, more politically sophisticated than the other parties and that is why we make a claim upon the nation and ask to be elected. If this is true, and I

Introduction

believe it to be true, then one can only conclude that the PNM should be in the advance guard of the nation. As such the party does not place its interest above the nation, it argues simply that its positions are coterminus and in harmony with the nation's highest aspiration in a way that the UNC or the NAR is not which is another reason why the "boys" ought to make and are entitled to have the first claims on the ruling party in government.

"Being a member of the PNM should mean that we are here to serve, not to get."

How is one to serve if one does not get? Take a hypothetical situation. One of the boys has served his party faithfully and well for twenty years. The party wins. Does it not seem consistent that this person ought to be given greater opportunities to continue to serve that party and, in the process, the nation? Isn't that the identical situation in which Mr. Manning finds himself: that having served he has now received. It seems to me that serving is a necessary precondition to receiving and that if one does not receive very soon he learns to limit his service. In some cases he terminates his service, and if this happens in a large-scale manner there soon would be no PNM, nothing to give, nothing to get, and no service to be rendered.

"Still people feel as though something is owed to them and maybe it is."

This statement is self-evident and follows from the proposition advanced above. When people serve they legitimately expect to receive and a statement that reads "no jobs for the boys" is as silly as it is self-defeating.

This, then, is the state to which the "official voice" of the party has descended: making contradictory statements and parading nonsense under the guise of political wisdom. When a society begins to degenerate, it is the party, the advanced consciousness of the masses, that emerges as the necessary instrument to see the society through. In this regard, the PNM has failed (or is close to failing) if, as we say, it does not pull up its socks. Such an occurrence cannot necessarily bode well for the nation. And just in case

Mr. Greaves and the present leaders are unaware of what a party newspaper means to a party and how it needs to function, it is necessary to quote Eric Williams on the fundamental importance of a party newspaper. He says:

> We give public notice that we propose in the near future to launch a public company which will invite all sections of the public to participate in order that we should publish here a daily paper devoted to the nationalist aspirations of the West Indian people and the people of Trinidad [and Tobago], a paper based on the popular democracy, a paper appealing to all good West Indians, party members or not, a paper of the People for the People by the People.
>
> Beside [these] concrete proposals we have to organise the education of the Party, because all these projects we must undertake would be nothing without a Party and public educated to take advantage of the opportunities we propose to create.[30]

As to who ought to be the editor of the party's newspaper, Williams was as eloquent as he was clear: a person who sees his or her task "as sufficient to occupy the greatest talents and energies [s/he] has."[31]

Under the current circumstances, no such scenario (the separation of party from government, or the importance of a party newspaper, the education of its members and members of the community about its aims, objectives, and programs) exists. The party seems to be synonymous with the government, and the party leader believes that a cadre of closely tight-knit southerners should take the place of a democratically run party. Any legiti-

---

[30] Eric Williams, "Perspectives for Our Party," the Third Annual Convention, October 17, 1958, p. 11.

[31] Ibid.

mate attempt to challenge the ruling orthodoxy is stifled, and every effort is made to eliminate such unregenerate underlings. In August 1992 the PNM constitution was changed to ensure that anyone with any organic link to the grass roots of the party would not be elected to serve in the capacity of general secretary of the party. A "professional administrator" under the direct control of and selected by the prime minister was thought to be the best way to prevent any independent candidate from being elected to such a powerful position. Surely this is not the best way to conduct the business of a serious political party.[32] I suspect that this is one of the many reasons why Merle Hodge has argued that "a kind of right-wing, middle-class coup within the party" has now taken over the party and that "there is really too much to suggest that the PNM is changing colour, abandoning some of its strongest principles. And this is precisely what its present leader is being patted on the back for."[33] Under the present circumstances, it should be made extremely clear that *autocracy* within a party can never produce or lead to *democracy* within the larger society. Sooner or later the contradictory and warring impulses of the former betray the symmetry and harmony of the latter. So that when we see a "Magnum" published in the *Trinidad Guardian* with some simplistic articles that amount to very little and the party's constitution changed to fit the whims of an ever-encroaching bureaucracy we know that the party has betrayed its commitment to the poor and impoverished and is moving more and more to accommodate the aspirations of the privileged.

The publication of a party newspaper serves another important function of actively rallying party members around a cause. Because a group of people have to work together week after week to produce a paper, it becomes an instrument through which party members can connect with one another, a vehicle whereby

---

[32] See Article 16 of the *People's National Movement Draft Report of the Constitution Review Committee*, August 5, 1992, p. 11.

[33] Merle Hodge, "Coup in the PNM," *Sunday Mirror*, June 21, 1992.

important ideas can be debated, be they about socialism, liberalization, racism, or privatization. It also offers an opportunity for party members to go out to the public to sell their papers (and by extension, their ideas), which means that they have to explain the ideas that appear in the party organ, and so on. In fact, the publication of a party newspaper becomes an alternate manner in which a party converses with itself, and its society and that is the necessary and indispensable prerequisite for a strong party and the base upon which any public discourse is conducted. Indeed, growing up in Tacarigua, I remember the stalwarts of the PNM such as Jack Alexis, Cecil Roberts (Churran), and others walking around the village to sell the *PNM Weekly*. These were party advocates who, in the earliest days of the party, would explain who and what the PNM was. This was serious business, and they took their business seriously. Now, in many ways, under Prime Minister Manning, the PNM has degenerated into a mechanism that uses the PNM faithful to get elected, reserving the right to dictate to the party at all times. This surely is not democracy within the party; it certainly is not the way a democratic society is nurtured and developed.

I have listed only some of the advantages that accrue from the publication of a party newspaper as opposed to the infinitely lazier task of throwing ideas together that amount to nothing more than a few announcements of the party and calling it an organ of the party. To any serious observer such a state of affairs cannot be acceptable.

There is a final question one needs to raise particularly with the Jobs and the Chambers of Commerce and Industry: what is the proper moral reaction to the monstrous cruelty and injustices perpetrated against the Amerindians, the Africans, and the Indo-Caribbean peoples in the Caribbean? And, as Bill Donovan has asked, is there "something intrinsically immoral in the West's ethos [that] has underlain all Western/non-Western relations from the earliest discovery?"[34] Perhaps there are no simple answers to these questions, but the vulgar manner in which the Jobs

Introduction

and the Chambers of Commerce and Industry proceed and their inflammatory response to Williams and Rodney demonstrate that the aim of these exercises in duplicity is to mislead rather than to enlighten.

It is important that the essays included in this volume be made available to the public. At their best, they speak to the rich legacy left to the people of Trinidad and Tobago by a party in its ascendancy as it moved to understand itself, forge its own destiny, and give voice to the hopes and aspirations of an essentially voiceless and silenced people. These essays remind us that the battle for self-autonomy and the dignity of our people cannot be seen as over. Slavery and colonialism cannot be theorized as being only and exclusively economic ideas and practices that were designed to exploit our society of its natural resources. They also involved the cultivation of what one theorist called "ideological apparatuses" that ensured intellectual and ideological hegemony over the colonized, which in turn coincided with the extermination of the Amerindians, the slavery of Africans, and the indentureship of the East Indians. Certainly, in the age of political independence these are legacies with which we must still come to grips. When, in 1992, African peoples can be called "savages" and "animals," the author of these sentiments feted at the country club of the elite and described as a misunderstood prophet in his land, it is time to revisit the scene of the crime and understand why Massa or Sahib Day Isn't really Dead and why we need to learn anew the lessons of our intellectual inheritance.

Bereft of facts and figures, these essays show Williams as the political philosopher that he was. In another context, I have argued that Williams was an intellectual descendant of John Locke, William James, John Dewey, and their brand of empiricism and pragmatism, intellectual-philosophical tendencies that were reinforced at Oxford and Howard universities. In these essays, we get a glimpse of Williams's break from those rigid methodological

---

[34] *The Devastation of the Indies: A Brief Account*, p. 23.

bounds and his ability to theorize about the society and its direction. I also believe that many of Williams's academic critics err when they fail to recognize that once Williams entered politics on a full-time basis he ceased to be an *active* historian, a craft that he practiced sporadically during the latter period of his life. Thus, in evaluating the last thirty years of his career, his role as a political theorist ought to be given greater academic attention. After all, from 1956 to 1981 *politics* rather than *history* was his major vocation. It is my belief that if Trinidad and Tobago is to go forward politically it must build and expand upon the political and philosophical base that Williams laid. In retrospect, Williams certainly looks much better in not having embraced the bureaucratic imperatives of the socialist system as comprehensively as some other thinkers did. I continue to believe that a philosophical marriage of the ideas of Williams and James offers us a way out of the ideological maze in which Trinidad and Tobago finds itself. Such theorizing, I argue further, can only come from an intelligent mixture of the indigenous practices and theories and an enlightened understanding of our historical past.

There is another reason why a collection of the best of Williams's political speeches ought to be republished. If, as I have argued, Williams reflects the best within the society and his ideas represent the seminal outpourings of a moment when our political life and thought were at its fructifying best, it seems obvious that one should be able to turn to a ready compilation of his speeches to get a sense of the way Williams theorized about his society. With the exception of *Forged from the Love of Liberty* (1981), there is no easy way to get hold of Williams's major speeches. The other pieces included in this collection supplement and contextualize Williams's addresses. "Eric E. Williams and the Politics of Language," a contribution by the editor, examines the nature of Williams's language and argues for the *how* rather than the *what* of Williams's rhetorical and oratorical contributions to our society. James's "Convention Appraisal" gives us a sense of Williams at his political best, at a moment when he and

Introduction

James shared many convictions. George Lamming's "Trinidad and the Revolution in Political Intelligence" captures the excitement that accompanied the rise of the PNM and the arrival of Williams in the political arena. Erica Williams-Connell, while acknowledging her father's shortcomings, reiterates his love for his country and the contributions the PNM made to the society. Her father's cadences, phrasing, humor, and rhetorical asides, as well as his penchant for figures, are reflected in her speeches. That twenty thousand people came out to see and hear her address her people during a preelection campaign is a reminder that the spirit and the legacy of Williams live, hence the need to meditate anew on the spirit of his work.

From time to time, a nation needs to reengage and to reflect upon itself. A careful study of Williams's essays and the accompanying pieces allow us to reflect upon some of our present political practices and to suggest some ways out of our present political dilemma. Lionel Seukeran, a prominent member of the opposition party during Williams's leadership, has written:

> Trinidad and Tobago and the West Indies will long remember his [Williams's] genius, this brilliant son of the soil, for the sense of direction he gave us all and for the tireless service he rendered the region. Never within a century will we be able to produce his equal. When future historians chronicle his achievements, they will have inscribe his name in the hearts of his fellow men.[35]

Eric E. Williams Speaks makes for intelligent reading and thus ought to be engaged. My hope is that this collection fills a gap in our nation's history, in Williams's scholarship, and in our nation's self-knowing.

Tacarigua/Ithaca/Wellesley
April 1993

---

[35] Lionel Seukeran, "Eric Williams in Retrospect," *Caribbean Affairs* 4 (April–June 1991): 123.

ERIC E. WILLIAMS AND THE POLITICS OF LANGUAGE

by Selwyn R. Cudjoe

Williams in a pensive mood as he cleans his pipe.

ERIC. E. WILLIAMS AND THE POLITICS OF LANGUAGE

> Some people are born writing, some achieve writing and some have writing thrust upon them. My belonging is to the last group, coming slowly to accept the blessing and yoke that is writing, and in so doing I have come upon an understanding of language—the anguish that is english in colonial societies. The remembering—the revolutionary language of "massa day done"—change fermenting not in the language of rulers, but in the language of the people.
> —Marlene Nourbese Philip, *She Tries Her Tongue*

The capacity for "ole talk," "mauvais langue," and the ability "to give fatigue" are all important ways in which the language of Trinidad and Tobago is used to help people survive and to create new spaces for historic possibilities. The history of Trinidad and Tobago abounds with examples of how language was used in the daily lives of our people to enable them to cope with the historic conditions of oppression and the irritations of the present day that attend their lives. Perhaps one of the most important examples of the way our people have used their tongue/language to defend themselves can be found in the early history of the society when the local English planters protested against the attempt by the British Parliament to ban the practice of whipping women slaves. In recognition of their powerlessness if such a law was passed, the planters met in Tacarigua in 1826 at the house of William Burnley, the leading slaveholder at the time, and asked in utter seriousness: "How are we going to control these slave women when we cannot control 'their tongue' through our whippings?" The attempt to control the tongue and, inherent in this symbolic act, to control the language of the people showed how potent the slaves' language was in Trinidad and Tobago. It was through the medium of silence, as Edouard Glissant called it, that they honed their language as a vehicle of resistance during the slave era.[1]

Another aspect of language use in Trinidad and Tobago also demonstrates its important role in the lives of Trinidadians and Tobagonians. There is a flair for language and a certain amount of enjoyment in its use. J. H. Collens, a Baptist minister and superintendent of the Boys' Model and Normal School in Port of Spain in 1888 and a resident of Trinidad for ten years before his writing *A Guide to Trinidad*, notes the love for the master's language that he observed among the "lower classes" in Trinidad and Tobago:

> In my capacity as Dominie I continually had to check the disposition of my pupils in Trinidad to use long-winded words and high-flown phrases. Boys and young men spend hours poring over dictionaries, simply to try and master the meanings of words which for length might be measured by the yard. They positively do not believe in the sweet simplicity of the Saxon tongue. Only to-day, in the street, one man talking to another, in the usual loud tone, said, while passing me, "I estimate it to be my particular and elementary duty." I should like to have discovered what duty combined those two essentials, but the speaker was out of hearing. I have heard, too, a woodcutter gravely tell his employer, "It was with the utmost difficulty that I managed to disintegrate those logs, sir."[2]

The carnival tradition also provided examples of linguistic exuberance and excitement. Within the tradition, two characters were known for their love of and dexterity with language. First, there was the Pierrot Grenade and the Pierrot. As Andrew Carr

---

[1] See the introduction to Selwyn R. Cudjoe, *Four Caribbean Slave Narratives* (forthcoming) for a discussion of language in the slave epoch. See also Glissant's notion about the development of creole language in the Caribbean: *Caribbean Discourse: Selected Essays* (Charlottesville: University Press of Virginia, 1989).

[2] J. H. Collens, *Guide to Trinidad* (London: Elliot Stock, 1888), pp. 38–39.

noted, several months of careful work went into the Pierrot's making of elaborate carnival costumes and "the memorising of parts of English History dealing with great kings and their successful exploits in war, to form the basis of the Pierrot's highly boastful speeches of his own personal prowess either as prime character or lineal descendant. . . . Some Pierrots have been known to recite also the orations from Shakespeare of such characters as Julius Caesar, Brutus, Mark Anthony, Othello, as well as excerpts from English classical literature."[3] The language of the Pierrot was Creole or French Patois, which, as Carr noted, demanded "a versatility with the dialect to play the part."[4] His speeches, used to parody the behavior of politicians, demonstrate his powers in spelling and their capacity for ad-libbing and verbal inventiveness.

The second carnival character that embellished the linguistic tradition was the midnight robber, a figure who delighted in making long speeches or addresses that are usually full of hyperbole. Daniel J. Crowley, who examined some of the speeches of the midnight robber, noted that they provided "worthy opportunities for the ever-glib West Indians to show their sensitivity and skill with words and their delivery."[5] As a society, Trinidad and Tobago prized the midnight robber and his "robber-talk," which was looked upon as "a kind of heritage received from the past and passed on to the future. Maskers take themselves and the masque they play very seriously. There is no question in their minds of the importance of their esthetic activities, and the real achievement

---

[3] Andrew Carr, "Pierrot Grenade," *Caribbean Quarterly* 4 (March–June 1956): 282.

[4] Ibid., p. 285. The practice of speaking in French Creole died out at the end of the 1950s. In 1956, Carr observed: "Some trend may appear to rescue the satirical jesting, badinage and 'erudition' of Pierrot Grenade through the medium of Creole-English, but such an innovation may not long survive as it will not preserve by any manner of means the spicy and pithy witticisms which can be so successfully conveyed through the expressive medium of French Patios or Creole" (p. 286).

[5] Daniel J. Crowley, "The Midnight Robber," *Caribbean Quarterly* 4 (March–June 1956): 265.

of obtaining recognition as a great masker from the critical Trinidad public."[6] In a society that values robber-talk, the ability "to talk for oneself" is a valued asset. One had to be good or ridicule would follow surely.

This ability "to talk for oneself" and use the language carries over to the written language. In 1956, in his application to join the People's National Movement, a newly formed party of Trinidad and Tobago, an unknown member of the lower classes wrote: "For years, for generations, even a forsaken people may pray for deliverance while they languish in near despair, pray for a light to show them hope and the way to better things. But when that light does glow, it is up to the people to recognize it as theirs too, fan it to greater brightness, to shield it from extinction. There is a tide in the affairs of men."[7]

And then there was Brother Boynes, a shoemaker, who sat at his last openly in the streets of Port of Spain. According to De Wilton Rogers, he "knew . . . Robert Emmett's speech by heart, and could tear to bits any specious arguments put forward." He, too, was forged in the crucible of a culture that prized language and rhetorical skills. Such love of language and argumentation permeated the society.

Language usage, then, has always been serious business in Trinidad and Tobago. Trinidadians and Tobagonians took sensuous delight in the subtle play of language for its own sake. People liked to listen to the sounds of their own voices and would use language to impress others and to denote status. Some members of the lower classes took the study of language seriously and tried "to speak properly." From the formation of modern Trinidad and Tobago, language and its usage have been of utmost importance to its inhabitants.

---

[6] Ibid., p. 271.

[7] Quoted in De Wilton Rogers, *The Rise of the People's National Movement* (Port of Spain: De Wilton Rogers, n.d.), p. 67.

When Eric E. Williams, prime minister of Trinidad and Tobago from 1962 to 1981, entered the political arena in 1955, he was certainly aware that the use and control of language would be a barometer in judging his appeal to the people. Thus one of Williams's more significant achievements during the years he led the country was that he mastered the language in a way no one else before or after him has been able to do. As a leader, his greatest strength lay in his ability and capacity to take the language of his people (unofficial, vernacular, and colloquial), fuse it with the language of the oppressor (official, classical English), and wield it into a weapon of great potency and fury. He could use the language to cajole as well as to offend; he could be sweet (that is, he could "sweet-talk"), yet he could be rambunctious. He could tear at the heartstrings of his people and play on their humorous side. He was also a master of picong, the ability "to give and take a joke," hence the ability to use language at another's expense and vice versa. In a land where picong was king, Williams, versed in this art form, proved to be one of the reigning monarchs.[8]

At moments of his people's greatest dissatisfaction, Williams could allay their fears in words that were appropriate and apt. One of his greater moments came on one occasion when he was under attack. He ended a speech with the words of a song that was popular at the time: "If loving you is wrong/Then I don't want to be right." Another time, when he contemplated giving up the leadership in the party and argued that "like a bridge over troubled

---

[8] In Trinidad and Tobago the relationship between language and power is inculcated also in the educational system and the cultural stereotypes of the society. In her thesis, "Education and Cultural Imperialism: Gender and Ethnicity in Reading Textbooks Used in Trinidad and Tobago," Josephine Mary Milne-Home writes, "In many ways, Annancy resembles the Black Adult Male stereotype in Trinidad and Tobago (and the Caribbean generally), who 'limes' in the street with other men, and whose aspirations for a certain style of life far outweighs his efforts toward, or means to support it. So his skill is wrapped in his charm, or 'sweet talk', and his wit and will to coerce others into supporting him and the schemes that he devises to reverse the status quo every once in a while" (University of Alberta, Edmonton, Alberta, 1980), p. 139.

waters, I'll lay me down," his audience responded: "So true, brother," or "Please, don't go." It was his use of metaphorically rich and vividly appealing language that led to the almost mythical status Williams assumed in his society. Even the tone of his voice became a trademark of his unique style. At the height of his popularity, people not only spoke like Williams, they tried to look like Williams. I will argue that his capacity for language went a long way toward explaining Williams's appeal to his people, a dimension of his personality that has not been given the scholarly attention it deserves. Most Williams scholars have concerned themselves with his intellectual brilliance (and rightly so), but none has examined the politics of his language. This essay delineates Williams's use of language in his interactions with his people. I am concerned to show the social and political realities that were encoded in Eric Williams's language and how that language, almost in a Whitmanesque manner, became a celebration of himself and his people. I will do this by examining some of Williams's most important pamphlets and locating their place within the construction of his political identity.

LANGUAGE AND THE TRINIDAD & TOBAGO EXPERIENCE

> [It] was the perfect lecture in timing, content and delivery. It was as the flow of a well-timed stroke from the bat of the late Sir Frank Worrell.
> —De Wilton Rogers, *The Rise of the People's National Movement*

Although the language of Trinidad and Tobago possesses a rich mixture of African, Indian, and European languages, during the colonial period most Trinidadians and Tobagonians were taught to privilege the language of the colonizer and were consciously aware of the difference between the language of the educated class, a classically based English or French, and that of the vast majority of the people, a rich, colloquial vernacular that reflected the richness and diversity of the people's culture.[9] Linguistic distinctions differentiated the populace for even though 99 percent of the people spoke a Creole language, it was not unusual for the dominant culture to dis-miss and de-mean the vernacular language of the people and call it bad English.[10] Because most members of the bourgeois class aspired to "speak properly" it was not unusual for a person who wanted to be perceived as being educated to spice his language with as many Latin quotations as possible to show his distinction and difference from the ordinary masses.[11] In colonial Trinidad, the capacity to "speak properly" was indeed a weapon in the hands of the "educated" and colonial elite to indicate their superiority over the ordinary masses of people. To lapse into "bad English" or colloquial language would taint one with the mark of "natural" inferiority, an indication that one had not quite washed away one's peasant's origins or "boorish" sensibilities.[12]

---

[9] Until 1865, the dominant language of the people of Trinidad was a French-based patois, a large part of the French population having come into the island through the Cedula of Population, 1783. See J. J. Thomas, *The Theory and Practice of Creole Grammar* (1869; rpt. London: New Beacon, 1969).

[10] In the current sense of the term, to "dis" someone is to demean or to disrespect him or her.

[11] See V. S. Naipaul's *Mystic Masseur* (London: Andre Deutsch, 1957) for a good example of this straining to acquire a classically based language as a mark of social superiority. This behavior is personified in the behavior of Indarsingh, an Oxford-educated character in *The Mystic Masseur*.

[12] Merle Hodge responds to this linguistic coercion with great clarity and enormous perspicacity when she observes: "Ninety-nine percent of Caribbean people, for 99 percent of their waking hours, communicate in a Creole language that is a fusion of West African syntax, and the modified vocabulary of one or another European tongue. These languages have stubbornly survived generations of disrespect and active suppression in the home and in the education system. Possibly they have survived because they express *our* personality, our reality, our worldview in a way no other language can. Caribbean Creole languages have been fashioned to fit our communication needs, and they have not only survived but developed—and they continue to develop as our communication needs become, perhaps, more complex" ("Challenges of the Struggle for Sovereignty: Changing the World versus Writing Stories," in Selwyn R. Cudjoe, ed., *Caribbean Women Writers* [Wellesley: Calaloux Publications, 1990], p. 204).

Eric E. Williams and the Politics of Language

The ability to "speak properly" and to manipulate language has always been of enormous importance to Trinidadians and Tobagonians. Apart from an oral, storytelling tradition that allowed self-expression in any manner that one chose and with a great deal of flexibility, skill, and diversity, the concern for the "proper" use of the classically based English language always seemed a preoccupation of the society. As a result, in the early part of the twentieth century there arose a number of literary and debating clubs whose main concern was to master the master's language. This concern with language use and the mastery of language skills became a part of Williams's social reality while growing up in the household of his father, a member of the civil service, which occupation was a sure indication in the colonial society that one had arrived. In those days, teaching at the public schools or working in the civil service provided a certain degree of respectability and demanded that one "speak properly." Williams grew up in a social environment in which the proper use of language was of utmost importance.

Williams was very much a product of his local environment. As he noted in his autobiography, his immersion in the intellectual culture of the society began from the cradle. He notes that his father "had read in a magazine about a nurse teaching a young child the alphabet and nursery rhymes. He promptly bought an alphabet card and began to put me through my paces. When I could recite the alphabet I received a tricyle."[13] Tranquillity Government School, the primary school that Williams attended, emphasized English grammar, spelling, and dictation. The core curriculum at Queen's Royal College, the secondary school he attended, included modern and classical languages. Williams recalled that on his first day at secondary school he was placed in a special class and requested to learn a few tenses of the Latin verb

---

[13] Eric Williams, *Inward Hunger: The Education of a Prime Minister* (Chicago: University of Chicago Press, 1971), p. 31.

amo for the next afternoon: "Within a short period at home that night I had learned not only all the tenses of *amo*, but of *moneo, rego* and *audio*, that is to say, all the conjugations; I was fully conversant with the cases of nouns, and had made my first acquaintance with the ablative absolute. I walked up and down the house, reciting all the tenses, beginning with *amo, amas, amat, amamus, amatis, amant*, my father beaming indulgently the while."[14] At secondary school and university Williams demonstrated an aptitude for languages.

Williams's love of language was not a unique phenomenon. In the early years of the colonial struggle, when the attempt to articulate an identity was paramount, the question of linguistic control and the delight in rhetoric were evident throughout the society and revealed themselves in the plethora of literary and debating societies that were formed. Victor Bailey, a resident of Tacarigua, speaks about how he and his friends walked around carrying grammar books and pored over them in their attempts to articulate words and to develop a facility with the English language.[15] This intense attempt to organize, control, and manipulate language set the stage for the modern nationalist movement in Trinidad and Tobago. Williams was a product of that struggle.[16]

The Teachers' Economic and Cultural Association, founded in 1942 and forerunner of the People's Education Movement (PEM), was a manifestation of the society's concern for language and an attempt to privilege local intellectual culture. In *The Rise*

---

[14] Ibid., p. 32.

[15] Conversation, January 2, 1992.

[16] Basdeo Panday, political leader of the United National Congress, perhaps the most charismatic leader of Trinidad and Tobago and certainly one of the most articulate spokesperson of the laboring classes of the society, was also formed in the crucible of the nationalist struggle. Like Williams, one of the major figures whom he acknowledges "influenced his thinking," Panday possessed a great command of the language and is one the most effective orators in the society. Panday is also an accomplished dramatist who acted in London while he studied there. See Samaroo Siewah and Roodal Moonilal, *Basdeo Panday: An Enigma Answered* (Port of Spain: Chakra Publishing House, 1991).

of the People's National Movement De Wilton Rogers makes three important observations about the transition from what can be considered a polemical to a more practical, down-to-earth treatment of ideas and language. First, he argues that between 1940 and 1955 a cultural transition took place: "The age of polemics was coming to a close. Such debates as: 'Was Brutus justified in killing Caesar?', 'which is the greatest incentive to crime, wealth or poverty?' drew people from far and near to listen to *quasi-forensic skill*. These were giving way to more topics. 'Should women have equal pay with men?', 'Is the food given to our children sufficient and enough?'" Second, he argues that between 1950 and 1955 less emphasis was placed on words than on action (after all, PEM was an "action organization"):

> We want to eradicate from our ranks all satisfied sectarianism, in the place of dead doctrinarianism, we want the spirit of live positivism. WE WANT TO END the scholastic tinkering with WORDS, WORDS, WORDS. We know where our vital interests lie. We want to get at them in the shortest possible time.
>
> We want soberly to take into account all the problems facing our people and to offer a solution. We are the enemies of all cut and dried schemes as far as they follow any beaten track of dogmatism. We must not be stereotyped.[17]

This movement from *words* to *action* had the important consequence of bringing attention to everyday problems. Individuals in the movement brought their forensic skills to bear upon the problems of the day rather than indulging in the glorification of language for its own sake. Yet even though action-oriented activities became more important, the reliance on and

---

[17] Rogers, *Rise of the People's National Movement*, p. 29.

love for linguistic skills still remained an integral part of the political culture. Even as they moved from a polemical to an action-oriented emphasis, the very presentation was articulated in a peculiarly Trinidadian "styling" of discourse. The evolution of the People's National Movement (PNM) intersected with the cultural patterns of the society. As Rogers notes, under the lamp-post "with its lamp light after dark, clustered knots of youngsters debating and discussing who is the better bat, Hobbs of England or McCartney of Australia? France's Maxim Gun was more affective [sic] than the German's Howitzer. Gaston Johnson was a better lawyer than L. C. Hannays! These meetings were not spasmodic but night after night. It was under the lamp light that a lawyer, the political adviser, the champion chess player debated and discussed."[18] This was the culture of the lime which was noted for endless discussions of a myriad of topics with the aim of persuading rather than bullying and manhandling.

Drawing from this linguistic culture of "Behind the Bridge" the PNM conducted open-air lectures in Woodford Square, later renamed the University of Woodford Square. From June 1955 to January 1956, the month the PNM was formed, more than fifty-two lectures were given under the auspices of the PEM. The PNM and its mode of discourse emerged directly from the oral literary culture of the society, from the energy and excitement of the folk. As Rogers noted, "The People's Education Movement had captured the imagination of the citizens and the folk—from Charlottesville to Scarborough . . . from Port of Spain to Point Fortin." Most of the initial support for the PNM, Rogers says, came from "the Behind the Bridge school masters [who] were members of the People's Education Movement."[19] And many of the leaders and influential members of the PNM such as Arnold

---

[18] Ibid., p. 33.

[19] Ibid., pp. 35, 46. C. L. R. James also came out of this culture. For a time his father, Robert James, was a principal of Eastern Boys Government, one of these "Behind the Bridge" schools. See the Appendix for a chronological listing of the 154 lectures that Williams delivered from June 21, 1955, when he delivered *My Relations with the Caribbean Commisssion*, to June 14, 1956, when he delivered a statement of the fundamental principles of the PNM.

Thomasos, John Donaldson, Donald Granado, C. W. and W. J. Alexander, Donald Pierre, and others honed their linguistic skills in these societies. According to Rogers, "The Reading Circle produced two ministers [of government]. The Thistle Debating Society of which the T.E.C.A. was a lineal descendant not only produced two other ministers but an agitator in the form of Clement Payne."[20]

It is well-known that language always preexists a speaker in that one is born into a language that is already formed. To survive in any society, an individual must be versed fully in the codes of its language. But to be successful in the use of politically oriented speech one must not only master the codes of the language but also its nuances and a people's understanding of themselves as generated by and through that language. In this sense, language/conversation can be seen as the reproduction of a *habitus*, that is, "a system of depositions ... that functions as a system of generative schema that generates strategies which conform to the objective interests of their authors without having been conceived distinctly as such."[21] Thus, a speaker presents him or herself to another according to the cultural coded linguistic, gestural, proxemical codes of the society.[22] As Teresa Jillian notes, "Conversation is always presentational and always engaged in full knowledge of the rules of the exchange, rules which differ according to the relative social position of the participants and to the general context of the exchange. In conversation a speaker sup-

---

[20] Ibid., p. 25. Arnold Thomasos was the speaker of the Legislative Council, John Donaldson, a minster of government, Donald Granado, a minister of government, C. W. Alexander, a deputy speaker, W. J. Alexander, minster of government and adviser to the prime minister, and Donald Pierre, a minister of government. The People's Education Movement sponsored the early speeches of Eric Williams. In 1956 it was dissolved and inculcated into the People's National Movement.

[21] Pierre Bourdieu, *Question de sociologie* (Paris: Les editions de Minuit, 1984), p. 119–20. See also Pierre Bourdieu, *Outline of a Theory of Practice* (Cambridge: Cambridge University Press, 1977), chapter 2, for a good discussion of the notion of the "habitus" (p. 11).

[22] Proxemics is the study of the nature, degree, and effect of the spatial separation individuals naturally maintain (as in various social and interpersonal situations) and how this separation relates to environmental and cultural factors.

plies the required material for exchange."[23] To be sure, Williams understood the rules of exchange that existed in his society. His power to ennoble and reinvigorate every aspect of his people's life arose in no small manner from his ability to use language to penetrate into the innermost recesses of his people's being and to strike the sensibilities that most needed to be soothed.

Therefore, when one examines Williams's language or, what I call the politics of Williams's language, one turns first to his language as a conversation. Although his speeches were written (that is, they were published as pamphlets), they were rendered first as part of a public discourse and so were meant to be *heard* rather than read. In large part, he was engaged in a public conversation with his people and so his meaning and eloquence depended upon the dialogic nature of his presentations. Thus, in large measure, the conversational mode became a very important aspect of Williams's linguistic engagement with his people. Because Williams was a consummate conversationalist, understood the linguistic codes of his society and his people's capacity for ole talk and *mauvais langue*, he became a "giant" in his people's eyes. As one listener noted after one of his early speeches: "That is man. He is the Saviour of the Negro. He expose them slave drivers. Look all those names, the man know what he is saying. We must follow him. Never before the Negro had such a champion."[24]

Undoubtedly, Williams understood the role that language played in the historical development of his people as well as the nature of its theatrical appeal. As early as 1938, Williams's ability to challenge the prescriptions of the dominant colonial class in the arena of language became evident when, taking his oral examination in French as a doctoral candidate at Oxford University, he believed that his colleagues laughed at him rather than at

---

[23] Teresa Jillian, "Working Women's Words and the Condition of Their Production(s)," Working Paper #5, Susan B. Anthony Center for Women's Studies, University of Rochester, p. 13.

[24] Rogers, *Rise of the People' National Movement*, p. 42.

a mistake he made in his translation. This is Williams's account of the episode:

> The examination included an oral translation from a foreign language. . . . The student had to enter a long room, in which he found some forty Fellows seated around a table. In the course of translation, I made a horrible mistake. The crowd roared. I received the distinct impression that the roar was aimed at me and not at the mistake. It sobered me at once, I lost all my nervousness, I looked all around the room, at one individual member after the other, until quiet had been restored. I felt like a schoolmaster upbraiding by looks a group of unruly pupils; some began to pick at their nails, one looked out of the window, one twiddled with a book in front of him. When there was absolute quiet I resumed translation in a cold, unemotional voice. At the end I came to a passage of which I could not make head nor tail. I declined to translate. The warden pressed me three times to have a go at it. I refused. To set the matter at rest, I told him on the final occasion that I did not wish to give rise to another such guffaw as I had already listened to. He thanked me for coming, and I took my leave.[25]

It is significant that Williams's "real" entrée into the public sphere occurred when he debated Dom Basil Matthews, the leading intellectual light of the time, at the Port of Spain Public Library, on the merits of Plato's philosophy. Williams's victory in this oratorical contest (for contest it was) and the demonstration of his mastery of the language and subject matter of the master philosopher signified an important moment in the launching of Williams's public career. Because of his mastery over the classics, in the public's eye, Williams assumed the role of the prodigal son

---

[25] Williams, *Inward Hunger,* pp. 46–47.

in possession of the full power and mastery of the master's language, ready to unravel its codes and thereby lead his people out of the bondage of a slave and colonial past.[26] As a scholar, Williams understood that simultaneously, language defined one's class, one's standing in the society, and the validity of one's public position. Used correctly, it could lead to political power. No wonder, in describing Juppy's contribution to the 1889 Franchise Commission, Williams enthusiastically endorsed Juppy's contribution and noted that it might have been poor language but it was pregnant with political content.[27] According to Williams, "Mr. Juppy would not have passed an English examination in Standard 1 but his political acumen was absolutely impeccable. He wanted to appoint the members of the Legislative Council himself and he did not want the Queen to do so. He could see them but he couldn't see the Queen. Mr. Wood agreed: with his own representatives he would have a better chance of getting better roads."[28]

In ruminating over Juppy's comments, Williams must have been reminded of the many petitions that were submitted to the British Parliament in the early nineteenth century by British citizens who demanded the extension of universal male suffrage only to be turned down because they did not use correct or acceptable language. By the time Williams became a polemicist on behalf of his people, he understood just where the battle lay: the strident use of language and the need to empower a society through its language. As he noted in "Two Worlds in Conflict," an

---

[26] In this context, see C. L. R. James's lauding of J. J. Thomas's intellectual victory over James Anthony Froude and the manner in which James spoke of this contest. He claims Thomas had won the contest because he "overwhelm[ed] the great historian" and thereby defeated the colonizer at his own game (*Froudacity* [1889; rpt. London: New Beacon Books, 1969]). See also Wilson Harris's response to James's position in *History, Fable and Myth* (Guyana: Ministry of Information and Culture, 1970).

[27] Mr. Juppy, a former indentured Indian immigrant who had lived in Trinidad for 34 years and who supported constitution reform, testified before the Wood committee. See Eric Williams, *History of the People of Trinidad and Tobago* (Port of Spain: PNM Publishing, 1962), p. 193.

[28] Ibid., p. 194.

article that appeared in a Special Supplement of the *PNM Weekly*: "The Old World is the corbeau declaiming against the brilliant plumage and the graceful flight of the Scarlet Ibis of the New. . . . It is a conflict between those who take up the sword and will perish by the pen, a conflict between obscene language and university analysis, a conflict between Patois and Latin, between the mauvais langue whispered from house to house, and the democratic, well-behaved, intelligent mass meeting of the age of political education dispensed by this P.N.M." [29]

It is easy to see that Williams privileges the proper over the "improper," the language of the colonized (Latin) over the language of the people (Patois) even though he manages to get the contrast between the corbeau and the Scarlet Ibis correct. Suffice it to say that at this point in his political development he was aware of the conflicts inherent in these opposed ways of seeing. By the time he arrived at *Massa Day Done* such ambiguity would be absent completely from his discourse.

WILLIAMS'S ENTRANCE INTO TRINIDAD AND TOBAGO'S POLITICS

> Knowing how eager Williams was for more active association with West Indian affairs, I did my best to secure his appointment, when the post of Economic Adviser to the Trinidad Government became vacant, but my colleagues had already begun to suspect that he nursed secret ambitions and accordingly opposed it.
> —Albert Gomes, *Through a Maze of Colour*

Williams's entrance into the politics of the society was not as unplanned or as accidental as his initial public speech, *My Relations with the Caribbean Commission,* might lead one to believe. His work at the Caribbean Commission was a conscious prepara-

---

[29] Quoted in Rogers, *Rise of the People's National Movement*, p. 84. In this context see also George Lamming, "Trinidad and the Revolution in Intelligence," *PNM Weekly,* August 30, 1956.

tion for his political participation in the society. James's accounts of Williams's visits to him in New York during the 1940s and Albert Gomes's suspicions of Williams's political ambitions in the early 1950s were not entirely off base.[30] His treatment at the commission gave Williams the excuse he needed to enter the political arena, especially when his capacity to express himself freely was threatened. Yet when Williams stated his intention "to lay down his bucket" in his society, it was not so much the content of that speech that was important as the way he connected with his audience that made the difference and eventually paved the way for a smooth entrance into the political arena. Because Williams understood the linguistic codes of his society, he was able to exploit the sensibilities of his people in a way that few did (I use the term *exploit* in its best sense) and so was able to "ground" with his people in a masterful way. Williams's formal entrance into the politics of Trinidad and Tobago constituted a conscious political act and a realization that his language had to be adequate to the occasion.

Although Williams formally entered the politics of Trinidad and Tobago in 1955, his association with the political issues and organization of the society had begun much earlier. In June 1950, at the invitation of De Wilton Rogers, director-general of the PEM, from which the People's National Movement sprung, Williams became a consultant to the organization. In his reply of acceptance, Williams noted:

> I have always had the view that the work of organisations such as the Caribbean Commission can very easily degenerate into a mere collection of papers and documents unless vitality is injected into it by the people whom it is designed to serve. In addition, as you know, I am consistently fighting against that West Indian complacency

---

[30] See James's letters to Constance Webb and Albert Gomes, *Through a Maze of Colour* (Port of Spain: Key Caribbean Publications, 1974).

which is prepared to sit down and await official pontification, to applaud publicly and grumble privately, and I feel that wherever possible, the people, the ordinary people should be encouraged and stimulated to look themselves into the problems of the area, discuss them and develop their own point of view.[31]

The memorandum the PEM sent to the Caribbean Commission asking for the use of the library facility and the circulation of its books had all the nuances of Williams's prose and the education positions that he outlined in his book *Education in the British West Indies* (1950). The book was published by the PEM, which in one of its circulars in 1951 urged all members of the organization to be sure all the teachers in the island bought a copy.[32] The PEM made Williams's entry into the formal politics of Trinidad and Tobago possible.

In entering the political arena of Trinidad and Tobago, Williams did what no other politician before him had: he not only delivered political speeches all over the country, he also made those speeches available to the public through the production of inexpensive pamphlets, the first of which was *My Relations with the Caribbean Commission, 1943–1955*, a public lecture delivered under the auspices of the PEM in Woodford Square, Port of Spain, on the night of June 21, 1955, and repeated under the auspices of the Caribbean Women's National Assembly at Harris Promenade, San Fernando, on June 28, 1955. The cost of the pamphlet was twelve cents. Other pamphlets on constitution reform, economic matters, and party politics followed. What is significant about the publication of these pamphlets was Williams's understanding of the importance of propaganda and the need to educate the masses of the people. As a historian, Williams knew the power of the written and spoken word, the impact that pamphlets had in the

---

[31] Rogers, *Rise of the People's National Movement*, p. 15.

[32] Ibid., pp.17–18.

development of a political culture, and the self-conscious awareness of a people in the construction of their political selves. Although printing was introduced to Trinidad during the latter part of the eighteenth century, Williams can be considered the first political pamphleteer in the society. He was the first person to address his audience with a mixture of standard and colloquial language and to explore social and political ideas that up until that time had remained largely unexplored at the public level of discourse. In this, Williams had much in common with Edmund Burke.

In writing about the importance of Edmund Burke's *Reflections on the Revolution in France,* Olivia Smith argued that "Burke established a background which enabled others to recognize their own thought. Ideas which had previously been unformulated were now held consciously or disowned. By writing about politics in an unusual manner, Burke made the radical position more capable of being articulated. Making political thought more conscious, in itself, makes it more expressible."[33] Soon after Williams arrived on the political scene, most Trinidadians and Tobagonians became politicians in their everyday lives, and for the first time they spoke about political matters in a politically conscious way.[34] People became so excited that many Trinidadians began to imitate Williams's manner of speaking (because he was deaf, Williams possessed a low baritone voice that was monotonous in its flatness and thus had a very distinctive style) and to wear dark shades as Williams did. Because Williams read late into

---

[33] Oliva Smith, *The Politics of Language* (Oxford: Clarendon Press, 1984), p. 37.

[34] As a young boy growing up, I remember Learie Constantine addressing an audience at the Tacarigua E.C. School and making the point that Williams was the first person to "bring politics to the society," that is, to make politics a self-conscious activity to which Cecil Ifill, a distinguished headmaster of Curepe E.C. School, disagreed violently. He argued that even housewives who had to manage the financial matters of their households were involved in making political decisions. He never went back to another PNM-sponsored event but such exchanges give an idea of the kinds of debates that were taking place in even as remote a village as Tacarigua once Williams arrived on the political scene. This meeting would have taken place around the middle of 1956.

the night, he usually wore dark shades to protect his eyes from the sun. This, too, became fashionable during the heyday of his reign. In a way, what Williams did for his society was to re-turn a people unto themselves by releasing them into their language through which they could begin to "speechify" about their social reality with a new vigor, enhanced sophistication, and a deliberate self-consciousness.[35]

In a society that understands the interplay between speaker and audience, a call and response mode, and the give and take that ensues, Williams's linguistic style and his understanding of his audience were very important. As is generally understood in the culture, if you "can't a take" fatigue, you don't give one and usually it is better to remain outside the arena of social discourse. The correlation to this position is that "if you playing sailor you car 'fraid powder." When Williams entered into his first public conversation with his nation (*My Relations with the Caribbean Commission*), in a particularly poignant Trinidadian way he had declared that he "had come out to play" and God help any man who got in his way. When he announced in that conversation that "the conservative-minded among you may accuse me of melodrama, or, to use a phrase that has already been used about me, of playing to the gallery. You would be quite wrong."[36] In his own eminently sensible way, Williams knew what he was doing. Playing and "gallerying" became important aspects of his public demeanor and discourse.[37]

Although Williams's public behavior always involved a certain amount of "gallerying," it was always serious. He always regarded himself seriously and granted the same seriousness of purpose to his audience. Even when he joked with his public, he never let them forget the ultimate seriousness of his purpose. In

---

[35] Selwyn Carrington makes a distinction between "speechifying" and "conversing" within the Caribbean context.

[36] *My Relations with the Caribbean Commission* in this volume.

[37] "To gallery" in Trinidadian language is "to play one's self" or to show off.

a society accustomed to "skylarking" and ridicule, such a posture could easily lead to a reverse form of ridicule. "Who you think you is" is a common epithet of ridicule. One had to "come good" or not at all.[38]

The response to Williams was quite the opposite. He demanded seriousness from his audience and it was returned. A good example of this behavior occurred when Williams met with the steelbandsmen in his first efforts to make contact with the lower strata of the society. At that time, steelbandsmen were disorganized, viewed as social outcasts, and meeting with them was sure to result in social scorn.[39] George Goddard, president of the Steelband Association for a long period, tells about Williams's second meeting with this organization. After subcommittees were formed to report on various aspects of the organization's affairs, a follow-up meeting was arranged but the members did not produce the reports they were required to and many of the sub-committee members did not attend the second meeting. Williams's response to this event was instructive:

> Mr. Crichlow [who had presided over the first meeting], I am going to be frank. I'm afraid that you will not like what I am going to say but I am going to be frank. You asked me to meet the steelband boys and we met three Sundays ago. We met, and assignments were given to some of you to report back here today. Where are the members of that sub-committee? Some of them are not here. But you bring a set of irresponsible people to take up two hours and ten minutes of my time talking foolishness, and if I don't put an end to it they will take up another two hours and ten minutes of my time talking more foolishness. I

---

[38] See "Trinidad" in V. S. Naipaul, *The Middle Passage* (London: Andre Deutsch, 1962), for a very good analysis of this kind of ridicule and suspicion that is placed usually upon achievement.

[39] See The Mighty Sparrow, "Outcast" (1963) on this score.

heard it said when I was in England that all Trinidad people like is old talk, I am not against the old talk, but not in my house.[40]

When Uriah "Buzz" Butler, the chief servant and an important people's politician until the entrance of Williams, tried to ridicule Williams by calling him "Monkey Eric" it backfired and Butler's downfall began. Williams was perceived as being serious, and the society treated him accordingly.

Language, then, in Trinidad and Tobago was of extreme importance. Williams, a consummate student of the needs of his people, understood that his task consisted of identifying with his people and releasing them back into the power and beauty of their language. To give voice to their aspirations in ways that were peculiarly theirs was Williams's overall and consuming task.

MY RELATIONS WITH THE CARIBBEAN COMMISSION

To articulate the past historically does not mean to recognize it "the way it really was." It means to seize hold of a memory as it flashes up at a moment of danger. Historical materialism wishes to retain that image of the past which unexpectedly appears to man singled out by history at a moment of danger.
—Walter Benjamin, *Illuminations*

My Relations with the Caribbean Commission, Williams's first political conversation with his people, is a tour de force in its linguistic style and demonstrates a knowledge and understanding of his audience. On June 21, "the longest day of the year," as Rogers characterized it, Williams had come out to play and no one

---

[40] George "Sonny" Goddard, *Forty Years in the Steelbands* (London: Karia, 1991), p. 80. See also C. L. R. James's "A Convention Appraisal" (reproduced in this volume) in which he argues that Williams was "extremely impatient" with "fools" who wasted his time. He notes, "Time is very precious to him."

was going to stop him. Over twenty thousand persons had come out to hear him speak, and speak he did for five hours. In graphic detail, Rogers outlined the scene:

> On that night, 21 st June, 1955, there was a scene as never was before in our island. The People's Education Movement had come of age. Cars ringed Woodford Square within the precincts of the Anglican Cathedral. Hundreds of cars with head peering out as so many Flintstones, listened. The whole of Trinidad and Tobago was represented. The merchant class, the planter class, it was as classless as Carnival only that there were no pockets or enclaves of bands.... The point chiefly discussed was the [sic] West Indianization. The discussion under the lamplight was always West Indianization. There was sympathy for the past treatment towards the lecturer [Williams]. But there was more empathy than sympathy. One of the Behind the Bridge [boys] drew an analogy.... "We are all like dogs with tails between our legs. This man has come to make us take our tail from between our legs."[41]

The address, then, had less to do with the manner in which Williams was treated by his superiors at the commission as it had to do with the way in which Williams presented himself to the common person, the manner in which he identified his cause with that of the public interest, and the bravery with which he acted in the face of the hostility of the oppressor. As Williams described the events, all he was doing when he lost his job at the commission was championing the cause of the masses within the context of a semigovernmental organization. It was not so much that *he* had defied the commissioners as *they*, his audience, thought. He had told *the man* where to go and what he could do with his job, and for this his audience was eternally grateful. In

---

[41] Rogers, *Rise of the People's National Movement*, pp. 36–37. See also Winston Mahabir's account of this not so unplanned address in Mahabir's *In and Out of Politics* (Port of Spain: Imprint, 1976).

their daily lives they wanted to say similar things to the master but could not. As he reminded his audience (at that moment they had become his parents, brothers, and sisters) they had paid for his education and so he (their son, or, "a son of the soil," as they called him with great reverence) would consecrate his life to their service. This was both serious business and, undoubtedly, high drama. No longer would white men (the colonial masters, the police heads, and so on) be able to kick around colonial people as they had done previously. Williams had stood up to them; he would be the people's champion. He had served the oppressor class (he would sometimes call them the imperialists), he understood them, and he would use that knowledge to advance the cause of his brothers and sisters. The stylistic dimension of Williams's conversation was an important part of that performance, as was its theatricality. They were geared to respond to the particularity of his audience. If one loses sight of these aspects of *My Relations with the Caribbean Commission,* one loses sight of an important aspect of Williams's persona and his contribution to political discourse of the society's political history.

Williams begins *My Relations with the Caribbean Commission* in a very direct manner: "I stand before you tonight, and, therefore, before the people of the British West Indies, the representative of a principle, a cause, a defeat. The principle is the principle of intellectual freedom. The cause is the cause of the West Indian people. The defeat is the defeat of the policy of appointing local men to high office."[42]

To impart a certain amount of seriousness to the occasion, Williams states the facts and gives historical and personal examples to demonstrate his position. The syntactical arrangement of the conversation is as follows: Such and such happened, I did such and such, and was treated in the following manner. In light of my behavior, was the commission's treatment of me justified?

---

[42] Since these addresses are reproduced elsewhere in this text, I will only note the specific address from which the excerpts used in this essay are taken.

I ask you to draw your own conclusions. Because he seeks to impart information, the syntactical emphasis of the conversation is on the nouns, pronouns, and verbs. Few adjectives and adverbs are used, and no maudlin prose is present because he does not seek to elicit the sympathy of his audience. That would distract from the seriousness of his presentation to his people. The effect that is conveyed to his audience is one of utmost seriousness, and all ears and emotions are given over to this confrontation between their son and the colonial master. As Williams spoke—and whenever Williams spoke—it was customary to boast that "if a pin drop, it could be heard miles away." As the people listened, a nation was engaged in a conversation with itself and thus utter seriousness and attention were demanded.

The cause to which Williams alluded was the freedom of West Indian peoples to express themselves as fully as they wished, and that capacity for unfettered expression constituted freedom. In later years, Bob Marley put it just as well: "Every man has a right to decide his own destiny." Williams's achievement, even though he said what had happened to him represented a defeat, was a jump from being a common citizen to the triumph of achieving the highest position the colonizer could offer. But, sly and manipulative as they were, they denied him the ultimate achievement, that of being made the chairman of the Research Division of the commission when he deserved it, and that was not really playing fair. They were not playing by the rules of the game, and so their treachery had to be unmasked. By identifying *his cause* with *their aspirations* Williams established a common bond with his audience, and from that point on he literally speaks for them. In other words, he becomes the spokesperson of their cause.

In conversing with his people, Williams does a number of things. First, he identifies his accusers: "The cause of the war [between himself and the Caribbean Commission] was [Williams's] *The Negro in the Caribbean.* The enemy was the sugar planters of Antigua with my superior officers as their standard bearer." Second, he ridicules the intellectual standards of the dominant planter class: "I was not impressed by planters' standards of research or definition of society." Third, it is he rather than they who speaks on behalf of the masses of the Caribbean:

> Every step that has been taken in the West Indies during the past ten years [1942–52] has been in the direction of the strengthening of the freedom of opinion and free discussion so as to develop the masses of the people in the practice of democracy and to enable them to express their views, and if possible implement them against the wishes of many of these vested interests [of the planters].
> ... I am pained to have to say that the situation in which you now place me leads me to believe that, in this instance at any rate, your request and the circumstances surrounding it represents a complete reversal of what I and, I am certain, many others have understood to be the recent trend in West Indian government ... and what I have considered to be a guiding principle of the Anglo-American Caribbean Commission.

Fourth, he establishes his intellectual and moral superiority over his superiors and, in the process, describes how he rendered the former speechless; that is, for a moment, he had taken away his speech. In fact, Mr. X, his superior, had not only become speechless, he was at a loss even to construct meaning. The young colonial had made the colonialist incoherent. This is a remarkable achievement: Williams had literally beaten his "superior" (both figuratively and literally) at his own game and rendered him mute, one of the major weapons that the colonizer always held over the heads of his subjects. While speaking with his "superior" Williams recounts that he was conscious of two impressions: "a) that Mr. X was literally flabbergasted. I doubt that he had ever expected *any colonial to write or speak to him like that;* b) that morally and physically I was his superior. That he should be evasive and apologetic I fully expected. But he was more than that. *At times he was quite incoherent, and I had to ask him at least twice to explain what he meant.* He placed the blame on fatigue. When we were through he had had enough; I could have gone on for three hours. On one occasion he conceded that I was fundamentally right. I replied that I was fundamentally, legally, morally and intellectually right. I refused to yield one millimetre of ground" (emphasis added). Later, he says to his superior with regard to a particular bit of contested information: "He also challenged my interpretation of the colonial regime in the thirteen mainland colonies of North America before the War of Independence, but he subsequently withdrew his opposition when I asked him to send to the library for any book on the subject." His mastery over the colonialist was supreme and assured.

At the end of his conversation, Williams identified totally with his audience. After speaking of the innumerable burdens he had to endure, he ends by confiding to his audience: "But you may ask why I tolerated those conditions for twelve years?" He answers: "I represented in the Commission's Secretariat the cause of the West Indian people. I had also had more personal reasons. My connection with the Commission brought me into close contact with present problems in territories the study of whose history has been the principal purpose of my adult life, while association with representatives of the metropolitan governments enabled me to understand, as I could not otherwise have understood, the mess in which the West Indies find themselves today." In other words, he is saying, I did it all for you. I was your legal spy in this mess of madness and den of intrigue. Hence the justification of his actions: "Obviously, the cause and interests of the West Indian people needed to be defended in such an organization, at least in two ways: first, the scope of the work to be done and the priorities to be given to it; second, the selection of the persons to do that work. *I became the watchman* for and the *spokesman of the West Indian people in the Secretariat* with respect to these two questions, and by my visits to territories and my attendance at meetings and conferences I was in a position to express the West

Indian point of view and to influence West Indians in attendance." Later, he says, "I missed no opportunity of getting close to the people. The expatriate missed no opportunity of getting away from them. . . . It is the power of the people that the imperialists feared most."

At this point, his identification with the people of the Caribbean and Trinidad and Tobago is complete. The issues that led to his firing from the commission and upon which he conversed with them were "not personal but political, they involve not a single individual but the West Indian people." As a result of such scandalous treatment, he vows to stay in his homeland and makes it very clear:

> I was born here and here I stay, with the people of Trinidad and Tobago, who educated me free of charge for nine years at Queen's Royal College and for five years at Oxford, and who have made me whatever I am, and who have been or might be at any time the victims of the very pressures which I have been fighting against for twelve years. . . .
>
> I am going to let down my bucket where I am, now, right here with you in the British West Indies.

In this speech, Williams represents himself as the people's champion, a native son of the soil who had returned to stay. In his conversation, he missed no opportunity to speak on their behalf and to represent their interests. The cut and thrust of his rhetorical skills are remarkable and his resentment against the commission's treachery and deceit is obvious. In his conversation with his people he brings together formality ("proper" grammar and scholarship), which gives his conversation, its authority, and colloquialism, which gives his audience a feeling of familiarity and warmth and a sense of connivance in this deadly serious game of defiance against colonial authority. The informality of his Trinidad speech rhythms and the taking of the people into his confidence are reminiscent of the traditional oral mode of storytelling. Yet the conversation possesses the elements of the lime and the authority of the schoolmaster and has all the trademarks of the general introduction to a long-awaited story: "Now, it can be told!"[43] It is this bringing together of formal syntax, vernacular diction, and the rhetorical asides that gives this conversation the mark of authority.

While his initial conversation with his people uses a language that depicts this oppressed mass as capable of understanding the injustice perpetrated against him, seeing their condition reflected in him, and participating in the activity of unmasking the treachery of the master, it would take a little more time before he began to formulate a narrative discourse that was adequate to his/their political ideas/ideals. As engaging and emotional as *My Relations with the Caribbean Commission* is, it lacks the syntactical tightness, the ready scatological thrust, the underlying sarcasm, and the deft rhetorical force of *Massa Day Done* (1960). At this point in his career, the personal still overwhelms the political, the appeal to sentiments still supersedes the need to engage in honest political dialogue that would come when the serious business of building a party began and the organization of political discourse arose. *My Relations with the Caribbean Commission* was about Eric Williams. His other pamphlets would speak more specifically to the needs of the people.

According to Colin MacCabe, "the writing of history is as much a specific practice as that of the novel." Arguing that the past does not have an order independent of its present enunciation, he quotes Benjamin to argue that "to articulate the past

---

[43] In a remarkable event during the last elections, Eddie Hart (M.P., Tunapuna, 1990–), a very popular sports figure of Tacarigua but not a person who is formally trained, was asked by one of his friends (Archer Morris, better known as Skip Jack) during a late night lime in Tacarigua in Kenny Traboulay's (better known as Baba's) backyard, "How come you were selected to run for the constituency?" In typical style, Hart began, "As the fellars used to say long time . . ." and went on to reveal the circumstances that led to his running for political office. Hart never held an elective position before this run for office.

historically does not mean to recognize it 'the way it really was.'. .. It means to seize hold of a memory as it flashes up at a moment of danger."[44] Williams's recapitulation of the events at the Caribbean Commission, as he acknowledged, was in no way an innocent, nonpolitical act. Its telling constituted a moment of danger in which he attempted to transmit to his people the predicament of what it meant to be helpless and alone against an indifferent enemy whose only concern was the maintenance of its own power. Yet, this specific practice involves the organizing and shaping of events to fit one's present needs, and that was Williams's task when he presented *My Relations with the Caribbean Commission*. Power, he argued, would have to be transmitted to the people, and he was prepared to work with them toward that end. Only by organizing the people as a coherent whole could such power be forthcoming. But the manipulation of language in a way that his people understood would also be of enormous value in presenting his case. *The Case for Party Politics* is the necessary culmination of that initial act of defiance: the organization of a people through the skilled use of language.

THE CASE FOR PARTY POLITICS, 1955

> The object of the institution of the *polis* is for him [Pericles] the creation of a human being, the Athenian citizen, who exists and lives through the unity of these three: the love and "practice" of beauty, the love and "practice" of wisdom, the care and responsibility for the common good, the collectivity, the *polis*. . . . Among the three, there can be no separation; beauty and wisdom such as Athenians loved them and lived them could exist only in Athens.
> —Cornelius Castoriadis, *Philosophy, Politics, Autonomy*

---

[44] Colin MacCabe, *Tracking the Signifier; Theoretical Essays: Film Linguistics, Literature* (Minneapolis: University of Minnesota Press, 1985), p. 110.

Thus far, I have argued that Williams was a conscious performer, aware of historical precedent in that he was conscious of what he wanted to achieve. I also drew on Edmund Burke to suggest that not only did Burke's book initiate the great debate in England "by which he . . . opened unto us the dawn of a glorious day," I also intimated that the publication of Burke's work "established a background which enabled others to recognize their own thought" and made "political thought more conscious, in itself . . . [and] more expressible."[45] It would also be remembered that Williams concluded his speech on his relations with the Caribbean Commission by characterizing Trinidad as being "politically the most backward area in the Caribbean, except for those monuments of backwardness, Martinique and Guadeloupe." As Williams saw it, his political task consisted in leading his society out of political darkness into the light of modern political arrangements.

As Williams started his tours around the island to engage his people in political discussion, one of his most important addresses was entitled *The Case for Party Politics in Trinidad and Tobago*. As usual, the tour, given under the auspices of the PEM, commenced at Woodford Square and the speech was delivered in eleven sites around the country. This lecture reflects a much more confident Williams, much more sure of himself and what he wanted to achieve and how he intended to do it.

In *The Case for Party Politics*, Williams began by accusing Trinidad and Tobago of being "the sick man of the Caribbean. Our principal handicap to recovery is our [political] doctors. Five years ago we called in a new team of local doctors to look after us. Five years they have neglected us; they have been too busy growing rich in private practice, and in having tea in the House of Commons, sightseeing in Scandinavia, and not sleeping a wink in Montevideo." The analogy of political sickness is right on the mark and gives his audience a way of speaking of the political malaise of the country in terms that they understood. His repeti-

---

[45] *The Politics of Language*, p. 37.

tion of "five years" reminded his audience of how they had been deceived.

Next, he accuses the Albert Gomes regime of being "political frauds" who must be dealt with by "political methods" and then demands the creation of an Opposition "so enlightened, an Opposition so alert, an Opposition so relentless, that long before those eight months have ended our Legislators and our Government will be wishing that the Secretary of State for the Colonies had saved them from themselves. We are going to do it right here in the University of Woodford Square." Woodford Square, then, would become the base of operations and Williams and his party (soon to be formed) would become "the organised expression of that overwhelming public opinion which the Legislators, the Government, and the Colonial Office have so flagrantly disregarded in prolonging the life of the present Legislative Council."[46] The need, he argued, was for a political party that would fulfill the legitimate aspirations of a people for the organized articulation of political expressions. To be sure, there were a few organized parties based on discussion and democratic decisions but, according to Williams, they were not as fully organized as they might have been nor did they have a coherent plan about how to solve the problems of Trinidad and Tobago.

As far as the language of the document is concerned, Williams effectively deconstructed the fifty-two manifestoes that were presented in the 1950 elections. His critique of the previous party system and the matter of individual representation was a masterpiece of what one might call a close reading of political texts. For example, he demonstrated the folly and miscognizance of those candidates who offered themselves for election and the loose syntactical construction of programs that called for, among other

---

[46] One is reminded of Cornelius Castoriadis's notion that "democracy is a regime founded explicitly upon *doxa*, opinion, the confrontation of opinions, the formation of common opinion. The refutation of another's opinion is more than permitted and legitimated there; it is the very breath of public life" (*Philosophy, Politics, Autonomy* [New York: Oxford University Press, 1991], p. 7).

things, "to demobilize unemployment" or to grant "more social securities" to the people. Yet, it was obvious that with Williams we were in the presence of one who was much better versed in the vagaries of economic and political theory and had a better sense of the realities of the contemporary international economic and social situation. As Williams noted in his document, "One of the fundamental deficiencies in the political life of Trinidad and Tobago is precisely this low level of political intelligence reflected in such appeals to the electorate." In one fell swoop, Williams lifted the intellectual level of the political debate in the society and took it to a much more sophisticated intellectual level. After 1955, candidates for national elections had to be more responsible, possess a better grasp of political, economic, and social issues, and think more carefully before they spoke or wrote. Perhaps because of these higher and more stringent demands, after 1956 independent candidacies disappeared from the political scene.

Williams used Edmund Burke, noted his people's capacity for greatness and enlightened understanding, and ended with Pericles and the promise of making Trinidad the Athens of the Caribbean. Certainly, the mood of this piece has changed: the emphasis is on the political rather than the personal; his excoriation is no longer for the expatriate exploiter but is directed against the local petit-bourgeois of the society who have betrayed the promise of universal adult suffrage and thereby the people's trust. Through the syntactical tightness of the piece and a careful appeal to reason, he seeks to define what is possible through the united efforts of the people. It is in this sense that he quotes Edmund Burke:

> Certainly, gentlemen, it ought to be the happiness and glory of a representative to live in the strictest union, the closest correspondence, and the most unreserved communication with his constituents. Their wishes ought to have great weight with him. It is his duty to sacrifice his repose, his pleasures, his satisfactions, to theirs; and

above all, ever, and in all cases, to prefer their interests to his own.

But Parliament is not a *congress* of ambassadors from different and hostile interests; which interests each must maintain, as an agent and advocate, against other agents and advocates; parliament is a *deliberative* assembly of *one* nation, with *one* interest, that of the whole; where, not local purposes, not local prejudices ought to guide, but the general good, resulting from the general reason of the whole. You chose a member indeed; but when you have chosen him, he is not member of Bristol, he is member of *parliament.*

Although Burke was identified as a model of reaction, his influence on Williams and James revolved around his (Burke's) capacity to see history as movement and his talent for writing elegant prose. As Consuelo Lopez says of Burke's influence on James, and this can be applied to Williams, "Because he [Burke] had the power to express the swift movement of time in daring images and classical allusions, Burke enticed James into a world of breathtaking oratory where the past danced circles around the present and waltzed the future into current view." [47]

But if Burke, the exemplar of party politics, constituency rule, and stunning oratory, was the means whereby the people of Trinidad and Tobago could be raised out of the political "ditch," ancient Athens provided the model for the new democracy. Drawing on the funeral oration of Pericles, Williams ended his discussion on party politics as follows:

> Its administration favours the many instead of the few; this is why it is called a democracy. If we look to the laws, they afford equal justice to all in their private differ-

---

[47] Consuelo Lopez, "C. L. R. James: The Rhetoric of a Difiant Warrior" (Ph.D dissertation, Indiana University, 1983), p. 36.

ences; if to social standing, advancement in public life falls to reputation for capacity, class considerations not being allowed to interfere with merit; nor again does poverty bar the way, if a man is to serve the State, he is not hindered by the obscurity of his condition.... Our public men have, beside politics, their private affairs to attend to, and our ordinary citizens, though occupied with the pursuits of industry, are still fair judges of public matters; for, unlike any other nation, regarding him who takes part in these duties not as unambitious but as useless, we are able to judge at all events if we cannot originate, and instead of looking on discussion as a stumbling-block in the way of action, we think it an indispensable preliminary to any wise action of all.

According to Rogers, *The Case for Party Politics* "plummeted Dr. Williams straight into the hearts of the people. It was considered the gem of his lectures," and as a member of the audience noted: "In amplitude of comprehension and richness of imagination he has out-burked Burke!"[48] The political had transcended the personal and Williams was on his way toward becoming a linguistic force to be reckoned with in the society.

PERSPECTIVES FOR OUR PARTY

Dear Jimmy. Your godchild!/ In appreciation./ Bill./ November 21, 1944
—Eric Williams to C. L. R. James, Dedication on the publication of *Capitalism and Slavery*

Perspectives for Our Party, delivered three years after *The Case for Party Politics,* is one of Williams's most theoretical speeches. In showing the ideological and intellectual development of the party,

---

[48] Rogers, *Rise of the People's National Movement*, pp. 43, 46.

it signifies another milestone in the history of the PNM and Williams's political development. In this essay, Williams is at his best when he seeks to point his party in a theoretical direction having realized that, though broadly nationalist in scope and fairly well organized, it had to some degree become an election machine. In his address to the party Williams identified three stages of its development and insisted that the time had come to organize it so that "it lives a political life of its own." Indeed, Williams's addresses to the third, fourth, and fifth Conventions were designed to examine and strengthen the apparatus of the party and to plan for its future development.[49]

In a strange way, this address reflected a culmination of yet another kind of partnership, the culmination of a process that had started some thirty years previously at Queens Royal College, Port of Spain, when Williams was a student and James was his teacher. Moreover, the views expressed in this address represented the theoretical result of a friendship and mentorship that were born in Trinidad, matured in Britain and the United States, and reached its apogee when James returned to the island in 1958–60. Indisputably, the thoughts contained in *Perspectives for Our Party* resulted from the fusion of Williams's and James's intellectual collaboration in that James's fingerprints can be seen throughout this document. And though Rogers contends that many of the principles articulated in this document were not put into practice (precisely, I suspect, because so many of the ideas belonged to James), it still remains an important address in the

---

[49] The reason for this strengthening of the party is obvious. A nationalist movement takes into its grasp all and sundry (that is, varying interests) who are opposed to colonialism. As the march toward independence proceeded, the party needed to organize and systematize the progressive strand within its movement, that is, those who were genuinely committed to social (and even socialist) transformation of the society. Only a purposefully organized party can provide such leadership to the society. This was precisely the content of C. L. R. James's objection to the lack of party building he noticed in the PNM and lack of interest that was paid to strengthening the party. See C. L. R. James, *Party Politics in the West Indies* (San Juan: C. L. R. James, 1962), for discussion of this problem.

party's history and in 1993 challenges the members of the PNM to give substance to its pronouncements.[50]

James always had been in conversation with Williams. Although their relationship deteriorated after 1960, the important point is that they enjoyed a very close and warm friendship until that time as Williams's inscription in November 1944 to James attests on the publication of *Capitalism and Slavery*, an extension of Williams's doctoral dissertation. The inscription read: "Dear Jimmy./ Your godchild!/ In appreciation."[51] James, in turn, referred to Williams affectionately as his son and always took great pride in Williams and his achievement. Thus, on April 8, 1944, he wrote to Constance Webb, his second wife: "I have a son you know. He is thirty years old. I watch over him like a trainer and prizefighter. Of course, he is not my son really. He is a young West Indian, a scholar of repute, who wrote a superb thesis at Oxford for his doctorate—The Economic Basis of the Slave Trade and Slavery. For nearly 12 years now, I have watched him come along. He sometimes is very thoughtless and selfish. But I don't mind. Seeing him develop pleases me."[52] This relationship, cultivated over a period of thirty years, had a major impact on Williams and the PNM and, to a large degree, fashioned Williams's conversations with his people.

---

[50] In repudiating Williams's position, Rogers also used very colorful language to express his disagreement. He says: "In 1956, the silver tongued picoplat, the golden-throated acravat, the ramougaing semp, even the dark-hued assonant atawatwas [sic] were not heard or was not, allowed to be heard at all in the Legislative Council.... At the present one does not even hear the toc-toc of the carpenter bird nor the tweet tweet of the sesizeb" (p. 120). Even the language of discontent, one must admit, was redolent with color.

[51] The copy of *Capitalism and Slavery* to which I refer is in the possession of Marty Glaberman, one of James's most faithful lieutenants.

[52] There is no doubt that *Capitalism and Slavery* owes much conceptually to *The Black Jacobins*, a point Williams acknowledges in one of his footnotes. To argue, as some persons have, that James wrote *Capitalism and Slavery* (a point made recently by the editors of *An Enigma Answered*) is to negate James's own testimony to the contrary and to misunderstand how influences and collaboration work in writing and research. See my discussion on James and Williams in *Movement of the People* (Ithaca: Calaloux, 1983).

From the inception of the relationship the intellectual approaches of James and Williams differed as did their theoretical conceptions of the world. They also went in quite different directions. Williams proceeded to Howard University and later to the Caribbean Commission and concerned himself with the facts and figures of the colonial economy, whereas James turned to the working class, explored theoretical questions (such as the nature of the "Russian Question" and the "Negro Question"), and involved himself in the Marxist debate that raged at the time. While Williams's engagement with his world led to publications such as *Education in the British West Indies* (1950) and *Documents in British West Indian History, 1807–1833* (1952), James's involvement led to the publication of *Notes on Dialectics* (1948), a major philosophical text, and *Facing Reality* (1957), a work on the Hungarian Revolution. In contrasting these works, one can argue, as I have in another context, for what I called Williams's empiricist-pragmatic approach to the examination of social-historical phenomena as opposed to James's dialectical method.[53]

But despite such divergence of interest, the love and respect they had for each other and their political collaboration continued. In 1956 Williams took the first draft of the *People's Charter*, the founding document of the PNM, to London, where he discussed it with C. L. R. James, George Padmore, and Arthur Lewis.[54] Also, it is very clear that James had a chance to discuss the ideas contained in *Perspectives for Our Party* with Williams. Grace Lee, a member of the Johnson-Forest Tendency, James's American party of the 1940s, and a close collaborator of James, writes that while she and James were in London in 1957, "Eric Williams visited often and told colorful stories about PNM struggles in Trinidad. Tom Mboya, Basil Davidson et al. also came to lunch. [Kwame] Nkrumah came for the First Commonwealth Prime

---

[53] See Cudjoe, *Movement of the People*, p. 200.

[54] See Williams, *Inward Hunger*, p. 143.

Ministers' Conference attended by Third World independence leaders and we (CLR, Selma [James, James's third wife], [George] Padmore, Williams and I) spent an afternoon with him at the Dorchester Hotel."[55] The next year James went to Trinidad, and his collaboration with the PNM and Williams intensified. James became the editor of the *PNM Weekly* and on December 6, 1958, changed the name of the paper to the *Nation*. James's account of his stay in Trinidad is recounted in *Party Politics in the West Indies* (1960). In *Inward Hunger* (1969), Williams gives little recognition to his association with James and dishonestly dismisses James when he argues that the latter deserted West Indian politics for "the absurdities of world revolution."[56]

In *Perspectives for Our Party*, Williams advances notions about the relationship between leaders and the masses ("the West Indian masses are . . . travelling fast . . . all party leaders . . . should be kept constantly aware of it"), the laying down of the broad party philosophy for the second-level leaders to follow ("It is not writing articles in the Press that is important. It is to lay down the lines along which articles should be written and to find and develop this talent in all sections of the organisation"), the importance of theory in building the party and the distinction between the political leader and the theoretical leader (Lenin's role in the Bolshevik party "was above all that of theoretical guide and source of inspiration" and the "political leader and the theoretical leader need not necessarily be one and the same person") all of which come straight out of James's work of the 1940s and early 1950s. I suspect, however, that the distinction that Williams made between the political and theoretical leader may have been a ploy—a testing of the waters, as it were—for James's entry into the

---

[55] Personal correspondence with Grace Lee, June 1992.

[56] Williams, *Inward Hunger*, p. 77.

formal leadership of the PNM. To do so, Williams had to sterilize James, the malignant Marxist.[57]

Yet the nuances of Williams's rhetorical strategy remain within the texture of this address to his party. Once more, he uses the cultural symbols of his society and draws upon the most popular cultural form, the calypso. In urging the members of his party to become financially responsible and to support the party, Williams reinterpreted the Mighty Sparrow, both in language and in cadence, to read:

> De doctah say to pay as you earn,
> PNM say you paying to learn.

By substituting PNM for Sparrow in the second line of the chorus Williams appropriated a very popular calypso—it was the road march for 1958—with all of its cultural symbols and popular sentiments and clothed them with the aura of the PNM. More important, the signature of "de doctah" is conflated with that of the PNM, thus the sacralizing of "de doctah" and the PNM is complete. This technique was not new. He had used it from the inception of the party.[58]

In winding up his address, Williams turns to the Bible when he talks about "the personality of the PNM." "The Lord said unto Peter upon this rock I will build my church" becomes "I say to you,

---

[57] James's close relationship to Williams during the 1958–60 period led an influential figure in the PNM to remark: "For a year Nello [C.L.R.] was number two in the Party. If fact, there were times when we thought he might have been number one." Quoted in Ivar Oxaal (Cambridge: Schenkman, 1968), p. 128.

[58] Rogers notes that at one of the earliest meetings of the PNM, when it was unknown and just getting started, Williams encountered an ill-disposed group of men, the Red Cap Boys, in his opponent's territory, who were intent on disrupting his speech. Making a similar substitution of lines from Sparrow's "Jean and Dinah," ("The Yankees gone, PNM take over now") Williams was able to ameliorate the crowd. After invoking Sparrow, Rogers notes, "the audience was responsive and began to look upon the Red Caps as a nuisance" (*The Rise of the People's National Movement*, p. 68). In his *Calypso and Society*, Gordon Rohlehr posits a link between the emergence of The Mighty Sparrow and the PNM (Port of Spain: Gordon Rohlehr, 1990), pp. 526–27.

you are the PNM, and upon this rock we will build the edifice of West Indian nationalism, and the gates of reaction would not prevail." There is no demonstrable evidence that Williams was a Christian in the narrow, dogmatic sense of the term (he decreed that his body be cremated at his death) even though he was a deeply religious man.[59] Yet he was not above using biblical allegories and religious imagery to dramatize the importance of his point. On important occasions he drew upon the Bible for inspiration and to inspire the nation. Because the base of his party were God-fearing people—for a long time the Spiritual Baptist was the base of the PNM—he knew that to connect with them, as he delivered this important theoretical message, he had to integrate the political with the theological. A more vivid image could not be found nor, for that matter, a more appropriate one for the purposes intended. After all, a speaker always presumes a listener and discourses are intended always to persuade. For Williams, biblical images were always important.

But Williams did not wish to confine himself to the limits of the biblical text. While the Bible verse ends with Peter founding his church upon a rock—the implied image being that building on firm ground ensures a strong foundation—Williams maximizes the conceptual reach of the biblical story and argues that if his party members lay the party's edifice upon/within the rock of West Indian nationalism, "the gates of reaction will not prevail against it." PNM had become coterminous with the progressive agenda of the society.

But the question must be asked: Who were the forces of reaction against which the society had to protect itself and why the coincidence of party building—the move from a nationalist movement to a more structured and organized party—with the society's approach to independence? To be sure, at the time of this address, the goal of the party was the independence of the

---

[59] Williams was believed to be a member of the Spiritual Baptist faith.

West Indian Federation by April 22, 1960, but circumstances thwarted that goal. Enormous enthusiasm was pushing the society forward but organized planning, at the level of the party, toward the achievement of independence was not keeping pace with the forward momentum of the masses. But the hand of colonial-capitalist reaction was reaching out to turn the society backward. *Massa Day Done* was an attempt to deal with that problem head-on.

MASSA DAY DONE

> "Rhetoric demands that the user has some perspective, something to which he is pointing." In this sense, "rhetoric can be used and will be used by revolutionaries; but it will be part of a movement, a revolutionary movement.".
> . . It is not some words that can be erected, put in or taken out as time goes on; not at all, it's part of a movement.
> —Consuelo Lopez, "C. L. R. James: The Rhetoric of a Defiant Warrior"

By any yardstick, *Massa Day Done* marks the apogee of Williams's rhetorical skills and political acumen. In this piece he brings together all the political wisdom five years of active politics had taught him and for which thirty years of scholarly research had prepared him. He combines the fierce sternness of the schoolmaster (remember *Inward Hunger*, "you are not laughing at my mistake, you are laughing at me") with the righteous indignation of a colonial subject (and by extension, a people) who had suffered centuries of indignities at the hands of Massa. For the first time since his departure from the Caribbean Commission, Williams seemed to have had a clear path in which, unrepentantly, he could repudiate every evil that had been thrust upon the African slave, the Indian, and the Chinese indentures and, in so doing, disdain for the system that had welled up in him over the

> I repeat, more emphatically than when I said it the first time, Massa Day Done. I accuse the DLP of being the stooge of the Massas who still exist in our society. I accuse the DLP of deliberately trying to keep back social progress. I accuse the DLP of wanting to bring back Massa Day. . . .
>
> This pack of benighted idiots, this band of obscurantist politicians, this unholy alliance of egregious individualists, who have nothing constructive to say, who babble week after week the same criticisms that we have lived through for five long years, who, nincompoops that they are, think that they can pick up any old book the day before a debate in the Legislative Council and can pull a fast one in the Council by leaving out the sentence or the paragraph or the pages which contradict their ignorant declamations—for people like these power is all that matters. They have not the slightest idea as to the constituents of progress in our society and the elements of our historical evolution. All that they can see in the slogan, Massa Day Done, is racial antagonism. This is characteristically stupid. Massa is not a racial term. Massa is the symbol of a bygone age. Massa Day is a social phenomenon: Massa Day Done connotes a political awakening and a social revolution.

In this address Williams's attack on the colonial *other* had come full circle. He had moved from stressing the wrongs against an individual that had cluttered *My Relations with the Caribbean*

---

[60] Williams's response to colonialism is certainly much more complex that this. In another context, I have argued that Williams felt a certain amount of ambivalence toward colonialism which drew him in different directions. Certainly his acceptance of a peerage, which I understand was very important to him, contrast sharply with his insistence of Massa's sins. See *Movement of the People* for a discussion of this aspect of Williams's behavior.

Commission to the expression of the common sentiment of a society as a collectivity that had been scorned by the colonial master. He had captured the inner vibes of the progressive strata of a nation and took its sentiments to the bitter end. Through the use of antithesis Williams contrasted the old days of slavery and colonialism with the new era of internal self-government; the sins of the colonial master with the liberation tendencies of the nationalist leaders. Thus the repudiation of Massa was concomitant to a social revolution of values, a freeing up of the national soul. No longer could the mere political association of a white person (Sir Gerald Wight, a massa, at that) with a reactionary party bring fear and trepidation into the nationalist camp especially at a time when the colonialist-capitalist enterprise appeared to be on the brink of visible destruction, lying on its febrile head and exposed to the naked glare of a nationalist movement (the party never really got itself going) that was just beginning to feel its spurs. Indeed, Williams's brilliant move was to link his opponents (the Democratic Labour Party [DLP]) with the taint of reaction, years of servitude, and then to counterpoise them against the progressive impulses of the nation.[61]

Massa Day Done was also about loyalty to a society and a people in struggle, a call for self-dignity and self-responsibility. In this conversation, all of the correct symbolic codes and representations were present: those of Massa and the slaves; concepts of subservience and defiance; racial inequality versus racial equality; notions about the brutality of the system and the search for personal and political autonomy. Contrasted with Williams's intellectual sophistication and commitment to his society was the specter of absentee landlords who had exploited the society economically, deliberately underutilized its human resources, and demeaned the human personality. As Williams argued, Massa

---

[61] For a boy growing up in Tacarigua and going to school with the son of an estate manager, whose mother told the workers to call his father "Massa," the energy that Williams's castigation released can only be imagined some thirty-two years later.

was "an uncultured man with an illiberal outlook." By putting Massa on one side of the social divide and linking the DLP with the forces of social reaction Williams had won an enormous victory. In the end, his address did not turn on *what* he said about Massa but on what Massa *symbolized* to the society: the worst elements of our social development as a people.

At its best, *Massa Day Done* is an oration that privileges the activities of the working people over those of the dominant exploiter class; employs the vernacular rhythms and melodic pairings of the folk; and anticipates "the-grounding-with-my-brothers" sentiments that are expressed in Walter Rodney's *Grounding with My Brothers* (1969) and Amilcar Cabral's solidarity with his traditional culture that is affirmed in his *Return to the Source* (1973). In this address, Williams has moved rapidly from the ambiguities articulated in "Two Worlds in Conflict" to a complete identification with the scrunting masses of his society and, to the degree possible, liberated himself from the psychological constraints of his formal academic training. There was little obsession with facts and figures for their own sake. There was only the controlled emotion of a people-centered discourse; the linguistic rendering of a people's suffering; the attempt to voice "the growing national and [liberated] consciousness" of a people on the move to national independence.

Within this context, the strength of this brilliant and sophisticated address lay in Williams's capacity to subvert "linguistic representation by his refusal to treat language in terms of meanings but rather in terms of a constant battle for power between speakers."[62] Williams's attack was launched first against the *Trinidad Guardian,* a perennial enemy, which he attacked for its "slave mentality." Here, the contest was between those who controlled the word and the way they represented colonized people. Next, there was the attack against those who left out sentences, paragraphs, and pages from their discourses in a deliberate at-

---

[62] MacCabe, *Tracking the Signifier,* p. 117.

tempt to distort the record (historical or otherwise), to misuse language and obfuscate meaning to satisfy their own ends. And then there were those who had refused to accept the fact that a new day had dawned upon the horizon.

In this discussion, then, not only were the questions of who controlled meaning or who was responsible for the representation of a people at stake. The critical question revolved around who had the power to control these practices. In *Perspectives for Our Party* the formation of a party press was one of the major recommendations that was made. By the time we arrive at *Massa Day Done* the question of who spoke for the people and who produces and reproduces meaning for society was still within the realm of contested ground. In other words, the question is posed: Who speaks for the people? Is it Williams, the enlightened son of a progressive age, or Wight, the benighted son of a reactionary past? Surely, the battle for power and control of the society was what the people's struggle was all about from the time the Maroons took up arms in Jamaica in the seventeenth century against the English to the moment Williams joined the nationalist struggle. As Williams insisted: "When they ask me to withdraw my banner, Massa Day Done, they are in fact telling the people of the West Indies that they want Massa *to continue in social control, monopolising political power,* stultifying economic development, [and] disciplining the workers" (emphasis added).

For Williams, part of this struggle over contested ground involved the struggle for intellectual freedom, the right to pursue knowledge wherever it leads and the capacity to control language and its meanings. In accusing the DLP of "intellectual dishonesty," Williams may have been a bit disingenuous, but it is wise to remember that the argument was not so much about morality as it was about the power of rhetorical skill, philosophical subtlety, and intellectual persuasion. For as James noted in another context, "Within revolutions . . . rhetoric is the highest development of a tremendous force of expression which is utilized by one force against another. Rhetoric was of use in fighting against slavery; it was of use in fighting against the bourgeoisie, and rhetoric will be of use in fighting against the modern bureaucracy."[63] Williams, a conscious and informed rhetorician, recognized what he was doing. By reducing the arguments of the Opposition to *absurdum* he is able to heap scorn upon its proposals. For even though there might have been some validity to the arguments made by the DLP (for example, their concern for small farmers) Williams's equation of its arguments with factors outside PNM's control ("All that is left for them to do is to blame P.N.M. for the fall in world prices") was designed to show how ignorant the DLP was of economic realities and how out of touch it was with the historical time and place. Certainly, the images of newness and rebirth embodied in the PNM contrasted with the moribund and decay of the DLP and suggested that the society had no choice but to stick with the PNM. Moreover, by portraying the PNM as the embodiment of progress and the DLP as the embodiment of reaction, he sought to demonstrate how necessary it was for the PNM to begin to represent itself in a way that was consistent with its image of a progressive nationalist movement which, to some degree, was part of the context out of which *Massa Day Done* arises. No wonder Williams could announce: "Now that the principal obstacle to a daily issue of the *Nation* [the PNM newspaper] has been removed from the scene, P.N.M. has its own contribution to make to the promotion of political education through the press and to the maintenance of the press from monopolistic control." The latter—the control of images and nature of representation—I suggest was part of the subtext within the entire debate about what *Massa Day Done* meant or did not mean.

Although *Massa Day Done* signified the acme of Williams's political career as an orator and the embodiment of a people's hopes and desires, it also signified the culmination of a particular manner of rendering the society's experiences and returning a

---

[63] Quoted in Lopez, "C. L. R. James: The Rhetoric of a Defiant Warrior," p. 41.

people to its own voice. For reasons that are outside the scope of this paper, at that historical point Williams had gone as far as he could as an innovative leader of his society. For example, Rogers argues that the degeneracy of the PNM began when Williams became "the Social Brain" and democracy within the party began to perish.[64] *Massa Day Done* also marked his break with James and robbed the society of two enormously politically gifted men who could have carried the society yet further.[65] Everything that Williams did after this moment was an apostrophe, a turning away from a mission—the denial of a historic collaboration—that could have had important consequences for the direction of our society.

LANGUAGE AND THE COLONIAL SUBJECT

> The necessary presumption of Milton's poetic practice is an epistemology in which truth can actually reside in the process of language and not *simply* in an external world which language is called to represent.
> —Colin MacCabe, *Tracking the Signifier*

Thus far, I have concerned myself with language and discourse and the way they are reflected in Williams's political speeches as he conversed with his people.[66] In this context it is wise to remember that all of these speeches (conversations) were offered at public forums to audiences of over twenty thousand

---

[64] See Rogers, *Rise of the People National Movement,* pp. 196–205.

[65] Williams said of James: "All . . . who wish to confuse, who seek to climb on P.N.M.'s back to achieve their own mental aberrations, . . . all these imps of Satan will be dealt with in due course. C. L. R. James' case has been sent to our Disciplinary Committee for action; when it is no longer *sub judice* I shall deal with it fully and publicly, and with all of those who seek to use him in their struggle to defeat the PNM and to destroy me." James's response to these charges are contained in *Party Politics in the West Indies.*

[66] In this section, I draw heavily on "On Discourse" in Colin MacCabe's *Tracking the Signifier.*

persons. Using discourse as language in motion and as action, I have sought to demonstrate that truth, as MacCabe has argued, "can actually reside in the process of language and not *simply* in the external world which language is called to represent."[67] Linguistically, *Massa Day Done* signified a very important moment in Trinidad and Tobago's history: that of a nation finding its own voice and positioning itself within the community of nations. It was almost as though a nation had found its identity, clothed in its own linguistic distinctiveness.

In examining *Massa Day Done* one can argue that the figure of the essayist/speaker (Williams) plays a very important function in the narrative. The narrative begins with Williams's recognition that the entire controversy started because "I reported to the people the outcome of the Chaguaramas discussion in Tobago, I poured scorn on the *Guardian*, reminding them that our population of today was far too alert and sophisticated to fall for any claptrap. I told the *Guardian* emphatically: Massa Day Done." Moreover, the first three introductory paragraphs of this address are filled with the first person pronoun "I" while the rest of the address is given over to the sins of Massa. Yet, throughout the address, the omniscient author displays his authority through "the wealth of detailed aorists which guarantee the truth of the narrative and, by metonymy, of its writer."[68] By providing a host of historical examples to prove the destructiveness of Massa which he argues continues into the present via the activities of the DLP and its cohorts, Williams seems to propose that the PNM represented the completion of that phase of Trinidad and Tobago's history, a social phenomenon, he argued, that it shared with the rest of the progressive world. Hence his conclusion:

---

[67] Ibid., p. 121.

[68] The language is that of MacCabe and is used to define the role of Balzac in one of his novels. See *Tracking the Signifier,* p. 91.

Massa Day Done, Sahib Day Done, Yes Suh Boss Day Done. All decent American public opinion is nauseated by Little Rock. The horrors of the Congo, deplorable though they are, represent the struggle between Massa and Massa's former exploited subjects. Massa is on the run right now in Portuguese Angola. The pressure from India and Ghana, Malaya and Nigeria in the Commonwealth Prime Ministers' Conference has forced South African Massa out of the Commonwealth.

Massa Day Done everywhere. How could anyone in his senses expect Massa Day to survive in Trinidad and Tobago? That, however, is precisely what [Ashford] Sinanan and the DLP stand for. Because for them to ask me [a return once more to the present and the use of the personal pronoun] to withdraw the statement, Massa Day Done, and, adding insult to injury, to demand that I apologise for it, is to identity themselves with all the forces of reaction which have been overthrown or are at bay in all the other countries of the world. What they seek, Sinanan and the DLP, is actually to restore Massa Day. For Massa Day Done in Trinidad and Tobago, too, since the advent of the PNM in 1956.

But as we examine the sweeping historical summary that Williams advances in his condemnation of Massa it is very clear that the force of the incitement comes not from one incident of malfeasance but from a varied set of alternatives that were possible within the contours of the colonial and slave systems. In fact, what we see in the narrative is the attempt by Williams to retrieve certain selected items from the preconscious of our collective historical memory and to place them at the disposal of the present. Taking especial care to displace himself from the narrative, Williams is able to guarantee the truth of his accusation against Massa through a very detailed and careful parading of the historical record. In a way, he allows history to speak for itself (or so he thinks), even if, all the while, he is the one who arranges the record so that it speaks the truth he wants to have told.

But having delivered the news is not the only problem. The historical site from which the news is offered is also very important. The news is delivered at the very instant that national independence is being spoken about, at a time when most nations of the Third World are assuming their sense of personhood, so that the acquisition of one's voice and the displacement of the *Other* is not an unimportant or incidental matter in a nation's history. In fact, so important was the announcement (*Massa Day Done*) that it generated a tremendous amount of uneasiness within the society. After all, it must be remembered that what led to this speech was the impertinence (or so it seemed) of a member of the Opposition asking the chief minister of the nation to apologize to Massa for his unfounded statement and hence the vehemence of his response: "I categorically refuse to withdraw my statement or to make any apology for it, qualified or unqualified. I repeat, more emphatically than when I said it the first time, Massa Day Done." Too much was at stake. At that point, he dared not turn back.

What, then, was so crucially at stake was the emergence of the colonial subject, out of a state of subjection, after centuries of servitude and silence, and hence the need to ask a very basic question: Who speaks for this *new* subject? Williams had taken it for granted that he, as representative subject, would do so. The DLP had said that he must apologize for speaking to Massa as he did and so he either had to bow his head, cap in hand, and run off to the nearest hole; or, as they say in Trinidad, "he had to stand up as a man and fight or forever hold his peace/voice." He chose the latter. But MacCabe has informed us that

> the crucial nexus in the acquisition of language (an acquisition which, on this account, must be understood as constant, as interminable) is the moment at which the child grasps the systematic substitutability of pronouns. The moment introduces . . . the big Other, an introduc-

tion understood *not* as the encounter with the parents on the level of demand but as the encounter with the parent as the site of language and desire which outruns any particular statement of demand. *This encounter turns on the parents' speech with each other about the child* [emphasis added]. It is this experience of articulation which produces the divided subject of psychoanalysis, for on the one hand the speaker is caught up in the play of signifiers, of the differential oppositions which produce meaning independently of the activity of the individual, and, on the other, the child takes its place as the "I" of experience and language, the unified subject of classical philosophy and modern linguistics.[69]

I wish to use the analysis above to argue that this description of the child's attainment of language and, with it, the assumption of its individuality, is precisely what was at stake at that moment of national self-consciousness and self-understanding. I argue that the sheer narrative thrust of *Massa Day Done* carries within it that same encounter between the symbolic parent and child of the colonial experience and out of this encounter there emerges a unified subject that is recognized by and through its own voice. In this encounter, the subject of the enunciation is caught up in the enounced not as a disinterested party but as a very active subjectivity. Williams represents the colonial subject who attains to language and, in his assertion of his independence, demands that the *Other*/the parent be silenced as the necessary condition for him to take his place as the "I" (that is, the new subject), or, as the Rastafarians would say, as the "I and I" within his discourse. Thus, in a curious way, independent of the subject, the narrative, caught up in a play of signifiers, produces a meaning independent of the subject/Williams. As such, this narrative can be placed at a moment of national beginnings, a linguistic articulation of our

---

[69] Ibid., pp. 100–101.

national being; a moment when Massa can no longer speak for the child; a moment when the child assumes language and speaks for itself. At that important moment of national self-beginning, Williams had achieved and fulfilled many of the objectives to which Lamming alluded in "Trinidad and the Revolution in Political Intelligence." He took the history of the society, "the infinite, barren tract of documents, dates and texts," and transformed it into senuously lived human experiences in which the people became participants. By objectifying Massa, Williams allowed a people to reside and revel in their subjectivity once more.

Apart from articulating a national sense of self, *Massa Day Done* is also important because of its ability to render a clear and powerful portrayal of the common person. Not only does the essay champion the latter but, in a way, Williams presents himself to the listener as the fundamental proof that massa day was truly finished. He, "William, the Conqueror," as he was called in the early days of the movement, was proof positive that a people could overcome its negative experiences and assume an autonomous role in its communities and in the family of nations.[70] No wonder, then, that in *The Chaguaramas Declaration*, he celebrated the ordinary citizen, whom he called "the small man," gave more emphasis to "grassroots involvement," and advocated "wide-spread popular participation" in the affairs of the society and the need to cultivate "the formation of indigenous values" as opposed to "metropolitan norms." For many Trinidadians and Tobagonians *Massa Day Done* was one of Williams's finest oratorical efforts and one of his finest re-presentations of the common man and woman of the society.

---

[70] In 1956, when the PNM won the elections, the Mighty Sparrow, who identifed closely with the PNM, rejoiced at its victory and lauded Williams in the following verse: "For we have a champion leader/ William the Conqueror." See "The Mighty Sparrow" in James, *Party Politics in the West Indies,* pp. 164–70.

INDEPENDENCE DAY ADDRESS

Our National Flag belongs to all our citizens. Our National Coat-of-Arms, with our National Birds inscribed therein, is the sacred thrust of all our citizens. So it is today. Please, I urge you, let it always be so. Let us always be able to say, with the Psalmist, behold, how good and how pleasant it is for brethren to dwell together in unity.
—Eric Williams, *Independence Day Address*
August 31, 1962

In retrospect, all of Williams's previous addresses were a preparation for his *Independence Day Address* and his address to the youths at Queen's Park Oval on August 30, 1962. Terse in style and aphoristic in content, it suggested that the truth of the "independence" moment was a culmination of all that had transpired during the previous six years. Most assuredly, the compactness of the piece had as much to do with the occasion as with the medium through which it was delivered.[71] Williams was accustomed to the interplay with a live audience and aware of the informal and theatrical nature of any public address (the dynamic interplay between speaker and audience). This *Independence Day Address* was a more formal performance presented in a demotic idiom yet somber enough to make the populace aware of the gravity of the step that it had just taken.

The *Independence Day Address* also signified the ability of a nation to speak for itself and to assume its public voice, a condition for which Williams and the nationalist movement had fought so gallantly. Such an achievement gave Williams the right to speak for or on behalf of his people and hence the direction of his broadcast to the nation on the morning of Independence Day, August 31, 1962. In this terse discourse on democracy, Williams is economical, taut, pointed, and direct. In clear and simple language he drew his people's attention to what it meant for a small

---

[71] This address was delivered to the nation over the radio.

nation to function in a large, indifferent, and hostile international environment. Urging his listeners to take pride in the new symbols of their nation, he was quick to reiterate the central concerns of *Massa Day Done* when he noted: "You are nobody's boss and nobody is your boss." As he reflected upon his society, he realized that although his people had come a long way, they still had an equally long distance to travel before they could call themselves independent.

The language of this *Independence Day Address* is down to earth and stern in that he wishes to persuade his listeners about the importance of this new social enterprise. The verbal images are concrete, and once more he uses verbs and nouns to give his address a tone of seriousness. Absent is the combative, emotional, and evocative tone of *Massa Day Done,* which was designed to annihilate a well-defined enemy. The concern of the independence moment is the conferral of an obligation upon new sovereign subjects: the need to assume new responsibilities in a world that is not particularly concerned about their welfare or the promulgation of their individuality.

The *Independence Day Address* also calls for a new sense of sociability among his people and the need to divest themselves of a particular manner of thinking about the world. Having been nurtured in a culture that demanded that one labor for the benefit of another, now one must work for oneself; having matured in a culture that promulgated and emphasized differences, all groups must now work together and seek out similarities of interest; having pursued individual and/or ethnic agendas, one must now seek to promote *the* national agenda; having seen labor as antagonistic to the development of the self, one must now see labor as a means of realizing the self. In other words, national independence must mean the development of a new social being.

To understand the importance of Williams's *Independence Day Address* it is necessary to know the context in which it was written and the place it assumes within the evolution of Williams's rhetorical positioning. While Williams drew on Pericles and Burke initially, the conditions of independence demanded a more concrete frame of reference within which to address his people. Under the circumstances, the rhetorical style of an Abraham Lincoln rather than a Pericles or Burke provided a more apt comparison for Williams's *Independence Day Address*. Writing about Lincoln in the *Nation* in 1959, James noted that "Burke, Demosthenes [and] Pericles may have excelled him [Lincoln] in range and sustained power. None of them has his simplicity."[72] That simplicity, James added, came from the peculiar nature of his social and political origins.

In very much the same breath, when Williams spoke about the society he envisioned after indpendendence, he could do no better than turn to the simplicity of Lincoln's addresses, particularly the Gettysburg and his Second Inaugural addresses. In fact, the former address changed the reading of the United States Declaration of Independence, argued convincingly that the United States descended from the Declaration rather than the Constitution, and, in a way, inaugurated the United States as we have come to know it.[73] In very much the same sense, one can argue that the simplicity and terseness of Williams's *Independence Day Address* arose out of the peculiarity of his society and inaugurated modern Trinidad and Tobago. To be sure, all of his earlier speeches had prepared him for this terse address of national beginnings. But this address, coming just eighteen years after universal adult suffrage had been granted and seven years after he promised to lay his buckets down in the society, suggested that he had completed a large part of the task he set for himself. Speaking at the birth of a nation that very much had been constituted by and through his language, he signified that an intellectual revolution of thought, particularly at the public level, had taken root in the

---

[72] Quoted in Anna Grimshaw, ed., *The C.L.R. James Reader* (Oxford: Blackwell, 1992), p. 284.

[73] See "Revolution in Thought" in Garry Wills, *Lincoln at Gettysburg* (New York: Simon & Schuster, 1992), for a discussion of this point.

society. Even if Pericles' idea of discussion as "an indispensable preliminary to any wise action of all" and Burke's ideal of political discourse about "the general good" among members of the society had not achieved their fullest realization, at least political independence, placed them within the realm of being attainable.

THE CHAGUARAMAS DECLARATION

> We must devise a system which gives a central place to the idea of the sovereignty of the people. The people must participate actively in the decision-making in political and economic matters; they must shape their own culture, welding all the separate strands that have been imported into our society into one new composite national culture. In other words, they must, after more than four hundred years of being acted upon, act for themselves. From being passive objects of history, they must become the active agents. They must shape their own future and their own destiny.
> —Eric Williams, *The Chaguaramas Declaration*

Indubitably, the Black Power rebellion of 1970 caused Williams to take another look at the direction in which the PNM was going and the nature of the course he had set for the party. In 1960 he had announced boldly that *Massa Day Done,* but quite clearly the young students at the University of the West Indies, some members of the trade union movement, and the armed forces did not believe that massa had left the social and political arena. In 1960 Williams had proclaimed "Massa Day Done, Sahib Day Done, Yes Suh Boss Day Done" and went on to link the national-colonialist struggle with the international struggle of colored people all over the world. Sadly, the forces noted above were content to argue that though Massa Day may have been finished, it was still particularly difficult for those persons possessing a black skin to find "an equal place" in the society.[74]

The Chaguaramas Declaration: Perspective for a New Society (1970), a last revolutionary gasp on the part of Williams and the PNM, was a response to the Black Power rebellion of 1970 and a telling indication that there was still much work left before the national ideal of economic and social equality could be achieved. The principles enshrined in the *People's Charter* (1956), the founding document of the PNM, were not sufficient to address the new questions that arose in 1970. In going back to the drawing boards, Williams realized that any new document had to embody the sentiments of a generation of Trinidadians and Tobagonians who were not as familiar with Massa as his generation was. Massa Day may have been finished and the *People's Charter* may have been appropriate for 1956, but both these manifestoes had to be rewritten from the bottom up to satisfy the aspirations of the 1970s.

In this conversation, Williams's rhetorical strategy is of enormous importance. First, he appropriates much of the language of the Black Power advocates to appease a sense of dissatisfaction that the masses of African people in the society felt. Second, he overdetermines certain clusters of words and concepts to obtain certain emotional effects. Williams, who never willingly used words such as "revolutionary change" and the like, seems to relish such terms in this address. Thus in the first three and a half pages he uses the word "revolution/revolutionary" eight times, "violent/violence" four times, and "change" thirteen times. Also, he contrasts *peaceful* means of change with *violent* means of change and the advantages of the privileged groups with the disadvantages of the dispossessed groups. Needless to say, Williams identifies with and is on the side of change and revolution in opposition to those who are on the side of massa and white

---

[74] The words of the National Anthem which Williams asked all citizens to respect in his Independence Day Message, in part noted:
"Here every creed and race find an equal place/ And may God Bless Our Nation."

privilege. Williams knew he had to identify with the Black Power advocates if he wished to survive that revolutionary upheaval. It may be remembered that Williams's rhetoric was always that of nationalist radicalism, never that of revolutionary socialism or Marxism. Yet, in this essay, he has no compunction whatever about declaring that "the word 'revolution' has always held terrors for the privileged groups in the Caribbean. This is one of the principal characteristics we have inherited from the period of slavery and colonialism. In part also it is an indication of our lack of awareness of the world in which we live."

The question here is, To whom is Williams really speaking and what does he hope to achieve? To ask this question, however, is to realize the ironic nature of Williams's discourse. Here is a man who, after having held the reigns of power for fourteen years and against whom, ostensibly, the revolutionary uprising was directed, has no compunction in saying to the nation: "Revolutionary change is not only demanded in the Caribbean today; it is also, in view of our past history an historical imperative necessary to confer real and meaningful power, self-discipline and self-determination upon those who have been historically dispossessed." In fairness to him, he recognized that any reconstruction of the society "must be guided by a philosophy and a sense of direction rooted in the history and in the potentiality of the dispossessed peoples of the Caribbean," but then again he had fourteen years in which to organize and orient such a direction. To speak, then, as though he bore no responsibility for what was taking place in the society at the time represented the height of irony.

In light of these concerns, the task of *The Chaguaramas Declaration* was to articulate a "clear-cut philosophy" to guide "a New Society." Apart from *Perspectives for Our Party,* Williams had never attempted seriously to engage in a disquisition about the philosophical direction the society ought to take. Not that he had not spoken about various aspects of the nation's direction before; it is only that this document was the first comprehensive attempt to outline a cohesive, integrated political, economic, and cultural approach of speaking about the nation "within the framework of a humane, cohesive and self-determining society where the individual can fully realise his or her full human dignity."

But if Williams attempted to appropriate the language of the Black Power advocates, he sadly misrepresented/misinterpreted the cultural dimension of what was at stake at that critical moment of awakening. In spite of his nationalist rhetoric, Williams seemed uncertain about the relative autonomy of his society's culture. Picking up on V. S. Naipaul, Williams believed that Trinidad and Tobago possessed a borrowed culture and, rather than being "true men [and women]," Trinidadians and Tobagonians were really "mimics," a position that he took earlier in his book *From Columbus to Castro*.[75] In this address, Williams also argued that Trinidadians and Tobagonians must "make their own culture." Williams was unable to see that, in spite of slavery and colonialism, a people always, inevitably, make their own culture—in fact, are defined by that culture and could not possibly exist outside of it. In this context, a people *make, are made,* and constantly *remake themselves* within their culture. That the upper classes may have looked outside the society to acquire certain rudiments of the master's culture is certainly true because their function was to maintain and to perpetuate a certain kind of rule and, by extension, a particular cultural order. Nevertheless, it also remains true that through their daily activities the lower classes drew their spiritual sustenance and constructed themselves from within their culture. As Mrs. Carmichael remarked about what she called "a singular song" that she heard among the African slaves in Trinidad in 1828:

---

[75] See Eric Williams, *From Columbus to Castro* (New York: Harper & Row, 1973), p. 502. See also Gordon Rohlehr's sparkling reply, "History as Absurdity," in Orde Coombs, *Is Massa Day Dead?* (New York: Anchor, 1974), pp. 69–108.

Fire in da mountain,
Nobody for out him,
Take me daddy's bo tick (dandy stick),
And make monkey out him.

Chorus.
Poor John! nobody for out him, &c.

Go to de king's goal
You'll find a doubloon dey;
Go to de kings goal,
You'll find a doubloon dey.

Chorus
Poor John! nobody for out him, &c.[76]

In *The Chaguaramas Declaration,* then, Williams attempts to appropriate the language of the dispossessed masses, turn it upon its head, and use it for his own sake and for radical purposes. In an interesting way, this last and important conversation represents an attempt to recoup what he had lost: that instinctive understanding of and empathy with his society and an ability to

---

[76] Mrs. Carmichael, *Domestic Manners and Social Conditions of the White, Coloured, and Negro Population of the West Indies,* Vol. 2 (London: Whitetaker, Treacher, 1833), p. 301. The slaves explained "this revolutionary song" to Mrs. Carmichael in the following manner: "When the bad negroes wanted to do evil, they made for a sign a fire on the hill-sides, to burn down the canes. There is nobody up there, to put out the fire; but as a sort of satire, the song goes on to say, 'take me daddy's bo tick,' (daddy is a mere term of civility), take some one's dandy stick, and tell the monkeys to help to put out the fire among the canes for John; (meaning John Bull). The chorus means, that poor John has nobody to put out the fire in the canes for him. Then when the canes are burning, go to the goal, and seize the money (p. 302)." These sentiments would seem to be those of the "field slaves" to whom Williams, using Malcolm X, referred in *Massa Day Done.* The only problem is that he didn't take this insight to its fullest development in *The Chaguaramas Declaration.* Surely, the field slaves, as Cabral noted in *Return to the Source,* are the ones who kept the culture of their societies alive during the trials and tribulations of slavery and colonialism.

recreate/recapitulate the people's feelings through a richly evocative prose. In his address, he seemed to be playing catch-up and even though he caught some of the nuances of the popular sentiment and made a tolerable attempt to articulate the people's anguish and pain, time had passed him by. At best, he was *reacting* more than *acting*, *following* rather than *leading* his people as they tried to deepen and expand an understanding of themselves. Indeed, there seemed to be a dissonance between his understanding of their reality and the defiance that their expressions revealed. *The Chaguaramas Declaration* symbolized an attempt to catch up, the contradiction between the old and the new, and the recognition that the struggle for social and cultural expression had reached another level. *The Chaguaramas Declaration*, it can be argued, was the last important conversation Williams had with his nation.

WILLIAMS AND THE HISTORY OF POLITICS

> "When I use a word," Humpty Dumpty said in rather scornful tone, "it means just what I choose it to mean—neither more nor less."
> "The question is," said Alice, "whether you can make words mean so many different things."
> "The question is," said Humpty Dumpty, "which is the master—that's all."
> —Lewis Caroll, *Alice in Wonderland*

Williams's entrance onto the political stage in Trinidad and Tobago signaled an epistemological break with the previous manner of speaking with and about the society. Although I do not mean to suggest that the political episteme that developed when Williams arrived was a monolithic entity that forswore/rejected all previous modes of discourse (such a statement would be an anachronism), I wish to argue that Williams inaugurated a new way of formulating political ideas in the society, opted for a new manner of organizing the political culture, and, most especially, developed a new way of discoursing about it.[77] In other words, we may theorize this phenomenon to say that before Williams there existed *a history of politicians*, each with his or her own views and problems, bereft of a common political program or clearly formulated ideology or a shared vision of how the society, as a whole, ought to function or proceed.[78] Each proceeded in his or her own way. During the 1950 elections over one hundred candidates ran for eighteen seats and produced over fifty manifestoes. Because they ran for election as independent candidates (that is, their affiliations were precisely that, independent), they reflected a diverse, somewhat anarchist approach to the politics of the society. Because the structured political participation of the whole society began only in 1946 with the introduction of universal adult suffrage, most of the politicians who took part in the process were in search of political office and were not too concerned with working out a common approach to the society's problems. The coming of Williams ushered in what can be called a *history of politics*, the first generalized elaboration of a common political ideology and the construction of the first genuine political problematic of the society.[79] As Max Ifill noted, "The introduction of

---

[77] In this sense, I see the larger vanacular discourse of the society, the alternative creole tradition of discourse, as being a diachronic phenomenon. Its synchronic moments are marked by persons such as J. J. Thomas, Trinidad's first and most important philologist, Arthur Cipriani, the champion of the barefoot man, Butler, the hero of the working class person, all in a line to persons such as Williams and Macandal Dagga.

[78] See "A Convention Appraisal" in which James speaks about the development of a particular type of politician before the arrival of Williams and the rise of a different kind of politics after he arrived.

[79] I use the term *problematic* in the sense that Gaston Bachelard and Michel Foucault used it to mean the development of "particular objects in a specific scientific domain, contemplated in its cognitive dynamic." Such a formulation does not arrive from an intellectual or cognitive void but "in response to a specific problem or set of problems." See J. G. Merquior, *Foucault* (London: Fontana, 1985), pp. 39–40.

adult suffrage [in Trinidad and Tobago] in the 1940s helped to bring racial and ethnic particularities to the fore in the society. But this consciousness took a significant leap forward when Williams began his political campaign in 1955."[80] Although Ifill is concerned to show the manner in which Williams exploited racial fears, it is very clear that Williams's entrance into the political arena generated a particular kind of cognitive dynamic within the body politic that transformed the manner in which political discourses and practices were conducted. In more scientific terms we can argue that with the emergence of Williams and the PNM there emerged a different "conceptual grid" and a grammar of cognitive language respectively through which the society organized its political practices and discourses about itself and its political realities. With the latter, a specific *politics of language,* necessary to signify this new discursive formation, was also inaugurated. As James noted, Williams was "an academic of a particular kind. He is an intellectual with an abiding faith in the power of the intellect."[81] The development and nurturing of this process, I hope I have demonstrated, was one of the central contributions of Williams to the political history of Trinidad and Tobago.

In the end, Williams's language of defiance and cajoling, bombast and humor, came at a time when colonial peoples were tired of submitting "to their betters, lowly and reverently," as one Anglican hymnal puts it and our primary education taught us. Language that inculcated elements of submission and emotional and psychological terror and was associated with slavery and indentureship certainly acted to cripple a people's sense of themselves. In speaking of Thomas Paine's view of language, Olivia Smith noted: "Language usage is creative in Paine's view in the sense that it defines and perpetuates political relations. Changing

---

[80] Max B. Ifill, *The Politics of Dr. Eric Williams and the PNM* (Port-of-Spain: Vanguard Printery, 1986), pp. 1–2.

[81] James, "A Convention Appraisal."

the style of language is a means of political and moral reformation."[82] Williams, aware that there exists always a public understanding of language, suggested in his discourses that the members of his society were intellectually adroit enough to examine issues in a sophisticated manner and to draw their own conclusions once the issues were presented in a clear and logical manner. He realized that the trick was to present that information so that it could be absorbed by the general audience and made intelligible. In his formal conversations with his people, by disrupting the artificial distinctions between leader (lecturer/politician/scholar) and his listeners (ordinary people/illiterates, and so on) Williams was able to communicate with the latter group very easily. Through his adroit use of humor, folkloric wisdom ("Every zandolee 'no he hole"), aspects of popular culture ("Like a bridge over troubled water, I will lay me down"), and his "robber talk" ("This pack of benighted idiots, this band of obscurantist politicians, this unholly alliance of egregious individualists"), he was able to touch his people's soul in a way that others could not, and therein lay his magic and his popular appeal.

Thus to attend an Eric Williams public meeting was like going to a calypso show at the Queen's Park Savannah or a Port of Spain calypso tent. It always possessed a dramatic air of the unexpected, an element of the festive, and a shared sense of participation in a common experience. Knowing the mood and timbre of his audience, Williams played to their expectations unashamedly, especially to the patrons in the North Stand.[83] If that section of the audience approved, his performance was deemed successful and,

---

[82] Smith, *Politics of Language*, p. 51.

[83] The North Stand of Queen's Park Savannah is constructed during the annual carnival season to accommodate the overflow audience. The seats are usually less expensive so that the clientele in that stand represent the ordinary person. To a large degree, however, they represent the heart of the culture. Almost invariably, the calypsonian plays to that audience which is notoriously hard to please. They are not beyond booing a calypsonian if his performance is not up to expectations. Needless to say, approval of one's work by this group is the mark of ultimate achievement, they being the ultimate connoisseur of the art form.

instead of responding with the words "Kaiso," or "Dat is kaiso," they said: "Dat is man! He could *really* talk." In exasperation, Basdeo Panday, the leader of the Opposition, would characterize Williams's "languaging" as unacceptable and the editors of Panday's writings accused Williams of practicing a form of "verbal terrorism."[84]   As Panday noted in 1966:

> Brothers and sisters, I end by leaving you to reflect on a recent development. Are you happy or comfortable with the *bad public image* Eric Williams is projecting to our Caribbean neighbours? Williams argued about Aristotle [sic] ten years ago; now he has *descended* to the level of talking about Zandolee, Cobo Jaw Bone, Ambakaila and Maka Fouchette. One may wish to argue that Williams should bow his head and walk out of the country if he had any character or integrity as it is not good for the nation to be continually taught such words. Maybe the time has come for him to step down gracefully from the government. [Emphasis added.][85]

The point is that Zandolee, Cobo Jaw Bone, Ambakaila, and Maka Fouchette (incidentally, characters about whom the common folk were knowledgeable) are words that are familiar to the public and suggest certain images and meanings to them. The genius of Williams was to bring these words into acceptable public discourse and then to manipulate them for his purposes. Because Williams understood his people as few politicians could and loved them as no one else did he could take people's language, transform it, and give it back to them in a new and reinvigorated manner. This is one reason why he is remembered as the "Father of the Nation," one who always understood that he was in conversation with his people (some say his children) even

---

[84] Siewah and Moonilal, *Basdeo Panday,* p. 322.

[85] Ibid., p. 328.

though he did not always expect them to talk back to him. In fact, Williams became so central to his nation's hopes and desires that at the height of his popularity one calypsonian observed:

> Annabella stocking want patching
> She want de doctah help she wid dat
> Johnson trousers falling
> He want de doctah help he wid dat
> Some want a zephyr motor car
> Others want a piece of land
> [Now] Dorothy loss she man
> She want to complain to Doctah Williams.[86]

His was part of the founding discourse of the nation.

To be sure, there came a time when Williams not only lost touch with his society's discourse, he also seemed to become deaf to some of the things his people were saying. Indeed, it can be argued that inherent in the very aesthetics of his discourse were certain contradictory impulses: that is, in giving speech to his people, he appropriated their voices and made them his own. In the process, however, he not only silenced them, he also became deaf to their entreaties and ceased to listen to what they had to say. In fact, this was the complaint of many of the PNM stalwarts who started with Williams in 1955 but eventually left the party. In a particular manner, it was an appeal to listen that James had in mind when he wrote *Party Politics in the West Indies*. It was not only that Williams was not listening to what he was saying, he was also telling Williams that to recapture what he lost he had to move the basis of the party from an *individual* to a *communal* project. It had to become a national movement. To achieve this end, there had to be a process of genuine listening to the masses and a renunciation of what became uneven relations of power that inhered within the discourse that Williams carried on with the

---

[86] Quoted in *Inward Hunger*, p. 269.

nation. As long as they (Williams and the masses) were in conversation, Williams kept his ears open and listened to what they were saying. Once he ceased to listen, he merely uttered himself and thereby estranged himself from his people. Once he uttered himself, he was unable to hear what others were saying and thus destabilized the dialogic project and dislocated himself from the discursive process. As a result, his conversation with his people ceased and his discourse ran into a dead end. Where in 1955 he spoke for most of the people, in 1972 he spoke for few and, paradoxically, the privileged class looked to him as their savior from the barbarous hordes. They felt that only he could save them from the Black Power advocates. By 1972 the symbolic universe of meaning had changed. The society had moved on, Williams had forgotten how to listen to his people, and so, once more, someone else arose to speak for and on behalf of their repressed aspirations. Nature, they say, abhors a vacuum and so Macandal Dagga and the Black Power advocates seemed to be the ones who were capable of speaking for the people. Both the names that Dagga assumed were those of Caribbean heroes of African descent who had risen to speak on behalf of their people. Williams, no longer able to make words mean as many things as he did when he walked onto the national stage in 1955, ceased to be master of the public discourse.

Yet, through his conversation with his people, Williams provided his nation with more than a political ideology: he gave the people a mirror through which they could see themselves and participate in a discourse with and about themselves. He allowed them to feel and believe in themselves again and shed light and understanding in areas where there was darkness and ignorance. No wonder that when he died all the candles in the twin-island republic were sold out. Each person wished to burn a candle for the father; each wished to testify to the light he had brought through his mastery of the word and its possibilities. If, as Jacques Lacan noted, language is a script of the unconscious, then it can be argued that through his use of language Williams unveiled/

revealed many aspects of his society's unconscious via his articulate and sensitive probing of the collective self. In the process, he became their hero: a person they loved and admired even if some did not always care for his biting wit and sarcasm.

CONCLUSION

> To establish his identity, Caliban, after three centuries, must himself pioneer into regions that Caesar never knew.
> —C. L. R. James, *Beyond a Boundary*

We can draw some conclusions about Williams's linguistic achievements and the manner in which they challenged imperialist discourses. I do not want to argue for one moment that Williams challenged the deep structures of meaning that existed in imperialist discourses except to suggest that within the colonial context there existed a parallel creole language, which, as Merle Hodge has argued, has never depended entirely upon the discourse of the other.[87] It was from this alternative tradition of discourse that Williams derived his strength and within which one can make certain claims for his use of the tradition. First, he took the political address, as an art form, to its highest level. Although the Caribbean has produced many political orators of tremendous stature (Norman Manley, Michael Manley, Forbes Burnham, Walter Rodney, Maurice Bishop, C. L. R. James, Fidel Castro, Winston Mahabir, George Padmore, and others), Williams certainly was among the best. Like Lincoln, Williams "was an artist, not just a scholar."[88] Second, as a student of classical, British, American, and African-American orators and their rhe-

---

[87] I do not mean to suggest that the official and creole languages did not intersect at any point. In fact, they did, and this led to a rich fusion in many instances. Also see Paget Henry's "Caliban as Deconstructionist: C. L. R. James and Post-Colonial Discourse" in Paget Henry and Paul Buhle, eds., *C. L. R. James's Caribbean* (Durham: Duke University Press, 1992), pp. 111–42.

[88] Wills, *Lincoln at Gettysburg*, p. 52.

torical strategies, Williams drew on the examples of and modeled his speeches after outstanding orators such as Pericles ("Funeral Oration"), Edmund Burke (*Reflections on the Revolution in France*) Abraham Lincoln ("Second Inaugural Address"), and Booker T. Washington ("Atlanta Address"). From the Greeks, he acquired a vision of democratic society and the role of oratory in expressing the concerns of the people; from Burke and Whig historians, he learned to see history as movement. Third, Williams drew on the rhetorical strategies of his own society. From his local culture, he learned the art and style of picong and its capacity to play on the sentiments of his people; from the midnight robber and calypso tradition he learned the art of wrenching aphorisms from their religious context and affixing them to serve ironic or didactic purposes; from the Pierrot Grenade he learned oratorical style and the art of pacing his dialogue. Fourth, following Aristotle's rhetorical guidelines, his proofs combined logical and emotional appeals while his erudition, clarity, and dry wit enhanced his capacity to communicate with his people. Fifth, his profound understanding of history (he was a historian by profession) allowed him to interpret the present in relation to the past, which he then elaborated into political policy. Indeed, this knowledge of history allowed him to speak with enormous authority and to face the future with unbridled confidence.

In the end, Williams's language, a political act in itself, played a large part in his political success. In characterizing the evolution of Williams, the impact that he had on his society, and the political content of his language, James noted:

> I have never seen or heard of any political forum (in non-revolutionary periods) where addresses of the level of Dr. Williams's speeches have been consistently listened to by popular audiences. The credit has to be divided equally between the confidence and courage of the speaker and the receptivity of the audience. *That, in the last analysis, is the secret of Dr. Williams's politics.* Every-

thing he has ever learnt, and he has learnt a great deal, he is able to stand and say and his popular audience listens for three, four, five hours at a time. This is the West Indies at its best. There is the promise that we shall achieve equality with other peoples and have the immense satisfaction and stimulus (very important to people with our history) that we do not only receive but are giving to the common stock of culture. This is Dr. Williams's own special contribution, the impact of his individual personality, the historical accident. And yet in the Hegelian dialectic the organic movement proceeds by way of accidents and the sum of accidents constitutes the organic movement. (Emphasis added.)

Williams, a social and cultural phenomenon, represented the best in his people and articulated their aspirations in a way that few did. As Lamming noted as early as July 1956, Williams never "talked[ed] down to his people." He respected their intelligence and demanded "at all times an adult attention and response to his lectures. This was an example, probably the first of its kind in our part of the world, of the teacher, in the noblest sense of teacher, turned politician, and of the politician, in the truly moral sense of politician, turned teacher." In Williams, the people of Trinidad and Tobago had discovered themselves and, in his turn, Williams realized himself in his people and thereby assumed his highest and noblest vocation. The following portrait, by an unknown midnight robber, best addresses Williams's intervention in the social and cultural history of Trinidad and Tobago. At his most risqué, he might have approved such a characterization of himself:

> For the day my mother gave birth to me, the sun refused to shine, and the wind ceased to blow. Many mothers that day gave birth, but to deformed children. Plagues and pestilence pestered the cities, for atomic

Williams and his daughter, Erica, at a calypso tent in early 1970s.

eruption raged in the mountains. Philosophers, scientists, professors said the world is come to an end, but no, it was me, a monarch, was born. Master of all I survey, and my right there is none to dispute.[89]

As we strive to find meaning in ourselves and the world around us, a reading of Williams's political texts becomes important. If we understand *how* he read his world we may arrive at a better appreciation of *what* he made of it and that even may stimulate our desire to know what our contemporary world means to and for us.

Ithaca
July 1992

---

[89] "The Midnight Robber," 269.

BOOKS CITED

Bourdieu, Pierre. *Outline of a Theory of Practice.* Translated by Richard Nice. Cambridge: Cambridge University Press, 1977.

———. *Questions de sociologie.* Paris: Les editions de Minuit, 1984.

Carmichael, Mrs. *Domestic Manners and Social Conditions of the White, Coloured, and Negro Population of the West Indies, Vol. 2.* London: Whitetaker, Treacher, 1833.

Carr, Andrew. "Pierrot Grenade" *Caribbean Quarterly* 4, Nos. 3 & 4 (March–June 1956).

Castoriadis, Cornelius. *Philosophy, Politics, Autonomy: Essays in Political Philosophy.* New York: Oxford University Press, 1991.

Collens, J. H. *Guide to Trinidad.* London: Elliot Stock, 1888.

Crowley, Daniel J. "The Midnight Robber." *Caribbean Quarterly* 4, Nos. 3 & 4 (March–June 1956).

Cudjoe, Selwyn R. *Four Caribbean Slave Narratives.* Forthcoming, 1993.

———. *Movement of the People: Essays on Indpendence.* Ithaca: Calaloux, 1983.

Gomes, Albert. *Through a Maze of Colour.* Port of Spain: Key Caribbean Publications, 1974.

Goddard, "Sonny" George. *Forty Years in the Steelbands.* London: Karia, 1991.

Glissant, Edouard. *Caribbean Discourse: Selected Essays.* Translated by J. Michael Dash. Charlottesville: University Press of Virginia, 1989.

Harris, Wilson. *History, Fable and Myth in the Caribbean and Guianas.* Georgetown, Guyana: National History and Arts Council, Ministry of Information and Culture, 1970.

Henry, Paget, and Paul Buhle, eds. *C. L. R. James's Caribbean.* Durham: Duke University Press, 1992.

Hodge, Merle, "Challenges of the Struggle for Sovereignty: Changing the World versus Writing Stories." In Selwyn R. Cudjoe, *Caribbean Women Writers: Essays from the First International Conference.* Wellesley/Amherst: Calaloux/University of Massachusetts Press, 1990.

Ifill, Max B. *The Politics of Dr. Eric Williams and the PNM.* Port of Spain: Vanguard, 1986.

James, C. L. R. *A Convention Appraisal: Dr. Eric Williams, First Premier of Trinidad and Tobago; A Biographical Sketch.* Port of Spain: PNM Publishing, 1960.

———. *Party Politics in the West Indies.* San Juan: C.L.R. James, 1962.

Jillian, Teresa. "Working Women's Words and the Condition of Their Production(s)." Working Paper #5, Susan B. Anthony Center for Women's Studies, University of Rochester, Rochester, New York.

Lopez, Consuelo. "C. L. R. James: The Rhetoric of a Difiant Warrior." Ph.D. dissertation, Indiana University, 1983.

MacCabe, Colin. *Tracking the Signifier: Theoretical Essays: Film, Linguistics, Literature.* Minneapolis: University of Minnesota Press, 1985.

Mahabir, Winston. *In and Out of Politics.* Port of Spain: Imprint, 1976.

Merquior, J. G. *Foucault.* London: Fontana Press/Collins, 1985.

Milne-Home, Josephine Mary. "Education and Cultural Imperialism: Gender and Ethnicity in Reading Textbooks Used in Trinidad and Tobago. M.A. thesis, University of Alberta, Edmonton, Alberta, 1980.

Naipaul, V. S. *The Middle Passage.* London: Andre Deutsch, 1962.

———. *The Mystic Masseur.* London: Andre Deutsch, 1957.

Rogers, De Wilton. *The Rise of the People's National Movement.* Vol. 1. Port of Spain: De Wilton Rogers, n.d.

Rohlehr, Gordon. *Calypso and Society in Pre-Independence Trinidad.* Port of Spain: Gordon Rohlehr, 1990.

———. "History as Absurdity." In Orde Coombs, *Is Massa Day Dead?* New York: Anchor, 1974.

Siewah, Samaroo, and Roodal Moonilal. *Basdeo Panday: An Enigma Answered.* Port of Spain; Chakra Publishing House, 1991.

Smith, Olivia. *The Politics of Language, 1791–1819.* Oxford: Clarendon Press, 1984.

Thomas, J[ohn] J[acob]. *Froudacity.* 1889. London: New Beacon, 1969.

———. *The Theory and Practice of Creole Grammar.* 1869. London: New Beacon, 1969.

Williams, Eric. *From Columbus to Castro.* New York: Harper & Row, 1973.

———. *History of the People of Trinidad and Tobago.* Port of Spain: PNM Publishing, 1962.

———. *Inward Hunger: The Education of a Prime Minister.* Chicago: University of Chicago Press, 1971.

Wills, Garry. *Lincoln at Gettysburg: The Words That Remade America.* New York: Simon & Schuster, 1992.

MY RELATIONS WITH THE CARIBBEAN COMMISSION, 1943–1955

by Eric E. Williams

Williams addresses a political crowd at the early part of his career. With him are Mr. John Donaldson, secretary-general of the Teachers' Economic and Cultural Association, and Mr. Hugh Harris, a member of the party.

My Relations with the Caribbean Commission, 1943–1955. A public Lecture given under the auspices of the People's Education Movement of the Teachers' Economic and Cultural Association, in Woodford Square, Port-of-Spain, Trinidad, June 21, 1955, and repeated under the auspices of the Caribbean Women National Assembly, Harris Promenade, San Fernando, Trinidad, June 28, 1955.

MY RELATIONS WITH THE CARIBBEAN COMMISSION, 1943-1955

Mr. Chairman, Ladies and Gentlemen:—

I stand before you tonight, and, therefore, before the people of the British West Indies, the representative of a principle, a cause, and a defeat. The principle is the principle of intellectual freedom. The cause is the cause of the West Indian people. The defeat is the defeat of the policy of appointing local men to high office.

I joined the Anglo-American Caribbean Commission, the predecessor of the present Caribbean Commission, in March 1943, one year after its establishment by the British and United States governments. I was then Assistant Professor of Social and Political Science at Howard University in Washington, D.C., the headquarters of the Commission. I was also the author of a book entitled *The Negro in the Caribbean*, a copy of which I presented to the British official who interviewed me for a post with the Commission in November 1942. My second book, *Capitalism and Slavery,* was published two years later, in 1944.

My initial appointment was a very modest one—work as a consultant for one afternoon a fortnight collating the prices of essential foodstuffs and bringing up to date the laws of the territories. I therefore retained my job at the university, and insisted that I must be free to continue my lectures and writings, as such activities were rated very highly among the criteria for promotion at the university. Both the British and the United States governments agreed to this. A year later, with the University's approval and the necessary leave of absence, I accepted a full-time appointment on the Commission's staff to work with the Research Council, my salary being paid jointly by the British Colonial Office and the State Department of the United States. My freedom to continue my writings and speeches was again acknowledged. The permission was in fact extended to the West Indies, subject to the condition that I should submit an advance copy of my lectures to

My Relations with the Caribbean Commission

the Colonial Secretary in the British West Indian areas.

As soon as *The Negro in the Caribbean* was published, a joint African-West Indian group in London sought and obtained permission from the publishers and from myself to bring out a separate edition in England. I had not then joined the Commission's staff, but owing to the paper shortage the publication was delayed until at the end of 1944, I learned that it was due to appear. I promptly reported the matter to both Sections of the Commission, explained the circumstances, and made it quite clear that the English publishers were a radical, anti-imperialist group with which I was not affiliated. My British superior officer, whom I had given a personal copy of the book, asked me to put my statement in writing for the Colonial Office, so that, as he put it, it would not be taken by surprise and lose confidence in me. I did so. My United States superior officer, who was very familiar with the book and who knew how widely it had circulated in the United States, and especially the State Department, advised me that the thing above all which I was not to do was to attempt to prevent publication. The English edition was published in 1945 and was soon selling widely in the British West Indies.

About the middle of 1945 the Commission began to give consideration to the transfer of its headquarters to the West Indies. The British government had also appointed a commission to consider the question of a West Indian University. I had for years been preparing myself for precisely such a development, and, as I had become very genuinely interested in the Commission and its work in the field of Caribbean cooperation, which I had independently recommended in *The Negro in the Caribbean*, I seriously considered resignation from Howard University and removal to the West Indies with the Commission, pending the establishment of the West Indian University. Just at this time, however, Howard University declined to renew my leave of absence for another year and invited me to return to take one of ten professorships being created that year. No teacher as young as I could take lightly such a recognition of his work expressed in a jump from Assistant Professor to Professor, bypassing the intermediate grade of Associate Professor, within six years of his first appointment. I thought that it might be more strategic to transfer to the West Indian University from a United States professorship than from a research job with the Commission.

Before making up my mind, I decided to consult my British superior officer who was then stationed in the West Indies. In reply to my letter he sent a telegram to the Colonial Office, dated June 18, 1945, asking for instructions. A copy of the telegram was given to me. It stated that he hoped to retain my services indefinitely in connection with the research work of the Commission, but that security of tenure or a position in the West Indian University could not be guaranteed to me. In the meantime he asked me to defer a decision until he visited Washington in the following month, and negotiations about my salary were begun.

I was in no hurry. I waited, confident, with no thought of danger, secure in the phenomenal success of *Capitalism and Slavery*. One of the most distinguished of modern United States historians had reviewed the book in the *New York Herald Tribune* of February 4, 1945. After describing it as "this learned and illuminating monograph," he concluded with the following paragraph:

> "Mr. Williams' monograph is one of the most learned, most penetrating and most significant that has appeared in this field of history. It would be cause for gratification if he would turn his attention to the economics of American abolitionism."

I had drawn the review to the attention of my superior officer. He had expressed the hope to me that my hat would not get too small for my head as a result of the adjectives used by the reviewer. I had assured him that I never wore a hat.

On May 26, 1945, an even more famous journal, Britain's *Times Literary Supplement,* had ended a long review of the book with this sentence: "this is an admirably written, argued and original piece of work." Reviews in this journal are never signed.

My Relations with the Caribbean Commission

But I learned privately that my book had been reviewed by one of Britain's greatest contemporary scholars. I had sent a copy to my superior officer, who had specifically asked me to show him copies of all reviews so that he could forward them to the Colonial Office.

The reception of the book in official circles had been no less gratifying. I had had a copy sent to the Secretary of State for the Colonies, Colonel Stanley, a direct descendant of the author of the British act emancipating the slaves, and another to one of the highest ranking Colonial Office officials. I had met both of them in Washington. Colonel Stanley had written to me thanking me for the book; he said that he had read it with the greatest interest and regarded it as a valuable addition to his library. The Colonial Office official had complimented me on my most admirable presentation of what was to him a new approach to the question, stated how really impressed he was with the masterly fashion in which I had marshalled authorities collected from so wide a range, both in time and place, and concluded that, even though he would personally have given the humanitarians rather more credit than I did, my book certainly did much to convince him that I was putting the matter in truer perspective than he had hitherto seen it.

Financially, too, the book had exceeded all expectations. First published in November 1944, by June 1945 all 1,500 copies had been sold, the subsidy insisted on by the publishers repaid, and a second printing of 1,500 copies begun.

Thus, when I was called in to my superior officer on July 24, 1945, shortly after his arrival in Washington, I was totally unprepared for an attack and the ensuing bitter struggle for intellectual freedom.

The cause of the war was *The Negro in the Caribbean*. The enemy was the sugar planters of Antigua, with my superior officer as their standard bearer.

After a few pleasantries, my superior officer, whom I shall call Mr. X, abruptly changed the subject from the discussion of the

Howard offer which I had wasted no time in introducing. Let me read here from my personal record of this conversation, written up immediately after.

> "Quite suddenly, he spoke of 'echoes' of *The Negro in the Caribbean.* He read to me a letter he had received, carefully concealing the letterhead. The writer admitted that he had not read the book, but quoted the passage about 'government of sugar, for sugar, by sugar', and called the book 'propagandist'. I was nonchalant. I told him I had seen a hostile review in *The Antigua Star* and another in the *West India Committee Circular,* both papers of the planters. I took the opportunity to emphasise that I stood by everything I had written, that the planters' attitude did not surprise me, that I was not in the least bothered by it, and that I was not impressed by planters' standards of research or definitions of sociology.
>
> He said it was all right, they knew the English edition was coming out, etc., it was a pity the book was not objective, there were other points of view on sugar, etc., etc., and there was nothing to worry about 'unless things got worse.' I asked him what he meant. He said: 'If that sort of criticism got around and I became the subject of general controversy.'
>
> I then asked him point blank what, in his opinion, 'looking at the matter in its worst light', as he had phrased it, would or could be the result? He replied, after a little hestiation: 'I would want to ask you to resign, but I could not do anything because of your 18 months' contract.'
>
> We finally agreed that he would discuss the whole mattter with the United States Section. He said that if I had the Commission behind me, it was o.k.
>
> My impressions are as follows:—
>
> 1. Mr. X wishes to force me out. I think this is connected with the fact that I am insisting on a well-paid job on a high executive level.

2. He does not want me in the West Indies if he can help it.
3. He is trying to queer my pitch with the United States people, but before he squeezes me out he wants to see if they will back him or me.
4. He was clearly quite nonplussed by my combination of nonchalance to the criticisms and firmness on the basic issue.
5. He was most uncomfortable throughout as was clear from his great efforts to prove to me from newspaper articles, etc., how the situation with regard to sugar had changed, and how there could be no possible abandonment of sugar.
6. Here and there I seemed to see a broad hint that I should recant, with the alternative of the stake. . . ."

The discussion was continued two days later at an official cocktail party, in an atmosphere charged with tension—the British Labour Party had just won the 1945 election. I learned that my future had that afternoon been discussed by the Commission for an hour and a half, and that the United States Section, which had at first suggested that the Commission should stick by me, later decided that I might be happier at Howard. Mr. X tried to make me admit that, if the Howard offer had been made two years before, I probably would never have joined the Commission. I dissented vigorously, whereupon he called me "stiffnecked". He said that if I talked to some 'reasonable' sugar planters, I might probably have different opinions.

Another brief and inconclusive discussion followed on the next day, and it was agreed to postpone the issue until the following week. I went immediately to the President of Howard University, explained the circumstances to him, and stressed that if I returned to the University that year, the impression would be left that I had turned tail and run away. The President agreed with me, assured me that he was 100% behind me, and authorised leave of absence for another year. With my back door thus fortified, I wrote Mr. X a long letter dated July 28, 1945.

I dealt fully with the background of the book and the appearance of the English edition, reminded him of his telegram to the Colonial Office a month earlier, and informed him that I was unable to reconcile the freedom of speech and expression given to me in 1945 as a member of the Commission's staff with retrospective criticism of what I had written in 1942 before I joined the Commission's staff. My letter continued as follows:

> The only reason that you give for your present attitude is a letter which presumably represents the hostility of vested interests to my writings. The representative of those interests whom you bring to my attention has not even read the book. You will pardon me if I draw the only conclusion which you leave open to me. It is that in June my work was in every way satisfactory, or, to put it as moderately as possible, I was rendering satisfactory service to an organisation as important politically as the Anglo-American Caribbean Commission. In July, however, as a result of pressure, unofficial, anonymous, and, if you will allow me, with no visible basis either for criticism or positive statement, at the first hint of this I became a liability and am asked not only by you, ... but, according to your statement, by the entire Commission, to consider retirement from the work to which I have given, as far as was possible, devoted service.
>
> I, for my part, would have expected from you and I am certain that any other subordinate, in a department would expect, not a request which virtually amounts to pressure in my opinion absolutely unwarranted, but a vigorous defence of my rights as a satisfactory servant of the Commission. I would remind you that the opinions I have expressed of the vested interests in the West Indies have been expressed in various forms by government commission after commission.

My Relations with the Caribbean Commission

It is largely upon the opinions of these commissions that I have based the ideas that I now hold of the past, present and future of the West Indies. Every step that has been taken in the West Indies during the past ten years has been in the direction of the strengthening of the freedom of opinion and free discussion so as to develop the masses of the people in the practice of democracy and to enable them to express their views, and if possible implement them, against the wishes of many of these very vested interests. There is not a single person in the West Indies who does not, for instance, interpret the constitution that has been granted to Jamaica in that way. It seems to me that not only in the West Indies, but even in Great Britain itself, the recent elections show precisely the same tendency. I am pained to have to say that the situation in which you now place me leads me to believe that, in this instance at any rate, your request and the circumstances surrounding it represent a complete reversal of what I and, I am certain, many others have understood to be the recent trend in West Indian government, stated repeatedly by some of the highest officials whom there is no necessity for me to quote, and what I have considered to be a guiding principle of the Anglo-American Caribbean Commission.

In view of these facts I see no alternative but to inform you that under no circumstances will I entertain any request for my resignation. I consider myself to be under an eighteen months' contract beginning March 1, 1945, with the understanding that from September 1, 1946 we shall revert to annual contracts. I may also add that I expect to be appointed Secretary of the general Research Council in accordance with the various discussions that we have had since the recommendations at St. Thomas last year. If, through the pressure of vested interests, I am to be removed from the Commission, it will be done not only without any assistance from me, but against every effort which I can make.

I have discussed with you very freely, and in as honest a manner as possible, my personal hopes for the future and the pros and cons of the post at Howard. But I could not now consider a post at Howard, whatever the personal consequences to myself. I do not propose to seek a post at that University as a refuge from the hostility of West Indian planters.

Three days later, on July 31, 1945, Mr. X called me in for a discussion which lasted two hours. I was all set for it. I was a very angry man, and I went prepared to give no quarter and ask for none. I knew that if I yielded, they would wipe the floor with me forever after. My notes, as I wrote them up immediately after, read as follows:

"Mr. X began by saying that he had never been more hurt or pained in his life, that he had not been able to sleep because of it, that it was a complete shock to him to come back on Monday to find a 'stiff official letter' in reply to unofficial, friendly conversations. He stated that I had completely misunderstood him, and that the Commission had decided nothing. It was merely that they considered that the security of tenure at Howard University was better than what the Commission was in a position to offer. I listened patiently and politely.

"Mr. X however, insisted on discussing *The Negro in the Caribbean*, emphasising that it was not a matter of the correctness of my views but rather of the smooth running of the Commission. In the course of conversation he admitted that he had not read the book beyond 'page 40 or 60'—an admission that I did not allow to pass unnoticed. As an example of the reaction to the book that might be embarrassing to the Commission, he cited as a hypothetical case a Research Council meeting in Antigua where the governor might be hostile to me as the author. I knew immediately that the letter had been written by the governor of the Leeward Islands. I stood about as much of this as I could, and then told Mr. X with deliberate heat that I could not agree to take part in any further discussion of the book. I had written it. I stood by it, and I would never repudiate it or one single line of it. Everyone knew of the book's existence, the Colonial Office had given me my appointment, and at one time the State Department was the best single purchaser. I had been taught the skills of my trade and I had learned them well. I was not prepared to listen to any criticism about my research standards and my methods from any vested interests in the West Indies. I would not capitulate for one moment to those interests. No question of unfavourable reaction to my book could be entertained. I refused to take responsibility for the fact, as he argued, that the planters may not have read the book before 1945. I said I did not want to hear any more about the subject, and if the Governor of the Leeward Islands were to take the hypothetical attitude attributed to him, I expected the Commission and the Colonial Office to give me full support."

Mr. X then stated that my appointment as secretary of the general Research Council would create a new situation by creating a new post and requiring a new contract. In view of the fact that I would probably be in the West Indies, this would be an opportunity for 'reconsideration' of the former latitude I had enjoyed with respect to speaking and writing. I suspected either (a) an attempt to make the post so unattractive that I would resign or (b) that muzzling me would be thrown to the planters as a sop in lieu of my resignation. I decided, therefore, to fight the issue. I denied that the appointment would create a new situation. I said that I had taken the original position on the understanding that I should have liberty to write and speak subject to the necessary controls by the Commission. I reminded him that I was not a civil servant and would not be in the new post. The argument was prolonged and at times heated. I said that I could not but associate this entirely new interpretation of my position with the very pressure from the sugar planters that I was fighting against. The upshot was that he agreed to the continuation of the existing system, 'made tighter'.

In the course of the discussion Mr. X used such phrases as: he did not want to 'bandy arguments', I had used 'threats' in my letter (the reference was to my statements about my contract and my appointment as secretary of the Research Council), and that I seemed very insistent on my 'rights'. I asked him who else would insist on them? I pointed out that the very raising of the issue of *The Negro in the Caribbean* made it imperative for me to get everything quite clear for the future. I told him that I was sorry that he had used such expressions and lost his temper. If anyone had the right to feel aggrieved, I thought it was myself, for his attitude was as if I had committed a crime in writing the book, and if I had concealed from him that the English edition was due to appear, he could not treat me worse. I added that, after my long association with him, I was bitterly disappointed to find that his approaches to me left me only one conclusion; that he was acting as the virtual agent of the West Indian plantocracy. He winced visibly."

Throughout the discussion I was conscious of two impressions:

(a) that Mr. X was literally flabbergasted. I doubt that he had ever expected any colonial to write or speak to him like that; (b) that morally and physically I was his superior. That he should be evasive and apologetic I fully expected. But he was more than that. At times he was quite incoherent, and I had to ask him at least twice to explain what he meant. He placed the blame on fatigue. When we were through he had had enough; I could have gone on for three hours. On one occasion he conceded that I was fundamentally right. I replied that I was fundamentally, legally, morally, intellectually right. I refused to yield one millimetre of ground."

I concluded my notes thus: "The snake has been scotched, not killed. But it has been scotched very badly." I forgot that a snake sheds its skin.

My Relations with the Caribbean Commission

It was eventually agreed that I was a jolly good fellow and that I would keep my job. But I was not deceived. I knew, as everyone of you here tonight knows, that I was a marked man after that. I knew, as you know, that the whisper campaign would be launched, that I would be denounced as a trouble maker, that a price would be set on my head, that the axe would be sharpened in readiness, and that sometime, somehow, somewhere, it would fall. But I preferred to stretch out my neck to the executioner than to crawl on my belly and coat my tongue with the polish from his shoes.

The conservative-minded among you may accuse me of melodrama, or, to use a phrase that has already been used about me, of playing to the gallery. You would be quite wrong. Let me give you a simple illustration of the hostile climate in which I lived in official wartime Washington. The British Section of the Commission used to receive information leaflets prepared in the British Embassy in Washington. These leaflets gave, among other things, advice and data on topical questions. One of them which was passed to me suggested various points which a British official might make if he found himself in a group discussing the problems of Palestine, India and other British headaches of the day. It gave point one, point two, point three, point four, etc., stated the American case, suggested a reply to it, and ended up by indicating how one might introduce the Negro question if the situation became too hot to handle. I went to an official cocktail party the very afternoon I read the document. I drifted across to where a British colleague was standing and holding forth with someone. I recognised point one of the document. A few minutes later I found myself within hearing distance of the head of my office. He was most eloquent, repeating point four almost word for word. It was the dissemination of ideas on the assembly line principle. I knew, that afternoon, as one who not only had his own ideas but also defended them, that I could not follow the party line, that I could not serve the god of intellectual freedom and the mammon of official propaganda at the same time.

I had been initiated into the theory of bureaucracy. It served to illuminate the practical difficulties which I had encountered from the very beginning of my connection with the Commission. The day before I was to leave for Boston in May 1943 to be the principal speaker at a conference of Jamaicans on the theme, "The Four Freedoms for Jamaica", my British superior officer, Mr. X's predecessor, came to my office. It was the first time he had done so. After some chit-chat, he told me that there was a very great difference between the demand for self-government in Puerto Rico and the demand for self-government in Jamaica. He explained it in this way: Puerto Rico was asking for something which it had won from Spain in 1898 but which had been withdrawn by the United States in the same year when the island was annexed whereas Jamaica was asking for something it had never had before. He concluded by saying that that was a good point which I might wish to use one day in one of my lectures. I thanked him politely, but told him that he was wrong—the Jamaicans were asking for something which they had enjoyed up to 1865 when the self-governing constitution were freely surrenderd by the planters, and the crown colony system substituted. He walked out without another word. I knew irrevocably after that that the price of intellectual liberty is eternal vigilance.

The official was shortly after appointed Governor of a British West Indian territory which I visited in 1944. Having obtained permission from my office to lecture on the proposed West Indian University and on representative government, I accepted invitations on my arrival to give these lectures and this was reported in the press. When I saw the Governor, he expressed regret that I had agreed to lecture on representative government. In his opinion the timing was not right; he preferred me to speak on slavery, the proposed University, federation. I thought this a very strange attitude to take, as the island was about to be officially launched on the road to representative government. It seemed to me, therefore that far from my timing being wrong, it was absolutely right, and I said so. But, as he was the Governor, I apologised for

My Relations with the Caribbean Commission

announcing the lecture and stated that I would immediately cancel it. He advised against this, as he felt that some explanation might be requested. But he asked me to delete from the copy I showed him a short paragraph which included a question from the great British authority on representative government, John Stuart Mill. He also challenged my interpretation of the colonial regime in the thirteen mainland colonies of North America before the War of Independence, but he subsequently withdrew his opposition when I asked him to send to the library for any book on the subject.

Faced with these British frontal attacks, I had also to cope with a United States attack from the rear. My tour of duty included Puerto Rico and the Virgin Islands. Just before my departure I was asked by the editor of a well-known quarterly in the United States, *Foreign Affairs,* to write an article on race relations in those two areas. On my return to Washington, I completed my article and submitted it to the United States Section of the Commission for review in accordance with the rules of the State Department. Every effort was made to persuade me to withdraw the article and not submit it for approval, on the ground that the timing was not right. It struck me that if West Indians are to think only when Britain and the United States consider it is the right time for them to do so, we will never think at all. I disagreed with the argument. I consider that each and every moment of each and every day is a fit and proper time to attack racial discrimination, and I said so. I was then asked whether I would similarly consider the time appropriate to discuss, for example, the Guatemalan claims on British Honduras. I replied that I would, and indicated how I would treat the subject—by discussing first the Guatemalan claim, then the counter-claim of British Honduras and Great Britain after which I would sum up judicially. Against this the argument was advanced that one engaged in public affairs at a semi-government level should not write about public affairs. I replied that the Prime Minister of Great Britain, Winston Churchill, wrote his own version of public affairs; the then Vice President of the U.S.A.,

Henry Wallace, wrote his own version of public affairs which not infrequently differed from the Government's policy, and Lord Olivier, a former Socialist governor of Jamaica, had thirty years before written a well known book on *White Capital and Coloured Labour* even though he was in the British Colonial service. I was challenged as to a statement I made to the effect that a coloured visitor to hotels in Puerto Rico would not be refused a room or service, but would be placed in the annex; I replied that it had happened to me on all the many occasions I had visited the island up to that time. Eventually it was agreed to submit the article for approval. It was returned to me with one insignificant amendment, and about a month later it was cited as a reference in an official United States document on Puerto Rico.

My victory over *The Negro in the Caribbean* was the signal for a number of sniping attacks on me in official quarters which were so regular that I could not possibly regard them as anything else but a deliberate campaign, well planned and carefully directed. At a conference in 1946 I met the Economic Adviser of a certain British territory. He greeted me with these words: "I hear you have written a book called *Capitalism and Slavery*. I understand you take the view that slavery was abolished for economic and not humanitarian reasons. Well, I don't agree with you. Of course, I haven't read the book myself." I suggested we defer discussions until he had read it. I had sent a manuscript I had written on education in the British West Indies to one of the highest British educational authorities in the area. He drew me aside at the same conference and spoke to me as follows: "I want to talk to you very seriously, but not about your manuscript. In fact, I haven't read it. But I want to talk to you about the fact that an increasing number of white people in the West Indies are beginning to express concern about your views." I bade him good day. Some time after my return to Trinidad in 1948, a government official wrote to me for a list of my authorities on a particular point I had made in one of a series of articles on Caribbean history. I was very busy at the time, and, as his letter was rather impertinent, I was in no hurry to

My Relations with the Caribbean Commission

reply to it. I woke up one Sunday morning to find that he had publicly accused me in the press of distorting the facts for what he called the morbid purpose of telling coloured people that they are not inferior. Some of you may remember how he was reminded that, where ignorance is bliss, 'tis folly to be wise.

Every effort was made to keep me out of the West Indian University College. From the time that the proposed establishment of the college was announced I began to make a serious study of university development in the past hundred years, with the emphasis on the colonial or semi-colonial countries. This study convinced me that our university must develop a curriculum suited to the Caribbean environment and to this end, with self-government ahead, it must be a fully self-governing university, not affiliated to any British or Canadian university. At the request of the chairman of the University Commission, I prepared a long memorandum on the subject which I sent not only to him but also to the two Sections of the Commission and to the official in the Colonial office I have mentioned earlier. The Colonial Office official replied that my study, for care, thoroughness and close reasoning, must rival *Capitalism and Slavery.* The chairman of the University Commission assured me that the commission was in agreement with my views, that for the most part the essentials of my scheme found a place in its recommendations, and that, approaching the problem from a somewhat different angle, it had come to decisions not far removed and not differing in any material sense from my scheme with the exception of the factor of residence. Notwithstanding these assurances, I heard nothing more of the question of an appointment until some five years later a close friend of mine on the University Council, a prominent lawyer in the Leeward Islands, advised me that the view held in the highest quarters in the University was that, when the time came to make a certain appointment, they would be sure to find a much better man than I.

I later expanded my memorandum and published it as a book, *Education in the British West Indies.* My views, especially those on the West Indian University, so appealed to the late John Dewey, the great United States scholar and philosopher, that he wrote a foreword to the book, describing it as "a case study of a world problem" in which the United States itself was involved. Thus if the chairman of the University Commission and the Colonial Office official were sincere in the views they expressed to me, why was I kept out of the University? The only possible explanation is the battle over *The Negro in the Caribbean*. If my superior officer sent to the Colonial Office copies of reviews of *Capitalism and Slavery*, asked me for a note on the English edition of *The Negro in the Caribbean* to transmit to it, and consulted it on every single detail of my appointment, it is unthinkable that he did not report what had happened over *The Negro in the Caribbean*.

Here was I, therefore, a member of the Commission's staff, being attacked right and left by sugar planters, bureaucrats and a governor for writings which none of them had ever done me the elementary courtesy to read before condemning me. I learned then how the imperialists operate—by condemning colonials without giving them a hearing. It all reminded me of a British publisher, notorious for his publication of revolutionary literature, who in 1939 angrily told me, though he had not read my doctor's thesis which later became *Capitalism and Slavery*, that he would never publish a book which took the view that Britain abolished slavery for economic and not humanitarian reasons, because it would be contrary to the British tradition.

Whilst the heathen raged, my senior colleagues in the university fraternity commended. The contrast was strikingly exemplified when *The Colonial Review*, the monthly journal of the Institute of Education of one of Britain's greatest universities, the University of London, thus reviewed *The Negro in the Caribbean*, two months after I was nearly dismissed from the Commission for being its author:

My Relations with the Caribbean Commission

"Eric Williams' scholarly and carefully documented study gives us a survey of the Caribbean in the perspective of its historic past and presents existing problems in a constructive interpretation looking towards its future. He is concerned mainly with economic questions and he views educational and political problems from this angle. It is interesting to note in view of Colonel Stanley's recent dispatch to the Governors of the West Indian Colonies (on federation) that Eric Williams' study led him to believe that the future progress of the Caribbean lay in political and economic federation."

I showed the review to Mr. X, who had tried to force me out of the Commission. He never said a mumbling word.

What was all the fuss in Antigua and Washington about? My book was a thorough and careful analysis of government commissions and statistics for the entire Caribbean area. It dealt as much with conditions in Puerto Rico as with conditions in the British West Indies; I described the sugar industry as an industry which combined the vices of feudalism and capitalism with the virtues of neither. I contrasted the dividends distributed to the shareholders and the wages paid to the workers. I quoted a Barbados commission which warned that a fundamental change in the division of earnings between the employer and his employees is essential if hatred and bitterness are to be removed from the minds of the majority of employees. I quoted a Puerto Rican government agency which insisted that the sugar industry did not satisfy the requirements of the economic life of the island and should be adjusted in order to meet the needs of the people. I quoted a Puerto Rican scholar who concluded that the sugar plantation economy with its seasonal employment does not offer any hope for the amelioration of social and economic conditions; rather it aims to perpetuate the present deplorable situation. I stressed that, except in times of crisis, adequate subsistence for the workers and the social stability which comes from a diversified economy have meant no more to foreign capital than to the man in the moon. I quoted a Barbados commission to the effect that Barbados planters claimed that the worker does not take milk in his tea because he does not like milk. I quoted a British aristocrat in the House of Lords who asked whether Trinidad is the only place where there are bad houses, no roads, no water, no sewerage; I could have asked him why he did not come to live in John John and help our tourist trade, but I did not.

I quoted a Puerto Rican study which attributed the incidence of malaria to the fact that houses were only too frequently built by the workers on swampy lands, so that they should not encroach on the sugar plantations and that nine out of ten houses on the sugar plantations lack bathing conveniences. I quoted a British philanthropist, a great friend of Mahatma Gandhi, who was told on a visit to British Guiana that the London directors of one of the sugar companies would vote money for new machinery but not for demolishing the barrack rooms in which the workers lived. I quoted the warning issued to company directors by the Disturbances Commission in Trinidad in 1937 that the claim of the workers for the common decencies of home life should be one for primary consideration, and that by maintaining existing conditions they are providing ground for justifiable discontent. I quoted Mr. Lloyd George who described the British West Indies as the slums of the Empire. I quoted a British Guiana Nutrition Committee which advised that a concerted drive against malnutrition in the Indian population and the raising of their nutritional standard of living would result in immeasurable benefit to the sugar industry. I quoted the famous statement of Munoz Marin, now the first elected governor of Puerto Rico, that Puerto Rico was Uncle Sam's second largest sweatshop.

I stressed the necessity of peasant proprietorship, I traced the growth of the labour movement, I warned that for the Caribbean as for the rest of the world, for the Negro as for the rest of mankind, there are only two alternatives—greater freedom or greater tyranny. I concluded: "Full and unqualified democracy—nothing less. The true Magna Carta of these colonies is economic emancipation, but the road to economic emancipation demands political democracy."

This is what I wrote in 1942, in the midst of a war based on the Atlantic Charter and the four freedoms. This was what the sugar planters of Antigua, with the governor of the island as their spokesman, wished to crucify me for. The Governor had only to denounce me, and Mr. X of the Commission, who had not read the book himself beyond page 40 or 60, promptly obeyed orders; Mr. X did not stop to inquire whether the duty of a governor is to govern his territory in the interest only of one class. He did not stop to ask why he should attach any importance at all to the governor and planters of one wretched little impoverished island. No other governor, no other planters attacked me. In fact Mr. X knew very well that the governor of another territory had said exactly the opposite about me. On April 19, 1944, on the occasion of my first visit to Trinidad since I had left for Oxford in 1932, I lectured to a packed house at the Public Library on "The British West Indies in World History". It was a preview of *Capitalism and Slavery*. The Acting Governor, who was in the chair, introduced me, and in a reference to my island scholarship, spoke thus as reported in the *Port-of-Spain Gazette* two days later:

> "Dr. Williams has come home, and he has brought with him scholarship and learning of which anyone, anywhere, however talented, might be proud. Seldom can a Government investment be so well placed. He has passed from the field of study to the field of action, as Secretary of the Caribbean Research Council".

Who was right—the Governor of Trinidad and Tobago or the Governor of the Leeward Islands? Did the former speak as he did in 1944 because he had not yet seen *The Negro in the Caribbean*, whereas the latter wrote as he did in 1945 because he had seen it? Do governors say one thing in public and the opposite in private? How could the Governor of Trinidad and Tobago commend my scholarship and learning which went into *Capitalism and Slavery* and the Governor of the Leeward Islands try to crucify me for them because they went into *The Negro in the Caribbean?* Was the Trinidad Government's investment in my scholarship well placed in 1944 and badly placed in 1945?

Ten years have elapsed since the controversy. Look back on these ten years, Ladies and Gentlemen, and tell me whether I should have been crucified in 1945 for advocating as a writer some of the very things which by 1955 have either been translated or are now being translated into action by the chosen leaders of the West Indian people. Perhaps you can't answer my question. Then ask Munoz Marin in Puerto Rico who came to power, with a majority unequalled in any election in any democratic country, on the slogan, "Bread, Land and Liberty", who has created 20,000 new jobs in industry to reduce the dependence on the sugar industry, who has raised individual and family incomes in Puerto Rico, who has given to the people of Puerto Rico a vitality and confidence which have no equal anywhere in the Caribbean, and who has given Puerto Rico complete self-government! Ask V. C. Bird in Antigua, who has built up one of the most powerful labour movements in the Caribbean, which brought to their knees in a strike not so long ago the very sugar planters who attacked me in 1945 and which swept the field in recent elections! Ask Robert Bradshaw in St. Kitts who has done exactly what Bird has done in Antigua! Ask Norman Manley, who is now in England demanding complete self-government for Jamaica, who is planning to create 150,000 new jobs in the island, and who is going in the next five years to transform the island into something which no one familiar with it today after 300 years of British rule will be able to recognise! Ask the sugar workers in Trinidad whose union has just been recognised by the manufacturers! Even the British Government has seen the light. The Soulbury Commission recommended the establishment of a fund for loans to sugar workers and cane farmers for building or repairing or enlarging their houses and for getting rid of the unsightly barracks which I condemned.

My Relations with the Caribbean Commission

It is not I whom the Antigua planters should have crucified but Munoz Marin and Norman Manley, Bird and Bradshaw, the Trinidad sugar workers and Britain's Soulbury Commission. That they should oppose me was not unnatural. But that the Anglo-American Caribbean Commission should persecute me for showing how badly needed was the improvement of the conditions it was set up to improve, that the conservative Governor of a British territory should hound me at exactly the time when the British people were about to transfer their allegiance to the Labour party which nationalised Britain's sugar refining industry—those injustices were hard to forgive. It turned out, however, that I had the last laugh. In 1947 I went to Antigua on official duty. By then the Governor had been transferred. I was met at the airport by the aide de camp of the Acting Governor, who has since become one of the principal officials of the sugar manufacturers' association in a certain British West Indian territory. The aide de camp brought an invitation from the Governor that I stay at Government House as his guest. The Acting Governor, however, was a West Indian.

I laughed even louder and longer last year when it fell to me, Public Enemy No. 1 of the Antigua planters in 1945, to propose the line of action for the defence of the sugar industry to be taken at the London Conference on the General Agreement of Tariffs and trade. It was the leader of the Jamaican Sugar Manufacturers who first saw the merit of the argument I advanced on which the whole British West Indian case was subsequently made to rest. My argument was that the protection of West Indian products by Britain and Canada long antedated GATT, and was acknowledged by Britain as a part of its moral responsibility for slavery and indenture. Such protection, I continued, was the economic expression of the constitutional relationship between Britain and the West Indies. It was therefore no more the subject of international review than was the protection accorded by the United States and France to Puerto Rico and Martinique respectively. The products of these Caribbean countries enter the metropolitan markets free of duty, this protection being only the economic expression of the constitutional relationship between them and their respective metropolitan countries.

To complete the record of this aspect of my subject, let me state that the whole question of freedom to write and speak was settled in the West Indies by the staff rules of the Caribbean Commission. These rules provide that the permission of the Secretary General must be sought for any public lecture, and that any lecture or article or book on subjects within the Commission's terms of reference must be approved by the Secretariat's Editorial Board. I have lectured and written principally on historical, cultural, literary and educational subjects. It is only within the past years that the Commission began to deal with education, and the other subjects are ignored by it. But I have always sought the necessary permission in writing and always obtained it in writing, the particular subject being clearly indicated. I have not spoken on a single subject within the past five years without official permission. As the rules do not specify that the content of lectures must be approved, I have never submitted any lectures for approval. Let me add that the Commission has more than once gone on record as welcoming lectures by members of the Secretariat staff.

You are now, Ladies and Gentlemen, better able to understand the feeling of relief at separation from the Commission which I expressed in a recent press interview. But you may ask why I tolerated those conditions for over twelve years. The answer is that I represented in the Commission's Secretariat the cause of the West Indian people. I also had more personal reasons. My connection with the Commission brought me into close contact with present problems in territories the study of whose history has been the principal purpose of my adult life, while my association with representatives of the metropolitan governments enabled me to understand, as I could not otherwise have understood, the mess in which the West Indies find themselves today.

My Relations with the Caribbean Commission

The principal functions of the Caribbean Commission are to concern itself with economic and social matters of common interest to the Caribbean area, and to study, formulate and recommend measures, programmes and policies with respect to social and economic problems designed to contribute to the wellbeing of the Carribean area. There was not really any need for the Commission and its predecessor. The West India Royal Commission of 1938 had thoroughly studied the British West Indian problem, and formulated and recommended measures, programmes and policies designed to contribute to the wellbeing of the British West Indian area. Many similar studies had been made in Puerto Rico. Whilst there was and is still room for study, the basic problem was to implement the recommendations made. But the two Commissions were a part of the price extracted by the United States for aid to the European governments during the war. These governments could not resist the pressure actively, so they resisted passively. The European governments have always been determined not to make the Commission work. The Americans, busy with more important commitments elsewhere, have been content to play ball in order to retain their foothold in the non-American area. I was told by many important American officials in 1946 that they preferred to set up the Commission's headquarters in Trinidad with an American boss, rather than in St. Thomas with a British boss, so that they could have a listening post in the British West Indies. The Commission has from the beginning been the stage on which the rivalry of the four powers has been fought out.

The Commission organisation consists of four parts—the Caribbean Commission itself, the Caribbean Research Council, the West Indian Conference, and the Central Secretariat. The entire organisation is dominated by the four governments—Britain, France, Holland and the U.S.A. Whilst each Section of the Commission includes West Indian representatives, few of these have been in any sense representatives of the West Indian people.

Moreover, each Section has a Co-Chairman, who is a metropolitan representative. Only the British Co-Chairman has any direct connection with the West Indies. The four Co-Chairman have the right to decide themselves, without reference to their other Commissioners, matters other than those relating to procedure. The Commission meets twice a year; in the interim decisions are taken by a Working Committee located in Washington, comprising representatives of the British, French and Dutch Embassies and of the State Department—four people who have otherwise not the remotest connection with West Indian problems. The Research Council consists of fifteen representatives of the four governments; it has five committees, each consisting of one member from each government. The Puerto Ricans and the Virgin Islanders apart, there are very few West Indians. The British Section is packed with advisers of the British Development and Welfare Organisation; there is only one British West Indian on the Committee. The French Section is similarly packed with representatives from metropolitan France, birds of passage who come and go frequently. The West Indian Conference which meets every two years, is attended by delegates chosen by the respective legislatures in the British West Indies or by the governments in other territories. But these politicians, who can only make recommendations to the Commission, have advisers, the majority European, in addition to which the four governments bring their own advisers, sometimes in vast numbers, so that one wonders what West Indian discussion there can be in such an atmosphere. There have been two Secretaries-General to date one American, the other Dutch; when the Secretariat was transferred to Trinidad in 1946, there were five senior officers, of whom one was American, one a Frenchman from France, one an Englishman, one a Dutchman, the fifth was a French West Indian.

Obviously the cause and interests of the West Indian people needed to be defended in such an organisation, at least in two ways: first, the scope of the work to be done and the priorities to be

My Relations with the Caribbean Commission

given to it; second, the selection of the persons to do that work. I became the watchman for and the spokesman of the West Indian people in the Secretariat with respect to these two questions, and by my visits to territories and my attendance at meetings and conferences I was in a position to express the West Indian point of view and to influence West Indians in attendance.

When the Commission transferred its headquarters to Trinidad in 1946, I resigned my post, for reasons that I shall make clear later, but agreed, at the request of the Secretary General, to continue as a consultant in charge of a Washington branch office specially maintained for the purpose of my continuing and completing some studies on crops and trade on which I had been engaged. During this period the research work at the headquarters in Trinidad, under the direction of an Englishman, was devoted almost exclusively to a study of dunder disposal from sugar factories. The European head of the Commission's research work might readily agree to be a dunderhead. In fact, he might be a quite admirable dunderhead. But any West Indian worth his salt would obviously give priority to the disposal of the sugar rather than the dunder from sugar factories. But when I proposed this, the Commission said no. It said that the sugar industry can take care of its own marketing arrangements, as if West Indian Ministers don't go time and time again to England to fight its battles.

I promptly put a stop to the dunder nonsense when I arrived in Trinidad in 1948 to head the Research Branch. I proposed that the Research Branch should publish an economic journal and a statistical handbook and should continue its trade studies. The British fought tooth and nail against my proposals, but at the same meeting the Commission accepted unhesitatingly a proposal for annual meetings about hurricane warnings. The Commission was much happier dealing with the damage caused by nature than with that caused by man. Working with committees preparing the agenda for conferences, I was able time and again to orient the discussions towards West Indian needs whether the subject was agriculture, livestock, education or trade. I proposed from time to time various important problems as the subject for conferences, such as small scale farming and trade statistics.

The next hurdle was who was to do the work? An imported expert is very expensive: much time and money are consumed in familiarisation tours running all over the damned place as if he is a Minister; in the course of these tours the expert falls victim, as hundreds have done throughout the centuries, to the hospitality offered by the vested interests. What he learns on the tour is of no value to the West Indies, for he takes his knowledge with him when he leaves. More often than not, his contribution has little value. Let me give some examples.

The Commission once approved a proposal of the American Secretary General for a regional survey of transportation facilities to be made by a highly paid Dutch expert ignorant of the area. This survey is alleged to have cost U.S. $20,000, according to a rumour circulating among the delegates to the Third Session of the West Indian Conference held in Guadeloupe in 1948, which rejected it out of hand and recommended against its publication. The survey was eventually made by a West Indian member of my research staff as a part of his normal duties, though he had to visit again the very territories previously visited by the Dutch expert. Another survey, this time of industrial development in the area, was made by a panel of reports, one appointed by each of the four Governments, the four reports being collated by a fifth expert. One member of the panel was British, another Dutch, while the co-ordinator was French; they brought to bear on the question the traditional metropolitan hostility to colonial industrialisation. The report took years to complete. Before it was finished, I succeeded in getting Arthur Lewis, the distinguished West Indian economist, appointed as a consultant to the Secretariat to study industrial development in Puerto Rico and make recommendations for the British West Indies. Dr. Lewis took three months, over the study, which cost little more than a single month's salary for the French coordinator, while other aspects of industrial development were later studied thoroughly by the West Indian economist on my research staff as a matter of routine.

Ever since its inception the Commission has talked about promoting Caribbean trade, especially trade between the different territories of the Caribbean. I had a Dutch expert on my staff. Never was expert more inexpert; in five years he analysed exactly nothing, and some of his work had to be transferred to a West Indian member of my staff, while I undertook the rest. The West Indian Conference which met in Jamaica at the end of 1952 then proposed a comprehensive programme of market research. The Commission accepted this recommendation. Last year, however, the Secretary General proposed to me that the project be abandoned; the principal responsibility for work in this field has now been assigned to specially appointed French and American officers, one of whom has no knowledge of the West Indies. I recommended a series of crop studies to supplement the market research programme. The Commission approved, but later agreed to abandon the project on the recommendation of the Secretary General.

The most recent manifestation of metropolitan influence is technical assistance—the provision of experts to study this, that and the other by other international organisations or by the United States Government. One such expert, brought down to study fundamental education, has publically advised that the training of voluntary workers should begin with community singing and games and proceed to specific training in such subjects as how to brighten meetings, conduct community games and curry eggs. Teaching us how to lay them before we curry them was possibly too fundamental for him. He ends this fundamental nonsense with some points for consideration when framing the proposed training course. His second point is:

> "It should never be forgotten that a community consists of both men and women, and that in the Caribbean the woman is very important. Indeed, it is proper to think that every man, woman and child is a member of the community."

So now you know, Ladies and Gentlemen, it is proper to think that every man and woman here tonight is a member of the community. Your children are, too.

Some very good work is being done by some of these experts in the field of housing and home economics, though I once shared an apartment with an expert whose services were requested by the local government but who for three months was not told what work he was required to do. He drew three months' pay without working, while I sat down night after night doing overtime work for the Commission without pay. From the research centre specified in the international agreement setting up the Commission, the Secretariat has become a clearing house, a post office, and the West Indian research worker making fundamental studies has been replaced by the imported administrative officer writing letters or progress reports.

These difference of opinion as to the work to be undertaken by the Commission in fulfilment of its obligations and the persons who should carry it out, important as they are in themselves, spring from a basic difference in perspective between West Indians and non-west Indian. Let me again give you examples. The American Secretary General once suggested to me that the Secretariat should strongly advocate United States capital investment in the Caribbean. I demurred, pointing out that that was a matter for the individual governments: the Secretariat should advocate investment, not investment from any particular country. I once proposed to a meeting one of my pet ideas—the publication by the Commission of a book describing the various territories as a natural implementaion of its principal purpose, cooperation between the territories and helping each one to know the other better. The proposal was attacked by a British chemist, who had been in the West Indies a few months, and who was attending his first meeting of the group involved.

On another occasion I proposed to a conference on trade promotion that the Commission should organise an exhibition of

My Relations with the Caribbean Commission

non-perishable products native to the Caribbean area for display in the various territories, partly for trade purposes, partly for educational purposes. I explained my reasons for the proposal—I had a few months before seen a similar exhibition in Amsterdam which had been attended by 40,000 people; people in Trinidad do not know that Jamaica produces some of the best coffee in the world, which is cheaper than imported United States blends, and a very good coffee liqueur, etc., etc., etc. One American claimed that I wanted to set up a museum; I had to ask him what the devil did it matter to him what we set up in the Caribbean. My proposal was passed by the Conference, but the Commission has retired it to a newly appointed American officer for study, which means that it is as good as dead. If I had only thought early enough of taking the proposal up with the Junior Chamber of Commerce in Trinidad on the occasion of the recent Trade Fair, you would have seen the exhibition for yourselves.

When the work for the conference was under way the Secretary General asked me what was meant by trade promotion—was it the promotion of metropolitan trade or the promotion of West Indian trade? I told him that I was astonished that such a question should come from the head of the Commission's Secretariat, which by its term of reference, was required to concern itself only with the promotion of West Indian trade, and leave the metropolitan governments to look after their own interests. He said he saw my point. But did he really? Shortly after the conference, the Trinidad Chamber of Commerce passed a resolution calling on the government to send a trade mission to the United Staes. After consulting informally the Chamber's President, himself a West Indian, I proposed to the Secretary General that my staff should proceed to complete a study of the details of British West Indian trade with the United States which I had begun myself in the course of a paper I had prepared for the conference. I explained that such a study would be of the utmost value to the Trinidad delegation. The Secretary General vetoed my proposal. Present indications are that it is metropolitan interests which will receive priority in the Commission Secretariat. This is nothing new. The Dutch market analyst on my research staff moved easily after his resignation into a position promoting Dutch exports to Trinidad; but I had not been able to get him to take the slightest interest whilst in his job in the possibility of selling Montserrat tomatoes in Curacao.

I took the Commission seriously and was determined that it should be made an effective force and brought close to the people. The imported officials, on the other hand, looked upon the Commission as a final resting place before retirement, and restricted their activities to palavers with "big shots." For example, I protested year after year against the expenditure of U.S. $3,000 on entertainment, whilst out junior staff had to work overtime without pay, the official attitude being that the Commission, which enjoys diplomatic immunities, can't be sued. The Commission eventually reduced the entertainment allowance and overtime pay was approved for the junior staff. The American Secretary General opposed my proposals, claiming that he did most of his work at cocktail parties. I thanked him for the information, advised him that research and cocktails did not mix, and I stopped going to official parties. A few years later a conference on home economics was convened here in Trinidad. I thought the occasion an excellent opportunity to invite social workers to meet the delegates from different territories at one of the evening seminars organised at such conferences. I had to fight to get the Secretary General's approval for this, and even then he insisted on restricting the number of invitations to fifty. When the conference was over, I had a good laugh. Trinidad's most prominent social worker, a legislator, wrote a stinging letter criticising the Secretariat for inviting so few people. I missed no opportunity of getting close to the people. The expatriate missed no opportunity of getting away from them.

My Relations with the Caribbean Commission

* * *

This conflict between the West Indian and the metropolitan point of view, between West Indian and metropolitan interests, revolved in the last analysis around the question of the appointment of local men to senior and professional posts in the Commission's Secretariat. This is a definite requirement of the Agreement signed by the four governments for the establishment of the Commission.

The rule reads as follows:

> "In the appointment of the Secretary-General, officers and staff of the Central Secretariat, primary consideration shall be given to the technical, qualifications and personal integrity of candidates and, to the extent possible consistent with this consideration, such officers and staff shall be recruited within the Caribbean area."

This brings me to the third part of my story, the defeat inflicted by my dismissal on the policy of appointing local men to high office in the Commission's Secretariat.

The basic conflict between the United States and the European governments to which I have referred earlier was reflected in the struggle over my appointment. The United States Section of the Commission did not see eye to eye with the British Section on my modest responsibility of one afternoon's work a fortnight, and under pressure from it my duties were steadily increased, both in quantity and quality, until the month before my permanent appointment, I was working a 30-hour week. The United States Section brought a similar pressure on the British Section to set in motion the machinery at the British Embassy to prevent my induction into the army, two days before I was due to report for military service. I was left under no illusion as to the reason for this—I was told that if the British had my right leg the Americans had my left. The speaker had a broad smile on his face, but I knew it was no laughing matter. I symbolised the British West Indian people, governed by Britain, with naval bases leased to the United States. The British never liked this arrangement and tried to get me out of Washington by offering me the post of Agricultural Economist in Jamaica. I declined the offer, on the ground that I am not an agricultural economist.

By 1945, however, the position had changed, in two respects. In the first place, the steadily increasing United States commitments all over the world pushed the Caribbean question into the back ground. In the second place, it was clear after the war over *The Negro in the Caribbean* that I did not propose to allow either of my legs to be tied down. Therefore, having failed in its efforts to dismiss me, the Commission resorted to other tactics. In appointing the first Deputy Chairman of the Research Council, I as a West Indian who know the West Indies was passed over for a British representative who knew nothing about them. He was a retired officer from the administrative service in an African territory, and was a sick man who within a year and a half had to be invalided out of the service. He had just stopped off in Washington on his way home to say hello to my superior officer, a former colleague of his, and landed a job in the West Indies. It was in protest against this discrimination that I resigned from the Commission.

But, as I have indicated above, my resignation was immediately followed by my appointment as a consultant remaining in Washington. Despite consistent British opposition, my Washington branch office was given increasing responsibility until I was working full time for the Commission over and above my duties at Howard University. I was able to do this by working nights and weekends.

The Washington office lasted from September 1946 to May 1948. The Secretary General then proposed to the Commission that I be appointed to take charge of its research activities in Trinidad. Opposition to my appointment came from the Dutch; it was obvious that they were merely pulling the chestnuts out of the fire for the British, who were handicapped by the fact that the British West Indian representatives on the Commission gave me strong support. Eventually a compromise was reached. I was appointed to act for six months in the post of Deputy Chairman of the Caribbean Research Council, with the understanding that a final decision would be made at the next meeting of the Commission. The Dutch Co-Chairman angrily complained in my presence that this decision was as good as giving me the job then and there.

It was absolutely necessary, therefor, to find some plausible reason for getting me out. The Commission picked upon communism.

The full significance of the accusation can only be appreciated in the light of certain facts. Shortly after the entry of the United States into World War II, I learned that the entire faculty of the Division of Social Sciences of Howard University had been summoned to the Department of Justice for questioning. But I was not called in. On June 19, 1942 I was advised by one of the most important wartime departments of the United States Government, the Office of Strategic Services, that I had been appointed a consultant to prepare a brochure on the Caribbean for the use of United States troops to be sent there, subject to a favourable report of the character investigation which was then being made by the United States Civil Service Commission. I later received a copy of a communication from the Civil Service Commission to the Office of Strategic Services, dated November 6, 1942, advising that investigation, without finger print clearance, had disclosed nothing reflecting unfavourably on my suitability.

No similar communication was addressed to me when I was appointed full time to the Anglo-American Caribbean Commission. But the appointment itself, which placed me for a while on the State Department's payroll, obviously proved that I was not unsuitable.

When, therefore, the charge was made against me in December 1948 that I was a communist, it was clear that it was merely an attempt to evade the crucial issue then pending, whether I was to be confirmed in the post of Deputy Chairman of the Research

Council. The charge was based on a sentence which was included in a document prepared for the third session of the West Indian Conference in Guadeloupe, in which I had, on the suggestion of the Secretary General, incorporated a letter I had written to him some months before from Washington. Overwhelmed with work, and forgetting that it was a confidential letter, I had merely given instructions to get the letter out of the files and quote it in the document; I had not even proofread the document. The sentence made some reference to the abolition of private property. The Commission decided not to confirm me in the post, pending investigation. I had never had any connection whatsoever with any political organisation at all, except that at Oxford I had attended regularly meetings of the Indian nationalist students in their club, the Majliss. So I refused to fall for the bait and resign in disgust. A few months later I was advised privately that the F.B.I. in the United States had cleared me completely of all suspicion. The British endeavoured unsuccessfully, as I learned from friends, to persuade another British West Indian, of whom they were sure, to take my post. He was a lawyer, who knew nothing of research, and he declined the post.

Consequently in June 1949 my appointment was confirmed without any fuss and I was given a five-year contract. This explains how I travelled freely and without hindrance in United States territory. Immediately after the conference I visited the U.S.A. on official duty in January 1949. I then went to the Virgin Islands in December 1949 for a meeting of the Commission, Puerto Rico in March 1950 as the Secretariat's representative at a Conference, the U.S.A. in September 1950 on six months leave, and Puerto Rico in April 1952 on official duty. Every time I travelled on re-entry permits issued by the Department of Justice of the U.S.A. I was never once challenged, questioned, or denied entry.

That the charge was not taken seriously even by those who made it is illustrated by an attempt made by some British West Indians to lure me away from the Commission to the post, which

My Relations with the Caribbean Commission

had shortly before been created but not filled, of Economic Adviser to the Government of Trinidad and Tobago. I declined the offer, as I would decline it today, on two grounds: I am not an economist, and I do not wish to be a civil servant. In addition, in 1948 no less than in 1945, I did not want to run from the enemy.

But the most amusing part of the story connected with this accusation of communism comes from Trinidad itself. Not long after my permanent appointment, I delivered a lecture at the public Library on Communism, as one of a series of twelve lectures on the development of Western civilisation. The following day I received a telephone call from a certain government department. I was told that someone, out of interest in the subject, I was assured had taken down the lecture in shorthand, it had been typed up and was considered so excellent that the department wanted my permission to use in in the government's anti-communist drive. I wondered what the Governor and planters of the Leeward Islands or even Mr. X would have thought. But I objected strongly to this attempt to take my views out of their context, to select one lecture only for publication, and to link me up with police measures, and I warned the department in the strongest terms of what would happen if it published the lecture. It did not do so. I wonder what whisper was begun about me then.

Throughout all these struggles and intrigues I had one enormous advantage—the unflinching support of Mr. Norman Manley and the Puerto Ricans associated with the work of the Commission, that is to say, the two most important democratic and nationalistic parties in the Caribbean, the People's National Party of Jamaica and the Populares Party of Puerto Rico. It is the power of the people that the imperialists fear most.

I met Norman Manley for the first time in 1944. Since then we have been the closest of friends. He congratulated me on my first appointment and agreed that I had acted wisely in seeking it. In 1947, when a determined effort was made to close down my Washington branch office, it was Norman Manley who defeated it. About the same time the President of Howard University requested me, together with other members of the faculty, to make a nomination of some prominent West Indian or Latin American personality for the honorary degree of Doctor of Laws, as the University wished to show publicly its interest in both areas. I nominated Norman Manley. My colleagues made other nominations, but the President, who was himself fully conversant with Manley's work and prestige, and who then had over 300 British West Indian students at the University, accepted my nomination, and an address given by Manley to the students and faculty was one of the greatest occasions during my long connection with Howard. In 1948 Manley led the fight for my appointment as Deputy Chairman of the Research Council, describing me as the most knowledgeable man in the West Indies. In 1949 I discussed with him the charge of communism. He told me he would take the matter up with the Labour Secretary of State for the Colonies. In 1952 at the West Indian conference in Jamaica he publicly praised the principal document which had been prepared by me. I told him about the difficulties in the Secretariat when I saw him late last year in Jamaica. As late as March of this year, when I again discussed the situation with him during the Immigration Conference held here in Port-of-Spain, he advised me to stay with the Commission as long as possible.

    The Puerto Rican members of the Commission also supported me unhesitatingly in my struggle for survival. They continued the fight for the maintenance of my Washington branch office where Manley left off. They supported Manley in his fight for my appointment, and in his absence at the 1948 West Indian Conference, insisted that the charge of communisn be investigated, and urged me not to walk out in disgust. The Puerto Rican delegates to the conference told me that they had positively refused to agree to a proposal that the conference—that is to say, the West Indian politicians—should denounce me as a communist. Twice in that year the Puerto Ricans worked out with me a programme of Caribbean research which I would be invited to

My Relations with the Caribbean Commission

undertake at the University of Puerto Rico if I were dismissed by the Commission, about the very time when the British West Indian University College was confident that it could find a better man than I.

I was also strongly supported at all times by the various American Negroes who served on the Commission.

Another powerful weapon which I dangled over the heads of my British opponents was the British Labour Party. The personal opposition to me over a period of time of the Colonial Attache at the British Embassy in Washington, who was one of the British Commissioners, because so serious that once, when I learned that Mr. Creech Jones, the Labour Secretary of State for the Colonies, was in New York, attending a meeting of the United Nations, I wrote to him requesting an interview. Unfortunately he had departed before my letter reached him, but he wrote me from London saying that he would have liked very much to discuss the Commission's work with me. I told the Colonial Attache that I would have asked Mr. Creech Jones for an assurance that I would not be disqualified from making my contribution to the commission merely because my views did not coincide with those of hidebound conservatives in the British Colonial service and were quite close to those of the Labour Party. He turned yellow and trembled in every limb. During the conference at which I was accused of being a communist, I asked the British Co-Chairman what reply he would make to his boss, Mr. Creech Jones, if he were asked whether he did not know that the sentence held against me was not communism at all, but very good socialism. He remained silent. It was with Mr. Creech Jones himself that Norman Manley took up my case. When I was in London last year attending the London conference on GATT, I discussed the difficulties which had arisen in the Secretariat with one of the highest officials of the Labour Party. It is of the utmost significance that my successful struggle to save my job over *The Negro in the Caribbean* was fought in the context of the British Labour Party's victory in the

1945 elections, while I received the official notification of the Commission's decision not to renew my contract on the very day the Labour Party was defeated in the 1955 elections.

I must turn now to the difficulties in the Secretariat.

Just prior to my taking up my appointment in Trinidad in 1948, the Secretariat was in the middle of an upheaval involving a serious conflict between the American Secretary General and all his senior officers, including the British Deputy Chairman of the Research Council. The Commission appointed a one-man commission of inquiry from the Colonial Office. What his report contained I do not know; it was never published. But it was common knowledge that the Commission stressed that the research section of the Secretariat was more important than the administrative, and that the Secretary General should in future have some research experience as well as administrative. The Secretary General himself told me in most bitter tones that he had never been more humiliated in his life. He had every reason to think this; the Commission had in fact attacked him. Thereafter the Commission took action to implement this decision at the very meeting at which I was appointed to act as Deputy Chairman of the Research Council. It very clearly and precisely prescribed the functions of the Deputy Chairman, and stated that he should, under the Secretary General, be the principal officer for all research activity of the Commission and should devote his full time to research work. Norman Manley, the leading figure in this reorganisation, told me at the end of the meeting that it would in future be impossible for the Secretary General, to interfere with me as Deputy Chairman of the Research Council. A year later the Commission underlined this new arrangement, by equalising the salaries and rank of the three Senior Officers under the Secretary General, thereby entitling me as Deputy Chairman to the privileges and immunities accorded up to then only to the Secretary General and the Deputy Secretary General by the Trinidad government.

My Relations with the Caribbean Commission

A Dutch Secretary General replaced the outgoing American at the beginning of 1952. Our relations from the very outset are indicated by the fact that, within three months of his arrival, I found myself obliged to tell him that if he had been appointed for the purpose of getting me out of the Secretariat, he would have done exactly what he had been doing. After that the situation steadily deteriorated and matters went from bad to worse.

We were preparing for a session of the West Indian Conference held in Jamaica at the end of the year; it was rumoured that the European governments were determined to close down the Commission. I assumed personal responsibility for the principal document, an appraisal of the work of previous sessions of the conference. Over and above this I was assigned by the Secretary General five other papers, one of which was his own report to the four governments; they had not been done properly either by the staff member responsible for them or the authors outside the Secretariat. I also had to perform the administrative duties of the Deputy Secretary General who was on leave for some months, and of the Secretary General who went on tour for a period. It was very fortunate for me that their duties are not particularly onerous. My overtime work was excessive—for every three hours of normal work for which I was paid my salary in the four months August to November, 1952, I gave the Commission two hours of overtime free.

Notwithstanding all my work for the conference the Secretary General wished to keep me away from it. There is a Commission regulation to the effect that authors of papers must attend conferences to defend their views and assist the delegates in their deliberations. I asked him whether the author of one paper must attend whilst the author of six papers must stay away. He then withdrew his opposition, and after more pressure from me, decided that I should attend also the Commission meeting which followed the conference.

My work at the conference was as heavy as my work before the conference, which was quite astonishing in view of the fact that I was to have been left out. I was assigned by the Secretary General to work with one of the three conference committees, to coordinate the reports of the three committees into a single conference report, and to work with one of the three committees of the Commission to which the conference recommendations were assigned for consideration. At this committee meeting I proposed a particular method of handling the large number of recommendations. The committee was so impressed that it requested me to repeat my proposal to the Commission in plenary session. I did so, and the Commission accepted my proposals without amendment. Thereafter, however, some doubt was expressed as to the Secretariat's ability to cope with the heavy workload entailed. The Secretary General, after consulting me, asked the Commission to allow me, as the officer in charge of the section of the office on which the work would principally fall, to explain how the Secretariat could handle it. The Commission accepted my proposals, which I had previously cleared with the Secretary General, without amendment. These were the proposals on which almost the entire Secretariat programme for 1953 and 1954 was based.

The conference was for me a resounding personal triumph. I was commended on all sides. One United States Commissioner, who was unable to attend the conference because of illness, wrote to me privately complimenting me in the warmest terms on the appraisal of the work of the previous sessions of the conference: he told me that he had written officially to the Secretary General. Coming as it did from the man who had taken the lead in refusing to confirm me in my post in 1948 on the ground that I was a communist, this was no idle praise. Another United States Commissioner greeted me most enthusiastically at the Conference, explaining that after my appraisal there would be no difficulty in getting his government to vote the annual appropriations for the Commission. The Conference itself included in its report the following commendation of the appraisal proposed by Robert Bradshaw, the delegate for St. Kitts-Nevis:

My Relations with the Caribbean Commission

The Conference commended the Deputy Chairman of the Caribbean Research Council and his colleagues on the Secretariat's staff for the painstaking research involved in the preparation of this full and extremely enlightening report, which is of valuable assistance not only to participants in the Conference but to the Member Governments, the Governments of the countries served by the Commission and all those interested in the work of the Commission. The Conference further recorded its high appreciation, personally, of Dr. Eric Williams, Deputy Chairman of the Caribbean Research Council, for the elevated standard of the work contained in the appraisal and its general clarity.

The Conference also commended the high quality, the form of presentation and the conciseness of the report of the Secretary General which I had prepared.

At the Commission meeting each of the four National Sections, one after the other, complimented me publicly on the proposal I had presented regarding the action to be taken on the conference recommendations. The chairman of the British Section suggested that, as the greatest compliment to me, the first part of my proposal should be taken on trust, and one of my personal friends on the Commission, the Leeward Islands lawyer to whom I have already referred, told me later that the Chairman had said to him that he did not know how I had done it. It had sounded like a gramophone record. The Commission later complimented me again on the lucidity with which I had presented the Secretariat's work programme, and on the assistance I had rendered in enabling it to complete its work so quickly. I left the meeting with my friend's stern warning ringing in my ears—look out for jealousy. It was no idle warning. One of the United States advisers had asked me, in the presence of the Deputy Secretary General, what sort of Secretary General we had who needed to call on a subordinate to outline the Secretariat's programme.

153

I returned to Trinidad to equally heavy responsibilities. I had to prepare the Conference report for publication, to pilot its recommendations through the Research Council and its Committees, to help lay the foundations for a future conference, and to advise the Secretary General so meticulously on modifications in the work programme for the Commission's approval that he asked me to dictate even the language and took it down word for word, urging me more than once not to go too fast. Then I went to Europe on long leave for a little over five months, the Secretary General taking charge of the research department in my absence. My leave was interrupted, at the Secretary General's request, to prepare drafts of letters to various people about action entailed in preparations for a conference on education and small scale farming, to consult with the United Nations Educational, Social and Cultural Organisation in Paris about the availability of the expert to assist in the work for the conference, to visit in Mexico a Unesco project for community education and assess its relevance for West Indian conditions, and to hold discussions with Unesco's Latin American Office in Cuba regarding collaboration between the Commission and Unesco.

I was called back from my leave ahead of time to attend a meeting of the Commission to Trinidad. At the opening session the Dutch Co-Chairman paid public tribute to the fact that the trade promotion conference scheduled for the following year was in good hands, mine, whose services to the Commission, he added, everyone appreciated. The meeting complimented both the Secretary General and myself on the work we had done in enlisting Unesco aid, and decided that my contract was to be renewed for five years, after the Secretary General had ascertained that I was willing to accept. The Chairman of two National Sections congratulated me privately on my decision to remain with the Commission. This was in December, 1953.

There followed another period of heavy overtime work for the trade promotion conference. The introductory paper was written by me, and most of the other papers were written by members of my research staff. We were complimented on all sides, publicly and privately, some of the warmest praise being reserved for my own contribution.

A few days later the Dutch Co-Chairman came to see me, to say goodbye, as he had been promoted to a new post back home. We had a common interest in West Indian history and had been on quite friendly terms for some years. Two hours after his departure I received a memorandum from the Secretary General, replying to one of mine in which I had drawn his attention to the excessive overtime being worked by my research staff. The memorandum criticised me for the delay in getting out conference documentation, and stated that I should not be writing papers at all but should be planning the work of my staff and guiding them in it.

To say that I was flabbergasted is to put my reaction mildly. I wrote a long memorandum in reply based on the following points:

(1) I did not see how conference documentation could be expedited if I passed on to my already overworked staff work which I was not only best qualified to do, but which itself could be completed by me only on an overtime basis.

(2) I could not understand why he should criticise me in April 1954 for writing papers for conferences when throughout 1952 he had himself time and again assigned to me papers which were the responsibility of other staff members of persons outside the Secretariat, and when only a month before he would have passed on yet another paper if I had not had the sense to decline.

(3) It seemed to me that there was nothing wrong in my writing papers for conferences though I was the head of the research department, no more than it would be wrong for the head of a university department to give lectures or the head surgeon in a hospital to perform operations.

(4) Since the Secretary General felt so strongly about the matter, I proposed, even though I disagreed with him, to turn over to members of my staff two papers, which he and I had previously agreed that I should write for the conference on education and small scale farming.

(5) In any case the Commission had laid down that I was in charge of the Secretariat's research activities and had specifically included in my personal responsibilities such things as the preparation of documentation. I took the view, therefore, that as I had told him a year previously under somewhat similar conditions, if the Commission's regulations were to be changed, they should be changed by the Commission.

Notwithstanding his criticism of me for writing papers, the Secretary General replied that I must continue to accept responsibility for the two papers for the conference later in the year, but agreed that the matter should be put to the Commission for decision. He expressed regret that I was not going to be in attendance at the Commission meeting.

The next thing I knew was that I was handed a letter from the four Chairmen of the Commission in May 1954 advising me that the Secretary General had reported on the difficulties in the Secretariat, that they did not wish to enter into any discussion of the conflicting views, that the Secretary General was the officer responsible for running the Secretariat and responsible only to the Commission, that it was likely that the research activities of the Secretariat would be reappraised in the revision of the Agreement establishing the Commission then under consideration, and that, accordingly, they had instructed the Secretary General to renew my contract for one year. The letter was signed by three of the very men who had voted for my reappointment for five years six months previously, one of whom had joined in the public congratulations to me in 1952, and by a fourth who had been appointed to his position one week before the meeting and therefore was in no position to judge any question in the Secretariat.

My Relations with the Caribbean Commission

That is the high-handed manner in which these democratic governments operate. In 1945 a governor wrote a letter and the Anglo-American Caribbean Commission rushed to his support. In 1954 the Secretary General held a private chat and the Caribbean Commission rushed to his support.

In reply, I sent a memorandum to the Co-Chairmen making various points, as follows:

(1) I had conducted myself throughout on the basis of an organisation specifically laid down by the Commission, which the Co-Chairmen had refused to take into consideration. That was to punish a man for following constitutional procedures.

(2) I had been condemned in my absence, without a hearing, merely on the basis of a report by one of the parties to the cause, whose charges were not even stated so that I could have an opportunity to reply to them.

(3) I was at a loss to understand how an employee could be considered an asset an December 1953 and a liability in May 1954.

I concluded my memorandum as follows:
"It will not be possible for people to reconcile my role in the adult education movement with the dismissal by an organisation established to promote regional cooperation in the Caribbean of the very person who had made the study of West Indian affairs the exclusive concern of his adult life and who is, in some eyes, 'Mr. Caribbean.' I would necessarily have to defend myself. I do not see how the Commission's prestige would be enhanced thereby or its possibilities of service to the area improved."

At a subsequent meeting of the Commission, which was held in Trinidad, all that I learned of the charges against me was that, being always very busy, I kept papers a long time on my desk, and that, having a notoriously bad temper, I would send inter-office communications, not always polite, without sealing them in envelopes; it was claimed that the messengers might read them. I replied that if that was all the trouble, I was happy to be able to give an assurance that it would not happen again.

This was seized upon as the basis of another communication to me, this time in consultation with the Commission, advising me that the question of my contract would be deferred to the next meeting of the Commission, when it would be considered in the light of the assurance I had given regarding consideration. One of the Commissioners whom I knew, a British West Indian asked me privately: "If the man wants to run the Secretariat his way, why not leave him alone? What's all the fuss about?" I realized then what I was up against. This so-called representative of the British West Indian people is a man completely rejected by the electorate in his own territory. He, like many others, is our representative right enough, but only of the stooges in our midst.

There the matter ended, with my doing what I was told to do, but the work of one man and not four men, as previously, until I was notified by a friend of mine who attended the recent conference in Puerto Rico that he had been told by a member of the Trinidad delegation that I had been fired by the Commission. Thirty hours later I received official confirmation that the Commission, meeting in secret session, had decided unanimously that my contract would not be renewed when it expired. It expired at four o'clock this afternoon.

You see what all this means, don't you? In 1947, the Secretary General, an American, found himself involved in a conflict with the Deputy Chairman of the Research Council, an Englishman. What does the Commission do? It appoints an independent commissioner to investigate the matter, who questions everybody, after which it proceeds to reduce the Secretary General's power. In 1954, the Secretary General, a Dutchman, found himself involved in a conflict with the Deputy Chairman of the Research Council, a West Indian. What does the Commission do? It does not appoint a commissioner to investigate the matter, it questions nobody, it shoo-shoos with the Dutchman at a meeting

My Relations with the Caribbean Commission

where the West Indian is not present, it makes no charges against the West Indian and simply fires him. Need I say more, Ladies and Gentlemen? I shall not insult your intelligence. You know, each and every one of you, that we West Indians are the last to be hired and the first to be fired, in all positions and not only in the one such as that from which, thank Heaven, I have now departed, never, never to return, with the Commission's appreciation of my services conveyed to me through the Secretary General who successfully intrigued against me.

I don't care a tinker's damn for the Commission's appreciation. I take away something far more valuable—the appreciation of my junior colleagues. I received a simple note yesterday which reads: "With all best wishes." It was signed by 55 staff members, 51 of them West Indian, the remaining four non-West Indian. The list of West Indian names includes white and black, Chinese and Indian, lightskinned and darkskinned, some of whom I had myself recommended for appointment, others whose appointment it had fallen to my lot to disapprove, one or two whom it had been necessary for me to reprimand, and many who had come to me at one time or another for assistance and guidance with the pressures they faced. My mind went back to the days when I worked them to the bone, and they worked ungrudgingly because they all knew that if I worked them till midnight, I worked myself till two in the morning. My mind went back also to the French expert brought down to survey industrial development, who, over his whiskies at the Queen's Park Hotel, told me with one sip that the West Indian was lazy, and with the other that in this wretched climate he could not even work three hours a day. I thought of the differences I had had with some of the staff, bitter and sharp at times, but which we submerged in our work for the common cause. I felt then the only pang of regret I feel at leaving the Commission, that I shall no longer be connected with a group of people who, at the height of their morale some years ago, achieved feats which no other group anywhere in the world could exceed, until I remembered that this unity of races, colours and religions in work of little meaning is pregnant with possibilities for the future welfare of the British West Indies. I have always known that we West Indians have all the talent we need to improve ourselves; I learned from the printers and the typists and the messengers and the chauffeurs and the research workers at the Commission that we also have the necessary spirit. The names of my non-West Indian well-wishers, all below the level of policy making in the Secretariat, reminded me of something equally important. Two are English, one French, one American; one has been here so long that it is difficult to think of him as anything but a West Indian; the others are playing an important and constructive part in the cultural life of Trinidad. Their association with my West Indian colleagues I deeply appreciate, not only in itself, but also because it shows that, in our struggle for improvement, we can count on assistance from many non-West Indians in our midst, not offered on the basis of master and servant relationship. All foreigners, Ladies and Gentlemen, are not imperialists.

That is the story of my relations with the Caribbean Commission and its predecessor extending over twelve and a quarter years. I have told it for two reasons. The first is to clear my name and reputation from any imputations of inefficiency or failure or factious opposition or disloyalty to which the termination of service of a public servant frequently gives rise. The second is that the issues are not personal but political; they involve not a single individual but the West Indian people.

Even in the Commission's Secretariat mine was not an individual case. In one department notorious for its changes of imported staff, a white West Indian acted as its head for a longer period than the combined service of three outside officers; the first Secretary General positively refused to appoint him to the post, and he resigned in disgust. The second Secretary General once complained to me that a West Indian subordinate in the same department was too ambitious; he had applied for the post of head of the department within a few months of his appointment. But why shouldn't he? One American officer appointed by

My Relations with the Caribbean Commission

the American Secretary General had lasted three months; a Dutch successor appointed by the Dutch Secretary General had lasted sixty-eight days. The only fault I can find with the West Indian was that he waited so long to send in his application. The Secretary General told me on another occasion that he was very worried: the head of another department, a non-West Indian, had threatened to resign. I replied: "So what? Appoint his deputy." The deputy was a West Indian; all similar posts in the government of Trinidad and Tobago are held by West Indians. The Secretary General refused: instead he persuaded the non-West Indian to stay. His predecessor once asked me if I would agree to take as a statistician a British official whose contract in Trinidad had expired. The officer's job had nothing to do with statistics and the Secretary General knew it. I refused to agree, and insisted that if he wished to make the appointment, he must do so on his own responsibility. The result was I found myself saddled with a French statistician, imported all the way from France. One could not even understand the man, and so I left him to his own devices for several months. When I got tired of his inactivity, I turned the heat on. He got a nervous breakdown and had to be repatriated. In twelve months he had done nothing; he had drawn his salary and got a free holiday in Trinidad, with a familiarisation tour to the French territories thrown in by way of "laniappe". A Dutch official was appointed to my staff, over my protests, precisely because he was related by marriage to one of the Co-Chairmen. As a colleague he was insufferable. What other term can I use for a man who asked a West Indian typist to type a letter in which he said that every time he walked down Frederick Street on a Saturday morning he was conscious of the inherent superiority of the white race? We in the Secretariat were painfully conscious of his inferiority. His work was absolutely worthless, and I had to transfer a part of it to a Jamaican economist whose appointment I had to press for over a year before I could get favourable action on it, though I had interviewed the candidate myself. The Jamaican's salary was more than one quarter less than the Dutchman's yet when he asked for equalisation of his salary with that of the officer whose work was transferred to him, his claim was rejected, even though it was supported by me as the head of the department.

That is the Caribbean Commission. The four governments vote about half a million dollar a year for its upkeep, and in return the jobs go to imported officials. In my Washington branch office I got sick and tired of calls from Congressmen as to the number of Americans employed at the Commission; in Trinidad I got sick and tired of hearing Americans talk about the amount of money voted by the United States taxpayers for the Commission. As more and more Colonial areas shake off imperialist control, the pressure is increased on the remaining areas of imperialist influence to provide jobs for outsiders. Not the least significant feature of the Commission's decision not to renew my contract for another five years is that in 1956 the contract of the present Secretary General expires. According to the rule of rotation, the next Secretary General must be British or French. My claims to the post would have been difficult to resist, if my contract as Deputy Chairman had been renewed.

What does all this mean to you here in Trinidad and Tobago, Ladies and Gentlemen? The Financial Secretary, himself a son of the soil, who was appointed, however, only after public clamour, announced seven months ago that the "Government reaffirms its declared policy of giving preference to a local candidate provided that he has the necessary qualifications, merit and experience." Only three days ago His Excellency the Acting Governor informed the Civil Service Association that federation will bring many opportunities but they will come to those who merit them most. This is admirable. But the Caribbean Commission gave exactly the same pledge. What are the necessary qualifications for West Indians? My relations with the Commission make it difficult to answer the question. One of the arguments used in 1945 to try to force me out was that my qualifications were too high, just as in 1939 a Colonial Office official had advised me that my high qualifications were not needed in Trinidad; yet in every one of the cases

My Relations with the Caribbean Commission

involving my colleagues to which I have just referred the discrimination against them was rationalised on the ground that their qualifications were too low. It is a case of heads the imported man wins, tails the West Indian loses. What sort of merit must West Indians have? Take my own case. I did not have to beg the Commission for one blasted thing. I placed first in the First Class for my bachelor's degree at Oxford; I have been studying the history and problems of the West Indies for nineteen years. What has become of my merit, recognised time and again in the records of the Commission and its various bodies? Is the merit we need the merit of not having ideas about the West Indies unacceptable to an imported superior officer who knows nothing of them? Or is the merit of not having any ideas at all about anything and of expressing only those prepared for us in information leaflets? And what is the experience we need? My own practical experience in the job from which I have just been fired extends over twelve years. Was this too much experience or too little experience? What of the man who, after years of experience obtained by acting in a job, is passed over for an imported official without experience of the West Indies?

There is another aspect to this question. We have heard recently a great deal about partnership. I have frequently quoted this famous statement of the Secretary of State for the Colonies, Colonel Stanley, made in the House of Commons in 1943, the very year in which I joined the Anglo-American Caribbean Commission:

> "The people who will help the West Indies—the teacher, the nurse, the club leader—must come from the West Indies, be of the West Indies, and work with the West Indies, and it is upon them more than anything else that the future of the West Indies will depend."

I used to consider this statement an official pronouncement on the West Indianisation of our civil service. I now see it in a new light. Who are the people mentioned by the Secretary of State for the Colonies? The teacher, the nurse, the club leader. Junior staff! Is partnership, then, to be a partnership between European senior staff and Colonial junior staff? Was that the reason why two years after Colonel Stanley's speech, Mr. X tried to force me out of the Commission? The Commission has now said, by dismissing me, that there can be no partnership between a Dutch Secretary General and a West Indian Deputy Chairman of the Caribbean Research Council. Can we ever look forward to a partnership between a West Indian Secretary General and a European Deputy Chairman?

What has happened to me could not have happened in Puerto Rico, Surinam, Jamaica, the Gold Coast, Nigeria, which have either achieved self-government or will achieve it in the very near future. It can happen only in Trinidad and Tobago, politically the most backward area in the Caribbean, except for those monuments of backwardness, Martinique and Guadeloupe. Whether it is Queen's Royal College or the Government Training College, the Police Band or the Post Office, our local men have either to be content with a bone as a substitute for meat or have to seek outside of Trinidad what they are not allowed to find in Trinidad. My own record with the Commission is a never-ending story of such substitute inducements or offers.

Now the latest one has come—an offer which would take me outside of the West Indies in a job in no way related to fundamental West Indian problems and needs, and—this is the really amusing part of it—requiring me to work in a subordinate capacity to one of the very men who sat down in secret session in Puerto Rico and decided unanimously not to renew my contract with the Commission. I have rejected the job, as I shall reject all others like it. I was born here, and here I stay, with the people of Trinidad and Tobago, who educated me free of charge for nine years at Queen's Royal College and for five years at Oxford, who have made me whatever I am, and who have been or might be at any time the

My Relations with the Caribbean Commission

victims of the very pressures which I have been fighting against for twelve years.

A local newspaper, in a recent editorial, flung in my face a quotation from Booker T. Washington with which I ended my lecture at the Public Library in 1944. It advised me to "let down my bucket where I am, now". The newspaper and I don't see eye to eye on many things—federation, the tourist trade, West Indian history. But on this issue we do agree. For I have decided to do exactly what the newspaper recommends. I am going to let down my bucket where I am, now, right here with you in the British West Indies.

THE CASE FOR PARTY POLITICS IN TRINIDAD AND TOBAGO

by Eric E. Williams

Eric Williams addresses a crowd at Woodford Square during the latter part of the 1950s. Seated left to right are some of the early members of the PNM: Andrew Carr, A. N. R. Robinson (partly hidden), Isabel Teshea, Saied Mohammed, John O'Halloran, Learie Constantine, and Patrick Solomon.

The Case for Party Politics in Trinidad and Tobago, Teachers Economic and Cultural Association, Ltd., People's Education Movement, Public Affairs Pamphlet No. 4, September 13, 1955.

THE CASE FOR PARTY POLITICS IN TRINIDAD AND TOBAGO

We, the people of Trinidad and Tobago, are the sick man of the Caribbean. Our principal handicap to recovery is our doctors. Five years ago we called in a new team of local doctors to look after us. For five years they have neglected us; they have been too busy growing rich in private practice, and in having tea in the House of Commons, sightseeing in Scandinavia, and not sleeping a wink in Montevideo. Now they are afraid that we might call in another team more able and less expensive. So, aided and abetted by their foreign consultants, they have drugged us for eight months and brazenly threaten even now to extend the period of unconsciousness. It is the biggest fraud in the annals of political medicine in Trinidad and Tobago.

It is not the sort of fraud that the police can deal with. It is political fraud, which must be dealt with by political methods. This demands the creation of an Opposition we have not yet had; an Opposition so enlightened, an Opposition so alert, an Opposition so relentless, that long before those eight months have ended our Legislators and our Government will be wishing that the Secretary of State for the Colonies had saved them from themselves. We are going to do it right here in the University of Woodford Square.

The first essential of this Opposition is that it shall be the organised expression of that overwhelming public opinion which the Legislators, the Government, and the Colonial Office have so flagrantly disregarded in prolonging the life of the present Legislative Council. That opinion must be organised into an effective political party. I propose therefore to analyse tonight the need for and the nature of such a party.

* * *

We last went to the polls on September 18, 1950, under a new Constitution. Less that a year before this historic date, the people

The Case for Party Politics in Trinidad and Tobago

of Jamaica also had passed judgment on their government. Three months before the people of the United Kingdom had had their election. The election in Trinidad and Tobago differed fundamentally from the elections in the United Kingdom and Jamaica. In the United Kingdom the election was a contest between two equally matched, organised parties, with a few candidates belonging to a third party. The independent candidates, of whom there were a few, were slaughtered to a man, both by the organised parties and by the voters—the parties with their slogan, "outside *the party* there is no salvation"; the voters by the outlook expressed by one, "I would vote for a pig if (my) party put one up."

In Jamaica the election was also a contest between two equally matched parties. But whereas one was a democratically organised party with a positive programme, the other was a party organised around a single individual with no real programme to speak of, while there were hundreds of independent candidates, many of whom forfeited their election deposit, and only one of whom was elected; he subsequently accepted an important Ministerial post in the government formed by the majority party, whose leader had campaigned on the slogan, "If I tell you to vote for a dog, vote for him."

In Trinidad and Tobago, on the other hand, notwithstanding the existence of a party which contested all the seats, organised around the personality of a single individual who advised the voters to vote for a frog if he told them to do so, and three smaller parties limited for the most part to the urban areas, the election was a contest between a horde of independent candidates. There were 141 candidates in all, or one candidate for every 2,000 voters. In one particular constituency there was one candidate for every 1,000 voters. One-seventh of the candidates received fewer than 100 votes; one-tenth received more than 100 but less than 200.

The difference between Jamaica and Trinidad and Tobago is best illustrated by a comparison of the programme of Jamaica's democratically organised party with the programme of the one-man party and the manifestos issued by some of the independent candidates in Trinidad and Tobago.

The 1949 programme of the People's National Party in Jamaica began as follows:—

"TO THE PEOPLE OF JAMAICA
WHY YOU SHOULD READ 'PLAN FOR PROGRESS'

In December 1949, you will vote for a new Government of Jamaica. Normally, the citizens of a democratic community have a genuine CHOICE of programmes and reasoned statements of policy.

You will NOT have a genuine choice!

There will be ONLY ONE PROGRAMME prepared and endorsed by a great party of Jamaican citizens organised democratically throughout the Island.

THAT IS THIS PROGRAMME

You will read so-called statements of policy. There will be one-man programmes, statements issued in the names of self-interested cliques and self-opinionated persons. You will encounter many slogans, many catchphrases. But the ONLY democratic programme will be the PROGRAMME of the PEOPLE'S NATIONAL PARTY.

WHY?

Because the PEOPLE'S NATIONAL PARTY is the ONLY Island-wide party basing its policy upon the democratic discussion and decisions of its members.

IT IS NOT an amorphous mass drifting around a self-willed demagogue.

It is NOT the political expression of a wealthy and privileged class.

It is THE PARTY FOR democratic Jamaicans.

The P.N.P. provides the means for the only real expression of the will of the people of Jamaica."

The keynote of the P.N.P. programme was more production. The Party pledged the creation of a Ministry of Production, the establishment of an Industrial Development Corporation and a Small Industries Credit Corporation with emphasis on the food industries, the production of building materials, furniture and other household goods, boxes, packages and containers, and the development of the textile and shoe industries. The P.N.P. proposed to finance this economic programme by granting incentives to outside capital and by public loans, and by the establishment of a National Bank. The Party further pledged itself to public ownership of public utilities, the promotion of the tourist trade, the expansion of the social services, and the institution of public works to provide relief for the unemployed. The Party programme included comprehensive proposals for labour and education.

The labour proposals contained specific objectives of social legislation: adequate wage-scales; a 45 hour week; extension of the Workmen's Compensation Law to cover all workers, including agricultural; annual vacation leave with full pay; equal pay for women; enforcement of the laws governing shops and factories; abolition of child labor; establishment of effective industrial relations machinery for the settlement of industrial disputes; decent housing for agricultural workers. The programme pledged workers' representation on statutory bodies, and accepted the principle of Joint Production Boards in private industry as well as in industries publicly owned or operated.

The P.N.P.'s educational proposals included sufficient school accommodation to make possible universal and compulsory elementary education in five years; a national plan for the provision of school meals; a scheme for the emergency training of teachers; adjustment of secondary school fees to the means of parents; adequate facilities for teacher training; and a national plan for adult education and the conquest of illiteracy.

The P.N.P.'s programme ended with proposals for constitution reform and the following demand for honesty and integrity in government:—

"The last five years have witnessed a deplorable decline in the standards of public honesty. Revelations of graft and dishonesty have become all too common in the Island. When the currency of public life is depreciated, social standards debased, integrity and public trust abandoned, it is not only democracy but the people themselves who suffer. The present Government has NOT set a fitting example of rectitude and scrupulous conduct in public affairs. Its example has been unworthy, its conduct inglorious, its transactions dubious and its record tainted. Its proceedings have been conducted in an atmosphere utterly lacking in dignity or even common decency. It has used its power to deny work to opponents and to victimise and oppress those who do not give it support. The people of Hanover and Trelawny will not have forgotten that the government threatened them during their by-elections that they should not be allocated public money if they returned opposition candidates. Such intimidation destroys democracy. It thwarts the free expression of the people's will. It exposes a system of racketeering and boss-control.

It is not surprising, then, that the Government's wretched example of worthless representation, self-seeking and internal strife for the division of the spoils, has been reflected elsewhere in the Island.

The People's National Party is determined to conduct the affairs of Government on the highest levels of integrity and public morality. Self-Government for Jamaica will never be advocated until the stains of the last five years have been removed from our political system."

When we compare the People's National Party's Plan for Progress in Jamaica with the election manifesto of the party which won the largest number of seats in the election in Trinidad and Tobago, the first thing that strikes us is the fact that the Trinidad party's manifesto was couched throughout in the first person. It began by recapitulating the leader's sacrifices in the cause of the people and castigating some of his opponents by name. Then followed a string of reforms and pledges, in which one can find no plan, no pattern, no sequence: the right of self-determination; the right of recall of unsatisfactory legislators; three square meals a day; increased old age pensions; free secondary education; creation of suitable new industries and self-help occupations; first class recreation centres; health insurance; help for fishermen, ex-servicemen and seamen; intelligent and wise control of agricultural policy; "good and plenty water"; free nurseries and clinics; encouragement of efficient local industries; a housing scheme for various categories of government employees and for pavement sleepers; and nationalisation of the oil industry and all the major industries.

The only indication of the method of financing the programme was the following statement:

> "If the millions that are collected out of Oil by absentee shareholders in Britain are made to remain (by law) in Trinidad to be used by a government of the People of Trinidad and Tobago in the interests of the poor of Trinidad and Tobago specifically and everybody in the Country generally prove insufficient to give the People what they want and are entitled to enjoy in their own Country then a big loan shall be sort (*sic*) in America to be used in turning Agricultural Trinidad and Tobago into the greatest industrial Country in the whole history of British Colonial Lands."

It was recognised, however, that the millions distributed to oil shareholders might not be enough. The demands for free secondary education, free milk, free dental and medical attention, free books and free transportation ended with the statement:

"If there is sufficient money in the local Treasury, a free nice fitting uniform to boot."

The manifesto called on the people to support the programme and policy of the party. But it distinctly and emphatically stated that the programme and policy were the work not of the party but of the leader. The manifesto contains this paragraph:

"These are but a few of the many (Reforms) that I have personally thought and put into carefully prepared plans for Freedom and Independence of our Country... I have saddled myself to the very serious responsibility of preparing (and due to certain circumstances) alone and unaided this historic Document."

There is nothing historic, really, about this document. Its underlying philosophy is the familiar one of Hitler's National Socialist Movement, in which the leader was obviously the party and just as obviously the party was the is leader. What is most remarkable, however, is that the party in question, which is notorious for its condemnation of the Tories in Great Britain, is obviously similar in structure to that of the Conservative Party, a committee of which stressed six years ago that "the final proposals are normally presented in a Party Manifesto by the Leader on the eve of a General Election, and are his responsibility." In 1945, for example, the Conservative Party's election stand was entitled, *Mr. Churchill's Declaration of Policy to the Electors.*

The climate of Trinidad and Tobago was, however, hostile to the very idea of party politics. The supporters of one candidate, who subsequently became a Minister, sneered at one of his opponents who was the leader of a political party. They criticised him as a candidate "who always presents a Party only at Election time, and which fades into oblivion and completely disappears the day after Election." They supported their claim by a reference to the United Front in the 1946 election. They were at least honest in this, for the candidate whom they sponsored was himself a deserter from the United Front. But when they proceeded to condemn his opponent for his "audacity to come back to us again, at this election with another party, which is even less fortunate, as it cannot even find sufficient candidates for the eighteen seats," it was clear that they were opposing not the leader of a party but party politics itself.

Another candidate, whose claims to the votes of the people were sung in verse, boasted of the fact that he had "no axe to grind no Party Affiliation." Yet a third condemned the very conception of party politics. Flagrantly putting the cart before the horse, he advised the electors:

> "The claims of the leaders of these so-called Political Parties can be discredited at once, since every thinking person knows that the party system can only be effective among a people having some idea of tolerance, honesty and sincerity.
>
> "It is my personal conviction that real Political Parties will develop only after the people of this Colony have had a chance of learning to manage their own affairs. The New Constitution, although only a beginning in the matter of government by the people for the people, will nevertheless serve as a stepping stone to the development of Political Parties in this country."

What did these non-party candidates offer you five years ago? Everything under the sun. I have examined 52 of the manifestos; of these 13 were from successful candidates, two of whom became Ministers.

The most popular promise was employment. Listen to the slogans: increased employment; employment for all; regular employment. One candidate advocated greater economic prosperity and a census of the unemployed. Several looked to the establishment of industries as a means of achieving increased employment or reducing unemployment. One of the successful candidates who became a Minister promised "intensive Industrialisation, to relieve the ever increasing unemployment." Yet another future Minister advocated the policy, "Develop new industries". Recalling in his manifesto that he had raised the slogan, "Trinidad must industrialise or perish", and claiming that he had been instrumental in getting the Aid to Pioneer Industries Ordinance passed, he enthused over the textile industry which, he claimed, "will soon start operations providing work for over 500 of our jobless youth." Have the 1955 elections been postponed to give Trinidad time to perish because he now opposes industrialisation, to allow the Aid to Pioneer Industries Ordinance to be repealed, and to complete his operations for putting out of work the people employed by the textile factory?

The farmers and the agricultural workers were promised their place in the sun. Some of the specific proposals for agriculture included: acquisition and equitable distribution of agricultural lands; nationalisation of the sugar industry; a better price for farmers' canes and cane farmers' insurance; free holdings for agricultural labour; a grow more food policy; co-operative cane farmers estates; intensive agriculture with mixed farming; a tax on uncultivated land. With that vagueness which has characterised our Ministerial policy, one future Minister advocated "a sound agricultural policy" with "full prices for the colony's staple products." He merely forgot to tell us how he would fix it. Self-sufficiency in rice to eliminate rationing and find jobs for the unemployed was the contribution of another Minister in the making, little realizing that when he eventually eliminated rationing, it would be because Trinidad was so self-sufficient in rice that the price went up to 40 cents a pound.

Side by side with promises of employment in industry and agriculture went a concern with wages and social security. Some of the promises read as follows: a higher wage scale; better wages; a living wage for sugar workers; a real living wage for all; a minimum wage tied to the cost of living. A famous democratic slogan suffered a sea change into something rich and strange, when one candidate advocated a fair day's work for a fair day's pay; some capitalist wolf in the labouring sheep's clothing, no doubt! Another candidate advocated family allowances and what he called "more social securities"; two others pledged unemployment insurance; a future Minister called for a sound social security programme with improved working conditions and a living wage for all workers. The most precious gem was the promise of one candidate to "demobilise unemployment"; the electorate, however, was not amused and left him unemployed.

Where the social services were concerned the candidates were in their element. These are some of the promises regarding our health:—better health services, one candidate specifying the backward areas; improved medical facilities; more modern hospitals; health insurance; rural clinics and health offices. A future Minister took a world view: improvement of the colony's Health Services to meet adequately the needs of the people in association with the efforts of the World's Health Organisation. As he wrote this, he must have licked his chops in anticipation of all the trips promised by such an association.

In the field of education the consensus was that there was vast room for improvement. The slogans varied only slightly—larger and better schools; improved education and more schools; better education facilities; more elementary and secondary schools; more medical scholarships; more scholarships for Civil Servants; free secondary education; more money for education; or, simply, more schools. A future Minister called for the extension of adult education facilities. A future colleague advocated expediting the school building programme for the purpose of producing additional facilities for improving vocational and technical training as well as more secondary schools. One candidate pledged the substitution of Chambers and Royal Readers for the West Indian Readers.

The housing reformers had a field day. More houses for all; comfortable houses for workers; comfortable houses for all; housing at reasonable rentals; government loans for improving houses; better housing for teachers—these were the inducements held out to voters. Our old friend wanted to "demobilize" the barracks. A future Minister capped it all with a promise to further the people's cause by "a Housebuilding Programme to provide cheap and improved houses to take care of the ever increasing housing problem." You see how right I was when I suggested banishment of the Ministers to Shanty Town to live with the corbeaux.

And then there was the question of water. A comprehensive water supply; an island wide water supply; a better water supply; extension of water supplies; these were the hopes held out, a future Minister contributing the promise of improved water supply for the entire Colony. The omissions were more eloquent than the admissions; no one mentioned either the Caura Dam or the dammed Caura.

No one was left out. The aged were promised larger pensions, the fishermen better facilities, the workers restriction of freedom of movement in federation. An island wide electricity supply was very popular. Someone advocated protection of public funds and improved Civil Service. Many candidates pledged more efficient and economical transportation, cheaper transport, more and better rural roads. A few remembered responsible government. Many talked of reducing the cost of living. Some advocated subsidies on essential foodstuffs and the reduction of import duties on food. One candidate called for better protection by the police. A few promised jobs for local men in the Civil Service and in industry. Those who ran out of specific objectives made up for this by more general promises to honour womanhood, to raise the social and moral standard, or, in the words of one candidate, to do the things required to be done, but only what is just, upright, decent and good.

Where was the money to come from all these things? There was universal silence, broken only by the candidate who advocated higher taxation of the oil companies.

In commending themselves to the voters, the independent candidates, since they could claim no party allegiance, necessarily fell back upon their personal claims and past records. They emphasised their labour affiliations and their struggles in the cause of labour or their sympathy with the workers through their own experience. One candidate, for example, stressed that he "slaves like you". Others reminded the voters of their connection with Cipriani or with Uriah Butler.

One of the most common of the claims made to fame by the candidates was their experience in city or county councils and in ward work. The manifestos are full of boasts of standpipes erected, drains paved, roads surfaced, telephone booths installed or secured, traces improved, and cemeteries enlarged, undertaken, or under construction. If the candidate is not able to guarantee you living space, dying space is the next best thing; if you guarantee the candidate a happy hunting ground in this life, he will guarantee you a happy resting place in the next.

The candidates stressed their philanthropy, their social work, the trophies they had donated, the scholarships granted, the years of free teaching they had provided. One claimed that he had been responsible for introducing B.C.G. into the island; another emphasised the big shots he had interviewed; a third recalled that he had brought the Governor to see something or other; a fourth had sent a memorandum to the Secretary of State for the Colonies and had helped fishermen, cane farmers and municipal employees; others recalled their association with youth movements and cultural groups. Another, a future Minister, boasted that he had restored Carnival after the wartime ban. We can readily sympathise with his interest in "ole mas'". Several set great store by the delegations they had led at one time or another. It was better to say anything than nothing. One candidate raked up his connection with a hurricane inspection committee way back in 1930. It was fortunate for the voters that Trinidad lies outside the hurricane zone.

The self-portraits of the candidates also speak volumes as to the political climate of Trinidad and Tobago five years ago. Several had travelled, one was widely read. The people of Trinidad and Tobago could make their choice from men of sincerity, integrity, ability, experience, reason, dependability. Some were business successes; others were honest, brave, progressive, well-informed. Some had educational qualifications, others had clean characters. One had a sound mind in a sound body, another conduct and habits pleasing to God and man. There was one who advertised himself as a gentleman who knows poverty, and another who was friend to one and all, rich and poor. The fearless agitator and servant of the working masses rubbed shoulders with the war veteran. One emphasised that the candidate should be able to speak and understand English well; another insisted that the candidate's colour should not be such that he would be embarrassed in taking part in the community's social activities.

Great stress was laid on the fact that the candidate must be born in the constituency he aspired to represent. "Why did you leave your home then to fight the seat in this constituency?" was the question one candidate suggested as a must for the electors. That, however, was not enough. He went on to propose another question: "Have you associated with us in the past or did you feel yourself too big to attend our wedding functions, our child's christening or our grandmother's funeral?" One wonders what would have happened if the candidate to whom this question was directed had been able to reply that, though he had not attended Granny's funeral, he had enlarged the cemetery for her reception.

I have not told this story merely for the sake of being facetious or to draw laughs from the audience. The story is a desperately serious one. The whole future of Trinidad and Tobago is wrapped up in it. Let me now draw your attention to its two principal features.

The first is the utter impossibility of carrying out the promises made in the individual manifestos and the utter absurdity of the claims advanced by the individual candidates. No individual in his right mind can seriously promise regular employment for all. How is he going to achieve this? He can himself contribute to regular employment in a small way. For example, he can employ a domestic servant on the basis of his salary as Legislative Councillor if he did not have one before, and after increasing his salary he can then proceed to hire a yard boy. It makes no more sense for the individual to promise to establish industries. The establishment of an industry is principally a question of the requisite amount of capital and the requisite skill of labour. How can one man undertake to guarantee a tax holiday for ten years which might be the incentive needed to bring an individual capitalist to the country? How can he guarantee to train the necessary labour? More important, how can he guarantee to establish any industry at all in any particular constituency when the location of the industry will be determined by the investor in the light of the availability of raw materials, existence of the necessary amenities, proximity to specific markets, etc.?

For the same reason no individual can guarantee to his constituents houses for all, be they uncomfortable or comfortable; nor can he guarantee to all a higher wage scale, which is a matter to be determined by collective bargaining between the employer and the union. The individual who pledges himself to substitute one text book for another encroaches on the functions of the Education Department. No individual can guarantee an island wide water supply or an island wide electricity supply or better roads. Nor can he guarantee more schools; he can only approach the Education Department if the schools are to get subsidies from the state, unless he means that he will set up private schools. All these are in the last analysis financial matters which have to be decided in terms of the total resources of the community and the competing claims on those resources. It is not a question of whether these reforms are needed or not. Everybody knows they are. The question is how to translate the aspiration into reality. No one man can do that. His claim to this power is as absurd as the claim of one man that a major industry should be nationalised, when we so obviously lack either the technical skill or the resources to take over and run a nationalised industry.

If the individual claims were absurd, the basis of those claims was even more absurd. For example, one of the candidates who promised employment for all and facilities for industrial expansion urged the voters to ask the aspirants whether they were sufficiently qualified to hold a ministerial post. He went on to stress the distinctions he had got in nature study, handicraft and hygiene in examinations and the studies he had pursued in music and art. Another candidate, who pledged modernisation of the fishing industry and support of farmers, supported his election claim by reference to the thousands of dollars he had donated to charity and the ground he had graded at his own expense for the erection of a school. The candidate who promised "more social securities" and "more agricultural securities" upheld his claim by the fact that he had enlarged two cemeteries, repaired several drains and extended several water pipes, while he had the attention of the government engaged in the provision of a taxi stand and the construction of a sidewalk. One of the fundamental deficiencies in the political life of Trinidad and Tobago is precisely the low level of political intelligence reflected in such appeals to the electorate.

The second conclusion we can draw from an analysis of the independent manifestos is that it is folly to say that the cause of our present mess is that the people backed the wrong horses. In one case they clearly did, when they succumbed to the seduction of back pay. But for the most part following their instinct, the people preferred one candidate who said he would do this instead of another candidate who said he would do virtually the same thing. By and large there was a remarkable similarity between the promises. Change the present eighteen members and substitute another eighteen from the list of unsuccessful candidates in 1950, or send the present five Ministers packing and substitute another five from the eighteen successful candidates, and the fundamental situation in Trinidad would be today exactly the same except in one particular—one of the unsuccessful candidates in 1950 would make a terrific one-man opposition.

But this does not mean that those who were elected as legislators and those who were chosen as Ministers could not have done better. The Legislative Council had the choice between holding the elections on schedule or postponing them. It decided to postpone. It could just as easily have decided not to postpone. The difference is one of ethics and respect for the people's rights. The Minister who decided to close the textile and shirt factories could just as easily have decided not to close them. What matters is the perspective, the intelligence and the appreciation of economic realities. There is nothing in the world to have prevented the Constitutional Reform Committee from producing a sensible Constitution which would not make Trinidad and Tobago a laughing stock. It chose to do otherwise. But it was not inevitable that it should have stultified and frustrated the community as it has done.

This, then, is the lesson of the 1950 election: even though those elected might have done better, the individuals as individuals could not hope to implement individual programmes, many of which bore no relation whatsoever to fundamental economic realities and were totally innocent of the slightest conception of planning.

The conclusion is a very simple one: the case for party politics in Trinidad and Tobago is overwhelming.

What are the advantages of party politics over the present system of individual politics? Assuming that the party is a democratically organised party, the advantages are the following:

1. The electorate is presented with a coherent programme, representing not the personal thoughts of one man but the collective competence of its membership. This programme is a national one, presented on platforms all over the country without any deviation or alteration. The voters know that they vote for or against not the caprices of an individual but the decisions of an organisation.

2. The programme is a national programme, too, in the sense that it deals with national issues affecting the country as a whole and not parochial issues limited to a section of it. Standpipes, drains, sidewalks, telephone boxes, cemeteries are parochial matters, not national issues. They come within the jurisdiction of the County Council, not the Legislative Council.

3. The members of the party with its national programme themselves take a national viewpoint. They are not lobbyists or representatives of pressure groups as in the U.S.A. seeking legislation desired by sectional interests; they are members of a national team as in the United Kingdom, where every Member of Parliament has to sign the following declaration when he accepts appointment to a committee on a Bill:
    "I swear that my constituents have no local interest in this bill and I have no personal interest in it."

4. Party discipline ensures that the party members in the legislature vote as the party decrees. The party which wins a majority in the election can therefore carry out its election pledges. The alternative is removal of a Minister by the Chief Minister, or dismissal of members from the party. Expulsion is a dreaded weapon. It means that the member cannot count on party support in the next election. It is well recognised in the democratic countries that, as the saying goes, it is easier to go to the country than to return from it.

The Case for Party Politics in Trinidad and Tobago

But there are parties and parties. The party which won the largest number of seats in the 1950 election is not a party in the recognised sense of the word. It is a conglomeration of individuals around a certain man, and defection within its ranks was only a matter of time. A party which consists of individuals who come together only in an attempt to get power cannot last if it fails in its attempt, and is unlikely to last if it succeeds. It has no programme; in the case of the party to which I am referring, it was most distinctly stated that the programme was the leader's programme. It could be accepted for tactical reasons by the party candidates before the election only to be rejected after it. A political party, in other words, is more than a bunch of individuals grouped together to contest a specific election. Nothing is gained by substituting a group of ten individuals for ten separate individuals working in isolation.

The first prerequisite of party politics in Trinidad and Tobago, is therefore, the establishment of one good party. Such a party is now being organised and I am identified with it. I am authorised to indicate to you tonight the essentials of such a party, as my colleagues and I see them, in the light of the specific conditions which we face today in Trinidad and Tobago.

The very foundation of the party is that it must be dedicated to the satisfaction of the principal need of today—the political education of the people. All its activities must be subordinated to this, must draw sustenance from this, and must find their meaning in this.

Parties are nothing but an expression of the organised political opinion of the community or sections of it. Hence before you can have party politics, you must have a public opinion to organise. The organisation of that public opinion demands first of all education.

The most damming criticism of the present government is that is has taken no steps whatsoever to promote the political education of the people. Quite the contrary; it sought to deport journalists and it discontinued political commentaries on the radio. One naturally expects a Crown Colony government to keep the people in ignorance, to dictate to them and to take them by the scruff of their neck and push them into some measure on the ground that it is good for them. It may indeed be the best thing for the people, but a wrong decision made by the people is better a thousand times than the most correct decision made for them; and who in Trinidad and Tobago will have the temerity to say that Crown Colony decisions were correct in theory and the best thing for the people in practice? But what is unpardonable is the manifestation of the same contempt for the people and public opinion from our own flesh and blood, people whom we regarded as our transition to self government.

We hold therefore, that a proper party in Trinidad and Tobago must give the highest priority to the political education of the people. The people will need guidance in this, especially in one particular. They must understand that Mr. X, even though he represents Constituency Y, has been returned to the Legislative Council to serve not his constituency but the country. Here let me say as Edmund Burke said nearly two centuries ago:

> "Certainly, gentleman, it ought to be the happiness and glory of a representative to live in the strictest union, the closest correspondence, and the most unreserved communication with his constituents. Their wishes ought to have great weight with him. It is his duty to sacrifice his repose, his pleasures, his satisfactions, to theirs; and above all, ever, and in all cases, to prefer their interest to his own.
>
> But Parliament is not a *congress* of ambassadors from different and hostile interests; which interests each must maintain, as an agent and advocate, against other agents and advocates; parliament is a *deliberative* assembly of *one* nation with *one* interest, that of the whole; where, not

local purposes, not local prejudices ought to guide, but the general good, resulting from the general reason of the whole. You choose a member indeed; but when you have chosen him, he is not a member of Bristol, he is member of *parliament.*"

But political education of the people must not be limited to the party's guidance of them. By political education we mean that every step taken by the party must be a step calculated not only to do something in the interest of the people or for the good of the people but rather designed to get the people to do things for themselves and to think for themselves. After two months of intensive educational activity throughout the country, I can say without fear of contradiction, except by those who stand to lose by it, that the political intelligence of the masses of the people is astonishingly high, their political instincts astonishingly sound, and that they are the best and most vital students I have encountered in any university in my experience. The principal objective of the new party must therefore be at all times the dissemination of knowledge and of facts among the people to enable them to draw their own conclusions. Whatever conclusions the party itself draws can then be tested by the people themselves. The party is conceived of as a vast educational agency equipped with an important research department, the data being presented in simple language and an attractive manner to the people to encourage them to form their own opinions. This will involve a party newspaper, party information leaflets and newsletters, party pamphlets, to serve as the basis of discussion groups within the party. The party recognises that to educate is to emancipate.

If and when the party achieves power, its party education must be supplemented by a system of public service broadcasting designed to give the people of Trinidad and Tobago the political education which they do not now receive by radio. One of the principal features of this public broadcasting might be broadcasts of debates in the Legislative Council. Similarly the party must particularly explain to the people the reason, scope and likely effects of all bills, long before they are debated and passed, so that public opinion can express itself on them.

I may conclude thus: the party we conceive for Trinidad and Tobago is not only a party which has the confidence of the people, though that will be an enormous step forward, but also one which is much more than that, a party which has confidence in the people, which understands from the very beginning that its future depends on the development of an enlightened and politically educated electorate.

After the political education of the people the next most important prerequisite of a party, in our opinion, is honesty.

The dishonesty and immorality of political life in Trinidad and Tobago are now a byword. The population is tired of graft and corruption, sick to death of broken promises, fed up to the teeth with the squandering of the taxes for which is to dig deep into its pockets. The situation daily gets worse. Ministers come and go like absentee landlords paying routine visits to the Caribbean to check up on their plantations, to hush up a scandal, to open up the big house, and to enjoy a little of the sunshine. The disease is rapidly spreading to the Civil Service. We can find the money apparently to send someone to witness an air show in Britain. We are about to send a department head to a tourist conference in India and a Minister to another in Switzerland, while we have nowhere to put the tourists, unless indeed they are to be put in our newest tourist potential, the Caroni Swamp, to sleep with the scarlet ibises.

The poison is seeping through the entire body politic. The postponement of the elections in Trinidad and Tobago and will go down in history as the greatest dishonesty and iniquity we have ever had to endure. The responsibility for it rests squarely on the shoulders of our elected representatives and the Colonial Office. Our elected representatives know the demand in the community for constitution reform. They took power on the distinct understanding that theirs was a transitional constitution. They shirked the vital issue until they could claim that it was impossible to deal with the question of reform in the limited period left to the legislation before it expired. So they wangled postponement of the elections in order to propose constitution reform. Now, to add insult to injury, they have come up with a constitution which is yesterday's leftovers hushed up in new form, thus giving a semblance of popular acceptance to what was in the first instance dictated by the Colonial Office. Fully conscious of their failure to live up to their promises in 1950, they are doing their best to postpone the Day of Judgment. But the day will come, and when it does the people of Trinidad and Tobago have only themselves to blame if they fail to extract the maximum penalty for the offence.

The Colonial Office, too, must share the blame. The British Government has been shouting for years for free elections in different parts of the world. But it refuses to give Trinidad and Tobago free elections at the scheduled time. Even in the midst of the life and death struggle of the Second World War, the British or American people could go to the polls; we in Trinidad and Tobago are denied that right at the height of the peace which is killing us. The British Government suspended the constitution of British Guiana because it did not have confidence in the government in power; it has in effect suspended the constitution of Trinidad and Tobago because it has confidence in the government in power. I watched for years in the Caribbean Commission how British Government officials took sides against Norman Manley in Jamaica because they knew that he could not be influenced and because they preferred to deal with people who were, as they said, "pliable", who had no constructive plans to offer, and who would therefore be an easy prey to their own advice and wiles, whilst behind their backs they laughed at their antics. The Colonial

Office pays lip service to colonial self government for the benefit of world public opinion, while it surreptitiously tries to achieve the type of self government which it considers satisfactory.

The whole rotten mess has been stirred up by a section of the local press. The Secretary of State for the Colonies announced that constitution reform was a matter for the Legislative Council. One of the local newspapers however advised us some time ago that, even before the view of the Legislative Council had been presented to him, the Secretary of State for the Colonies had decided in favour of postponement of the elections and was only waiting on "the niceties of protocol." To aggravate the insult, we are now told that postponement has been decided upon not in order to reform our constitution but in order to ensure federation. Not a single denial has been issued about this, the most dishonest part of all. I am as good a federationist as any in Trinidad and Tobago. I was publicly preaching and advocating federation long before the community ever heard of some of its present supporters. I deny categorically that it is necessary to postpone the elections in order to achieve federation. I go further and I state, now that we have accepted the principle of federation, that the proposed federal constitution is totally absurd in the light of constitutional progress in Jamaica and Barbados since it was drafted and the widespread aspirations for reform in Trinidad and Tobago. There is not the slightest moral justification for associating with the final establishment of the federal structure a government which is not only totally discredited in its domestic policies but which is the only government in the British Caribbean which has not been drastically changed by the popular vote since the draft federal constitution was approved. I propose to deal at greater length with this in my final lecture in this series, in which I shall discuss federation.

The party now being formed must therefore place honesty in government high on the list of its priorities, and by honesty we mean not merely the elimination of the graft and corruption which are now eating away our society, not merely the drastic reduction of the indefensible cost of government. Napoleon Bonaparte, in an exhortation to his troops before the most famous of his battles, the battle of Austerlitz, urged them finally so to conduct themselves that, as he said, "it would be enough for you to say, 'I was at Austerlitz', for people to say, 'there goes a brave man' ". The party I am discussing tonight is one of which it must be enough for someone to say that he is a candidate of the party for the Legislative Council, or one of the Municipal or County Councils, for the people of Trinidad and Tobago to say, "there goes an honest man".

Some are born honest, some achieve honesty, some must have honesty thrust upon them. The party is of the opinion that every legislator, every Minister, every councillor, every top civil servant even, must be required by law to divulge annually all the sources of his income. In recommending similar legislation to Congress on September 27, 1951, former President Truman of the U.S.A. said:

> "As a general rule, I do not like to see public officials, or any particular group, subjected to rules and requirements which do not apply to the rest of the population. But at the same time public office is a privilege, not a right. And people who accept the privilege of holding office in the government must of necessity expect that their entire conduct should be open to inspection by the people they are serving.
>
> With all the questions that are being asked today about the probity and honesty of public officials, I think all of us should be prepared to place the facts about our income on the public record. We should be willing to do this in the public interest....
>
> I know of no other single step that will do so much good, so quickly, in protecting the reputations of our public servants and—at the same time—in producing concrete indications of any really questionable practices".

My colleagues and I are of the opinion that this legal provision for the annual disclosure of income must be required not only of the individual concerned but also of the members of his immediate family. Only by such a drastic step will the people of Trinidad and Tobago be convinced beyond a shadow of doubt that public office is not sought for personal gain. The necessary corollary of such a requirement is legislation to limit election expenditures and to make impersonation at elections impossible.

It stands to reason that a party dedicated to the political education of the people and infused with the spirit of honesty must necessarily be a democratic party. The conception of party in many quarters in Trinidad and Tobago, even in those whose honesty cannot be questioned, is that of a bunch of people who have climbed, for one reason or another, on to a bandwagon and then try to foist themselves upon the voters of the different constituencies, each one selecting his own, for all the world as if Trinidad and Tobago is a carved up chicken passed round to the guests at a Sunday dinner. This is utterly undemocratic and simply cannot be defended. As an example of an authentic democratic party in the Caribbean, we have chosen the People's National Party of Jamaica.

The basic unit of the P.N.P. is the Party Group, consisting of not less than six members. The group and the area covered by it are subject to the approval of the Constituency Group of the Party, which is based on the existence of not less than twenty Party Groups. The obligatory subscriptions of all members go into the Party's funds, but the Party Group retains one-third of all obligatory subscriptions collected by it, and the Constituency Group receives one-third. The Constituency Group organises Constituency Conferences, which are attended by the Party member in the Legislature and members of the Municipal and Parochial Bodies in the constituency. These Constituency Conferences select the Party Candidates for national elections, subject to the vote of the Party's executive; the candidates for parochial elections are elected by the groups within the division or area involved, subject to the approval of the Constituency Group. The supreme authority of the P.N.P. is the annual Party Conference which elects all the Party Officers except the Parliamentary Leaders and the Secretary and Treasurer. The P.N.P.'s Executive Council consists of the officers of the Party and 25 members elected by the annual Party Conference, plus two members from each constituency elected at Constituency Conferences. This National Executive Council meets at least once a month. In the interim the party's affairs are managed by an Executive Committee meeting at least once a week. The Executive Committee consists of the Party Officers, as elected by the annual Conference, the Parliamentary Leaders, three representatives of the Parliamentary Group chosen by the Parliamentary Group, and eleven members elected by the National Executive Council from their number. The National Executive Council enjoys the reserve power to veto the candidature of any person chosen to stand as the Party's candidate in national, municipal or parochial elections. It keeps in close contact with the Parliamentary group and maintains the funds of the Party. As in all democratic parties, the position and responsibility of Chairman of the Party, elected by the Party Conference, are separated from those of the Leader of the Parliamentary Group, who is the recognised leader of the Party.

The party now being organised in Trinidad and Tobago must ensure these cardinal principles of party democracy—the separation of Party Leader and Party Chairman, the supreme authority of the Party Conference and the selection of party candidates by the party membership in the appropriate divisions—groups or constituencies—subject to the right of veto by the Party's executive.

One further aspect of the party's democratic structure needs to be stressed. It concerns the party's funds. The U.S.A. has become the classic land of dirty money and dirty politics, with the domination of the major political parties by big business reaching the proportions of a regular national scandal. The danger is just as great in Trinidad and Tobago. The only solution is to have a mass party financed largely by dues-paying members and sympathetic individuals, some of the revenue being refunded to the party and constituency groups, as the P.N.P. constitution provides, rather than by undisclosed sources which might constitute pressure groups. If the country wants good government, it must be prepared to pay for it. The only alternative is to accept rum, roti and dollars as its price for misgovernment.

It goes without saying that the party I am describing must exercise strict party discipline. The spectacle of individuals moving from party to party, or abandoning a party as soon as the election objective has been achieved, or opposing party decisions, or publicly dissenting from them, is as notorious in Trinidad and Tobago as the sun at noonday. A Minister who stays in a government after publicly rebelling against government has become as characteristic of the political life of Trinidad and Tobago as that of the leader of an opposition who accepts an acting appointment as a Minister. Behaviour of this sort only illustrates that saying which epitomises the immorality of public life in Trinidad and Tobago, "in politics anything goes".

Such behaviour is contrary to the true party spirit. A proper party cannot possibly condone it. The need of discipline is particularly strong in a place like Trinidad and Tobago where the word is hardly known. It is necessary principally in three directions—(1) the refusal by the party's executive to admit anyone who, in its opinion, is not likely to abide by its decisions or whose past record is regarded as compromising to the party's reputation for honesty and ideals; (2) the expulsion of any member whose conduct has been in the executive's opinion contrary to the interest of the party or to its programme, policy or principles; (3) a clear prohibition by the party of any indulgence by its candidates in personal abuse in election campaigns.

This brings me then to the constitution and programme of the party, the two principal criteria by which the party will be judged by the electorate. The party's constitution must enshrine the principles of democracy already indicated. The party programme must clearly and precisely indicate to the voters what the party proposes to achieve and how it intends to do so.

When the party states that it proposes to build schools, or roads, or bridges, the people must understand that the party will build schools, roads and bridges. When it states that it will provide jobs, the people must understand that it will provide jobs. People dominated by the Colonial Office mentality still babble about agriculture being the basis of our prosperity, in the face of all the evidence that oil and not agriculture is the basis and that agriculture is steadily displacing labour and must continue to do so. The party must show the people clearly that it stands for a programme of industrialisation designed not only to provide jobs for the unemployed and for those whom agriculture will be forced to throw out of employment, but also to lead to the very expansion of agricultural activity which the agriculturists themselves wilfully refuse to understand. It must show the people also that it is industry alone which can guarantee a higher standard of living than agriculture and which will thus force agriculture to fall in line. The party programme will make these things absolutely clear, as clear as the Labour Party's promise in Britain to nationalise the steel industry and the Conservative Party's counter promise to denationalise it. It must show the people that a national programme requires a national outlook, that the representative of a constituency is also a trustee for the country as a whole, and that national progress is not a question of a standpipe in constituency X, a drain in constituency Y, and a cemetery in constituency Z.

Above all, the party programme must indicate the method of financing the economic and social objectives, while its political and constitution reform pledges must be designed to achieve and maintain the political power necessary to guarantee these economic and social changes. No such guarantee can be given if a nominated element locally and the Secretary of State for the

Colonies abroad can frustrate the people's will. The party programme must therefore unambiguously demand responsible government.

The party, finally, is conceived as a national party, of all and for all. It must be so not only in theory but also in practice. It must not be content to pay lip service to the ideal; it must be a living exemplification of its national outlook. It must appeal to all classes, all colours, all races, all religions. The party recognises that, to maintain their allegiance, it must prove to all in positive ways that each group can feel secure within its fold, that the contribution of each group will be welcome, and that its programme is designed to improve the community as a whole and not any part or section thereof. Let me give some specific examples.

Take the case of capital and labour. The national interest requires the active co-operation of both. The jobs needed today can be provided only by the large scale investment of capital. A great part of the capital needed will necessarily come from private sources. This requires inducements, incentives and guarantees to investors, not less than other countries offer, possibly more. The workers must understand that this is necessary if jobs are to be provided for them. They must understand that, once their organisations are secure, capital is nothing to be afraid of. The Venezuelan Government has for years been co-operating with the oil companies using excess profits from oil to develop Venezuelan agriculture and secondary industries. The secretary of one of the most powerful trade unions in the United Kingdom announced recently that his union had a health and welfare fund totalling $40 millions, which it intended to raise to $400 millions, making the union, as he said, the biggest capitalist in the country.

But capital must co-operate in all this. The jobs it provides must be adequate jobs, well paid, with the conditions of labour asociated with a modern democratic society. Capital must understand that the day when West Indians were content merely to hew wood and draw water for private investors is gone forever. The worker today requires inducements, incentives and guarantees, just as much as the investor does. The party must be the defender of the workers, the political arm of the labour movement, providing particularly the information and data so urgently needed by the workers in their organisations, as I was able to see for myself quite recently when I was asked to attend as an adviser a conference of sugar workers unions in British Guiana. It must not, however, actively intervene in the formation of management of trade unions; the people of Trinidad and Tobago are sick and tired of scheming politicians riding on the backs of the workers to gain the confidence of the Colonial Office and the Chamber of Commerce. I wish to make it clear, however, that I am referring only to leaders of the working class movement drawn from outside of the working class. If the workers wish to be represented by workers in the legislature, they are the best judges of their own needs and interests. I have already stated my personal opinion, in my lecture on constitution reform, that the workers' representatives should be elected and not nominated. But the party must give every encouragement to effective trade unionism, and must make it clearly understood that this includes the right of the workers to choose their own representatives. We repudiate unambiguously the indefensible efforts of the Ministers to intimidate the trade unions, split the workers' ranks, and set themselves up as little demigods recognising only those they consider amenable. That road leads straight to totalitarianism.

The party, further, must pledge itself to a comprehensive programme of industrial and social legislation designed to ensure to the workers an adequate share of the national income. It must encourage the profit-sharing schemes which are now a commonplace in conservative Great Britain and which were introduced several years ago into the sugar industry of Puerto Rico. It must above all insist, as the Latin American countries generally do, and as the oil industry is now doing to some extent, that investors train West Indians for the highest positions on the senior staff and promote them when they have been so trained.

As another example of the national outlook that needs to be cultivated today I turn to the question of race. The party must be open only to those who pledge themselves actively to oppose racial discrimination in all shapes or forms. It must proclaim as its principle a career open to talent, irrespective of racial considerations. But it must recognise that this is not enough. It must accordingly take active steps to discourage and eliminate that racial discrimination in employment which is so characteristic of our society. Once equal access to jobs is guaranteed, it only remains to respect the legitimate cultural aspirations of the several racial groups in our diversified society.

The religious question is yet another case where the national outlook of the party is of the utmost importance. This raises the whole question of the denominational school.

One of the distinctive features of our educational system is that never at any time have we, the people of Trinidad and Tobago, had self-determination in this important matter. Outside commissions of inquiry and experts have diagnosed our ills, prescribed for us, pontificated and departed, leaving us the headaches. My colleagues and I are convinced that it is for us at this crucial stage in our history to work out our own salvation. We must agree among ourselves; all efforts to impose agreement on us from outside have signally failed. We take the view therefore that the essential first step towards an amicable solution worked out by ourselves is the appointment of a commission of inquiry consisting of local people and those so long and so intimately associated with us that they belong to us, representative of the governing bodies, the teachers and the parents, to investigate the entire question, with specific reference to the necessity of developing a curriculum suitable to our needs, achieving the maximum possible integration of the diverse elements in our community, and maintaining the highest academic standards.

Here, I hope, you will permit me to introduce a personal note. I have uniformly held that this question of the organisation of our education is not a matter of individual prejudice but one for the people themselves to decide as their elementary democratic right.

The question has been raised, both publicly and privately, how to ascertain the wishes of the people? That is the easiest thing of all. Merely to ask the question is to emphasise the need for the political education of the people. Is there anyone today who can claim that he does not know the wishes of the people on the issue of postponement of the elections, after all the resolutions passed against it at meetings all over the country? Letters and editorials have appeared in the Press against my personal views and opposing the state school. Friends of mine have asked me whether I seriously expect them to support a state school system run by Minister X or Minister Y. There was not the slightest doubt in my mind as to the wishes of the audience a few years ago at a public forum in San Fernando when I stated that the people of the British West Indies feel a deep debt of gratitude to the churches for giving them education when the State deliberately refused to do so, and that any system of state control of schools has to face the fundamental difficulty that the State is identified by the people all over the area as their principal enemy thoughout their history. I concluded with a proposal for the appointment of a local commission of inquiry to go into the entire question of education in Trinidad and Tobago. The audience greeted my remarks with enthusiastic applause. My old friend, Dom Basil Matthews, suggested to me a few months ago that the disunity which might be promoted by the present system might well be controlled by a uniform curriculum coupled with rigid inspection of the schools. I regard the suggestion, and I told him so, as an honest and sincere effort to reconcile the wishes of the people with the attainment of our reasonable educational objectives.

One further illustration may be given of the national outlook to be cultivated by the party now in process of formation. It is that all available talent in the community, irrespective of its political affiliation, should be utilised in the service of the community. As matters stand today, the statutory bodies, public corporations, the civil service, the teaching profession and our cultural organisations are all dominated by nepotism and favouritism, and appointment and promotion are dependent to a very large extent on whether one is on a Minister's bandwagon.

I hope that I may be allowed to illustrate this point by reference to myself, merely because I know the relevant facts better than I know those involving other members of the community. I shall address my remarks particularly to the recent ministerial condemnation of some lonely genius in our midst, which, I gather, was directed at me. If this is true, it is rather curious, for I am not the least bit lonely. Some 27,000 people have endorsed my proposals for constitution reform, which were estimated to reach some 40,000 people in our University and its different colleges. Look around this vast audience and see how lonely I am, see if I want to be alone. I have been working for weeks with a group of some of the intelligent men in our community discussing and planning the organisation of a party.

The ministerial condemnation of me is even more curious, as all the evidence suggests that they wanted me to be lonely. Let me give some examples.

The former Governor of Trinidad and Tobago and one of the Ministers both asked me to do something, as they put it, about federation. I don't know what they meant by this. I never asked. I knew what I wanted to do, to popularise the view that federation is necessary for the development of the British West Indies in general and of Trinidad and Tobago in particular. I opposed all those who opposed the idea of federation. I made it quite clear that I was discussing the principle of federation and not the proposed federal constitution. I emphasised that the position I formerly held at the Caribbean Commission necessarily restricted me from expressing any view opposed to that of the Governor who had been chairman of the committee which drafted the constitution, and I stated quite distinctly that I had not read the Rance report. Sir Hubert Rance's resignation, however, freed me of this restriction. I studied the Rance constitution and I expressed strong criticism of it shortly after his departure. The

The Case for Party Politics in Trinidad and Tobago

Minister in question immediately endeavoured to stop my public lectures. It was quite clear that I had stepped on his corns, as he had signed the Rance report, and that he had had the audacity, misled no doubt by a section of the Press, to assume that I would for twelve years fight against four governments for the freedom to think only to end up as a ministerial stooge.

This lecture on the draft federal constitution was given under the auspices of the Extra Mural Department of the University College of the West Indies, which was refused by another Minister any use of government buildings for its course, on the ground, as I was given to understand, that I was connected with it. I was subsequently advised that the Minister vetoed two proposals made to him regarding my active association as director with two prominent cultural activities in Trinidad and Tobago.

I was appointed adviser to the Regional Economic Committee's delegation at the Commonwealth Conference on the General Agreement on Tariffs and Trade held in London last year. The appointment was based on a statement of the West Indian case which I had originally prepared for Mr. Robert Bradshaw of St. Kitts at his request and which the R.E.C. had endorsed at a meeting held here in Port-of-Spain. This statement eventually became the sheet anchor of the West Indian case. At the conference I found myself in sharp disagreement with one of the Ministers of Trinidad and Tobago on two issues; (1) his repeated reference to the political dependence of the British Caribbean on the United Kingdom; (2) my insistence that important pronouncements be read from a text carefully written and generally approved, as the important pronouncements of all heads of governments are read today. When I was left out of the delegation which attended the subsequent conference in Geneva in favour of new advisers not familiar with the subject, the only reasonable conclusion that I, and others with me, could draw was that I had offended the Minister. One of his friends said afterwards that I made the mistake on my return to Trinidad ahead of the Minister of speaking publicly and writing on the importance of the conference—thus stealing some of the Minister's thunder. My real mistake was, of course, in thinking that the economic interests of the British Caribbean were more important than the personal interests of the leaders of the delegation.

I have not said what I have said, Ladies and Gentlemen, in any spirit of spite or peevishness. What I am fighting is the attitude behind it all, the very attitude that I fought for years at the Caribbean Commission—that one can serve one's country only by being a yes-man to imperialists or Ministers, and that political power is a means of personal aggrandisement, an opportunity for rewarding friends and punishing enemies. If my case were singular, there would be no problem. But as you all know, it can be duplicated hundreds of times all over Trinidad and Tobago.

Yet these are the very people who accuse me of trying to pull down everything and everybody, of unwillingness to co-operate, and of aiming at one-man control. But it is they who refuse to recognise this or that trade union, who boast that this or that would be done only over their dead body. Where is the basis for co-operation? There is none on the issue of postponement of the elections or closing of the shirt factories or reactionary constitution reform. One either agrees with these policies or disagrees. I disagree. It is a matter of principle. The emphasis on the other side is on expediency. One of the elected members asked me to collaborate with him and his colleagues in drawing up a minority report. I declined, because I had by then already committed myself to a personal statement on the subject. It was lucky for me that I did decline, because the elected member has since signed the majority report.

And, in truth and in fact, I do co-operate and assist. I publicly opposed the policy of non-protection of local shirts and textiles. See what has happened since. Protection will soon be given to both industries. One of the newspapers asked me for data on tourism. Every two or three weeks it reproduces the facts I gave them, word for word. One of the Minister's capitalist friends has gone so far as to ask me to write an economic blueprint for Trinidad and Tobago. I laughingly accused him of trying to appoint me economic adviser to the government, without pay, since I have declined the paid post, and of trying to get ideas from me for the Ministers to carry out during the period of postponement. He replied that there was no harm in that. They seek my assistance privately, while they denounce me publicly as a lonely genius.

So you now have another reason for postponement of the elections—to give the Ministers time to put their houses in order. The teachers will get recognition; the federated workers have already got partial recognition. Oil will get its depletion allowances. The tourist hotel will be begun. One Minister has taken a trip to study industrialisation in Puerto Rico which I drew to his attention in one of my earlier lectures. The prospect of health insurance is dangled before your eyes. Paper houses are being built, but you must not apply too early for them. The boys are going to be busy in the next few months making frantic efforts to fool you. You see what I mean when I say we shall hereafter have an enlightened, alert and relentless Opposition. But don't be over optimistic. This is one case when it will not be true to say that anything goes. Legislators' and Minsters' salaries will not be reduced, the trips and travel will not be cut down.

Most important, of all, however, will be the attack on my colleagues and myself. Pressure and intimidation will be resorted to. They have in fact begun. One of my close friends has already been summarily dismissed. One Minister is reported to have said that when they are finished with me I shall be glad to take up my bucket and run. Efforts have already been made to close down our University. I warn them that we shall fight on the beaches, we shall fight in the carparks, we shall fight in the fields and in the streets, we shall fight in the hills; we shall never surrender, and even if, which I do not for a moment believe, this University were closed, then our colleges in the various parts of Trinidad and

Tobago would carry on the struggle for the right to think, to express our views and to work for the good of our community, each man and woman according to his ability.

They will denounce the new party as a party of inexperience and idealism. They are quite right. My colleagues and I are and always will be inexperienced in corruption, in changing our minds, in promising one thing and doing the opposite. We do have ideals and we do not propose to surrender them, ideals which will appeal to all those, especially the youth, the women, the middle classes, who in the past have for the most part been content to leave the corruption alone, to try to pass on the other side, rather than fight actively against it, as the workers have done. That great Negro American scholar, Booker T. Washington, once said that if you want to keep a man down in a ditch, you must get down into the ditch with him. We go further, and say, if you want to prevent yourself from getting into the ditch yourself, you must pull the man out of it.

The people of Trinidad and Tobago must either be kept down in the ditch in which they are or they must be pulled out of it. My colleagues and I lack the qualifications to keep you in the ditch. We believe that we can help to pull you out of it, and that the way to do this is by the organisation of a party such as I have described—a democratic party of men and women of honesty and incorruptibility, of all races, colours, classes and creeds, with a coherent and sensible programme of economic, social and political reform aimed at the development of the community as a whole, dedicated to its service, appealing to the intelligence rather than to the emotions of the electorate whose political education it places in the forefront of its activities.

Such a party will hold up to you the ideal of the ancient democracy of Athens which, limited though it was by slavery and the subordination of women, still represents one of the greatest achievements of man. I leave you tonight with a tribute to this small democratic state handed down to us in one of the simplest and at the same time most profound historical documents, the funeral oration of Pericles:

> "Its administration favours the many instead of the few; this is why it is called a democracy. If we look to the laws, they afford equal justice to all in their private differences; if to social standing, advancement in public life falls to reputation for capacity, class considerations not being allowed to interfere with merit; nor again does poverty bar the way, if a man is able to serve the State, he is not hindered by the obscurity of his condition.... Our public men have, besides politics, their private affairs to attend to, and our ordinary citizens, though occupied with the pursuits of industry, are still fair judges of public matters; for, unlike any other nation, regarding him who takes part in these duties not as unambitious but as useless, we are able to judge at all events if we cannot originate, and instead of looking on discussion as a stumbling-block in the way of action, we think it an indispensable preliminary to any wise action at all...."

Animated by the noble sentiments of Pericles, my colleagues and I humbly dedicate ourselves as from tonight to the service of all the people of Trinidad and Tobago through the party of which I have spoken. This party will shortly be formally launched. It will be designed, as its counterparts in Jamaica and Puerto Rico, as the key, to quote once more my friend and colleague, Dr. Arthur Lewis, needed to open the door behind which our dynamic energies are at present confined.

PERSPECTIVES FOR OUR PARTY

by Eric E. Williams

Williams at a steelband yard in the early 1960s.

Address delivered to the Third Annual Convention of the People's National Movement on October 17, 1958.

PERSPECTIVES FOR OUR PARTY

Our third Annual Convention convenes almost to the day two years and nine months after the inaugural conference of the Movement. Two years and nine months represent a very brief period in the life of an individual, a still briefer period in the life of a Party. Yet in this short period much has happened which responsible observers especially from the outside have been describing as "PNM Miracles". It is not inappropriate at this stage to recall some of these "miracles."

"PNM MIRACLES"

The first is the firm establishment of Party Government which has already brought the country to the threshold of internal self-government expressed through a Cabinet broadly on the United Kingdom pattern.

The Party, in the second place, has established a political leader who speaks with authority in the Party, in the Government, and in the country.

The third "miracle" is the establishment of the Party Forum, the University of Woodford Square. Through this forum it has brought political education to the people of the West Indies and introduced a new technique of cold intellectual political analysis based on reasoning and facts as against the empty emotionalism of the past. The participation on a large scale of thousands of citizens in this programme of political education has been described as revolution by intelligence and as one of the great contributions to twentieth century democracy. The international recognition of the University of Woodford Square is illustrated by the front page photograph in the current issue of PNM Weekly, which reproduces a German picture with supporting text of "Universitat von Woodford-Square."

In the fourth place the Party has established a weekly newspaper which, with all its obvious faults, represents a challenge to the daily press and the vested interests who control that press.

Fifthly, within the short space of a little over two years, the Party has captured the Central and Municipal Governments and has contributed to the capture by its West Indian affiliates of the Federal Government.

Further the Party has posed in Trinidad and Tobago and in the West Indies a conception of the new society to the point where the old situation will never again prevail. This is not merely a theory, in practice the PNM has tackled the big boys.

Finally, the PNM has become the spearhead of the nationalist movement in Trinidad and Tobago and in the West Indies as a whole.

All this has been accomplished between January 1956 and October 1958. The face of Trinidad and Tobago and therefore of the West Indies has been so radically altered that the report of the Mudie Commission on the Federal Capital Site had to be discarded into the waste-paper basket by the time it appeared at the end of 1956. What was undoubtedly true when it investigated Trinidad and was drafting its report ceased to obtain, as the Commission itself recognised, after September 24, 1956.

YOUR GOVERNMENT AT WORK

The General Elections of that date gave the Party the responsibility for organising the Government of the country and for translating into action the Election Manifesto pledges and ideals. During the less than two years in which the Government has been formally in power the Party has translated into reality the well known democratic ideal of Government of the people, for the people, by the people.

Government of the People

Never before in the history of the West Indies have so many average citizens been associated actively with the work of Government. These citizens men and women, of all races, faiths and classes, drawn both from the ranks of PNM and outside those ranks, have been appointed to Committees of Enquiry and Investigation and to Statutory Boards and Corporations. The West Indianisation of the public service has been vigorously proceeded with, and the whole question of the opportunities for appointment and promotion of West Indians to the highest positions in the public service and private employment is now being completely investigated.

At the same time, however, precisely because we are a Government of the people we are not going to allow any lowering of standards and competence. The West Indies cannot overcome overnight the present disability which rises from an inadequate system of education and an external political control prevailing over several generations. We simply do not have the local talent in several fields and we must call upon outside assistance whether in the form of members of investigating committees or of technicians on contract for carrying out a specific job.

This necessarily imposes on a Government of the people the obligation to accelerate and to reorientate programmes for training West Indians to meet the requirements of modern society and modern economy and to permit self-government in the economic and administrative life of the country to the same extent as we have it or will shortly have it at the political level. In this connection it is to be remembered that there are hundreds of Europeans and Americans who, tired of the contradictions of democracy in their own advanced countries, out of the same humanitarian motives which urged millions to support the abolition of slavery in the West Indies, are ready and eager to place their intellectual abilities and social vision at the disposal of the former colonial countries now facing the complexities inherent in the emergence from colonialism. The position is the same in Trinidad and Tobago as in Ghana and other countries which have newly achieved their independence, and one has only to refer in this connection to the British Labour Party or to the large trade union organisations in the United Kingdom, Canada and the

United States, which as part of their own struggle for recognition in their own countries recognise how essential it is to give technical assistance to less developed countries.

Government for the People

The Development Programme, patiently and faithfully incubated during the whole of the first year in office, is now in full swing, steadily gathering momentum. Persons who considered themselves eternally condemned to the backyards of 29 St. Joseph Road, Mango Rose and similar locations have today moved into aided self-help houses built by themselves with Government assistance to be repaid over a period of years on easy terms, in Morvant and Pleasantville, or are about to move in to rental mortgage houses in Morvant and Mount Hope, as the first practical step in the implementation of the Government's Housing Programme. The twilight of Port-of-Spain, San Fernando and Arima has been illuminated by the bright municipal lights provided from Central Government funds, and the darkness in which Rio Claro, Moruga, Mayaro, to mention only three rural areas, lived in the old world before September 24, 1956, has been pierced by the electric lights already introduced as part of the Government's Five Year $24m. programme for electricity.

As I speak to you, steps are being taken so that the residents of Moruga can have during the 1959 dry season for the first time in their lives, running water in the district to eliminate their former dependence on the truck home water supply with all its abuses; this is only one practical example of the improvement of the water supply centered around the large project of the Navet Dam calculated, with subsidiary projects, to make an adequate supply of water available to the population within our five-year term. The powerful tractor and bulldozer and hundreds of workers are now building roads where before there were no roads to increase the living space at our disposal, bring new lands into cultivation, make economic resources accessible which were formerly inaccessible, and stimulate the knowledge of our country by our own people and by visitors—linking up Maracas Bay and Las Cuevas linking up Roxborough, Parlatuvier and Moriah in Tobago, opening up the Platanal region in St. Andrew-St. David for the increased production of bananas, linking up Valencia and Toco, improving the roads in Moruga and to Mayaro.

The Port-of-Spain Community Concert Hall is well advanced; the Technical Institute on Wrightson Road, the Teachers Training College around Arima, the Hilton Hotel on the Lady Young Road, the Maternity Block and the Central Block at the Port-of-Spain General Hospital, will soon begin; work has already started on the Airport Terminal at Piarco and the Training School for nurses in San Fernando and the extension of the Sangre Grande hospital. Very soon the first steps towards the increase of agricultural and fisheries production will be taken when on the basis of subsidies given to farmers and fishermen by the Central Government, hundreds of acres will be planted in coffee and pangola grass, and refrigerated units established on the principal fishing beaches.

Public activity stimulates private enterprise. The aided self-help and rental-mortgage houses are matched by the private investment in housing in Goodwood Park, Diego Martin and Valsayn. Large scale investment of private capital has already brought to Trinidad important industries which are now being established and the factories being built—the fertiliser plant at Savonetta, the deep sea fishing industry for tuna and the canning plant soon to go up, the Nestles factory soon to go up around Arima for the production of sterilised and condensed milk, the large paper plant utilising bagasse which we hope will soon start in Caroni, and numbers of smaller industries.

But private enterprise must work in our interest, not against it. Circumstances have compelled the Government to take over the Angostura factory in order to keep the industry in Trinidad, and it is now possible to support local industry by buying State rum, and where teetotalers are concerned, to flavour their locally manufactured sweet drinks with Angostura Bitters. The Government has publicly announced its readiness to share with private enterprise the strain of the capital investment necessary for the extension of the telephone network.

Government by the People

The Party pledged to keep close to the people by monthly reports and in constituency offices and to keep the people fully informed of Government action, particularly by a re-organisation of the Government Information Services, with special emphasis on the radio. There are serious defects in our reporting service and constituency offices, and many of our legislators and councillors are not fulfilling our pledges. This is a matter that will have to be corrected and I shall deal with it when we come to the question of the reorganisation of the Party. At the level of the radio PNM's Government has initiated broadcasts of Legislative Council debates, as is done in Australia, and broadcasts of the Chief Minister's press conference, which follows the pattern of the American Press Conferences set by Presidents Roosevelt, Truman and Eisenhower and which are now televised. Reports have recently reached Trinidad indicating that the press conferences are heard in Sweden and listened to attentively, and there is every reason to agree with that ex-mayor of Kingston who has written to me recently to say that within the next ten years the Prime Minister of the West Indies and the Chief Ministers of all the unit territories will follow the example.

So here we stand in October 1958 at our Third Annual Convention with a past record extending over two years and nine months which is second to none in the early formative years of any Party elsewhere in the world and second to none in the history of any Party anywhere in the world during the same period. The question that faces us as Party Members is where do we go from here? What will be our record in the next two years and nine months?

SUBORDINATION OF THE PARTY

Let us first analyse generally the phases of development since January 1956. The first phase covered the period from January to November 1956 when we concentrated on the island wide dissemination of our principles, ideals and programme. All efforts, all energies were concentrated on this goal. The Party was subordinated to the Movement. The policy was strikingly successful— it won us the General Elections by a majority of 18 out of 24 seats and gave us a clean sweep of the 11 seats at stake in the Municipal Elections. The first year's effort placed us at the helm of the Central Government and the Government of the Borough of Arima, whilst we became a powerful opposition in the City Council of Port-of-Spain and San Fernando Borough Council.

From there we moved on to the second phase, the organisation of the Government and the translation of the election programme into a coherent and rational development plan for the country. This phase lasted from November 1956 to the end of 1957 when we presented the 1957 Budget and the Five-Year Development Programme; in the course of it we achieved power in the Port-of-Spain City Council and San Fernando Borough Council. It was a year of extremely hard and prolonged work, during which we had to face on the one hand a noisy and belligerent opposition which ultimately coalesced into the DLP opposition, spearheaded by the daily press, whilst on the other hand we had to make our contribution to the planning of the Federal Government. During the second phase the Party organisation and machinery were subordinated to the Party programme and to the Party Government.

The third phase began with the approval of the 1958 Budget and the Five-Year Development Programme. During this phase emphasis was concentrated on the implementation of the Development plan and on the checks and investigations associated with that plan in action. The programme has now gathered momentum, and the paper plan is being steadily transformed into houses, schools, roads, public buildings, and such amenities as water, electricity, and so on. Or to put the matter a little differently, the country which voted by majority vote for the PNM's conception of planned development is now steadily at work on the specific and concrete projects which have been formulated within the framework of that plan. In this phase therefore the Party was subordinated to the Government and its Development Programme.

Thus for two years and nine months the Party has had to play a subordinate role, subordinate to the Movement, subordinate to the Government. Party organisation, machinery, and planning have had to take a back seat, inevitably so, whilst the driver's seat was given over to the organisation of the Government, to the machinery of development, to the planning of the material foundations of a healthy society.

PRIORITY TO THE PARTY

So that when we ask in October 1958 the question where do we go from here? the answer is immediately obvious. We go to the Party. The Party, left to fend for itself two years and nine months, becomes automatically and necessarily the number one priority from October 1958.

WHAT KIND OF PARTY?

The question now arises, What kind of Party?

The distinctive feature of 20th century politics is the ever increasing role of the Party, either in active support of the Government or in actually taking over the Government. On the revolutionary side we have had the Bolshevik Party; on the counter-revolutionary side we have had the Fascist Party; in the former colonial countries we have had the Congress Party of India and the Convention People's Party of Ghana. This is due to the fact that, with the increasing complexity of Government on the one hand, and the need of the masses to participate in the organisation of their own affairs on the other, the only possible way has been to so organise the party that it lives a political life of its own. It must so organise itself and so act that the people recognise it as the indispensable complement and support of the Legislators and the Government. That is the task that now faces the PNM. That is the task it is proposed to leave to this Convention to carry out.

What is our condition at the present time? The plain fact of the matter is that in Trinidad and Tobago, but also in the West Indies, we have built up a trade union organisation, a political organisation, but what we are lacking in is the organisation of the party, and the weakness of party organisation weakens our effort in every sphere of government and of social life.

This is the key to the whole situation. If 25 years ago it was possible to foresee the rapidity of the development, today it is possible to see still further and with more concreteness. The West Indian masses are on a broad road, and travelling fast. Everything pushes them forward. Nothing holds them back. This is a theoretical point to be systematically and carefully developed so that all party leaders (and reactionaries also) should be kept constantly aware of it.

It is certain that no type of West Indian organisation so far has even caught up with where the people have already reached, far less being organised to handle and develop, or subjectively explore, all the possibilities and needs as they actually exist.

Former West Indian political parties organised around professional or businessmen who criticised, made suggestions, etc. But Government was carried on by Colonial Office officials.

There is a big break and a sharp turn in West Indian social and political life. It is inevitable that political organisation will carry a certain amount of old outlooks and habits from the previous period. The people are certain to have these hang-overs also. The old is not completely taken over in the new. But the general idea remains. Government was carried on previously by colonial officials. Government today is carried on by elected officials. Formerly the people elected representatives who did not have the power. Today, they elect representatives who have the power. That is how they see the change. It does not follow that this is all they want. It is absolutely certain that they want more, as the British Labour Party found to its cost in 1950, 1951, and 1956. What is needed is a clear, well organised, sharp break with the old. At such times it is necessary to swing in the opposite direction even to excess. The people have to be told that today the emphasis is on party organisation and mass activity. That the PNM was pitchforked so rapidly into governmental power is not the only reason why it is so weak in party organisation. Other West Indian parties older than the PNM are equally weak or even weaker in party organisation. The old system, and its dangers for the present, must be held up and exposed, and the new orientation towards party organisation made clear and explained in all its ramifications. That is not done in a day. At present it is not being done at all.

This is what we have to do. We have to build our party organisation from the bottom up. We have to reorganise our system of education so that, through the Party, it penetrates into the deepest masses of the people. We have to reorganise our press on the same scale. The whole constitutes what we have to look upon as the Development Programme of the Party, which involves above all the financing of these vast projects.

PARTY HEADQUARTERS

The first essential is a Party Headquarters.

The Party must act, it must show its power. In a small area like Trinidad, a party headquarters on an imposing scale is a political victory. We need a three storey building at least, with restaurant, offices and an auditorium to seat at least 600 people.

Headquarters of the kind proposed is not only a public political act. It builds the Party. And if, like the PNM, the Party is already the Government, the announcement and practical beginnings of such a structure signify—

(a) that the Party has the utmost confidence in its own future;
(b) that though it is the Government it is the Party of the people.

The construction of a building on the scale suggested is in detail a strictly business proposition to be placed in the hands of architects, lawyers, etc. What should be done as soon as possible is the acquisition of a piece of land and a substantial notice, well painted and planted in a prominent position:

SITE OF PNM HEADQUARTERS

This is what convinces and wins over people. Once this is done, the further raising of funds for this purpose assumes a different quality. The thing is to begin, and to begin boldly. Once this beginning has been made, here is one permanent topic for the Party Group meetings, until in a year or two the building is completed. This is something to be discussed, plans, finances, stages of progress, etc., become a part of the life of the Party, and seize the attention of the public.

Along with the Party Headquarters should be posed the question of a second headquarters in another constituency, preferably, San Fernando. One thing is certain. It is around such plans that the Party organises itself. It is such plans, boldly and resolutely posed and begun, that move the membership to sacrifice, and bring out financial and other assistance worth tens of thousands of dollars to the organisation. But you have to begin first. This is a sign and a national sign of a new regime and new politics.

REORGANISED CENTRAL OFFICE

The establishment of a Party Headquarters underlines the urgency of a vigorous Central office and the working out of a rational and effective liaison between Party and Government. Whilst today too many legislative representatives of PNM shirk their patent duties and there is far too much indiscipline among them, whilst too many regard the Constituency and Party organisation as their servant and not their master, the fact remains that far too much is expected of the Legislator and far too little envisaged for the Party. The legislator dominated in the individualism of the Old World; it is the Constituency organisation that must dominate in the party politics of the New. The key is a reorganised Central Office.

Three considerations emerge:

(1) The Party is to separate itself from the Government and live an independent life.

(2) The Party is represented in the Government by the Cabinet and the Ministers.

(3) The Party must have its own "Cabinet" and its own "Ministers" in the Central Office, centering around the General Secretary, who, in calibre and in status, must be on par with the legislative representatives of the Party.

The responsibility of the General Secretary must be the organisation of a Central Office functioning in such a way as to serve all elements in the Party as a guide; to train people; and to develop the talents of individual party members wherever they may be.

It is the simplest thing in the world for any capable and experienced individual to carry out the tasks. That would be of little value. What is needed is to create the basis by which the whole Party and the best elements in it will be set in motion and will be able to develop themselves and others. To take an easily understood example. It is not writing articles in the Press that is important. It is to lay down the lines along which articles should be written and to find and develop this talent in all sections of the organisation.

PARTY AND LEGISLATURE

The ultimate aim must be:

(a) to create an organisation which will develop and proliferate in such a manner that in three years' time the island will be aware that its future lies with the Party and the functioning of the Party. On such a basis, legislators can introduce the boldest and most far seeing legislation, confident that there can be no serious resistance because all reactionary and disruptive elements will be aware of the strength of the Party in the population surrounding them.

(b) Such an organisation from the very start will relieve the legislators to carry out the business of Government. Until they are thus supported, legislators will not know the real possibilities of shaping the destinies of the country. It is not only Trinidad as a territory that must be considered. It is the whole of the British West Indies and in the not very distant future, other non-British territories which one way or another will be driven to seek some sort of common West Indian confederation.

(c) This building of the Party cannot be carried out by legislators. If they attempt to do so, the only result will be that the scope and possibility of the Party will be cut down to the size which suits such time and energy and thought as the legislators can spare for it, and you know how precious little time and energy and thought some legislators have spared for the Party.

All this emphasizes the separation of the Party leadership in the Central Office from the Governmental functions. The result will not be to strengthen the Party functionaries as against the leadership in Government or in the Legislature. The result is exactly the opposite. The Legislature remains in theory and in practice the highest organ of Government. Power is concentrated in the hands of Ministers. Therefore the more powerful the Party in the community, the more powerful the legislative and ministerial arm of the Party.

That is Central Office in Party Headquarters which will set out to build the Party, in the same way that the Foundation Members set out to build the Movement and place its Government in power, and in the same way that the Government, when returned to power, set out to build the economy and the cultural life of the country. In the Government we have been impeded by all sorts of hangovers and by the squeaking and squawking of the Opposition. When we set out to build the Party we shall do anything that we have the vision to imagine and the will to carry out. Nothing stands in our way but our own weaknesses.

Our second task is the complete transformation of our Party Press.

TRANSFORMATION OF PARTY PRESS

The Party Press is not good. The documents presented to this Convention show that it is financially in a parlous state, and editorially even worse. The circulation should be at least twice what it is. Recent improvements notwithstanding, the need is for a paper so written that it is eagerly awaited by every literate person in the population, symbolising the new West Indies, a concrete manifestation of the transition from the colonialism of the daily press of the Old World. Our advertising machinery is hopeless; our dependence on private printing requires us to conform to such restrictions as our printers stipulate. First of all the Party leadership is to see to it that we purchase at the earliest possible moment our own printing machinery, our own linotype and all that goes with the publication of a modern newspaper even though it is only a weekly.

At once we are going to carry as soon as we can make the arrangements the Weekly to 16 pages. We do this merely to organise the staff and the preparation of the party and public for what is inevitably the next step. We give public notice that we propose in the near future to launch a public company which will invite all sections of the public to participate in order that we should publish here a daily paper, a paper devoted to the nationalist aspirations of the West Indian people and the people of Trinidad, a paper based on the popular democracy, a paper appealing to all good West Indians, party members or not, a paper of the People for the People by the People.

Such a paper fulfilling the role assigned to it in the Party and in the community, serving our Federal neighbours as well as ourselves, requires an Editor who, like the General Secretary, is in calibre and status on a par with the legislative representatives of the Party. Let me make it quite clear—the men to fill these two top posts, General Secretary of the Party and Editor of the Party papers must be men who look upon their tasks as sufficient to occupy the greatest talents and energies that they have.

This is what the Party leadership must do. But besides concrete proposals we have to organise the education of the Party, because all these projects we must undertake would be nothing without a Party and public educated to take advantage of the opportunities we propose to create. I turn now to what we need to set in motion for the education of the Party.

PARTY EDUCATION

A primary source of education for PNM members is PNM speeches in the Legislature or to the general public and the Press Conferences. There are Ministers whose education and faculty of expressing themselves are such that some of their speeches or statements are a contribution to the general education of the Party and the public. There are certain Ministries whose function in the community invites statements of this kind, such as for example the Ministry of Education and Culture. The journalists and the Party orators and speakers will make these ideas and facts their own. They will translate them into their own language. They will discover and develop apt illustrations. They are not supposed to quote these speeches as if they were quoting from the Bible. They must, however, use them as the basis of the approach to concrete matters. There should never be any problem for a speaker or a journalist when dealing with fundamental matters such as the Chaguaramas question, the Development Programme, the telephone issue, the attitude to the DLP, etc. In the Bolshevik Party, where sheer ideas were of infinitely greater importance than they are in a democratic party such as the PNM, the role of Lenin was above all that of theoretical guide and source of inspiration. To print columns of a speech in the Legislature or of a statement at a Press Conference and then to forget it as is repeatedly done by the journalists, the educationists and the others, is a source of graveness to the Party.

In addition to this, there are the communications which PNM representatives in legislative bodies make and should make to the Party and primarily to their own press. It is one of the strangest things in the present function of the Press that Party leaders or Ministers seem ready to give interviews and information to all sections of the public Press except to their own Party organ. Just as strange is the argument that dominated the Newspaper Convention last year as to whether Ministers should write in the party organ.

The PNM speeches or statements should be printed in a special section of the Party paper and if they are of sufficient importance to be printed in the Party Press as a whole, then they should be immediately reprinted in pamphlet form, so as to be available for discussion and education.

It is in this way that the ideas and conceptions that are so important in the state of transition acquire cohesion and at differing levels are disseminated through the Party organs and publications to the Party members and to the public.

There is one other source of Party education. The political leaders of the Party and the Staff of the Press must be on the alert for historical pronouncements by political leaders of other countries which have attained or are in process of attaining independence. These should be printed in full or almost in full with matters that are strictly local pruned away. There are also classic statements in the past history of national struggles which also, on suitable occasions, should be reprinted.

These constitute the basis of the education of the Party. All other talk about education is not only without any serious basis, it is actually misleading because it turns education into some sort of teacher and schoolboy relationship which the Party members and still more the public will not stand for. That is the method of political education of a Party and a people in the process of transition from the colonial status to the status of independence. It has to make its own way, and this is the only way that it can be done.

Upon the basis outlined above a structure of education which can mean something to the Party and the people can be developed.

Similarly a programme for the internal education of the Party has to be worked out. This also is a concrete matter to be done in strict relation to the concrete circumstances. Meanwhile, however, there are certain tasks which should be set in motion immediately.

1) Every encouragement should be given to individuals or groups to study questions arising from the general propaganda above or any question that interests them. After they have made their study it should be possible for them to give a course or a local seminar, and if the local seminar is successful, a regional seminar on the particular topic which they have studied to such people as are interested.

2) The Party should immediately establish a Party Library and begin to import books and from the Party Headquarters begin a book service. There are a mass of cheap books of great educational value which can be a source not only of education of the Party, but of income. The experiment should be begun on a small scale but in combination with the Press and the general ideas outlined above, it can rapidly develop until ultimately a Party bookshop or more than one is established.

3) In relation to the above there should be developed a core primarily of young people who act as researchers and gatherers of information for the Political Leader, the Party leaders in general and the editorial staff of the paper. These people are not functionaries. They work in their spare time. But such a core can be of immense value to the Party and also in training themselves for more responsible posts. I propose to set up such a group immediately.

PNM RECORD

4) It is one of the gravest weaknesses of nationalist parties, and in the West Indies in particular, that they do not solidify achievements and establish traditions until they are in power, and not always then.

The PNM must immediately seek the means to record in a book, intended for the public in general its origin, its achievements and its perspectives. The idea that people cannot be found to do this is totally false. Together with this should go a published account of each Convention, and I hope that we can begin with a report on this Third Convention with a historical summary of its predecessors.

These books are an absolute necessity for the consolidation and education of the Movement and the confounding of its opponents both at home and abroad. There will be no difficulty whatever in getting them to circulate both in Great Britain and in the United States. It would be a crime against the Movement not to begin this at once. It can have immense effect in an electoral campaign, and this should appeal to many.

WEEK-END SCHOOLS

The programme of internal education of the Party has, I am glad to say, now begun in real earnest. Two decisive events have taken place in the past month. The first is the establishment in the North

East Port-of-Spain Constituency of PNM's first library. The second is the organisation by the South East Port-of-Spain Constituency of PNM's first week end school, followed by the organisation of a second school in Diego Martin last week jointly by the Constituencies of South East Port-of-Spain, North East Port-of-Spain and St. George West.

The programme of the two week end schools dealt, respectively, with the West Indies, past, present and future, and with federation in various aspects. The schools drew on PNM's Legislative Group for the lecturers. The subject of the third week end school to be held next month is "Colonialism and Chaguaramas". Arrangements have also been made to hold a six month school of twelve fortnightly lectures on "The History of the West Indies."

INTERNATIONAL RELATION

Political education of the party which is the decisive force in West Indian nationalism must be international as well as national. The West Indian Federation is heading inexorably for independence by the deadline proposed by PNM at last year's Convention, April 22, 1960. This will give us responsibility in the field of foreign policy. We need to be prepared for this. Hence the new direction indicated in the relevant document presented to this Convention by the General Council's Committee on External Affairs. The party must look outwards; the national party must on the achievement of its independence be international in outlook. This involves the USA and Chaguaramas; Canada and external aid; Venezuela and the problem of fishermen; the United Kingdom and the racial problem; the non-British territories of the Caribbean and the possibility of a West Indian Common Market; Ghana, India, Pakistan and China whence we derive so much of our origins; the study of parties and party organisation in various countries. It involves also the international ramifications of our economy—GATT, oil, sugar, bauxite, bananas, citrus, cocoa. The

Institute of International Relations projected by the Committee will become one of the principal educational agencies of the Movement.

This is what has to be done and what is going to be put in motion by the powerful Central Office we are going to establish. But this will be as nothing unless it calls forth from the party members a new burst of party activity and participation in all aspects of party life. It is with the organisation of the Party that PNM can genuinely and truly become a way of life.

The Party must organise itself to correspond. Two main points emerge:

(a) Members must not be organised solely for electoral purposes.

(b) Members must not be educated solely on programmes and policies of the Party.

That is the surest way to demoralise them.

THE IDEAL PARTY MEMBER

Education and organisation must constantly bear in mind the following as the ideal Party member:

(a) Every Party Member must feel himself and be seen and recognised as the centre of a periphery of citizens or the members of any organisation in which he finds himself.

(b) The Party member must be looked upon as the active leader in all local progressive causes and nationalist aspirations. This does not necessarily mean being in the leadership although that is not excluded.

(c) The public must in time get to recognise the Party member as the person most likely to be well informed on all the multitudinous international, social and political questions which are pressing on the West Indian population from every side and to which they want answers.

THE POLITICAL LEADER

To this party organisation that I have described the Political Leader has a very clear and special responsibility.

The first is that, particularly at the present stage of development, he is the main source of its ideals and of its political and social attitudes. He must be free to develop these, to extend his knowledge in every sphere, to have at his command trained and capable collaborators and to exercise the all-important function of presenting these ideas in a manner that can be easily assimilated and grasped by the Party and the public.

As the theoretical leader, he is the source of inspiration, ideas and facts and research for journalists, orators and the innumerable other individuals and groups who transmit their ideas to the public. The Party journalists and the Party orators from the highest to the lowest take the inspiration and the structure and tone of their work from the theoretical leader. Political leader and theoretical leader need not necessarily be one and the same person. They may be two or three persons. History is full of such a natural collaboration of talents. George Washington from the beginning to the end was the leader of the American Revolution. He was soldier and after soldier political leader and organiser of the new state. Yet the fact remains that the educator of the people in that stage of transition and afterwards was Jefferson and, almost on the same level, Alexander Hamilton, Madison and others in their paper, THE FEDERALIST.

It is true that the Party journalists and orators also are the source of much of the Political Leader's facts and information and many ideas. But the grasp of the whole at any particular time is the work of the Political Leader of the Party.

Since the Party paper is the principal medium of Party education, the Political Leader also has a special responsibility to it. He should write a weekly article in the Party paper. He may take up a historical subject. He may write on foreign affairs. He may write on any topic of the day. The point is that in this manner he sets the tone for the Party and through the Party, the public. At difficult moments in the life of the Party, or in the life of a country, this can be of immense value in educating and lowering or raising the temper of the Party and the people. This is not an easy task. It requires that a special time and much thought be devoted to it. In certain parties, this task is performed by some highly qualified person apart from the Political Leader—like Harold Laski in the British Labour Party. Organs like THE TIMES and THE DAILY TELEGRAPH speak for the Conservative Party. In the present stage of transition in the West Indies this task cannot be left to any but the Political Leader of the Party with qualifications for so doing. This is the general guide as to what Party members should be thinking both in general and on particular matters. This must be the primary source of ideas and attitudes and this is the axis around which the Party revolves.

All this means that the Political Leader, who automatically becomes Chief Minister when the Party achieves power, cannot be part legislator, interviewing constituents; part Party organiser, supervising and reorganising the Party; part agitator at Party rallies; and general factotum of the Party editing reports of the General Council to the Convention; and expected to attend every social function of every Party group.

Many of the ideas that we have worked upon in the past and which are now being put before you, and others which will be put before you in the future, are ideas which I have had the good fortune to work over and discuss for many years with some of the finest and most devoted minds concerned with the problems of the underdeveloped countries. Fortune has so willed it that I have been lifted by you into a position where these ideas or some of them at any rate can be translated into positive action for the benefit of our people and as an example to other citizens of the world in our situation. I do not intend to shirk that responsibility, but the experience of the last two or three years has shown me that I can only carry it out fully and make the best of it when my colleagues and the Party members are themselves carrying out the kind of activity which is the responsibility of a political organisation today. What the leadership puts before you is not only a means for the Party to impress itself upon the public as the organisation on which the future of our society depends; it is also the means by which those of us to whom you have given high and responsible position will at last be able to carry out their responsibilities. This applies to all of us and to me in particular.

FEDERATION

The task before us, every word that we are saying here, every project that we propose, not only apply to Trinidad and Tobago but also must affect the Federation of which we are a part to whose success we are committed. Let me pause for a moment to give you an example. In our paper of 16 pages we should print in every issue a supplement which we would call the Federalist. That is the way in which we approach these problems. We hope to learn from what our fellow members of the Federation are doing. We hope also to set an example which they will follow with profit and with pride. PNM's Legislative Group is already well advanced with a detailed study of the Federal Constitution as the basis of constitutional amendments which it will propose to the WIFLP preparatory to the constitutional conference to give the West Indies Dominion Status by the deadline fixed at our Convention last year, April 22, 1960.

PARTY FINANCE

Party organisation, Party press, Party education—these are impossible without Party finance. Without Party funds, all of my fundamental thesis is so much hot air. Without the theoretical foundation, the raising of funds would be, at best to build up an electoral machine, at worst sheer adventurism.

A Party Headquarters, a Party linotype machine to print not only the paper but also Party pamphlets, cards and forms and circulars—these cost money. The Party needs also to provide for automobile transportation, loudspeakers, and a propaganda van equipped not only with loud speaker but also with literature, tape recorder and mimeographing machine.

PARTY DEVELOPMENT PROGRAMME

The Treasurer, when his turn comes, will present to you the first Party budget and indicate to you that the Party membership must finance its own organisation. I am dealing however with extraordinary as distinct from recurrent expenditure. Over and above the Treasurer's Budget, I present to you the Party's Development Programme to match the Government's Development Programme. His theme and mine are the same: The Party must systematically educate its members and the public in the conception that, instead of the Old World of politics where their votes were bought and their minds enslaved, in the New World of education which emancipates they must bear the main financial responsibility for an independent political organisation.

"De doctah say to pay as you earn,

PNM say you paying to learn."

I propose as an arbitrary figure a Development Programme to cost $100,000 a year and to begin with the acquisition of land for the Party Headquarters and the purchase of a linotype machine. This represents less than $5 per PNM member, less than $1 per PNM voter. The masses, and the middle classes for that matter, are more impressed by acts and facts than electoral speeches. A Development Programme of this kind carried out in this way is a gigantic political act. It must be an annual affair. That is what is in political parties abroad. When, however, for say two years, the headquarters have been built, a printing press bought, the Party newspaper developed to 16 pages, perhaps appearing twice a week, then, upon the basis of these successes, a public company seeking to raise a million dollars for the publication of a daily paper can be launched. It is because the public has seen for the previous two years (or perhaps only one year) that the Party is able to carry out a tremendous programme, utterly independent of the Legislature and Government, that it will be willing to subscribe.

I am posing these problems to you as the question of the organisation of the Party. We intend to make the public of Trinidad and Tobago, the West Indies and the whole world understand that the PNM simply proposes to lead the way in the political life of the country and as a force in every section of social life. But in so doing we are not merely pursuing party interests. We are pursuing party interests, yes, and in a moment I shall let those whom we are going to pursue know how this is going to affect them. But in reality we are laying the only sound foundation for democracy in these islands of ours. There is and there can be no other foundation, but a development along the lines that we began two years ago and are now carrying to a higher stage. There are many thinking people, both on the right and on the left, who know how serious a problem it will be to establish democracy in these parts once the colonial system has finally departed. Look at the whole of Latin America and you will see how difficult it is. This is the way to solve that problem. We do not only propose to do this for positive reasons. This is the way to finish once and for all with that figment of an Opposition which day after day in every issue shows itself the main obstacle to material progress and intellectual understanding in our country.

WHAT THE DLP OFFERS

This is our programme. We have to fight them and expose their bankruptcy. This is our programme and everybody knows now that what the PNM says the PNM strains every nerve to carry out. Look at the Opposition. What have they to offer? In what way do they propose to lead the West Indian people to independence and a fuller democracy? In four ways.

First, by Government of rewards, for rewards, by rewards, of personal appeals to individual problems, demonstrating the petty concerns of pettier minds. Generations of neglect and poverty combined with the emergence of standpipe politicians symbolic of parochialism and individualism necessarily expose the community to the complex that has been bred of concentration on purely local issues, small points and the demand for and expectation of handouts—Mrs. X's drain at the back of her house, Mr. Y's petition for reconsideration of his rejected petition twenty years ago, the personal problems of Annabella, Johnson and Dorothy, one wanting Zephyr motorcar, one wanting piece of land. To stoop to this in order to conquer, to fight the DLP with DLP weapons; to challenge colonialism in order to enthrone individual materialism; to belittle West Indian nationalism by the concentration on a gigantic election machine riddled with intrigues for nomination and lobbying for favours—that is to approximate PNM to DLP. PNM's must be a higher destiny, a nobler calling, a graver responsibility.

What does DLP offer in the second place? The continued domination of Big Business which feels at home with standpipe politics, opposes constitution reform, and looks for security to an outside arbitrator with armed forces not subject to local control.

FOREIGN SUBJECTION

DLP's third proposal for leading the West Indian people to independence and a fuller democracy is by keeping us in subjection to a foreign power. This is not a problem limited to Trinidad and Tobago and to the West Indies. The existence of the so called Loyalists in Northern Ireland associated with the United Kingdom has for generations strengthened colonialism in Ireland and strangled the Irish Nationalist Movement for an independent Irish Free State. The Parliamentary opposition in Canada for decades carried on a protracted struggle against Canadian federation and the establishment of an independent Canadian State, preferring instead to be an American satellite annexed to the powerful United States of America. We face a similar situation here in Trinidad and Tobago in respect of Chaguaramas, where it is now quite obvious that the DLP will play America's game and where the legitimate nationalist movement for ownership of its soil and for the moral right to independence in foreign affairs finds itself locked in conflict with an opposition party ready to sell out half of Trinidad for a few pieces of silver if only it can be guaranteed in its possesion of the other half.

RACIALISM

The DLP's fourth offering is racialism. To our programme of independence and democracy, they oppose what is called "the Indian vote." There are a lot of people who always speak about "the Indians" and sometimes that kind of phrase gets away from you. But in our thoughts we must not do the Indian people the gross injustice of believing or even pretending to believe that those Indians who claim to speak in their name are their genuine political leaders. The 1956 election showed that a large section of the population was waiting for people to come forward so that they would turn their backs on those who had led them or misrepresented them for so many years. Let us do our work as we should. Let us reorganise this party. Let us show the whole population—Africans, Indians, Chinese, Europeans, Syrians—what a democratic party is and can be. Already we have some of the finest Indians in the country in our ranks. In every constituency you will find them. As we build and develop, the genuine Indian leadership will emerge and we will meet it with outstretched hands, as Nehru's hands are outstretched to assist and to welcome West Indian democracy and nationalism as exemplified by the PNM.

ELECTIONS

I have not said a word so far about elections and it may appear that I have disregarded electoral victories. That is not so. What I have been trying to convey is that voters are more impressed by acts and facts, by vision and perspectives, than by electoral speeches. The finest speeches, electoral or otherwise, will not build a party or win elections, as we learned from the huge midnight audiences I addressed in Arima, Tunapuna, San Fernando and Point Fortin in the Federal Elections and in Sangre Grande in the resultant by-election. The basis of electoral successes is a party that is active in its own right in all sorts of political and social projects—a party which (a) provides an opportunity for the Party membership to give of its best and attract the best; (b) educates the masses and the middle classes to see politics and the Party as something else besides elections and Government handout; (c) convinces the general public as a whole that it is an instrument fit to govern so that they follow it in the need to create a society built on new instead of colonialist foundations.

All political experience shows that in a period like the present people are ready to follow and make great efforts, even sacrifices only when great ideas are placed before them and great efforts are demanded of them.

Furthermore, it is a vigorous political party, penetrating on its own independent basis all sorts of social activities and obviously the force upon which the new country depends, it is this which most impresses foreign capital and foreign Governments—foreign capital because it wants above all to see some force that is capable of keeping order; foreign Governments because with all their faults they want to see democracy flourishing in the colonial countries and in the final analysis respect a people who have thrown off the yoke of servility and emancipated themselves by their own peaceful but irresistible efforts.

THE PERSONALITY OF PNM

These are the perspectives for our Party which I hold out to you at this our Third Annual Convention. These are the opportunities which beckon to you, urging you to emulate the Congress Party of India, the Convention People's Party of Ghana, to blaze the trail for your West Indian affiliates ending in your own Conference of Independent Caribbean States as independence in Asia and Africa has produced the Asian Conference, the Conference of Independent African States, and the Bandung Conference. That is the destiny which awaits you—an independent West Indian foreign policy, independent West Indian representation in the United Nations. That is the responsibility with which, as Political Leader, I charge you—the responsibility of creating and writing the history of a free people. I say to you, you are PNM, and upon this rock we will build the edifice of West Indian nationalism, and the gates of reaction will not prevail against it.

MASSA DAY DONE

by Eric E. Williams

Williams examines African handicraft with Nigerian officials in the 1960s.

This address was delivered at the University of Woodford Square, Port of Spain, on March 22, 1961.

MASSA DAY DONE

On December 4, 1960 the *Trinidad Guardian* announced that Sir Gerald Wight had joined the Democratic Labour Party. The announcement was presented in such a way as to suggest that this was a feather in the cap of the Democratic Labour Party, and therefore the citizens of Trinidad and Tobago should follow the lead of Sir Gerald Wight. Consequently, in my address here in the University on December 22, in which I reported to the people the outcome of the Chaguaramas discussions in Tobago, I poured scorn on the *Guardian,* reminding them that our population of today was far too alert and sophisticated to fall for any such claptrap. I told the *Guardian,* emphatically: Massa Day Done. In other words it was the *Guardian* I attacked for its slave mentality. But if Sir Gerald Wight and his admirers thought that the cap fitted him too, that was nothing over which I should lose any sleep.

The Scribes and Pharisees had a field day. Someone wrote to the *Guardian,* to say what a gentleman Sir Gerald was, ever since he was a boy of eight on horseback. Another one wrote to say that Sir Gerald had got him a job. Farquhar, that notorious sycophant, called my statement mischievous and accused me of responsibility for all the evils of Trinidad society which he, from his pulpit, had not been able to exorcise. Finally the DLP in a statement which appeared in the *Guardian,* on March 5, 1961, called on me to withdraw what it called the wicked statement Massa Day Done, and to make an unqualified apology for introducing it.

I categorically refuse to withdraw my statement or to make any apology for it, qualified or unqualified. I repeat, more emphatically than when I said it the first time, Massa Day Done. I accuse the DLP of being the stooge of the Massas who still exist in our society. I accuse the DLP of deliberately trying to keep back social progress. I accuse the DLP of wanting to bring back Massa Day. Tonight I shall explain to you fully just what is meant when I say, Massa Day Done, and by the same token just what the DLP means and stands for when they not only object to the statement but even ask me to withdraw it.

This pack of benighted idiots, this band of obscurantist politicians, this unholy alliance of egregious individualists, who have nothing constructive to say, who babble week after week the same criticisms that we have lived through for five long years, who, nincompoops that they are, think that they can pick up any old book the day before a debate in the Legislative Council and can pull a fast one in the Council by leaving out the sentence or the paragraph or the pages which contradict their ignorant declamations—for people like these power is all that matters. They have not the slightest idea as to the constituents of progress in our society and the elements of our historical evolution. All that they can see in the slogan, Massa Day Done, is racial antagonism. This characteristically stupid. Massa is not a racial term. Massa is the symbol of a bygone age. Massa Day is a social phenomenon: Massa Day Done connotes a political awakening and a social revolution.

What was Massa Day, the Massa Day that is done? Who is Massa?

Massa was more often than not an absentee European planter exploiting West Indian resources, both human and economic. I had particularly referred in my address in the University before Christmas to a book well-known to students of West Indian History written by an absentee English landlord who visited his plantations in Jamaica for the first time around 1815. The author's name was Matthew Lewis. He had written a journal of his visits to Jamaica, and in my address I referred to one passage in the Journal when, as he went around the plantation, the slaves ran up to him with all sorts of complaints, saying "Massa this, Massa that, Massa the other". Massa lived in England off the profits of West Indian labour. He became a big shot and ostentatiously flaunted his wealth before the eyes of the people of England. He was a big noise in the House of Commons in the British Parliament. He could become a Lord Mayor of London. A famous play entitled "The West Indian", presented in Drury Lane in London in 1776, portrayed Massa as a very wealthy man who had enough sugar and rum to turn all the water of the Thames into rum punch. Massa's children were educated in England at the best schools and at the best Universities, and it was openly and frequently claimed in the long period of the British controversy over the abolition of the slave trade and abolition of slavery that Oxford and Cambridge were filled with the sons of West Indian Massas. When things got bad and sugar ceased to be king in the West Indies, Massa simply pulled out of the West Indies, in much the same way as the descendants of Massa's slaves today pull out from the West Indies and migrate to the United Kingdom.

We have a record of one such Massa in the small poverty-stricken island of Nevis. He arrived in Nevis about 1680 with ten pounds, a quart of wine and a Bible. He developed into a big shot, became planter, merchant, and Legislator, and when things turned sour in the 19th century, he invested all his wealth derived from the West Indian soil and the West Indian people in railways and canals and harbours in Canada, India and Australia. He went back to live in the old County of Dorset in England from which his ancestors had migrated to the West Indies, and his biographer tells us that today the same family occupies the same pew in the same church in the same village. What he does not tell us is that it was as if Massa had never emigrated to the West Indies. Massa left behind Nevis as under-developed as he had found it. The wealth that should have been ploughed back into Nevis to save it from its present disgrace of being a grant-aided Colony, went to fertilise industrial development everywhere in the world except in the West Indies. Today only a beach which bears his name survives to remind us that this particular Massa had ever existed in Nevis. His English biographer tells us that it was as if he had never left his English County. We tell him it is as if Massa had never been in the West Indian Island.

On his West Indian sugar plantation Massa employed unfree labour. He began with the labour of slaves from Africa, and followed this with the labour of contract workers from Portugal and China and then from India. The period of Massa's ascendancy, the period of Massa's domination over workers who had no rights under the law, the period of Massa's enforcement of a barbarous code of industrial relations long after it was repudiated by the conscience of the civilized world, lasted in our society for almost 300 years.

To his slave workers from Africa the symbol of Massa's power was the whip, liberally applied; records exist showing that 200 lashes were not infrequent, and a tremendous howl was raised by Massa when British law tried to step in and limit punishment to 39 lashes under supervision. To his contract workers from India the symbol of Massa's power was the jail. Massa's slogan was : the Indian worker is to be found either in the field or in the hospital or in jail. For such trivial offences as leaving the plantation without permission, being drunk at work, using obscene language, encouraging his colleagues to strike, the Indian worker, who was paid a legal wage of 25 cents per day, was sentenced to jail by the law of Trinidad and the law of British Guiana where Indians were employed in large numbers.

Massa's economic programme was to grow sugar and nothing but sugar. His table, one of the most glaring examples of gluttony that the world has ever known, was almost entirely imported, and as a Brazilian sociologist, Gilberto Freyre, has emphasised in respect of that country, it was the African slave who kept alive the real traditions of agriculture in the West Indies and concentrated on the production of food for his own subsistence. The Indian contract worker went even further than the African slave, and it was he who brought West Indian society to its present level in terms of the production of such essential commodities as rice, milk and meat. Massa's economic programme represented the artificial stunting of West Indian society, and a powerful Royal Commission sent out from Britain to the West Indies in 1897 condemned the emphasis put on a single crop peculiarly vulnerable in the markets of the world, attacked Massa for making it difficult for the West Indian peasant to get land of his own on which to grow food crops, and advised that there was no future for the West Indies which did not put in the forefront of the programme of economic development the settlement of the landless labourers on the land as peasant owners.

Massa's day should have been done then. But it was very easy in those days for Britain to ignore the recommendations of a Royal Commission and Massa was allowed to perpetuate his uneconomic and anti-social activities until 1930 when another Commission from Britain, at the height of the world depression, repeated the condemnation of the 1897 Commission almost in the identical language used by its predecessors. Massa's long economic domination of the West Indies reduced the population of the West Indies, whether slave, contract or free, to the drudgery of the simplest and most unedifying operations, almost unfitting them totally for any intelligent agricultural activity, and giving them a profound and almost permanent distaste for agricultural endeavours.

Massa was able to do all of this because he had a monopoly of political power in the West Indies which he used shamelessly for his private ends as only the DLP can be expected to emulate in our more modern times. He used this political power ruthlessly to import workers for his sugar plantations with no respect either for elementary economics of his time or of population problems of the future. Massa's economy was distinguished by perhaps the most scandalous waste of labour the history of the world has ever known. Forty house slaves in a Jamaican slave household was not unusual, and the domestic female slave who carried the cushion for Massa to kneel on in church in Surinam, or kept Massa's cigars lighted while he was being shaved in Brazil, typifies not only Massa's total contempt for the human personality but also his pathological unconcern with the most elementary considerations of cost of production. It was the same with the Indian workers brought in on contract. They were brought in without any consideration whatsoever as to the supply that was really needed, if any was needed at all, and a Commission from the Government of

India which visited the West Indies and Surinam in 1915 condemned as an unwarranted waste of labour the importation of four workers to do work which would have been light labour for three.

Massa was able to do all this because he controlled political power in the West Indies and could use state funds for his private gain. Whilst he imported African slaves out of his own personal resources, he dug into the purse of the West Indies Treasuries for public financing of Indian indentured migration to the tune of about one-third of the total cost of introducing the workers. This went on throughout the 19th century on Massa's insistence at the very period when, as thousands of Indians came to Trinidad and British Guiana, thousands of Barbadians and Jamaicans went to build the Panama Canal, or migrated to the United States of America to do unskilled work, or went to Cuba to work on the sugar plantations in that Island.

As far as Massa was concerned this organisation of West Indian economy, this dispensation of political power was one of the eternal verities. He developed the necessary philosophical rationalisation of this barbarous system. It was that the workers, both African and Indian, were inferior beings, unfit for self-government, unequal to their superior masters, permanently destined to a status of perpetual subordination, unable ever to achieve equality with Massa. It was there in all the laws which governed the West Indies for generations—the laws which denied equality on grounds of colour, the laws which forbade non-Europeans to enter certain occupations and professions, whether it was the occupation of jeweller or the profession of lawyer, the laws which forbade intermarriage, the laws which equated political power and the vote with ownership of land, the laws which, consciously or unconsciously, directly or indirectly, attempted to ensure that the non-European would never be anything but a worker in the social scale, the improvement of whose standard of living depended, as a British Secretary of State once told the workers in Jamaica in 1865, on their working on Massa's plantation for wages. That was why, when slavery was abolished in 1833, and Massa was afraid that the emancipated slaves would no longer accept the drudgery and exploitation of the slave plantation but would work for themselves on small plots, Massa in Barbados and Massa in British Guina destroyed the gardens and food plots which the slaves had been permitted to cultivate during slavery in order to force them, out of the threat of starvation, to accept starvation wages on the plantations.

Massa was determined to use his political power for his own personal ends. He had no sense of loyalty to the community which he dominated or even to the community from which he had originally sprung. When Massa in Haiti found that the French Government was ready to abolish slavery he offered the island to England. When Massa in Jamaica found that the British were ready to abolish slavery he entered into conspiracy with planters in the southern States of America. When Massa in St. Croix in the Danish Virgin Islands found that it was too difficult to deal with the emancipated slaves, he tried to sell the island to the United States of America. When Massa in Cuba on sugar plantation found himself confronted by a combination of abolitionist forces representing progressive metropolitan opinion, free white planters in Cuba growing tobacco and not sugar, and the slaves themselves, he too turned his eyes to the United States of America and plunged the country into civil war. When Massa in Jamaica in 1865 recognised that it was no longer possible to hold back the tide of constitution reform and deny the vote to the emancipated slaves, he brutally suppressed a revolt among the Jamaican workers and peasants and persuaded the British Government to suspend the self-governing Constitution of Jamaica and introduce the Crown Colony system. And when Massa in Barbados in the 1860's feared that West Indian federation might involve a large redistribution of his land among the workers of Barbados, Massa made official overtures for joining the Canadian Federation. Massa was always opposed to independence. He welcomed political dependence so long as it guaranteed the economic dependence of his workers. He was for self-government so long as it was self-government for Massa only and left him free to govern his workers as he pleased. Our whole struggle for self-government and independence, therefore, is a struggle for emancipation from Massa.

That was the West Indian Massa. There has been slavery and unfree labour in other societies. Ancient Greek society, precisely because of slavery, had been able to achieve intellectual heights that so far have had no parallel in human history. The ownership of a large slave empire in the West Indies did not prevent the flowering of intellect and the evolution of politics in the metropolitan countries of Europe. But the West Indian Massa constituted the most backward ruling class history has ever known. Massa in Jamaica had a contempt for education and the profession of teaching which scandalised even the commentators of the 18th century. A traveller in Haiti before its independence commented caustically on Massa's anti-intellectual outlook. He described the conversation of Massa as follows : It begins with the price of sugar and then goes on to the price of coffee, the price of cocoa, and the laziness of Negroes; and then it retraces the same ground beginning with the laziness of Negroes, and going on to the price of cocoa, the price of coffee and the price of sugar. Massa in Trinidad in the early 20th century asked sarcastically of what use would education be to the children of plantation workers if they had it. He stated unambiguosly in the Trinidad Legislative Council of 1925, in the age of Cipriani, that as long as Trinidad was to remain an agricultural country, the less education the children of the plantation workers had the better. As one of the abolitionists in the Colonial Office recognised a century and a quarter ago, there was no civilised society on earth so entirely destitute of learned leisure, literary and scientific intercourse and liberal recreations.

This was Massa Day. This was Massa — the owner of a West Indian sugar plantation, frequently an absentee, deliberately stunting all the economic potential of the society, dominating his defenceless workers by the threat of punishment or imprisonment, using his political power for the most selfish private ends, an uncultured man with an illiberal outlook.

But not every white man was a Massa. Las Casas, the Roman Catholic Bishop, condemned in Cuba, in Santo Domingo and in Mexico the iniquitous exploitation of the aborigines by the Spaniards. Thomas Clarkson, the humanitarian in England, and Victor Schoelcher, the radical politician in France, dedicated their entire lives to a relentless crusade against slavery. It was Clarkson who, 170 years ago, made one of the finest defences of the African against charges of inferiority, before modern sociological research and modern progressive ideas. It was Victor Schoelcher who provided the abolition programme in France in 1848 with the resounding peroration that the French Republic could not compromise with slavery and tarnish its immortal formula, "Liberty, Equality and Fraternity". It was the white Cuban philosopher, Luzy Cabellero, who coined the famous aphorism that "the blackest thing in slavery was not the black man." It was the white Cuban philosopher, Jose Marti, who educated Cuba in the view that man is more than white, more than Negro, more than mulatto. It was the white Spanish planters in Puerto Rico who themselves demanded the emancipation of the slaves. It was a white Danish Governor who on his own initiative abolished slavery in St. Croix and returned home to be impeached for exceeding his instructions. It was the white Missionary, John Smith, who died in imprisonment in Massa's jail in British Guiana because he insisted on educating the Negroes and teaching them to read in order that they could read the Bible. It was the white Rev. William Knibb who organised in Falmouth, Jamaica, a tremendous movement against Massa and swore that he would not rest until he saw the end of slavery, and who, once slavery was abolished, spent the rest of his life in providing schools for the children and in trying to secure land for the people. It was the white Rev. James Phillips in Jamaica who, as far back as 1845, put forward proposals for the establishment of a University College in Jamaica which, if the

British Government of the time had had the foresight to accept and to promote, would have changed the whole course of West Indian History in the past 100 years.

Here in Trinidad it was people like the Grants and Mortons who first undertook the education of the children of the Indian indentured workers on Massa's plantation. It was names like Lange which advocated the vote for Massa's workers. It was the Alcazars and the Stollmeyers among others in Trinidad who fought Massa on the question of Indian indenture; it was Sir Henry Alcazar who, in a memorable phrase in a memorandum to the Royal Commission of 1897, stated that the effect of Indian indenture was to keep the ruling class of Trinidad at the moral level of slave owners.

If Massa was generally white, but not all whites were Massa, at the same time not all Massas were white. The elite among the slaves were the house slaves. Always better treated than their colleagues in the field, they developed into a new caste in West Indian society, aping the fashion of their masters, wearing their cast-off clothing, and dancing the quadrille with the best of them. To such an extent did Massa's society penetrate the consciences of these people, that Haitian independence, which began with a fight for freedom for the slaves, ended up with a ridiculous imperial court of a Haitian despotism with its Count of Lemonade, exploiting the Negro peasants. The Maroons in Jamaica, runaway slaves who took refuge in the mountains from the horrors of the plantations and who became the spiritual ancestors of the Rastafarian movement of our time, after waging a successful war against Massa and forcing Massa to recognise their independence and to constitute them a veritable state within a state, accepted a peace treaty which required them to help Massa to put down any other slave rebellions. Emancipation of the slaves led in the smaller West Indian Islands to a gradual transfer of ownership of property to the point where, in such islands as Grenada and St. Vincent, whilst Massa remained, his complexion became darker.

This, then, was Massa in the West Indies. This was Massa Day.

The most savage condemnation of Massa in Trinidad came from the evidence of an Englishman who made Trinidad his home, Mr. Lechmere Guppy, Mayor of San Fernando, before the Royal Commission of the Franchise in 1889. Guppy related to the Commission a conversation between himself and a sugar planter with whom he had remonstrated about the condition of the houses provided for the Indian immigrants. **"The people ought to be in the field all day"**, the planter said. **"I do not build cottages for idlers".** When the Mayor reminded him that there might be sickness or children or pregnant women, the planter answered, **"Oh my dear Guppy, what do you talk to me about lying-in and nursing women; I only want working hands."** To which Guppy retorted, **"Then you will never have a settled population of labourers on your estates".** "A settled population", said the planter: **"I want two years of good crops and good prices, and then I will sell my estates and go to live in Europe".**

Guppy voiced the growing national and liberal consciousness when he unsparingly criticised the Indian indenture system as a selfish expedient pursued by a few Massas to the detriment of the community at large. Their chief aim by the policy, he emphasised, was to keep down the rate of wages, to force down artificially the price of labour and to confine it to the cultivation of the sugar cane. This they did "by importing labourers at the public expense to be indentured to plantations; by taxing the necessary food of the labourer; and . . . refusing to grant Crown lands to small settlers; by inequitable labour laws; by encouraging the unjust administration of the laws by Magistrates devoted to the wishes of the sugar planters; by refusal of practicable roads other than those required to convey the sugar planters' produce to the shipping place, and minor means tending to the same end. During all this time no men could be more grandiloquent about their intention, in all they proposed to do, being the development of the resources of the island; no men could be more determined, as shown by their measures, to do no other thing than bolster up the more or less normal owners of sugar plantations".

Life with Massa was summed up by me in a formal statement I made to an international conference in Geneva on October 20, 1955, when I acted as a spokesman of the International Confederation of Free Trade Unions at a meeting of the Committee on Plantations of the International Labour Organisation. In my statement I concentrated particularly on a reply on sick pay for plantation workers submitted by the Government of Trinidad and Tobago through its representative at the Conference, Mr. Albert Gomes. The reply of the Government of Trinidad and Tobago was as follows: **"The sugar employers do not consider it possible to provide sick pay to plantation workers".**

My formal statement at the Geneva Conference on this question read as follows:

"Let me emphasise in some detail the significance of this statement from the Government of Trinidad in the light of the views which have been expressed from time to time by the sugar employers of the Caribbean area on social questions and the conditions of the workers. I shall give some specific examples:

1. **In 1896, the British Government appointed a Royal Commission of Inquiry to investigate the difficulties then being encountered by the British West Indian sugar industry. The principal sugar employer in Trinidad gave evidence before the Commission to the effect that the plantation workers could live comfortably on 5 cents a day.**

2. **In 1910, before another Royal Commission of the British Government, this time on the commercial relations between Canada and the British West Indies, Canadian manufacturers and Trinidad merchants and employers indicated how it was possible to subsist on this low wage. They stated**

that what was rejected as stockfeed in Canada, was imported into Trinidad as flour, which was bought up like hot cakes by the plantation workers.

3. In 1915, a Commission of the Government of India was sent to various Caribbean territories to investigate the conditions of the indentured Indian immigrants. The Commission reported that the protection of the plantation workers against malaria by providing mosquito nets and against hookworm by providing shoes, would only involve unnecessary expenses for the sugar employers.

4. In 1926, in Trinidad, in evidence before a committee of the Legislative Council on the restriction of hours of labour designed principally to prohibit the labour of children of school age during school periods, one of the principal sugar employers stated in the most emphatic way that if they educated the whole mass of the agricultural population, they would be deliberately ruining the country. After this he proceeded to ask, of what use would education be to the children, if they had it?

5. In 1930, on a visit to British Guiana, a well known British Philantropist, a close friend of the late Mahatma Gandhi, was told unambiguously by one of the sugar employers that the London directors of his company would not provide any money for the elimination of the disgraceful workers' houses, though they would readily spend money for the installation of new machinery.

6. A Commission of Inquiry, which investigated widespread disturbances in Trinidad in 1937, was advised that sugar employers thought it unnecessary to provide adequate sanitary facilities for their employees, because the workers would not use them.

7. In Barbados in the following year, one of the sugar employers assured the members of the commission of inquiry investigating similar disturbances in that island that the plantation worker in Barbados did not take milk in his tea because he did not like milk!

I just leave to your imagintion the conditions which would prevail today in the British Caribbean territories if the views of the sugar employers had received the consideration which they thought should be attached to them."

The Second World War meant the end of Massa Day. Wendell Wilkie, the unsuccessful Republican candidate in the 1940 American Presidential Election, issued a general warning in his book **One World,** written at the end of a world tour. Wilkie warned the world:

"**Men and women all over the world are on the march, physically, intellectually, and spiritually. After centuries of ignorant and dull compliance, hundreds of millions of people in eastern Europe and Asia have opened the books. Old fears no longer frighten them. They are no longer willing to be Eastern slaves for Western profits. They are beginning to know that man's welfare throughout the world is independent. They are resolved, as we must be, that there is no more place for imperialism within their own society than in the society of nations. The big house on the hill surrounded by mud huts has lost its awesome charm."**

They marched everywhere, during and after World War II — in India, in Burma, in Indonesia, in Nigeria, in Ghana, in the Philippines, in Puerto Rico, above all in the United Kingdom. The counterpart of Massa in the West Indies was the squire in the United Kingdom. The welfare state has been super-imposed on the class society. The age of sweated labour in the factories has been abolished by the British trade unions. Oxford and Cambridge no longer serve exclusively the sons of the ruling class, and

Parliament and the diplomatic service are no longer the exclusive preserve of their graduates. Massa Day Done in the United Kingdom too. Here is an advertisement from the **Observer,** one of London's principal Sunday papers, on February 12, 1961:

"BUSINESSES FOR SALE
AND FROM KENYA, NIGERIA, CENTRAL AFRICA, MALAYA, INDIA and Other Corners of What Was 'The Empire' Of Sahib, Boss And Master, come a host of sadly disillusioned one time 'Empire Builders' to face the necessity of providing home and income for self and family — And to this problem the most certain answer is the purchase of A Village Store with maybe an appointment as Sub-Postmaster, or the purchase of a 'Pub, Filling Station, Tea Room or some such business. There is no better thought."

Massa Day Done, Sahib Day Done, Yes Suh Boss Day Done. All decent American public opinion is nauseated by Little Rock. The horrors of the Congo, deplorable though they are, represent the struggle between Massa and Massa's former exploited subjects. Massa is on the run right now in Portuguese Angola. The pressure from India and Ghana, Malaya and Nigeria in the Commonwealth Prime Ministers' Conference has forced the South African Massa out of the Commonwealth.

Massa Day Done everywhere. How can anyone in his senses expect Massa Day to survive in Trinidad and Tobago? That, however, is precisely what Sininan and the DLP stand for. Because for them to ask me to withdraw the statement, Massa Day Done, and, adding insult to injury, to demand that I apologise for it, is to identify themselves with all the forces of reaction which have been overthrown or are at bay in all the other countries of the world. What they seek, Sininan and the DLP, is actually to restore Massa Day. For Massa Day Done in Trinidad and Tobago, too, since the advent of the PNM in 1956. Let us assess the position in Trinidad today.

Massa's racial complex stunted the economic development of our territories. Today with the PNM, the cane farmer, the small farmer growing cane, pitting his puny weight against the large plantation, is receiving a recognition that he never anticipated, and is coming into his own, a man with a stake in his country, with the legal right to refuse his labour if he wishes to and to work his own land. The sudden and dramatic growth of industry, producing fertilisers, furniture, milk, textiles, paints, cement and a hundred other essential commodities, is vastly different from the monoculture society of Massa Day. In Massa Day the West Indies produced what they did not consume and consumed what they did not produce. Today, under the PNM, the slogan is, "Made in Trinidad".

Massa stood for degradation of West Indian Labour. PNM stands for the dignity of West Indian labour. The symbol of Massa's authority was the whip, his incentive to labour was the lash. Today, with the PNM, the worker's right to establish trade unions of his own choice and to bargain collectively with his employers is recognised by all but the obscurantist who still regard Trinidad, as Massa did, as a place to which the ordinary conventions of human society not to apply. Massa passed laws to forbid non-Europeans from being jewellers or lawyers. Today, under the PNM, the right of the West Indian to occupy the highest positions in public and private employment is axiomatic and is being increasingly enforced.

Massa stood for colonialism: any sort of colonialism, so long as it was colonialism. Massa's sole concern was the presence of metropolitan troops and metropolitan battleships to assist him in putting down West Indian disorders. Today, with the PNM, those who were considered by Massa permanently unfitted for self-government, permanently reduced to a status of inferiority, are on the verge of full control of their internal affairs and on the threshold, in their federation, of national independence.

Massa believed in the inequality of races. Today, as never before, the PNM has held out to the population of Trinidad and Tobago and the West Indies and the world the vision and the practice of interracial solidarity which, whatever its limitations, whatever the efforts still needed to make it an ordinary convention of our society, stand out in sharp contrast as an open challenge to Massa's barbarous ideas and practices of racial domination.

Massa was determined not to educate his society. Massa was quite right; to educate is to emancipate. That is why the P.N.M., the army of liberation of Trinidad and the West Indies, has put education in the forefront of its programme. If Massa was entirely destitute of a liberal outlook and learned leisure, the P.N.M., come what may, will go down in history as the author of free secondary education and the architect of the University of Woodford Square.

The D.L.P. statement of March 5 reflects the hostile forces which still exist in our society. There are still Massas. Massa still lives, with his backward ideas of the aristocracy of the skin. And Massa still has his stooges, who prefer to crawl on their bellies to Massa, absentee or resident, Massa this, Massa that, Massa the other, instead of holding their heads high and erect as befits a society which under the P.N.M. is dedicated to the equality of opportunity and a career open to talent. Farquhar is one outstanding example of this contemptible backwardness and this slave mentality. The D.L.P. is another. When they ask me to withdraw my banner, Massa Day Done, they are in fact telling the people of the West Indies that they want Massa to continue in social control, monopolising political power, stultifying economic development, disciplining the workers. They are in fact telling us that they are as much the stooges of the Massa of the 20th century as the house slaves were of Massa's 18th century counterpart.

We of the P.N.M., on the other hand, have been able to incorporate into our people's national movement people of all races and colours and from all walks of life, with the common bond of a national community dedicated to the pursuit of national ends without any special privilege being granted to race, colour, class, creed, national origin, or previous condition of servitude. Some of our most active and most loyal P.N.M. members are indistinguishable in colour from our Massa. In recent weeks I, with several top leaders in the P.N.M., have had the opportunity to meet privately with many representatives of business and the professions in our community, and we have all been struck, notwithstanding a little grumbling here and a little dissatisfaction there, with the large reservoir of goodwill and admiration which the P.N.M. is able to draw upon. You members of the P.N.M. must understand once and for all that you misunderstand your Party and you do a great disservice to your national cause if you think that every white person or every Indian is anti-P.N.M. or that every black person is pro-P.N.M. You shall know them not by their colour or their race but their fruit.

When, therefore, I categorically repudiate the D.L.P.'s impertinent suggestion that I should withdraw a historical analysis which is the product of more than 20 years of assiduous research on the problems of the West Indies in the context of the international community, I unhesitatingly condemn them for betraying, not for the first time and not for the last time, the vital interests of our national community. I accuse them of an intellectual dishonesty which is prepared to accept any bribe and to commit treason to their country in order to grasp political power for themselves. They serve to remind all of us here in the University, which like all reputable Universities must remain dedicated to the pursuit of truth and to the dispassionate discussions of public issues, of two important considerations which are fundamental in P.N.M.'s conception of the national community and in P.N.M.'s crusade for the interracial solidarity—first, not every white is Massa, second, not every Massa is white.

If Sininan attacks me for the statement Massa Day Done, where then does Sininan stand on the question of the canefarmers of Pointe-a-Pierre, Naparima and Caroni whom P.N.M. has just recognised as a vital force in our society, these canefarmers of today who were Massa's indentured Indian workers yesterday? If Sininan attacks me for the statement Massa Day Done, where then does Sininan stand on P.N.M.'s programme of housing for sugar workers and canefarmers which has accelerated the elimination of the disgraceful barracks in which Massa housed his indentured Indian workers against all the invectives of the Englishman, Lechmere Guppy? If Sininan attacks me for the statement Massa Day Done, where then does Sininan stand in respect of the Indians who, as indentured workers, adopted the slave terminology of Massa and were forced into the social and economic status which Massa carried over from the regime of slavery?

I must ask Sininan and the D.L.P. to answer these questions in view of their alleged concern with the problem of the small farmers. The D.L.P. has just published a plan for agriculture with the photograph of Stephen Maharaj; in it they ask for a sound credit system for farmers. Bryan and Richardson led last Saturday an agricultural demonstration from the Eastern Counties demanding aid for the farmers.

Let us recognise immediately the right of any group of people to demonstrate peacefully in our community. Let us recognise immediately that the agricultural demonstration was itself a tribute to the political awakening and the national spirit generated by P.N.M. But when all is said and done, the question remains: Who is the farmer these people have in mind? Massa? It is precisely Massa who has so far directed the operations of the Agricultural Credit Bank set up in 1945 and dominated the facilities extended by it to farmers. Here are some examples of the operations of that Bank:

1. A loan of $10,000 in 1955 for the development of cocoa and citrus; two years later it was ascertained that the estate had a large area in anthuriums, orchids, African violets and roses.

2. A loan of $25,000 in 1954 to pay off a bank overdraft for development; this was followed by another loan for $35,000 a year later again to pay off an overdraft.

3. A loan of $6,000 in 1955 to extend an estate dwelling house; the applicant already owed over $30,000 on two previous loans.
4. A loan of $43,500 in 1955 to an employee of the Bank to purchase an estate.
5. A loan of $13,000 in 1956 to purchase an estate which was sold two months later.
6. Loans of $50,000 and $68,000 in 1955 and 1956 to a large planter who used the money in part to make payments to the press and the church, and to pay dividends, income tax and auditors' fees.
7. Loans of $150,000 in each of the years 1955 and 1956 to a large industrial and commercial concern.

As against this emphasis on large scale agriculture and the big planter who had sufficient security to approach an ordinary commercial bank, the small farmers and agricultural societies were pushed into the background by the Bank. The average loan made to farmers in this category varied between $110 and $175 from 1950 to 1959. Thousands of dollars were left unutilised each year which could have been allocated to small farmers. Small farmers waited months and years for attention, whilst the big farmer was attended to in a matter of days. One such large farmer, who received a loan of $40,000 in August 1957, made his application in July; there were several applications there pending. A large loan of $26,000 was approved in two months in 1956; a small loan of $600 took eleven months.

What is the explanation of this system? It is fourfold — (1) the lack of any precise policy laid down by the Government for the guidance of the Bank; (2) the insufficient liaison between the Bank and the Ministry of Agriculture, which is the organ of Government responsible for agriculture in the country; (3) the composition of the Board and staff of the Bank; (4) the latitude given to all such statutory bodies to function in independence of the Government.

Bryan must have known all of this; if not, why did he not know? The P.N.M. had to learn it. Yet Bryan did not one single thing to correct it. The P.N.M. has had to take the necessary steps. First we transferred the Agricultural Credit Bank to the Ministry of Finance where, as a financial institution, it properly belongs. Second, as soon as the transfer had been effected, the Minister of Finance instituted an investigation into the operations of the Bank. Third, on the basis of that investigation, we proceeded recently to alter the composition of the Board of the Bank. Fourth, we are proceeding shortly to amend further the Ordinance governing the Bank to make available to it for loan purposes additional capital of 1 1/4 million provided in the Five Year Development Programme and to enable it to make loans to fishermen out of a sum of $500,000 earmarked in the Development Programme for this purpose. Finally, we have made available subsidies in many forms to the small farmers, and we are concentrating particularly on the prospects and problems in the world market for our export crops, whilst we have already taken large and positive steps to stimulate a greater production of local foodstuffs and fruits. A new market is now being built on the Beetham Highway to improve the distribution system, while, with the active encouragement of P.N.M.'s Government, a large new factory, Pacmarine, will shortly be in production on Wrightson Road canning local products and so providing an additional market for the farmers.

Bryan was Minister of Agriculture for six years and did none of these things. Now, as a member of the Federal House with not enough to do, he wants me to agree to a radio debate with him on agriculture. He had six years of radio time; now he wants a little lagniappe. Stephen Maharaj and Ashford Sinanan sat in the Legislative Council for six years before the P.N.M. and did nothing to help the canefarmer or the cocoa farmer over whom they now shed crocodile tears. Richardson was a member of P.N.M. General Council. Apart from lobbying to get a seat in a farming area, none of us in the General Council had any suspicion, either from his participation in the work of the General Council or from his silly articles in the Guardian, that he had any affection for the farmers at all. Now he wants a Small Farmers' Association. Will he please tell the small farmers how much money he has been able to borrow from the Agricultural Credit Bank, so that they can compare the Bank's tenderness to a doctor of medicine doing part-time agriculture with its disregard of the genuine agriculturists of the country? To avoid all further misunderstanding on this question of credit, I shall publish forthwith the investigation of the Agricultural Credit Bank which I was, for various reasons, reluctant to make public. Then the small farmers will be able to judge for themselves.

Why this sudden recognition by Bryan, Richardson, Maharaj, Sininan and the D.L.P. of the existence of the samll farmer, when in years gone by they never uttered one single word of condemnation of the Bank's neglect of the small farmer? All that is left for them to do is to blame P.N.M. for the fall in world prices. You know the explanation, Ladies and Gentlemen, as well as I. It is election year, and for guys like these, anything goes. They lack brains, perspective and principle. So they resort to confusion, intrigue and of course the **Guardian,** our old Public Enemy No. 1, whom we sent straight to hell on April 22, 1960.

It has recently been announced that the **Guardian** is to change hands and will hereafter form part of international chain. It is obviously impossible for us to anticipate the line of action that will be taken by the new Canadian owners. We can only wait and see. We note in the meantime that Monday's **Guardian** could find a lot of space for a report on the opening of a D.L.P. office in Gasparillo on Sunday, no space at all for a P.N.M. rally in Morne Diable on the same Sunday, and insufficient space for a truncated report of a monster P.N.M. meeting in San Juan on Saturday night. We can only conclude that the explanation lies in the fact that the D.L.P. function was attended by 125 persons (which no doubt explains the **Guardian's** photograph that suggested a death rather than a birth), while there were at least 5,000 present at P.N.M.'s Morne Diable rally. Monday's **Evening News** reduces the estimated 8,000 at P.N.M.'s San Juan meeting to 1,250; I suppose the reporter got tired of counting. We note also that Gomes today writes on everything under the sun except P.N.M., that Farquhar did not appear last Sunday, that we have been spared for some Sundays Forrester's idiocies, and that the voice in the wilderness of Cassandra seems to have been strangely silent in recent weeks. We watch with interest to see how long the absurd reveiw of the week's news will continue to disgrace the Sunday news. For the rest, as I have said, let us wait and see what the new Canadian ownership will produce. But whilst we wait and see, the danger of a press monopoly continues, with all the evils that that brings in its train even in the advance and diversified United Kingdom society, still more in Trinidad with its legacy of four and a half years of dishonest reporting, deplorably low intellectual standards, and partisan prostitution of freedom of the press. We shall continue our efforts to appraise and to counteract this monopolistic pattern. In these efforts our own Party organ, **The NATION,** has an important role to play as the intelligent voice of the national community, the trumpet of independence, the jealous protector of West Indian interests. In the impending revision of the Canada-West Indies Agreement of 1926, for example, whose side will the Canadian-owned **Guardian** take? The West Indies? or Canada? Now that the principal obstacle to a daily issue of **The NATION** has been removed from the scene, P.N.M. has its own contribution to make to the promotion of political education through the press and to the maintenance of the press from monopolistic control.

Let the D.L.P. know therefore that no amount of attacks on the P.N.M. by Sinanan or the **Guardian** will in any way stop the onward march to national independence and community dignity. No amount of stabs in the back from P.N.M. renegades will stop us either. After all, as a new party, nine months old when we won the 1956 elections, faced with ever-increasing pressures in four and a half years in power as a Government, it was inevitable that scamps and vagabonds and individualists should hop on the band wagon and seek to corrupt the party for their personal ends. We are now finding out those who pretended to support us on Chaguaramas because they thought we would not succeed in our declared policy to tear up the 1941 Agreement. They applauded loudly when I said that I would break the Chaguaramas problem or the Chaguaramas problem would break me; they saw me broken already. Now that I have broken the problem, lo and behold, all the scavenger birds of the P.N.M. suddenly suggest that I changed my direction and they don't like us West of the Iron Curtain. All those who see in Castro a precedent for a few persons lusting for power to take control suddenly begin to attack us for not emulating Castro; they forget we took power peacefully and did not take it from a fascist dictatorship. All such who wish to confuse, who seek to climb on P.N.M.'s backs to achieve their own mental aberrations, who want to abuse me because I refuse to condone corruption in any quarter, all these imps of Satan will be dealt with in the due course. C.L.R. James' case has been sent to our Disciplinary Committee for action; when, it is no longer **sub judice** I shall deal with it fully and publicly, and with all those who seek to use him in their struggle to defeat the P.N.M. and to destroy me.

We go on our way, confident and undaunted. We stand here tonight, we the P.N.M. enormously proud of the confidence the vast majority of the people have in us. We have seen it recently for ourselves, in Tunapuna, in Fyzabad, in Point Fortin, in Princes Town, in Sange Grande, in San Juan, and on Sunday in Morne Diable. If the people wish to abandon that confidence in us, because they don't have a secondary school in Fzyabad, because they don't have price supports in Sangre Grande, because they don't have rental mortgage houses in Princes Town, because they have a dirty drain in San Juan, because the oil companies are reducing their labour force in Point Fortin; if the people want to sell their identification cards to the enemy, or refuse to take their photographs because they have to go to a fete or play cricket or wappie, or can't be bothered to vote, if the people want to sell themselves back into slavery from which P.N.M. has emancipated them; if the people prefer Massa to P.N.M.—then they have the democratic right to make history that will be unique in the world. History is full of instances where slave owners restore or try to restore slavery. I know of no instance when the slaves themselves, once emancipated, return voluntarily to their former chains.

If you wish to do that, Ladies and Gentlemen you must do it without the P.N.M., certainly without me. We shall continue on the road of national dignity and national independence. It is we of the P.N.M. who brought the United States Government to you to renegotiate in Tobago a treaty negotiated for you in London twenty years ago. It is we of the P.N.M. who gave you your flag and ran it up at Chaguaramas to do the saga ting everyday in the breeze. It is we of the P.N.M. who will shortly renegotiate the basis of your relations with Venezuela with a view to removing the discrimination against you that is sixty years old. It is we of the P.N.M. who brought the Secretary of State for the Colonies for the first time in your midst to appreciate at first hand that the future destiny of the West Indies depends on you. With the new Agreement on Chaguaramas, we of the P.N.M. have been able to welcome Sir Winston Churchill to Trinidad. It is we of the P.N.M. who will take the United Kingdom Prime Minister around when he comes on Friday on his historic visit, and I hope hundreds of you will be at Piarco to welcome him. It is we of the P.N.M. who will show him around some of our development projects, who take him to Chaguaramas, who will take the lead in making representations to him in respect of West Indian migration to the United Kingdom, protection for West Indian products and economic aid to the West Indies, in order to assure economic stability as the foundation of our political democracy.

It is only left now for Her Majesty the Queen to visit us. After all we are an important part of the Commonwealth, and if Her Majesty can go to Australia, to India and to Pakistan, to Nigeria and to Ghana, she can come also to the West Indies. There will shortly be an appropriate occasion for so distinguished a visit. Her Majesty's sister, Princess Margaret, inaugurated the Federal Parliament on April 22, 1958. The Federation will arrange for its independence at a conference in London scheduled to begin on May 31. I now publicly propose that Her Majesty the Queen be invited to inaugurate the first Parliament of the Independent West Indies on April 22, 1962, at 11 o'clock in the morning.

And so we stand ready to meet the challenge of this year's election. The challenger calls himself the D.L.P. but he goes under many aliases and has no fixed abode. He stands for nothing in particular; he poses as the champion of labour and the small farmer but worships at the shrine of Massa. He has been repudiated by Britain and America and the **Guardian** has sold out under him. He has offices but no party. Like ancient Gaul, he is divided into three parts.

Defending our title is the P.N.M., the party of principle and not of wealth, the party of the people and not of Massa, the voice of the national consciousness and not of individual or sectional privilege, the mass movement of the national community and not the divisive tendency of an unassimilated splinter group. With our new electoral procedure we eliminate corruption, protect the living from the dead, identify the individual, and ensure free, honest and unperverted elections. With our free secondary education we safeguard equality of opportunity and a career open to talent.

With the University of Woodford Square in the lead, we have called upon the many rather than the few for financial assistance for our cause, to enable the Party as such not the individual candidate to finance the election campaign. By so doing we ensure greater discipline of and control over the elected representatives. The population is contributing magnificently. I have here with me tonight a dollar turned over to Dr. Solomon as a contribution to our Public Appeal for Funds by a young man, a member of the P.N.M., who was given it by an Opposition Member whom he assisted with changing a flat tyre in the early hours of one morning after a late sitting of the Legislative Council. Once again therefore, tonight, our Women's League will, with the permission of the Police, solicit your contribution in our official receptacles. Tonight of all nights I call on you to help us, for tonight of all nights Massa Day Done.

And so we proceed to the election bearing aloft proudly our banner of interracial solidarity, with the slogan inscribed thereon, Massa Day Done, and below it the immortal words of Abraham Lincoln who dealt Massa in the United States of America a mortal blow:

> *"With malice toward none; with charity for all; with firmness in the right, as God gives us to see the right, let us strive on to finish the work we are in."*

Williams speaking with Kwane Nkrumah of Ghana in 1964.

INDEPENDENCE DAY ADDRESS

by Eric E. Williams

Williams with his daughter Erica in 1956.

Eric Williams's Broadcast to the Nation, August 31, 1962, the first day of national independence.

INDEPENDENCE DAY ADDRESS

Fellow Citizens,

It is a great honour to me to address this morning the citizens of the Independent Nation of Trinidad and Tobago as their first Prime Minister. Your National Flag has been hoisted, to the strains of your National Anthem, against the background of your National Coat of Arms, and amidst the beauty of your National Flower.

Your Parliament has been inaugurated by Her Royal Highness the Princess Royal, the representative of Her Majesty the Queen. You have your own Governor General and your own Chief Justice, both appointed on the advice of your own Prime Minister. You have your own National Guard, however small.

You are now a member of the Commonwealth Family in your own right, equal in status to any other of its members. You hope soon to be a member of the World Family of Nations, playing your part, however insignificant, in world affairs. You are on your own in a big world, in which you are one of many nations, some small, some medium size, some large. You are nobody's boss and nobody is your boss.

What use will you make of your independence? What will you transmit to your children five years from today? Other countries have ceased to exist in that period. Some, in much less time, have become totally disorganised, a prey to anarchy and civil war.

The first responsibility that devolves upon you is the protection and promotion of your democracy. Democracy means more, much more, than the right to vote and one vote for every man and every woman of the prescribed age. Democracy means recognition of the rights of others. Democracy means equality of opportunity for all in education, in the public service, and in private employment—I repeat, and in private employment. Democracy means the production of the weak against the strong.

Democracy means the obligation of the minority to recognise the right of the majority. Democracy means responsibility of the

Independence Day Address

Government to its citizens, the protection of the citizens from the exercise of arbitrary power and the violation of human freedoms and individual rights. Democracy means freedom of worship for all and the subordination of the right of any one race to the overrriding right of the human race. Democracy means freedom of expression and assemble of organization.

All that is Democracy. All that is our Democracy, to which I call upon all citizens to dedicate themselves on this our Independence Day. This is what I meant when I gave the Nation its slogan for all time: Discipline, Production, Tolerance. Indiscipline, whether individual or sectional, is a threat to democracy. Slacking on the job jeopardizes the national income, inflates costs, and merely sets a bad example. The medieval churchmen had a saying that to work is to pray. It is also to strengthen our democracy by improving our economic foundations.

That democracy is but a hollow mockery and a gigantic fraud which is based on a ruling group's domination [of] slaves or helots or fellaheen or second class citizens or showing intolerance to others because of considerations of race, colour, creed, national origin, previous conditions of servitude or other irrationality.

Our National Flag belongs to all our citizens. Our National Coat of Arms, with our National Birds inscribed therein, is the sacred thrust of our citizens. So it is today, please, I urge you, let it always be so. Let us always be able to say, with the Psalmist, behold, how good and how pleasant it is for brethren to dwell together in unity.

United at home in the common effort to build a democratic Nation and ostracise outmoded privileges, let us present to the outside world the united front of a Nation thinking for itself, knowing its own mind and speaking its own point of view.

Let us take our stand in the international family on the basic principles of international rectitude. When our time comes to vote, let it always be a vote for freedom and against slavery, for self-determination and against external control, for integration and against division.

Democracy at home and abroad, the symbol of it is our Parliament. Remember Follow citizens, we now have a Parliament, we no longer have the colonial assemblies which did not have the full rights of a Parliament of a sovereign country. The very name "Parliament" testifies to our new Independent status. By that same token, however, we at once become the object of comparison with other Parliamentary countries, inside and outside the Commonwealth.

This is a consideration which involves not only the Members of Parliament but also the individual citizen. The Members of Parliament have the traditional Parliamentary privileges guaranteed in the Constitution. The Speaker, the symbol of the power of Parliament, has his status guaranteed in the Order of Precedence. We shall soon have a Privileges Bill protecting and prescribing the powers of Parliament itself. Measures are being taken to establish the responsibility of Parliament in the field of external relations.

The Constitution recognises the positon of the Leader of the Opposition and the normal parliamentary convention of consultation between Government and Opposition are being steadily developed and expanded. The Constitution itself, Independence itself, represent the agreement of the two political parties on the fundamental question of national unity. The ordinary citizen must recognise the role of the Parliament in our democracy and must learn to differentiate between a Member of Parliament, whom he may like or dislike, and the respect that must be accorded to that same Member of Parliament *ex-officio.*

I call on all citizens from now on to accord the highest respect to our Parliamentary system and institutions and to our Parliament itself.

Democracy, finally, rests on a higher power than Parliament. It rests on an informed and cultivated and alert public opinion. The Members of Parliament are only the representatives of the citizens. They cannot represent apathy and indifference. They can play the part allotted to them only if they represent intelligence and public spiritness.

Independence Day Address

Nothing has so demonstrated in the past six years the capacity of the People of Trinidad and Tobago than their remarkable interest in public affairs. The development and expansion of that interest is the joint responsibility of the Government, the Parliament, the political parties and relevant civic organisations.

Those, Fellow citizens, are the thoughts which, on my first day as Prime Minister, I wish to express to you on Independence Day. Your success in organising the Independence which you achieved will exercise a powerful influence on your neighbours with all of whom we are likely to have close associations in the next few years, the smallest and nearest, as part of our Independent Unitary State, the larger and more distant as part of the wider and integrated Caribbean community. Problems of difficulties there will be. These are always a challenge to a superior intelligence and to strength of character.

Whatever the challenge that faces you, from whatever quarter, place always first the national interest and the national cause. The strength of the Nation depends on the strength of its citizens. Our National Anthem invokes God's blessings on our Nation, in response to those thousands of citizens of all faiths who demanded God's protection in our Constitution.

Let us then as a Nation so conduct ourselves as to be able always to say in those noblest and most inspiring words of St. Paul, "By the Grace of God we as people are what we are, and His Grace in us hath not been void."

THE CHAGUARAMAS DECLARATION
—Perspectives for the New Sociey

by Eric E. Williams

Williams addressing an audience at Chaguaramas Convention Centre.

This address was delivered at a Special Convention of the People's National Movement, held at Chaguaramas Convention Centre on November 27–29, 1970.

THE CHAGUARAMAS DECLARATION
–Perspectives for the New Society

1—INTRODUCTION

On January 24, 1956, the People's National Movement issued its clarion call in *The People's Charter* for a national consensus with the establishment of a mass Party open to all classes:

> "... Nor are we an ordinary Party in the accepted narrow sense of the word. We are rather a rally, a convention of all and for all, a mobilisation of all the forces in the community, cutting across race and religion, class and colour, with emphasis on united action by all the people in the common cause...."

We were careful to emphasise further in the *Charter:*
> "We are not another of the transitory and artificial combinations to which you have grown accustomed in election years, or another bandwaggon of dissident and disappointed politicians each out merely to get a seat in the Legislature."

Our opponents confidently predicted that the PNM would not survive the 1956 General Elections. Parties have come and gone since 1956, too numerous to be counted. Parties will continue to come and go after 1970. The PNM was and is Trinidad and Tobago's first recognised national Party. PNM brought party politics to Trinidad and Tobago.

The PNM has, in its 14-year history, led Trinidad and Tobago first to self-government, then to Independence. It has made the voice of Trinidad and Tobago heard in the United Nations, the Commonwealth, the Organisation of American States, and meetings of the Third World countries. It played a leading part in the ill-fated Federation of the West Indies, and is one of the moving spirits in Carifta.

For fourteen years our party has been the symbol of stability and orderly and constructive change, the envy of our opponents, the whipping-boy of those who wish to see the substitution of

The Chaguaramas Declaration

undisguised ministerial individualism free from the fetters of either collective Cabinet responsibility or party influence.

In our Annual and Special Conventions which are incomprehensible to those who know nothing of how a reputable party operates, we have repeatedly raised matters of vital national concern and taken democratic decisions for the guidance of the Government which we of the PNM have put into power.

We need only recall here Chaguaramas (which we inherited in 1956 as a 99-year American naval base), Independence as against participation in a truncated federation, the Caribbean Economic Community (initiated by the establishment of Carifta in 1968), joining the Organisation of American States, Family Planning, and, most recently, the Republic.

The People's Charter of 1956 was not intended to be a final document for all time. Politics is the art of the possible. New circumstances constantly arise posing new challenges, demanding new emphases, requiring adjustment and emendation. In fact in 1956 *The People's Charter* was a revolutionary document. With the increasing tendency to fragmentation in the 1970s, PNM must continue to be revolutionary. For the urgent cry on all sides in 1970 in Trinidad and Tobago and indeed in the entire Caribbean is for further social and economic change to complete the process of Independence. In fact, the beginning of the Decade of the Seventies finds the Caribbean area in a revolutionary mood.

The word "revolution" has always held terrors for the privileged groups in the Caribbean. This is one of the principal characteristics we have inherited from the period of slavery and colonialism. In part also it is an indication of our lack of awareness of the world in which we live.

It is generally not understood that the constitutional and democratic form of government in the United Kingdom which the privileged groups so admire as the "Mother Country" was the result of a bloody civil war in the 17th century in which the King of England was decapitated. The American nation, to which the privileged groups increasingly look as the principal source of foreign investment, was the result of a revolution which we know as the War of American Independence. The triumph of liberal capitalism in Europe, which the privileged groups consider the only pattern of development for a developing country like ours, was the result of the French Revolution. The whole white world as we know it today is the product of change and upheaval—sometimes violent, sometimes non-violent, some of it fairly recent, some of it representing the reopening of old sores; one has only to look at Northern Ireland today.

We need not therefore be too haunted by the spectre of revolutionary change. What is involved is the way in which this change is to come about. Four specific questions arise:

(1) Will the change come through violence or through peaceful and orderly methods? To go a little further, will the change be guided by rational objectives and rational means, or are we to be caught up in the romantic, anarchistic fantasies (without programme or objective) of the "New Left" attitudes imported from contemporary Western Europe and North America?

(2) Will the change involve the emergence of a totalitarian society, or is it to take place within the framework of the democratic structure and organisation we are trying to develop—with all that this inescapably means in terms of dissent *as long as dissent does not mean sedition, mutiny and coup d'etat?*

(3) Will the change lead to a reduction in our standard of living or will it produce better material conditions with a more equitable distribution of the national product, and with enhanced employment opportunities for all?

(4) Will the change lead to greater tension between the two historically dispossessed groups in our society and between white and non-white, or to the achievement of self-respect by the two historically dispossessed races and to solidarity among

the diverse elements of our multi-racial Nation on the basis of genuine fraternity and mutual respect?

Revolutionary change is not only demanded in the Caribbean today; it is also, in view of our past history and historical imperative necessary to confer real and meaningful power, self-discipline and self-determination upon those who have been historically dispossessed.

Two main categories stand out among the dispossessed—the descendants of the African slaves and the indentured workers brought in from what are today India and Pakistan. We need change in order to carry to its logical conclusion the movement for political independence which we initiated in 1956 and achieved in 1962 as a part of the general world movement against colonialism which began in India in 1947 and spread to Africa in the sixties with the Independence of Ghana and the successful Algerian War of Liberation.

This change will come either through peaceful means or violence. If it does not come through peaceful means, the extreme and often despairing forms of Black Power concepts imported from the United States of America will ensure that it comes through violence. Just as we achieved political independence through peaceful means, so we can achieve meaningful economic and social change without resorting to violence.

But social and economic change will come through peaceful means only if our Government as well as other Caribbean Governments reconstruct and reshape the distorted, unjust, irrational structures inherited from our historical past. This reconstruction must be guided by a philosophy and a sense of direction rooted in the history and in the potentiality of the dispossessed peoples of the Caribbean.

The history of the Caribbean has failed to confer either power of dignity on the dispossessed. The manipulation of the economy, society and culture by external forces over the last four and a half centuries has undoubtedly contributed to a certain degree of material prosperity among many sections of the population (more so in Trinidad and Tobago than elsewhere, because of oil); but it has not conferred upon the masses the power of self-determination or dignity. They have no economic power; theirs is a largely borrowed culture and set of values; they need to have greater pride in themselves; they think of themselves not as a Nation but as an island still in the colonial period from which the only form of escape is emigration to the ghettoes of the United States of America, with the recent addition of the incipient ghettoes in the United Kingdom and Canada.

II—THE TASK OF RECONSTRUCTION

The task of reconstruction can thus be simply stated: to allow the West Indian people

- to acquire economic as well as political power, steps being taken to ensure that all people share equitably in the benefits of reconstruction and economic advancement,
- to make their own culture,
- to participate fully in both the political and economic process, and
- to become true men instead of what one critic has savagely called us mimics.

Considerable progress has been made in this direction in Trinidad and Tobago since 1956 when the PNM took charge of the destiny of the country. The achievement of first self-government and then independence has made it possible for the society to progress in a variety of fields.

One of the most important of these is education. Before 1956 secondary education was reserved to those who could afford the high fees charged in the few schools available. Between 1956 and 1969, the enrolment in secondary schools more than tripled. In 1960 secondary education was made free. In the subsequent nine years 46,718 free places were provided as compared with 1,116

The Chaguaramas Declaration

free places in the nine years before PNM took over.

The number of secondary schools increased from 15 to 44; in 1970 twelve Junior Secondary Schools are under construction.

In accordance with the original People's Charter, much emphasis has been placed on the small man, especially in the field of agriculture with the development of the Crown Lands Programme. Between 1956 and 1969, nearly 12,000 acres of Crown Lands have been distributed to small farmers. 866 small farms have been developed by the Government, and a further 468 are under development at a total cost, up to June 1970, of $11 million; and there have been large increases of production of meat, poultry, milk and food crops. In the field of business the small man is coming into his own and cooperatives are being actively encouraged.

In the field of housing, significant improvements have been registered. Between 1956 and 1969, 7,375 new housing units have been provided, exclusive of 6,058 in sugar areas; in 1970 a comprehensive attack had been launched on the urban ghetto and the unsatisfactory semi-urban and rural housing, with priority to the elimination of Shanty Town and the rehabilitation of John John.

Positive steps have been taken, especially under the Third Five Year Plan, drafted in 1968, to provide for participation by the Government of Trinidad and Tobago in many economic areas formerly left to the private sector, and especially the foreign private sector—oil, sugar, chemicals, banking, external and internal communications, hotels.

The PNM has consciously encouraged grassroots involvement through the Village Council Movement, has paid increasing attention to handicraft, and has taken steps to develop economic and social programmes for youths. One hundred and thirty Community Centres, four Youth Camps and six Youth Centres have been constructed at a cost of over three million dollars.

Great emphasis had been placed on the promotion of a national culture at the expense of foreign importations—assistance has been given to the calypso, steelband and Indian music, and folklore encouraged by the Best Village Competition.

Infrastructure development in the fields of electricity, water, sewerage, drainage and roads has been promoted—water production has trebled, electricity generated has increased nearly sevenfold, 30 miles of new roads have been built, 662 miles of water mains have been laid, while $5 million has been spent on public bus transport since 1965.

Prior to 1956, Tobago was the victim of gross neglect. PNM changed this—two new secondary schools, the North Coast Road, electricity in all but two villages, new dairy and pig farms, two new coastal steamers, drastic renovation of the airport, encouragement of new hotel construction, a new bus transport service, an improved water supply. In 1970 new houses are going up in Bon Accord and are soon to go up at Charlotteville, while the redevelopment of Lower Scarborough, with first priority to a new market and a bus terminal, is in progress.

The Trinidad and Tobago inherited by the PNM in 1956 has been changed physically beyond recognition in 1970.

But three serious shortcomings have emerged. The first is that, notwithstanding the establishment of three major centres of technical education, the vocational requirements of the country have been subordinated to the academic, thus perpetuating the colonial traditions of grammar school certificates and external examinations. This is being corrected with the decision in 1970 to construct 15 vocational schools, four of which are to be constructed in 1970-71—one of these is to be located in Tobago.

The second shortcoming is the slow rate of progress in the achievement of genuine equality between the various ethnic groups and the removal of discrimination and prejudice in employment in the private sector against non-whites, especially in banks and other financial institutions. This matter is now being competently investigated.

The third shortcoming has been the difficulty experienced in providing a satisfactory level of employment for our rapidly growing labour force. Between 1956 and 1969 the number of persons with jobs increased from 250,100 to 318,300— or by 68,200. At the same time the number of persons without jobs increased over the same period from 17,000 to 50,000—or by 33,100. In other words, we have succeeded in providing jobs only for two out of three persons joining the labour force over the past fourteen years.

This kind of experience with unemployment has been typical of nearly all the Third World countries. Much of the difficulty has had to do with the high rate of movement from rural areas and rural occupations to the towns.

While this factor has operated in Trinidad and Tobago, there have been other aggravating circumstances—such as large-scale retrenchment in the oil and sugar industries, the distorted pattern of wage and salary rates, the capital-intensive industries which have been established, and the high rate of population growth. Apart from the programme of Vocational Training now in progress, we shall need to devise a future strategy of development which will be more oriented towards employment creation than the previous one.

Thus, despite the concrete gains since 1956, much remains to be done, and determined efforts are required during the Decade of the Seventies to carry further the work of constructing a *New Society* in our country. This task must be guided by an articulated and clear-cut philosophy.

III—GUIDELINES FOR THE NEW SOCIETY

But what philosophy, by what set of concepts and values, will this task of reconstruction be guided? Should it be guided by liberal capitalism or by Marxism—the two mainstreams of social thought which Europe has produced?

The answer to this crucial question, in the opinion of the PNM, is that this process of reconstruction should be guided neither by liberal capitalism nor by Marxism, at least in their pure forms.

The respective merits of the two systems in promoting economic growth are still being hotly debated by their proponents.

Without going into their respective merits, we can say that both systems are capable under certain conditions of producing rapid economic growth. Certainly, we in Trinidad and Tobago must seek faster economic growth.

But we must seek more than mere growth. Our former metropolitan masters have in the past relentlessly pursued economic growth at the price of human degradation and at the price of creating an artificially fragmented economy and society, controlled from outside and relying on the indiscriminate importation of labour—from Europe, from Africa, from India, Pakistan, and elsewhere. Economic growth we must have, but growth within the framework of a humane, cohesive and self-determining society where the individual can fully realise his or her full human dignity. We must, therefore, judge the relevance of these two forms of social and economic organisation by criteria which include, but go beyond, their capacity to promote economic growth.

Liberal capitalism is patently inadequate as a guide; for, whether in its 19th-century Victorian form, analysed by Marx, or its 20th-century American form, it leads to inequality (tempered but not eliminated, by the Welfare State); denial of human values; lack of effective participation of the masses of the people; and at least in the 20th-century America, almost total alienation. Both the atomistic, competitive capitalism of 19th-century Britain and the 20th-century competition of large corporations, if adopted, will fail to involve the people and so lead to increasing alienation and lack of commitment.

The ideal of Marxism, with its ultimate vision of liberated, non-alienated Man making his own history, has not been realised. The Marxist state has not withered away, as the Communist propaganda has promised; rather, it has been strengthened. Where Marxism has been adopted, it has led to totalitarianism and the exclusion of popular participation in the political and economic process. In addition, it cannot yet claim to have satisfied the needs of the population for material benefits equitably distributed among all members.

Thus in Trinidad and Tobago, and in the Caribbean as a whole, we are thrown back upon our own resources in developing a philosophy. This, in the opinion of PNM, is all to the good. For a relevant philosophy, a relevant ideology, must arise from the specific historical experience of a people under specific conditions. The outstanding examples in today's Third World are Tanzania in Africa and Peru in Latin America. Even a cursory glance at Caribbean history will show that West Indian man is, because of his peculiar history, *sui generis,* almost unique.

We must devise a system which gives a central place to the idea of the sovereignty of the people. The people must participate actively in decision-making in political and economic matters; they must shape their own culture, welding all the separate strands that have been imported into our society into one new composite national culture. In other words, they must, after more than four hundred years of being acted upon, act for themselves. From being the passive objects of history, they must become the active agents. They must shape their own future and their own destiny.

Let us develop this central guiding idea under different aspects.

A—POLITICAL ASPECTS

(1) Political Independence

Politically, the Caribbean must be fully independent. It must shed the remnants of colonialism still existing and the bastard compromise of Associate Statehood foisted upon it recently. It is our political independence that makes it possible for the people to shape their future. We must preserve our political independence in the Caribbean, not only from the former metropolitan powers but also from the new substitutes that threaten to emerge. It is fashionable today for many of the young people in the Caribbean to sneer at the idea of mere political independence: they never had to live as their parents did, under the colonial regime. Political independence is the highway to the achievement of economic independence, popular participation in the economy and cultural autonomy.

(2) Popular Participation

In addition to political independence, there must be full popular participation in the political process. The Caribbean had to fight hard and long for universal adult suffrage and the removal of the abomination of Crown Colony rule which, in its purest form, permitted no elections and simply allowed nomination at the whim of the Governor responsible only to his metropolitan overlords. It is clear today, however, that while universal adult suffrage provides a necessary condition for popular control and participation, it is not a sufficient condition. Because of their long history of Crown Colony government, especially in Trinidad (though not in Tobago), the people are still to be brought into a meaningful participation in the political process. Hence the need for a greater degree of Local Government and a greater number of consultative mechanisms at various levels, including village councils, youth, and other grass-roots organisations. This applies with special force to Tobago, separated as it is by sea from the capital of the country.

(3) Constitution Reform

The question of Constitution Reform arises here. This raises two fundamental issues—the Republic and the Senate.

First, the Republic. A republican constitution, notwithstanding the antics that have been indulged in, is the obvious expression of our national identity and our psychological break with our former connection with the Imperial Power. It brings us in line with the Third World—Latin America, for example, has expressly repudiated monarchy. The question is, should we think in terms of an executive President, as obtains in Latin America, or in terms of a President who is Head of State but not Head of Government, as in India? The question is not really one of centralisation versus decentralisation of power, as some people seem inclined to think; for even in an executive Presiential type of system it is possible to provide a large number of checks and balances on the power of the Chief Executive and to develop a number of consultive mechanisms so that many shades of community opinion can be brought to bear upon important decisions.

The other issue is the nature, powers and composition of the Upper House. The PNM in 1961 made an advance on the Parliamentary practice in force in most of the developing countries in recommending the setting up of a Senate with representation for several community interests—such as Labour, Business and Religion. In fact the concept of a broadly-based Upper House for Trinidad and Tobago goes back to ideas first enunciated in 1955.* These ideas were based on two considerations deriving from an analysis of the special circumstances of Trinidad and Tobago— the fragmented and heterogeneous nature of our society caused by our peculiar history, and the need to involve as many sections of the population as possible in the political process. It appears to us now that we should carry the principle somewhat further and seek to provide representation on the Senate for Local Government representatives, Co-operatives and representatives of art and culture. But this is obviously not the place for specific detailed recommendations for Constitutional Reform. The PNM's specific proposals will shortly be presented in another document.

(4) Role of the People

The people can be involved in governing through elections; through the provisions of the Constitution, providing for example for more broadly based representation on the Senate; through more meaningful Local Government; and through activity in political parties. One other way which suggests itself is the estab-

---

*Eric Williams—Constitution Reform in Trinidad and Tobago, People's Education Movement, July 19, 1955.

lishment of non-partisan Local Committees (for example, Village Councils in rural areas and District Groups in urban areas) to advise on incompetence or corruption on the part of the Executive—at both political and official levels. This might have its dangers in that it may promote rumour-mongering and *mauvaise langue* but it is a democratic procedure, quite unlike the practice in totalitarian countries where Committees of Public Safety and the like are part of a monolithic Party-cum-State apparatus. New techniques of political organisation and Government would have to be employed.

(5) Confidence in the People

In the conception of the *New Society* based on active participation of the masses in all aspects of the economic, social and cultural life, the importance of leaders having confidence in the people is central. Attitudes which claim that as soon as the people assert themselves they are wishing to "create another Haiti" are not only colonialist; they are simplt based on fear of popular resurgence and cultural renaissance. Unless rulers have confidence in the people their rule will be highly authoritarian and they will never feel secure or legitimate in their power.

To say that leaders should have confidence in the people is not to deny the need for leadership; nor is it to forget that social discipline is of the utmost importance in achieving the goals of reconstruction.

Only the romantic anarchists of the "New Left" in America and Europe would carry populism to insane lengths and be blind to the need for the exercise of leadership. Indeed in any popularly based process of economic and social transformation, sound and intelligent leadership at all levels is required—unless the population is to rush blindly down the slope of perdition. Not just at the level of the ministerial arm of the central government, but also the party, the trade union, the public service, the local government body, the co-operative, the community group, the sports club, the social club—leadership should be seen as giving focus, direction and organisation to vaguely apprehended popular aspirations. In fact the real difference between authoritarian and popular systems is that in the latter case the number of leaders required to make the system work exceeds the number necessary in the former.

Moreover leaders in the popular systems have to be sensitive to popular aspirations and demands. Their role is that of providing coherence, organisation and inspiration. They have to give direction to (but not suppress) popular imagination by indicating the limits of the people and translating vague enthusiasms into concrete programmes.

Leadership implies organisation and organisation spells discipline.

But discipline in the *New Society* must not only be externally induced through leadership and organisation. It has also to be "internalised." And the "internalisation" of discipline in the masses comes about through commitment, which is essentially a moral relationship between the individual and a set of values, or an ideology, and between the same individual and leaders who share the set of values of ideology.

(6) Theory and Practice

A set of guiding principles on which national life is based is not a fixed guide, valid forever. These principles must themselves evolve in accordance with changes in objective circumstances and with changes in the people's consciousness and perception. They are also modified, enlarged and developed through practical activity—through the constant attempts to put them into practice and to achieve them as far as they are capable of being achieved. In the course of this practical activity they are tested and given more and fuller meaning. Thus the guiding principles of 1970 cannot entirely be the same as the guiding principles of 1956.

Moreover, we must not forget that an ideology has meaning only so far as the proponents seek to put it into practice, not only in relation to the nation as a whole through State laws, edicts and policies, but also in relation to the individual proponents themselves. The importance of this concrete translation of principle into practice is to be seen in the fact that the masses will seek to make efforts and sacrifices only if they know and are fully aware that all sections of the communtiy are sharing their efforts and sacrifices.

(7) Popular Participation and Totalitarianism

Many are of the opinion that a totalitarian system practising a high degree of centralised planning constitutes a better framework for effective rapid economic and social transformation than a more decentralised participation type of politics and political and economic system. Current experience elsewhere in the world does not support this argument. Apart from the certainty of such a system suppressing the potential and initiative of the people, the real question is: for how long can the leaders under such a system hope to secure commitment from the people? It would seem that this type of regime can continue to secure popular commitment (or at least to be able to maintain itself in power) for any appreciable length of time only if there is some external threat—in the case of Russia in the inter-war period, the capitalist countries, particularly Germany; in the case of Cuba, the U.S.A.; and in the case of China, the U.S.A. and the U.S.S.R.

Thus widespread popular participation would seem to be the only basis for hoping to secure long-run commitment to a drastic process of economic and social transformation demanding continuing sacrifices from the masses of the people.

In 1956 the P.N.M. propounded the concept of Morality in Public Affairs and was universally acclaimed for introducing this principle into the political life of Trinidad and Tobago. The party will pursue this ideal and will go further by ensuring that appropriate legislation is enacted to give effect to the principle.

B—ECONOMIC ASPECTS
(1) Ending of Foreign Domination of the Economy

Political independence sets the stage for, but does not guarantee, economic independence. If in the 1940s and 1950s the countries of the Third World fought against political colonialism, today they have to contend with the infinitely more subtle danger of neo-colonialism.

We have to recognise that too much dependence on metropolitan governments and metropolitan firms is incompatible with the economic sovereignty of the people of the Caribbean. (This has become a matter of concern even to some developed countries). Too much domination by the giant international corporations has the same effect in suppressing the potential of the West Indian people as did the mercantile links of the plantation economy of the 17th and 18th centuries.

Economic independence refers to a state of affairs in which major decision making on economic matters becomes internal to the country. It does not mean an end to contact with the outside world.

Once a country has, and intends to keep, the key sectors of its economy under control, it can then freely engage on a reciprocal basis in economic intercourse with other countries—through capital inflows and through international trade—without any undue fear of foreign economic domination. Indeed a country can be truly interdependent with the rest of the world in economic matters only when it has achieved a certain amount of economic independence. Where it has failed to achieve a certain measure of economic independence, its relationship with the rest of the world (metropolitan governments and the giant international corporations) is one of dependence and mendicancy. An economically independent country needs to trade; and the need to trade is greater, the smaller the size of the country. In fact, a reconstructed Trinidad and Tobago will have to attach supreme importance to the expansion of exports, particularly of manufactured goods and of new non-traditional agricultural products.

All this means that we have to strengthen popular participation in the economic life of the country. We have to localise decision-making over the key sectors of our economy. This can be done, as was indicated clearly in 1968 in the Draft Third Five Year Plan, in a number of ways:

- The assumption by the State of outright ownership (with compensation) of certain foreign controlled enterprises (e.g. The Bank of London and Montreal, Orange Grove Estate, Trinidad and Tobago Television (90%) and Radio Guardian);
- Fifty-one per cent participation by the State in foreign firms (Caroni, Cable and Wireless);
- Joint ventures on a fifty-fifty basis with foreign firms (Trinidad-Tesoro Limited and Telephones);
- Governmental regulation over particular enterprises (e.g. The Petroleum Act).

With respect to new enterprises, we have also to ensure that there is meaningful participation by the Public Sector, or by the National Private Sector, or by a combination of both. We must also move towards greater national decision-making in respect of the banking and financial system, which locates resources of capital and credit for the whole economy and therefore acts as its central nervous system. (We have in our time seen this happening not only in India, Tanzania and Uganda, but also in Canada).

Such regulatory policies designed to prevent complete economic penetration by highly efficient foreign enterprises well-endowed with capital, know-how and managerial and organisational skills, and to promote and develop a national economy are being resisted by some local businessmen. This is indeed strange, seeing that the very purpose of the policy is to protect and expand the area of decision-making (and profitable opportunity) for national enterprise—both public and private.

The only conceivable reason for this curious reaction, so different from that of the majority of Latin American and other Third World businessmen, is the long strangulation of local initiative by our centuries-old colonial economy to the point where there is not a large enough number of national and nationally oriented self-confident businessmen. Just as many among the dispossessed need to cast off their attitude of dependence on the government, so do many of the business people have to cast off their inferiority complex vis-a-vis the large international corporation and come to realise that they are capable of doing much of the job of developing the country. They must make up their minds—do they belong to the Nation of Trinidad and Tobago or do they belong to the international enterprise? Do they belong to a country of the Third World or do they belong to the metropolis? It is in the last analysis a question of identity.

Moreover, the population as a whole will have to be ready to face both external and internal pressures in favour of completely open-door policies for foreign investment and unregulated purchase of land by foreigners. A Caribbean country has always been expected to conform to what outsiders in the metropolitan countries ordain is best for it. No sooner does a Caribbean country analyse its situation for itself and formulate a new policy, than it attracts the disapproving attention of outsiders as well as insiders who speak for the outsiders. Such pressures are, therefore, inevitable. We must not lose heart, especially when we see that another Caribbean country is also valiantly trying to reshape its economy and society in the face of similar external and internal pressures. Sacrifices may well be necessary in order to withstand the pressures; and, if and when they do come, such sacrifice must be made from top to bottom.

All this does not mean that we should reject foreign private capital and foreign aid. What it implies is that we must ensure that such aid and capital must become adjuncts to our internal effort, not the centre-piece of our development strategy. Development is something which in the long run can be achieved only by the people of this country themselves. Foreign aid and foreign private capital are necessary to help us achieve this goal. We need and want foreign aid and foreign private capital, not foreign economic domination.

(2) The Role of the Public Sector

The Public Sector itself, as the instrument of the people, is one such means. In any programme for reconstruction the economic role of the State must go beyond the provision of economic and social infrastructure. It must engage in productive activities and generally act as an entrepreneur. This is because the State in a popularly controlled society represents the people. Consequently any activity of the State in productive activity represents at one remove the economic power of the people. The State must also, as we have seen, regulate the terms under which foreign private capital has access into the country, in order to make sufficient room for the flowering of national initiative and national enterprise and in order to provide opportunities for the maximum participation of the people of the country in the country's development with emphasis on equal opportunity for all and the elimination of all forms of discrimination.

This role of the State imposes heavy responsibilities on members of the Public Service, who often complain that their services in the past have received inaqeduate recognition and appreciation by the public. In the new dispensation this vital area of the State must receive greater recognition. Equally, when the Public Service secures better terms and conditions of service, the public is entitled to demand an even higher standard of performance and increased productivity.

(3) Encouragement of the National Private Sector

With regard to the local private sector we must not be doctrinaire and oppose the development of a national and nationally-oriented private sector. One of the goals of the *New Society* must be the promotion of a national and nationally-oriented private sector, with widespread diffusion of share ownership among the people. We must definitely avoid the mistake made by many so-called "Socialist" Third World countries in seeking State domination of the entire economy. There should in fact be every opportunity provided for a nationally controlled private sector, broadly owned, to expand. Every opportunity, too, ought to be provided for those of our nationals now living abroad in North America and Britain, who have accumulated some capital, some skills and some degree of entrepreneurial expertise, to return home and set up business, thus joining the national private sector.

The importance of wide diffusion of share ownership in the nationally controlled private sector is of the greatest importance. For it is possible to have a "nationalist" development policy where the prime agents and beneficiaries are a limited group of the society. But this option is simply not open to the Caribbean. The masses of the people, after their long period of dispossession, are no longer content to be precluded from participation in the economy. Whoever does not understand this in the Seventies understands nothing.

The task before us now is, therefore, to devise strategy, institutions and mechanisms for achieving the maximum degree of popular participation in the economy by those whom our history has dispossessed, particularly those whose ancestors came from Africa, India and Pakistan.

(4) Motivation of the People towards Self-Reliance

Apart from the operation of the public sector, the issue of shares to workers and the people generally is another means of ensuring popular participation in the economy. But we also need a more direct association between the people and economic activity. To achieve this association means emphasis on the co-operative which not only ensures direct participation by the small man but also produces motivation; and it is motivation which is needed among the dispossessed of our country.

This motivation is of greater importance to those whose

ancestry relates to Africa rather than to those whose ancestry relates to India and Pakistan. For historical and cultural reasons, the people of African descent in the country have not been sufficiently drawn to agricultural and business enterprises as proprietors and owners. It must be appreciated here that this was a conscious decision of the State, both local and metropolitan, in the period of slavery. There were laws which limited the ownership of land by Negroes, which excluded them from certain specified professions (e.g. lawyers and jewellers), and which specifically debarred them from engaging in commerce. That is why the history of the Caribbean indicates that the Black man of African descent in the Caribbean has excelled in the professions (including the law from which he was originally debarred), in scholarship, in politics, in the civil service, in the arts, but not as an entrepreneur or a proprietor.

There were not only historical reasons for this but also sociological ones, particularly the break-up of the Negro family through slavery and the proscription of African religious practices—hence the loss of a sense of continuity throughout the generations so important for success in business and agricultural enterprises. Our present day Caribbean society has to find an equivalent for a stable family life for the Negro in order to provide this motivation for him. This substitute is and must be the co-operative.

It must be appreciated that these particular disabilities on the people of African descent were not extended to the people who came from India and Pakistan. They were permitted family life and their religious customs, and were never as culturally deprived as the people who came from Africa—although numerous social and economic disabilities were imposed upon them by indenture and the sugar plantation system.

The *New Society* must seek to motivate all sections of the population to achieve material progress for themselves on an individual or, better still, on a group or co-operative basis, with the emphasis on the dignity of labour. Perhaps the PNM Government has sometimes in the past gone too far in being paternalistic in the face of severe lack of social amenities (particularly housing) and appalling levels of unemployment. But the *New Society* must now place greater emphasis on self-reliance and personal and group initiative. The urban dispossessed must still be assisted by the State in many ways, but they must learn to create employment for themselves, particularly through the co-operative. Hard work, thrift and perseverance must from now on become a way of life for most of us. Economic independence and popular participation have to be earned by the people, not handed down by the Government. What is more, only a bigot would deny that the people of African descent in the country need to develop greater pride in themselves and a greater degree of constructive consciousness in order to secure much of the necessary motivation.

This having been said, it must never be forgotten that Trinidad and Tobago belongs to Trinidadians and Tobagonians of all races, all shades, all colours.

(5) Promotion of the People's Sector

In the light of the historical and sociological factors influencing the attitude of the people of African descent, and in the light of the many economic and social liabilities affecting the numerous under-privileged people of Indian descent (particularly in the rural areas), it seems necessary for us in Trinidad and Tobago to evolve and implement a new concept in our economic organisation of a "People's Sector", consisting of small-scale Agriculture; small-scale Industry; Handicrafts; Small Service Activities such as Distribution and Transport; Small Hotels and Guest Houses; Credit Unions; Cottage Industries, and Trade Union enterprises. *The co-operative will be promoted as a basis for organising these activities; but the People's Sector will include activities organised on an individual, family or small partnership basis.* Government paternalism must be avoided in encouraging the growth of enterprises in this sector; but active Governmental financial and technical support—with greater emphasis on technical assistance—must be provided to make these enterprises self-reliant and viable.

Further, we should aim at ensuring that (leaving aside the Petroleum and Petrochemical sectors which are very heavily capital-intensive and which can be regulated in the national interest by legislative, fiscal and administrative measures) the Public Sector, the National Private Sector and the People's Sector all combined come in time to dominate the economy. Naturally, there will over time be continuous movement of particular enterprises, through their expansion, from the People's Sector to the National Private Sector; but this movement will be more than compensated by the establishment of new enterprises in the People's Sector as the population (particularly the youth) becomes increasingly motivated to seek self-employment on either an individual or group or co-operative basis. In this way the people will achieve real and direct economic power.

Thus the achievement of popular participation in the economy must be found under the specific circumstances of Trinidad and Tobago and the West Indies through a development strategy consisting of such varied means as:

(i) an active public sector which itself engages in productive enterprise and which also regulates the economy in the interest of nationals;

(ii) a vibrant, nationally oriented private sector; the elimination of unnecessary bureaucratic procedures within the administration will be given the highest priority in order to drastically reduce the period of time between decision-making and implementation;

(iii) widespread dissemination of shares in public companies among workers in the companies themselves and the people at large; and,

(iv) a large and growing People's Sector.

Foreign private investment will continue to be relied upon to supplement local efforts based on this development strategy.

(6) Income Distribution and Unemployment

If we adopt the system of liberal capitalism (accompanied by recourse on a large scale to foreign capital) the result will be increased prosperity for a relatively small group of people (including workers fortunate enough to get well-paid employment), accompanied by increasing unemployment and the maldistribution of income and wealth. The experience of certain developing countries, including one or two in the Caribbean, illustrates this.

The kind of system outlined above, combining elements of liberal capitalism, governmental regulation, participation and encouragement of national private enterprise, and a growing People's Sector of the economy will do much to promote a more equal distribution of income.

The People's Sector will also help with employment in several ways. First, the small-scale enterprises will be more labour intensive than the bigger foreign-owned industries. Second, with a more controlled type of development based largely on local and national initiative, the climate will be more favourable to a development of more suitable and less capital-intensive "intermediate technologies". Third, the promotion of popular participation, especially through co-operatives, will *motivate* people, particularly young people, to create work for themselves through *self-employment* rather than waiting to get employment and big wages and salaries in government or in the Private Sector. Popular participation in the economy means social justice and economic democracy. But, most important, it gives individuals and groups a *sense of motivation*. This cannot be stressed too much, given the specific economic, historical and sociological characteristics of the people of Trinidad and Tobago and the Caribbean.

A sense of motivation and of commitment is also important if the brain drain is to be stemmed. There is evidence to suggest that the brain drain in Trinidad and Tobago is due not only to salary differentials but also to a feeling on the part of the professional that in both the Public and Private Sectors at home his skills are not being used to their fullest advantage. In other words, at home, he is neither motivated nor committed.

(7) Trade Unionism and Popular Participation in the Economy
Trade Unions constitute an important instrument for popular participation in the economy. They protect the worker against the abuse of authority by the employer. They bring dignity to labour degraded by centuries of slavery and indenture. They ensure that the worker directly employed in the enterprise can share in its gains. They also represent the nuclei of popular power over both the economy and the political process. They can instruct the worker in the skills of organisation and group decision-making.

The difficulty with the traditional European and North American conception of trade unions when applied without modification to the Caribbean environments is that trade unions in privileged sectors (such as oil, bauxite and Government) can share in the productivity gains of their employing enterprises often at the cost of damage to other groups among the masses—such as the rural agricultural population, the unemployed and the underemployed, and the less privileged workers in less privileged establishments. In other words, trade unionism practised in the metropolitan style can add to the distortions and irrationalities of the inherited economic and social system rather than eliminate them. It should be emphasised that those observations are not an "attack" on trade unions or trade union leaders; they merely constitute an attempt to analyse objectively an important aspect of our peculiar economic system.

There are two ways out of this dilemma. The first is through the imposition by government fiat of a more rational wage and salary structure in both the Public and Private Sectors. This invites totalitarianism. It must therefore be categorically rejected. This, naturally, does not apply to minimum wage scales in occupations where workers are not unionized.

The other, and infinitely more preferable way, is through a mixture of moderate governmental influence (based on consultation with Labour and Business) on wage and salary determination; appropriate government price and fiscal policies; and a more active participating role of the unions in economic activity.

Thus trade unions should be encouraged to form co-operatives, to set up workers' banks and savings institutes, to participate in National Insurance and so obviate the need for government old age pensions, to enter directly into productive activities, and to purchase shares in public companies. To the extent that they do so, the more privileged workers who happen to be employed in the more productive and highly paid parts of the economy will be using their higher earnings to undertake more capital accumulation to the benefit of all the workers in the country.

The PNM, in this general context, re-affirms the following pledges made in 1956:

"(1) Promotion of effective democratic trade unions with a clear recognition of the workers' right to choose their own representatives.

(2) Adoption of a comprehensive modern Labour Code based on the following accepted international standards and practices:

   (i) improvement of the conditions of labour with special respect to hours of work, minimum wages, guaranteed wages, paid weekly rest, paid public holidays, annual holidays with pay, severance pay in the event of dismissal due to no fault of the worker, protection of the health and safety of the worker;

   (ii) protection of women, young persons and children—including maternity protection, abolition of child labour, limitation of hours of work of women and young persons, equal pay with men for women performing equal work;

(iii) social security—including workmen's compensation, sickness and invalidity insurance, unemployment insurance, old age pensions;

(iv) special incentives to the workers—including profit sharing, guaranteed employment, prosperity bonuses enabling the workers to participate in the benefits of higher prices.

(3) Reorganisation of the Department of Labour to make it an active agent for the protection of the rights of the workers, for the education of the workers in a knowledge of those rights, for the training of trade union leaders through appropriate courses, and for the constant review of international labour standards and practices.

(4) Adequate provisions of training facilities for all grades of labour and for educating them to realise responsibilities.

(5) Fair employment practices and the abolition of racial discrimination in employment.

(6) Insistence that employers train West Indians, without discrimination on grounds of race, colour or religion, for the highest positions on the senior staff in all industries, and promote them when they have been so trained—the continued importation of overseers for the sugar industry is an insult which will no longer be tolerated.

(7) Representation of the workers on public corporations, statutory boards, committees for public purposes, and in intra-Caribbean or international commodity negotiations."

The PNM calls on the government to continue to regulate profits by Corporation Tax, Personal Income Tax and Withholding Tax and, in the case of oil companies, by the Petroleum Act as well; to continue and expand the regulation of prices by the Prices Commission; and to expedite the operations of the Export-Import Company in order to assist in keeping down the prices of imports.

(8) Full Utilisation of our National Resources

The vesting of economic power in the people also requires that we use our local resources fully—whether these are resources of manpower, of capital, or natural resources.

Because of their long history of economic dependence on the metropolitan countries, the people of the Caribbean have never been forced to utilise their own resources. We have preferred to view our material progress in terms of handouts from the metropolis—handouts of aid, of capital investment, of sheltered and preferential markets, of opportunities for emigration and for the brain drain. We have never fully looked inwards. And when we do, we look towards the government as a source of handouts.

Our trained manpower resources are greatly under-utilised; in the civil service, in the professions, in the artistic and cultural field, in business, and even perhaps in sport. Our resources of unskilled manpower are under-utilised—witness the small number of genuine self-help projects undertaken. (A vital Local Government system will help considerably to mobilise labour for self-help schemes). Our resources of capital equipment are under-utilised—witness the schools, technical institutes and the University grossly under-utilised in the evenings and during the vacation. Our mass media are operating well (in fact maddeningly) below their real potential. We have local talent and imagination and need to reduce our dependence on imported radio and television programmes many of which are unadulterated rubbish. The country is rich is creative artistic talent; and yet this too is grossly under-utilised. Our national resources—natural gas, bagasse, forests, steel scrap, fish and shrimp—are also being under-utilised. The whole country is operating way below maximum capacity.

As a result of this under-utilisation of our own resources, we are forced to become more and more dependent on the outside world—for aid; for private capital; for technical assistance; for radio and television programmes; for outlets for both our skilled and unskilled labour force; for imports of food, raw materials and finished goods; and for ideas and institutional forms.

Reconstruction, if it means anything, must mean the maximum utilisation of our own resources and this in turn demands that our citizens produce the maximum of which they may be capable in all fields of endeavour.

(9) Rural Development, Urbanisation and Unemployment

Too many people at home and abroad think Trinidad and Tobago is an urban, sophisticated community. At one level this statement is correct. Only some 22 per cent of the population is engaged in agriculture, as compared with the much larger numbers in many of the other Third World countries. The conurbation stretching from Chaguaramas to Arima is both heavily and densely populated. The drift to the urban areas is indicated by the fact that the rate of growth of the urban population is higher than that of the rural population. At the level of perception, values and aspirations, the people are sophisticated and "urban", even many of those in the rural areas—thanks to the small size of the country, its topography, and its highly developed and relatively cheap transport facilities. The North American values propagated nightly on our radio and television programmes also add to the "urbanisation" of values.

All of this is correct. What is wrong is to draw the inference that rural development should be relegated to a minor role in our development strategy and that the only way forward is through manufacturing and service industries, massive urban infrastructure, tourism, and of course emigration. It is also erroneous to think that it is impossible to secure commitment to inward looking development based on hard work and sacrifice from a population so many of whom live in urban areas and are influenced through the mass media by the life styles and consumer aspirations of the more developed countries.

To accept all of this is in effect to say that the problem of development and unemployment is insoluble—except by massive inflows of aid and private investment into urban infrastructure, manufacturing industries and tourism, and by massive emigration.

The real solution lies in a renewed committment to rural development and the mobilisation of the people through an ideology which stresses the formation of indigenous values and the rejection of metropolitan norms and through a change in the educational system and the mass media.

To begin with values. Here our history is against us—the obsession with colour, the aspiration to white collar jobs, the rejection of agricultural occupations and even agricultural training. But the Decade of the Seventies begins with the young people well on the way to having effected their cultural revolution, reflecting in large part their search for new values and a new ideology.

The educational system must now stress agriculture, rural development and self-reliance. A reconstituted and revitalised radio and television service nationally oriented in the national interest has an important role to play in this regard. Relevant mass media services can have a profound effect in shaping values and the urge to "do their own thing."

We emphasise that, as part and parcel of the economic, social and cultural revolution, there must be a new thrust towards rural development in the broadest sense of the word. In this respect land reform is crucial. There is still a fair amount of unused and under-utilised agricultural land in the country, especially in the eastern part.

Self-reliance, as has already been pointed out, means the maximum use of our own resources, including land and labour. A new thrust to rural development does not mean, as so many people superficially believe, a return to the "simple" life. Rural development should be based on the concept of "agro-industries"—that is, manufacturing based on local agriculture. Even if people settling in the rural areas wish to keep in touch with the urban areas, they can do so easily because of the absence of transportation difficulties.

As in the rural areas, manufacturing industries in the towns should be based on indigenous resources and local raw materials—oil, natural gas, forestry, fish and sea foods, etc. Industries based on these resources should be planned, and foreign capital, when necessary, should be sought not only from North America but also from Europe, Japan and the socialist countries.

C—THE SOCIAL AND CULTURAL ASPECTS

(1) Values

But the sovereignty of the people is perhaps most critically compromised and suppressed by the residue of metropolitan values and values handed down to us by centuries of colonialism and by our willingness to import ever new forms of values and ideologies from the outside, such as the anarchic romanticism of the "New Left" from Europe and the United States of America; the despairing and therefore destructive forms of Black Power from the United States of America: the Welfare State from Scandinavia; and even classical Marxism from Europe of the 1930s.

The supreme revolution that is needed in the Caribbean today is a psychological revolution. We must make a clean break from the metropolitan notions (more often than not outmoded in their countries of origin)—whether in terms of hours of work or social norms and outlook, etc. The young people have already begun this psychological revolution, and this is one reason for the enormous "generation gap" in Trinidad and Tobago.

(2) Education

From the point of view of the PNM, the area where it is easiest to shape values is in the school. This has implications for the curriculum, the methods of teaching, and indeed teacher-pupil relations in the schools. There would seem to be no reason, for example, why each secondary school should not have fifth and sixth form committees to advise the Principal on administration.

The Chaguaramas Declaration

The personality of the child can also be shaped in the school. Our educational system must seek to shape a creative, innovative being who is prepared to evolve solutions to problems for himself. Thrift, civics, agriculture should figure prominently in the curriculum, and greater emphasis should be placed on radio and television as teaching aids.

Social attitudes in the society at large should be influenced in order to achieve, at all levels, the acceptance of the products of all types of education—technical, vocational and academic.

One should also not ignore the more materialistic aspects of education in our community. The PNM has, as we have already pointed out, expanded facilities for secondary education and took the initiative in providing free university education at St. Augustine. But PNM has not done enough for vocational and Technical Education. These forms of education must in the future be emphasised more, as must out-of-school training in skills in Trade Centres and Youth Camps. In fact, PNM must seek to end the almost complete divorce between school and work which we in the West Indies have inherited from the elitist educational system of 19th-century Britain.

We must also give greater emphasis in the secondary school curriculum to such subjects as cooperatives and business management; and training in these subjects must be provided for out-of-school youths and adults in University, in the Labour College, in community centres, in special institutes, and through the mass media. Finally, in the secondary schools Science, Mathematics and Agriculture should be taught to all students, as the government has already decided.

Attention will be given to the production of appropriate text books and curricula to give direction and effect to the development of ideas and attitudes consonant with the concept of this Declaration. And the fullest use will be made of television as an educational device.

The role of the University must primarily be to provide the skills which we need as a developing country against the background of a knowledge of the Caribbean past in the context of world history. We need a greater emphasis on Science, Mathematics, Agriculture and Engineering. At the same time, the University must develop in the student a sense of commitment to, and active involvement in, the national community—something which, it is gratifying to note, is already being developed, as shown in the community projects which students have for some time now been undertaking.

Finally, a University of the West Indies cannot fail, like universities everywhere else, to develop a body of thought which must be relevant and indigenous. But such critical thought must take place in the context of a University aimed primarily at turning out students with relevant skills and actively involved in community improvement. A university whose dominant preoccupation was critical social thought would be an expensive luxury which the community could not afford to support.

(3) The Legal System

Any legal system must be organic in the sense that it must be continually growing and changing to give effect to the aspirations, customs and needs of any people. In this sense the legal system and the laws must be an instrument of the people and for, *not* against them. The present structure of the courts and the delays encountered require a total reappraisal in order to eliminate frustrations, delays and injustices. Greater emphasis must be placed on legislation of a social nature and the laws revised generally to give effect to the aspirations of the people.

The party recognises that not enough has been done in the question of law reform—this notwithstanding the appointment of a Law Reform Commission, proposals for the complete removal of the Anglo-Saxon concept of illegitimacy and other significant measures.

Irrelevant concepts of land tenure still strangle the legitimate desires of our people to own their country and to develop affinity with the land. Examples can be multiplied.

The Chaguaramas Declaration

The PNM therefore advocates immediate and effective measures for drastic and fundamental law reform, with particular reference to the removal of obsolete laws relating to historical injustices and indignities that are totally out of place in a politically independent country.

(4) Race and Colour

Racism has been Europe's greatest gift to the world. Its legacy bedevils our path in the Caribbean after four and three-quarter centuries of European and American domination. As European colonies, Trinidad and Tobago and the other Caribbean countries were founded with their economic, political, social and cultural values based on racism—the assumed superiority of white over black. The most pernicious effect of colonialism (and therefore of the entire history of our communities) for the West Indies has been that many Black people have "internalised" this value system and have come to believe in the deepest recesses of their minds that black is in fact inferior to white.

The young generation is however rapidly shaking off this value system, and is asserting vociferously that black is beautiful and that all Blacks are brothers. They are merely making the central point of establishing their own worth in their own eyes. The tragedy is that in shaking off the feeling of inferiority of the older generation, they appear to be going to the other extreme and denigrating minority groups.

Black dignity in the Caribbean, as elsewhere in the New World, will be achieved only if this sense of worth is established. But the achievement of this dignity carries certain dangers for such a cosmopolitan country as Trinidad and Tobago.

The greatest danger is that of the likelihood of the creation of further division between the non-white of African descent and the non-white of Asian descent, both of whom have, historically, messed out of the same pot in their servitude to the sugar plantation. But there is one fundamental difference between the two groups that must not be lost sight of. The Indian in the West

Indies, although historically dispossessed economically, socially and politically, has never faced the cultural trauma which the African has had to face—forbidden his native languages and religions, prevented from using African names, proscribed from certain skills, occupations and professions, and not infrequently debarred from owning land.

Thus a certain amount of over-assertion of his dignity on the part of the young African, who is just discovering himself in the age of the political rebirth of the African Continent and its struggle against the apartheid of Southern Africa, needs to be understood. The assertion of Black dignity does not need at all to be and categorically ought not to be anti-Indian, though there are undoubtedly obscurantist elements who will so interpret it for their own political advantage.

We should also always bear in mind that the person of Asian descent has faced social, cultural amd psychological difficulties in the colonial economic, political and social system which we have endured for so long and are now aiming at casting off fully. If we are to become a genuine Nation, we all have to look at our society through the eyes of both the numerically preponderant under-privileged groups. The majority of persons of Asian descent are still rural and poor. They form the overwhelming majority of the sugar-estate workers and as such are subject to great economic insecurity.

Because of their cultural background, some have succeeded through hard work and perseverance in business and have been able to train their children for the professions. But it should be realised that until recently many Indians were not made to feel very secure in the community. The Government has recently, on the urgings of the religious groups themselves, proclaimed both Hindu and Muslim religious holidays and intends to provide specifically in the Creative Arts Centre facilities for Indian culture.

What is required in Trinidad and Tobago in the essentially transitional period of the next two decades is a certain amount of cultural and psychological "space" for each of the two principal ethnic groups within the larger confines of a wider and commonly shared national identity. There are more than enough commonly shared experiences and values between the two groups, especially among the young (who are now both sharing equally in the forbidden fruit of the plantation society, free education, especially at secondary level) to enable one to speak meaningfully of a common Trinidad and Tobago national identity and to permit the growth of such a national identity. Both groups will increasingly shed their Anglo-Saxon residue and evolve more in a common Trinidad and Tobago and Caribbean consciousness, even though that consciousness has and will increasingly have more "creole" than either Indian or African or Anglo-Saxon elements in it.

Racism (in the sense of open confrontation between non-white of African descent and non-white of Asian descent) should therefore not really be a problem over the years. At the same time local whites (including people of mixed blood, Chinese, Portuguese and Syrians) should have no need to fear the growing self-confidence and self-assertiveness among non-whites. These minority groups, many of them established here for long periods, most of whom are citizens, have every right to expect the state to protect their legitimate rights as citizens. They too are entitled to respect as human beings and not be made the object of inverse racism. What cannot be tolerated is that they should seek, as a group, to maintain their privileged status by blocking economic and social change and by denying equality of opportunity on the basis of merit and ability.

These groups must increasingly involve themselves, as many individuals among them already have, in the National Community. They must increasingly follow the example of Guppy and Alcazar in the 19th century and Cipriani in the 20th century—who fought, respectively, against colonialism, the brutality of indenture and the degradation of the common man. They have an important entrepreneurial role to play in developing the national economy. They also have a social role to play by giving of their talents in voluntary community work—in the social services and in training in business management, in cooperative organisation and in technical skills. They need to give voluntary service to the less fortunate in the community, not in the spirit of charity but as an affirmation to themselves and to others that they belong to a genuine National Community. In giving such practical expression to the idea of national solidarity and in actively promoting and supporting the People's Sector of the economy, they will be making an invaluable contribution to Nation-building.

Our Nation then is and must be multi-racial, with no racial group enjoying special privileges or suffering disabilities simply on account of race or colour. But since large numbers of the population are of African descent, we must have sympathy with Black people fighting for dignity in the United States of America, Britain, Canada, Southern Africa, and other parts of the world. And since the overwhelming majority of the population derive from Africa and Asia, we as a Nation must show solidarity with coloured peoples fighting the world over for dignity. And since we all (black and white alike) have for four and a half centuries been the victims of colonialism and external economic domination, we as a Nation must ally ourselves with all the peoples of the Third World (the Caribbean, Latin America, Africa and Asia) fighting for economic emancipation from metropolitan domination in respect of trade, aid, technology and capital. As far as the PNM is concerned, these affirmations are not new and go back to our support for the Bandung Conference as long ago as 1956.

(5) The Creative Arts, the Mass Media and Sport

The promotion of National Culture in the sense of the Creative Arts must also be an important end which the *New Society* should pursue. Creative Arts are rooted in, and a reflection (however indirect) of, social realities. They also make people in the community more aware of themselves and of each other and so bring the individual into closer relationship with the community. This is so, even though the artistic product may reach out to universal human themes.

Although the government has given some financial assistance to Carnival and to the Steelband Movement, the PNM has become increasingly conscious of the importance of promoting the Arts and Culture (especially Drama) as part of the process of Nation-building and achieving self-awareness. The building of the Creative Arts Centre should be of great assistance in developing this important aspect of our national life. And tourism in future should expose the visitor to a greater extent than hitherto to our cultural and artistic accomplishments. Our party has already expressed its reservations about the social consequences of uncontrolled tourism, divorced from the local community and harmful to the dignity of our people. At a recent Annual Convention the PNM called on the government to commission a study, now being undertaken by the University of the West Indies, on the sociological implications of tourism, with particular reference to Tobago.

The mass media are closely related to Culture. They are also crucial in building up a sense of national and Caribbean identity and promoting economic, social and political development. Radio and television in Trinidad and Tobago have to be given new bases, new directions, new orientations, and programmes must in future involve the ordinary people of the country to a greater extent. From being a barrier to all that we aspire to, they must be converted into an active agent of national reconstruction.

In addition it is essential for the citizens to be kept fully informed of all governmental activities and this implies drastic reconstruction of the existing information services.

It is also more than obvious that the promotion and development of all forms of sporting activity must receive greater emphasis in the *New Society*. Our people have long excelled in many forms of international sport; people abroad who had never before heard of Trinidad and Tobago now know of us through some of our great sportsmen.* An ever widening range of sporting activities attracts increasing numbers of both participants and spectators, particularly from among the young people. The *New Society* must carry further recent initiatives by the government such as coaching programmes and playing fields throughout the country and so develop the latent talents of our people and give them greater avenues for self-expression.

IV.—TRINIDAD AND TOBAGO, THE CARIBBEAN AND THE THIRD WORLD

A moment's reflection will show that the prospects of achieving a greater degree of economic independence for Trinidad and Tobago are enhanced by being set within a common Caribbean regional framework. The state power of the individual Caribbean countries needs to be combined so that the maximum power can be exerted by the region to promote the sovereignty of the Caribbean people over their economies.

This analysis helps to elucidate the paradox that the countries of the Caribbean region can enhance the sum total of their peoples' effective sovereignty only by pooling their separate state sovereignties with those of other Caribbean states.

It also helps to elucidate another paradox—namely, effective and meaningful Caribbean economic integration can only be achieved if each separate Caribbean country changes its internal development strategy from that of mendicancy to the achievement of economic independence based on local effort, local self-reliance and the use of local resources.

It follows from all this that reconstruction of Trinidad and Tobago's economy and society can best take place in the framework of similar efforts by other Caribbean countries. Neverthe-

---

*For example, Wendell Mottley, Edwin Roberts, Roger Gibbon, Christopher Forde, Hilton Mitchell, [Learie] Constantine, and [Sonny] Ramadhin.

The Chaguaramas Declaration

less, in the absence of unanimous agreement on a programme of action by all Caribbean governments, Trinidad and Tobago will have to press ahead, either on its own or jointly with some of the countries which also are seeking to reshape their inherited structures.

Our efforts at Nation-building in Trinidad and Tobago will also be facilitated by similar efforts on the part of other Caribbean countries. Although Trinidad and Tobago is probably the most fragmented and least cohesive, nearly all the countries of the region are lacking in consciousness and self-awareness. This is a legacy of Caribbean history: at a very early stage of European colonisation, the colonists tended to look outward than inward. The Spanish inhabitants of the Greater Antilles tried to get out of these islands and go to Peru or Mexico; the British planters in Jamaica and Barbados and the Leeward Islands were anxious to return to the Mother Country once they made money; nothing local was considered of value by anyone in any of the islands; getting out to the metropolis has always been the West Indian philosophy.

In the age of independence, many of the governments are now actively engaged in the task of Nation-building. This simultaneous process is bound to assist in the emergence of both a national and a Caribbean identity, especially if it is accompanied by a greater awareness of the Caribbean past and by the very real achievements of such great Caribbean leaders as Hatuey in Cuba, Enriquillo in Santa Domingo, Cuffy in Guyana, Toussaint L'Ouverture in Haiti, George William Gordon in Jamaica, Jose Marti in Cuba, Cipriani and Butler in Trinidad and Tobago. It must also be accompanied by a greater awareness of non-Commonwealth Caribbean literature—for example, Aime Cesaire in Martinique, Jacques Roumain in Haiti, Nicolas Guillen in Cuba.

The prospects are, however, favourable for the emergence of an identity among the peoples of the Caribbean in the light of the astonishing and growing congruence of views and outlook among the young people of the Commonwealth Caribbean. Indeed, when one speaks today to a young person from the Caribbean, it is difficult, apart from his accent, to tell which country he comes from. The government saw this hope for Trinidad and Tobago and the Caribbean as early as 1963, when it drew up its Draft Second Five Year Plan. The Plan listed the large percentage of young people in the population as one of the great potential strengths of the Caribbean, notwithstanding the overall density and rate of growth of the population. In this regard a vigorous Caribbean cultural exchange programme would be of inestimable value in forging the new Caribbean identity.

The Caribbean must also look increasingly towards the other countries of the Third World. There is Latin America, which is still struggling for identity and self-realisation. The Caribbean has for far too long been an outsider in the New World and needs to become more closely linked with the other under-privileged countries of the Western Hemisphere. There are also the countries of Africa and Asia which, like ourselves and Latin America, are suffering from deteriorating terms of trade and increasing difficulties in selling their products in metropolitan markets. We in the Caribbean and the other peoples of the Third World need each other in respect of markets and in respect of providing a common front against economic domination by the metropolitan countries and in favour of improving the structure of international economic relations to our benefit. These considerations make it imperative for us to maintain and develop diplomatic relations with the countries of Latin America, Africa and Asia—as we stated quite unambiguously in *The People's Charter* in 1956.

V.—THE NEW SOCIETY

Politically, the independence of the country must be maintained and the people, on the basis of Constitution Reform, changes in the system of Local Government, and the introduction and strengthening of consultative mechanisms, must be allowed to participate more fully in the political process.

The Chaguaramas Declaration

Economically, the goal should be the creation of a national economy, with decisions over the key sectors of the economy being made at *home*, with widespread popular participation and greater self-reliance by all groups in the economy, with a more equal distribution of income and with a greatly improved employment situation. There will of course still be a lot of trade with the outside world because of the small size of the country.

Production will be carried out by three sectors: the Public Sector; the National Private Sector; and the People's Sector. Foreign aid and foreign private capital will be useful *adjuncts* to meet shortages of resources in the three basic national sectors. The long-run goal is for the Public Sector, the People's Sector and the National Private Sector combined to dominate the economy.

Socially, the idea of solidarity between the two dispossessed groups—Negroes and Indians—must be all pervading as the basis of a new nationalism, which must consciously enlist the participation of women and youths. There can be no future for the country without such solidarity. We should strive to eliminate prejudice against local minority groups; but they, in turn, should realise that if they fail to support the effort to create a *New Society* they will be doing so at their own peril. The reconstruction effort will in fact, as has been pointed out, create opportunities for a vibrant National Private Sector, supported by national financial institutions and national services designed to encourage national production and exports.

Culturally, the reconstruction effort has already been started by the youth. It must promote indigenous and authentic values, give pride and dignity to the people, and motivate them to achieve in the economic and artistic fields. In other words, reconstruction must convert the Trinidad and Tobago citizen into being a *true man*, into a participant in a People's economy, instead of a mendicant for work in an extension locally of the metropolitan economy.

VI.—THE ROLE OF THE PARTY

In the past fourteen years a new generation has grown up, and the toddlers of 1956 have come of age. The increasing recognition of the importance of professional training, whether at home or abroad, has equipped us with hundreds of trained nationals to substitute for the skilled personnel formerly imported. Our party must recognise this and must consciously seek to attract to its fold, as a means of bridging the generation gap at the same time as it provides new and constructive ideas for the party to distil and translate into concrete proposals for effective political action, the youth of the country, our young professionals and technocrats, the writers, the artists and the artistes who are waging the cultural battle and carrying on the campaign for decolonisation in the cultural domain. The total membership of the PNM will be motivated and prepared for promoting the ideas and concepts contained in this *Declaration*, as a prerequisite for the motivation of the general public.

The achievements of the PNM from 1956 to 1970 have been the result of the dedicated work of thousands of loyal party members in their various party and constituency groups and in the Women's and Youth Leagues. The loyal and active party members will have an equally important role to play in the introduction of the *New Society*.

There are certain specific obligations which fall to the party members in the context of the *New Society*, with its popular participation in decision-making, its vigorous People's Sector, its dignity for the historically disadvantaged, its multi-racial character based on an equality that is *de facto* and not merely *de jure*. These are:

1 To make every effort to improve both the structure and the functioning of the party so that it becomes an even more efficient and democratic instrument for the achievement of the New Society.

2   To ensure that the party continues an independent existence separate and distinct from the government, but directing at all times the policies by which the party's government is guided.

3   To support positive and constructive constituency efforts, within or without the party, and/or to initiate such efforts where necessary, for raising the dignity of life in their respective constituencies with special reference to the following:

   (a) the purchase of shares by individual party members in all reputable cooperative endeavours:

   (b) the encouragement of the national culture in all its manifold forms—steelband, calypso, folklore, Indian music, to name the outstanding ones;

   (c) the support of local products, especially the small businessman;

   (d) consumer vigilance and initiative in respect of rising prices;

   (e) more active direct participation in cottage industries and handicrafts as one positive means of providing employment for women over 40 and girls under 20;

   (f) the expansion of sporting and recreational facilities;

   (g) the promotion of self-help efforts in various fields;

   (h) voluntary service, particularly by our women members, to assist the under-privileged, the aged, the poor, the retarded and the handicapped;

   (i) the development of a more vibrant youth arm.

4   To play an active role, as citizens, in all community organizations and centres in the effort to encourage the widest possible participation in discussion of public issues and in national decision-making.

5   To defend vigorously the human rights of all, without discrimination on grounds of race, colour, religion, sex or country of origin.
6   To present to the world a successful multi-racial society free of the tensions and turmoil so prevalent in the contemporary world.

Members of the PNM, old, young, and middle-aged, foundation members and new recruits: Forward to the *New Society* under the banner of the PNM.

The People's Charter of January 24, 1956, has guided us for fourteen years. Here is the revised *People's Charter* of 1970, *The Chaguaramas Declaration*, to guide us in the years ahead.

GREAT IS PNM AND IT SHALL PREVAIL

TRINIDAD AND THE REVOLUTION IN POLITICAL INTELLIGENCE

by
George Lamming

George Lamming

PNM Weekly, August 30, 1956.

TRINIDAD AND THE REVOLUTION IN POLITICAL INTELLIGENCE

It is easier to tell the excitement and the optimism I felt during my recent visit to Trinidad if I offer, in some way, a picture, an idea of the general impression, the whole experience which I was taking with me when I left in 1950. It helps too to explain the reason for these remarks, which I feel, should remain free from unnecessary argument or attack. For I am trying angrily not to make out a case for any person or group, nor I am trying to justify my own political position, whatever that may be. This is an attempt to describe two kinds of experiences which are different in quality, and the implications which emerge, however obvious they may appear, must be interpreted according to each individual temperament and intelligence. It is true that I make it clear what force of education and political organisation have been merely, if not wholly, responsible for the differences I shall mention, but even that commitment must be regarded as part of the total experience I am trying to relate.

 I arrived in Trinidad for the first time in 1946. It was the first time I had ever left my native Bardados, and the job I accepted was the first of any importance that I was going to do since leaving school the year before. I liked Trinidad immediately. The two years following on my arrival soon became and remained for a while the most pleasurable phase of my adolescence. I respond almost naturally to the rhythm of the place. I do not mean to suggest that my dancing improved or that I even learnt to dance. I mean simply the atmosphere seemed right for me, that I was an easy convert to something which I must have thought was not to be found in Bardados. As you would say in easy 'old talk' "it was nice, I liked it." But the pleasures of adolescence can become, with out any warning at all a very shaming rebuke. I would have thought this tendency to complain a sign of ingratitude if I weren't supported by my friends who were all Trinidadians. They had already started to quarrel, and one, in particular, had started to show signs of aggressiveness. He was continually rude to people who were much 'better off' and who, he felt, ought to understand. He was poor, he was young, he was intelligent, and he was angry. And this is an exceedingly dangerous combination in a man who is also healthy. When the arena of dispute is a colonial territory, anything can happen; and they are very stupid, whether European or West Indian, who cannot see this. I think this young man arranged a very convenient marriage some time later, but that, in some circumstances, can be very uncertain escape; and it is nearly always very exhausting.

The fourth year in Trinidad was the kind which many a young man in many parts of the world has written or talked about at great length. It was the kind of season which you manage to endure because there is nothing else for you to do, and there were many Trinidadians, I knew at the time, who were enduring their jobs and their bosses and their neighbours because there wasn't anything else they could do, short of getting into 'serious trouble'. It is easy for a few elderly gentlemen, with piles of rust accumulating round their brains, and very crooked notions of what they call experience, to dismiss this phase with words like 'let him alone, he will get over it'. It is easier to see, as I learnt, this IT getting over the victim. And this is exactly what happened to people I knew. They went under. Having no means of getting out, and losing confidence in their energies to transform, they became one with the atmosphere of the place, an atmosphere of sterility and final ruin. Interpret my motives as you like, but I scrambled a passage and got out. I left for England.

Why did I like Trinidad in 1946? And if I liked it so much even in 1947, why this accumulated hatred of the place in 1953? For that is exactly what happened. One answer seems clear to me. To a boy, who had just left school, migrating with a boy's dreams of freedom among people who knew nothing about him, a foreign territory becomes a kind of playground. And all of us know the immense relief which comes when aunts and well-meaning grandmothers and the whole tribe of well-wishers are not nearby. It quickly creates the psychology of 'at last nobody is looking.' I have tried to describe this kind of self-deception elsewhere, in *The Emigrants:*

> "Those four years in Trinidad now seemed nothing more than an extension of what had gone before, but for this important difference... I had won the right of the front door key, escaped the immediacy of privation, and walked, unrebuked, in the small dark hours. I felt my freedom fresh and precious. It was a child's freedom.... It can be felt, and it lasts if you remain what you are when you feel it. In the early hours of the morning I pulled myself out of bed and walked out to the savannah to watch the day break in a bubble of sunlight over the hills. There I felt it, and at other hours when the whores fixed their prices, talking leisurely about their difficulties, the sort of men they preferred, the careers of their rivals in the trade... I felt this freedom. It was a private and personal acquisition and I used it as a man uses what is private and personal....
>
> "And gradually as though there were a repetitive order in a man's experience, I felt precisely the inward discomfort I had known some years ago, when vaguely perceiving the meaning of a boy's enslavement, I said farewell to the climate that caught me at birth. It was the end of my freedom....
>
> That night a civil servant who under a false name had crept surreptitiously into the club broke news about the reduction of cheap passages. I scrambled fifty pounds from three sources and set sail for England."

This is an individual's experience of a period in the life of a certain generation in a certain British colony in the Caribbean. These of you who have any clear recollection of those four years I have mentioned may judge how widely this experience can be

Trinidad and the Revolution in Political Intelligence

extended to others. But it was for me a very memorable period; and some years later, when I wanted to invent, for the purpose of a novel, a place and a situation which represented the desperateness, the moral bastardy, the utter void in which a certain kind of energy and vision might be forever imprisoned, I chose that period in Trinidad as my raw material.

"Carrion Crows were collecting again over the iron shed, and the flies were busy devouring the wet entrails of the empty fish which had been stacked high on crocus bags. It was hot. People moved everywhere, wet and rough, through the loud swift traffic of the neighbouring town. The trains never stopped hooting, and the rails seemed to rock and screaming an agony of spinning wheels. And always the flies dispersed and returned in terror and delight. All the clocks contradicted each other. Only the weather seemed reliable in its oppressive steam, and the stale, familiar odour of the dead fish water. The dogs crept fearfully round the wire-turned fish pots, sniffing the rot of black bones and dead gray fish scales, until feet kicked them out of the street.

"Each road was like the beginning of a chase which led maliciously behind the houses, through crooked lanes of withering brown shrub, across sudden flat areas of red marl that burnt and spread with out flame towards an iron shed which expanded in all directions with its chaotic increase of scrap iron.

"Small boats were tied on the water with ropes which were made ready to snap, swaying under the hurrying feet of illicit workers who had their push-carts parked on the wooden bridge to carry off the stolen cargo. Everyone understood. The Indians worked furiously, hurrying up and down the pier. They were cruel with labour to their bodies, and their faces were labelled with secrecy and expectation. Some said they were going to rob the future of all its gifts. The negro workers were heavy, indolent, large, unwilling, furious, naive and destructive. And some said that others said they had always been so. They rebuked all possessions by a show of unconcern. They were killing time with their hands. Their labour seemed irrelevant and misplaced. The Chinese moved everywhere with severe and stoic reservation. They were not given to any interruption, and they were no part of any alliance, but some said that they were going to earn their share of everything, like a gang of willing exiles who watched the weather and anticipated every occasion of danger.

"The police arrived, withdrew and returned, rehearsing their role of privileged neutrality. They pretended not to noticed anything. Their visits were a formality, frequent and harmless. They spoke with their friends who invented information about the progress of the day. But whenever they arrived they had safely left the LAW behind. Everyone understood. They were part of a conspiracy of disorder. It was unfriendly to complain. The faces said simply; so what?"

I think this represents quite fairly, in terms of fiction, the kind of social situation which the People's National Movement found and which their initial efforts have managed, beyond all expectations, to survive and reform. Any serious political organising had to start from that point of crisis, and Dr. Eric Williams started in a way which, to my mind, is unique in the history of Caribbean politics. He started with an intensive and quite exhausting campaign of popular education. He turned history, the history of the Caribbean, into gossip, so that the story of a people's predicament seemed no longer the infinite, barren track of documents, dates and texts. Everything became news: slavery, colonisation, the forgiveable deception of metropolitan rule, the sad and inevitable unawareness of the native production. His lectures retained

Trinidad and the Revolution in Political Intelligence

always the character of whisper which everyone was allowed to hear, a rumour which experience had established as the truth. And whatever misgivings we may have about the ultimate value of popular education, this undertaking, it seems to me, has become an achievement of genius on the part of a teacher. Dr. Williams himself is already history, living history. No other British West Indian politician has exposed himself so consistently to that gravest of all political risks: the risk of refusing to talk down to an electorate. He distinguished very early and quite clearly the difference between formal education which is often wasteful and native intelligence; and having done that, he worked on the native intelligence by demanding at all times an adult attention and response to his lectures. This was an example, probably the first of its kind in our part of the world, of the teacher, in the noblest sense of teacher, turned politician, and of the politician, in the truly moral sense of politician, turned teacher. The result has taken a novel turn, a turn of discovery which is the beginning of action. Today's Trinidadian, who was very much a part of the ugliness I have described above, did not know that he was capable of understanding. And in a sense that is most urgent, and therefore absolutely important, he understands. It is this discovery which explains, I feel, the present character of that square which is today known throughout Trinidad and Tobago as THE UNIVERSITY OF WOODFORD SQUARE.

I try to recall a picture of Woodford Square in 1946. It was, as I remember it, a market for night-food. All transactions were done in the shadows. Women strolled about in search of male friends whom they had not yet known. Men sat on the benches in an attitude of tolerable and even pleasing boredom. And there were always a few lunatics who had either avoided or escaped the attention of the state. Today, this same Woodford Square has become Mr. Everyman's Academy. The same people who used it appropriately, or inappropiately, as you like, in the past, now assemble there to learn. It is this transformation of Woodford Square which is going to have the most profound effect on the

323

forthcoming elections, and the forthcoming elections will most certainly be the most interesting, the most serious and the most historic Trinidad and Tobago will have experienced so far. This is precisely what I mean by the phrase, Trinidad and the revolution in political intelligence. It is the first time that the meaning of the machine, political party, has taken practical shape among Trinidadians, and it is certainly the first time that many a student of Woodford Square will have come to respect the importance of that powerful little weapon, the vote. It is the first time that many will be using that weapon with intelligence and effectiveness.

And this raises the question of moral responsibility and what, to my mind, is the real significance of the People's National Movement. The significance which now expresses itself in political terms (and it is right in the circumstances that this should be its most urgent and important significance) is deeper than politics. It has to do with the whole man of which his political reason is only one aspect. The entire West Indies is doomed until the sense, the tradition of the individual's unconditional worth, is firmly established. Many of us can offer many reasons for the absence of this sense of worth, the humiliating failure of dignity in the Caribbean community. But it is not now very helpful to fret about reasons since a movement has been born which brings us face to face with our past failures. It is rather tomorrow's judgment which concerns us. The PNM has taken the Trinidad community, almost overnight, beyond the phase of complaint, and self pity. There is no need to fret any longer about what those 'people,' meaning the overseas law-makers, have done to 'us'. That is an experience which can now be put on the shelf for future reference, a kind of harmless, ghost story with which we may surprise and amuse our children. And now that this example of a story comes to mind, it is the moment to say that the PNM has succeeded, among other things, in turning what was once a power and a force into a memory and a ghost.

So this, then is my story. I do not know what strange conversion, what magic, if you like, took place in Trinidad between 1950 and 1954. But when I returned to Port of Spain in 1955 I did not believe the rumours I was told about the change brought about by the PNM. And I would certainly not have believed if I hadn't seen it myself then and during a later visit in 1956. The tidiness, the order, and that consuming sense of serious application which I experienced at the Party's headquarters; the competence, the precision and the range of the party's manifesto which I studied; the efficiency and the power of the whole Party machinery which rolled itself into every corner of Trinidad and Tobago, the excellent standard of its newspaper which is easily the best political weekly in the whole British West Indies: these are qualities and achievements which none of us could honestly have associated with Trinidad and Tobago before 1954.

As a result of this experiencing two things have become clear to me. The first is this: no Trinidadian in his right mind can in future undertake to go into politics without being prepared to work harder than he has ever worked before. The second lesson has to do with the future of the Trinidad Legislative Council. No opponent of the People's National Movement, for whom the words honour and dignity have meaning, can now escape a feeling of shame, regret and humiliation, produced by the terrific achievement of the PNM in so short a time. And after the September elections, the standard of debates in the Legislative Council will reach a stage of excellence and decency with which Trinidadians have never before been blessed. It is the first time the place has ever been offered what can frankly be called, A GOLDEN OPPORTUNITY.

A CONVENTION APPRAISAL

by
C. L. R. James

> Dear Timmy
>
> Your godchild!
>
> In appreciation
>
> Bill
>
> November 21. 1944

C. L. R. James; *A Convention Appraisal: Dr. Eric Williams, First Premier of Trinidad and Tobago, A Biographical Sketch* (1960).

A CONVENTION APPRAISAL

FOREWORD

This sketch of the career of the Premier of Tinidad and Tobago aims to give biographical material which will contribute to a better understanding of his politics. When it is convenient I shall try to relate Dr. Williams (and other prominent West Indian politicians) to the type of society which produced them. This of course will be much more difficult, but correspondingly, it will provoke more discussion, and I hope, more systematic investigation and thought. If we do not think for ourselves, then we perforce, use other people's thoughts. To demostrate for independence is good, but to think independently is much better.

May 12, 1960   C. L. R. J.

A Convention Appraisal

By Convention appraisal I mean an appraisal suitable for consideration before the Convention. I certainly do not mean a conventional appraisal, the origins of Dr. Williams; his intellectual interests; his taste in ties and that sort of business, all of which can have a place but not here. I mean simply this: certain ideas which should circulate in the Party and, more important than anything else, arouse discussions around Convention time. Far from being a personality parade, what I am aiming at is to place Dr. Williams, as far as this is possible, in the objective environment which has made him what he is, and will help to make him better understood primarily by his own party. A clearer grasp of what he stands for may not improve relations with his opponents or his enemies. It could easily make them more determined than ever to get rid of him. We, however, have our own tasks to tackle irrespective of what opponents may or may not do as a result.

Some such appraisal as this is overdue. Two dangers always are waiting at the heels of an inexperienced, i.e. four-year old political party, which has no long history of its own to chew upon. The first is seeing everything too much in terms of personality. The second is pursuing a particular point without reference to the total picture. Both are in reality examples of the same generic error, not keeping a proper balance between the universal and the individual, the part and the whole. This type of thinking is rampant in the West Indies today: X did this. Y did that. B failed here. C is a bad type. D did not do that................ This cannot go on indefinitely. If a group of individuals are in constant conflict and turmoil, then the reason for it almost always is, not their personal failings but the system they are trying to operate. Either it is a bad system or, *taken as a whole,* the body of men trying to run it are unsuited to it. Within such a general framework but only within it is personality decisive; for good or bad. Furthermore what is a personality? You have to work hard and long before you can arrive at some clear, i.e., workable conception of a strong political personality, a conception which enables you to understand why he does what he does. *The Guardian,* that ball and chain on the feet of the new nation, deals exclusively in ambition, chips-on-the-shoulder, would-be dictator, or in the case of its hero, Bhadase Maraj, illness which made him nervous and nervousness which made him etc. etc. It is my considered opinion that this is equivalent to injecting a slow but deadly poison into the body politic every morning. It is worse than lies or suppression of news. It is a systematic corruption of the thinking of the community. I happen to have had an exceptional opportunity to observe Dr. Williams during many years. Let us try to get some distance into the conception of a political personality.

ROLE OF PERSONALITY

Dr. Williams is a post-war (World War II) nationalist politician in an underdeveloped colonial territory which is still not independent. That is the primary generalisation. We can be a little more particular and say that whereas the general world movement to full democracy, self-government and independence began in the West Indies, in 1937, it seemed that in Trinidad, up to 1956, this movement, *a world-wide movement,* found impossible obstacles to getting under way. This was expressed by the apparent impossibilty of forming a political party, for without political parties, parliamentary democracy and independence are impossible. The nationalist idea in Trinidad seemed destined to fritter itself away in fits and starts, self-seeking, demagogy and individual struggles for power. Given such a situation as I have described, it was inevitable that it would breed a certain type of politician. If even an individual of ability, character, and dominated by the highest motives had appeared, he would have been worn down, corrupted, or demoralized and defeated by the objective circumstances. No individual by himself can conquer a web of circumstances which comprise a political system. If even he survives with his integrity, he is ineffective and useless, with a strong inclination to blame the backwardness of the people.

Someone has to change the system. It is here that personality, the subjective, enters into an objective situation. A comparable backwardness in British Guiana was entered into and shaped by Dr. Jagan. It was not bound to be Jagan. It might have been Burnham alone. (But even here, the weight of the Indian population made it more likely that the emergent political leader would be Indian.) There was no law that dictated that such a person would be an adherent of Moscow. These are the accidents of history. This one is an accident which has caused and is causing infinite suffering, frustration and disorder to British Guiana and, indirectly, affects the whole of the West Indies. Let us see what was objective and what was accidental, subjective, in the fact that Dr. Williams emerged as the political leader in Trinidad.

His policies previous to the formation of the Party and in the process of its actual formation, tell us much. The principles he established were Political Education, Nationalism, Morality in public affairs, PNM. Dr. Williams is a certain type of person. But it seems to me that the notorious corruption of Trinidad political life forced political morality inescapably into the forefront of the new politics. No emergent party leader could avoid it. Similiarly, in 1956, no emergent party builder in Trinidad could fail to raise the banner of nationalism. It was a natural. When we come to political education, however, we touch the personal, the individual contribution, the accident in history. As Dr. Jagan is a Stalinist intellectual, Dr. Williams is an academic, an academic and an academic of a particular kind. He is an intellectual with an abiding faith in the power of the intellect. There are not many such: that is why so few have ever created a University of Woodford Square.

BEST PREPARATION

He is no ordinary academic in another sense. I doubt if there is a single Premier in the Commonwealth, certainly in the underdeveloped countries of the world, who came to power so admirably suited for leadership in his own territory. He has been shaped by the circumstances of his life and they should be known and discussed and pondered over. He appears to be the result of an extraordinary series of coincidences and I have not had the time nor the opportunity to work at the organic connection between them. The facts, however, are striking enough. Of course Dr. Williams has brains as befits a scholarship winner. But when he took history at Oxford instead of law or medicine, he made a new significant break with the colonialist mentality. I remember meeting him in Warner or Marli Street in 1932, congratulating him on his scholarship and saying to him that I was glad to see that he had broken out of the law and medicine routine and was going in for history. I said: "You need not be afraid of the future. Trinidad and Tobago in 15 years will be a very different place from what it is now."

Thus early Williams had broken out of the spheres that colonialism had marked out for the local man of colour, who had no money. Some no doubt did law or medicine from choice. But in those days, to earn a living, you had to take one or the other.

It is impossible here to stay to analyse the reasons why an individual behaves in this way. In my own case I find that since I was ten, I had set my mind quite firmly against being a lawyer or doctor, making a lot of money and becoming an Honourable Member of the Legislative Council (Nominated). That was the career everybody marked out for me. I would have none of it. A writer I wanted to be and that I pursued, irrespective of everything and everybody.

Williams took history. Note that this is the best preparation for politcs if it is the right kind of history. And in England in the thirties it was bound to be the right kind of history. At no time since Chartism in 1848 was Britain in such political and intellectual turmoil as in 1933-1939. The Great Depression, the success of the first Russian Five Year Plan, the rise of Nazism, the threat of Hitler, the threat, and very real it was, of a Facist movement in

England, the spread of Marxism, the anti-imperialist struggle, all this contributed to making England a seething cauldron of political and social ideas. All traditional conceptions were examined and stripped to the bone. Williams was at Oxford where the ferment of ideas had penetrated. His holidays were spent in London, and in our various ways George Padmore, myself, Arthur Lewis were part of this tremendous intellectual and political training. Among much else this period produced the ideas and the leadership of the movement which immediately after the war opened up the era of the passing of colonialism. Much of the conflict in the West Indies today between Williams and his fellow politicians has some at least of its origins in the fact that he passed through this school and others didn't. That period left its mark on all who went through it. Fortunately for Williams (like most successful men in politics and war, he is very lucky), he had the priceless good fortune of studying history academically while all this actual history and thought was going on around him. The academic and the actual interpenetrated each other. To him history became real and actual politics historical. If you do not understand this, you do not understand him at all and much that he does and the way that he does it is incomprehensible and creates antagonism among his fellow politicians whereas it gives the mass a sense of participation in the historical process.

HIGHLY LITERATE BUT . . . . .

In this revaluation of historical and political ideas that occupied all thinking minds, the West Indies, as a nation, as a people, even as a colony, were out, out of history, ignored and forgotten. We were highly literate but intellectually and spiritually deficient as we still are. *The Case for West Indian Self-Government* and *The Black Jacobins* brought the West Indies into the historical and political current of the day and Butler's movement in 1937 made the ideas an actual force. Williams followed with *Capitalism and Slavery* as his thesis for his Doctorate. I remember the long discussions we had as to what the thesis should be and how it should be tackled. Those congenital idiots and backward people who talk about Williams having a chip on his shoulder on the race question should study all this, ponder over it and take a vow of silence for the rest of their days. West Indians and the West Indies were out of all that was going on in the thirties and we deliberately set out to bring them in. When Dr. Williams speaks of West Indian nationalism, independence, it comes from the very roots of his being. He passed from studentship to maturity by projecting West Indian history into the surging stream of modern history and political theory from which it was absent. His nationalism did not begin in 1956. Those who find his nationalist attitude strange and intemperate would do well to remember its origins. For my part I had had plans for doing more work on the West Indies. I put that aside for other things when I saw the powers Williams had developed and the direction of his mind. I felt that the intellectual basis of West Indian nationalism was in safe hands.

Out of *Capitalism and Slavery* Williams emerged with certain convictions which are the basis of his mind to this day.

1) The bankruptcy of the sugar-based economy.
2) The West Indies as a football for colonial powers.
3) The fact that if emancipation had not taken place from above, it would have taken place from below by a slave revolt. It is the ideas prevalent in Europe in 1932-1939 and his own studies in West Indian history which have given him his faith in the masses of the people.

Behind this were more subjective but no less significant ideas for his future development. I select two.

His academic study of history at Oxford and his experiences in England had given him a thorough grounding in the fundamentals of British parliamentary democracy. This is important because the basic training and experience of Nkrumah and Azikiwe of Nigeria was in the United States and the influence of that is appearing already in the new Ghana Constitution. Padmore and

I, on the other hand, made thorough studies of the Soviet system and both of us wrote and published books on this. In this respect Williams is as British as Nr. Nehru.

COLONIAL AT OXFORD

Closely allied to this is another experience: anyone who has read Dr. Williams's "A Colonial at Oxford" will see that Williams absorbed European culture through every pore and, what is very characteristic of the period and of him, integrated it with his academic studies: he does not like loose ideas or anything else straying about; it was in the thirties that the unity of all aspects of social and political life became a common property of English thought. The result is that he is a highly educated (in the Greek total sense of the word) citizen of the world rooted in the British civilization and the British culture. If 1935 were 1955 he would certainly have had a Blue for soccer at Oxford and he is a Centaur, a member of the Oxford Society for near-Blues. Crowds used to follow him around at Oxford to see him play for his college.

This consciousness of his personal equality with anybody of his generation was fortified by a special experience in the England of the thirties. Traditional England was under fire. And it was the regular habit of a number of us colonials to go to public lectures and meetings of some of the most celebrated lecturers and speakers in England and at question time and during discussion tear them to pieces. (Sometimes we astonished even ourselves but we soon got over that). I think it was the very famous Socialist lecturer at Oxford, G. D. H. Cole, whom Williams tore apart at one of his meetings. Curiously enough it was the Liberals we usually dealt with—the Conservatives we considered unworthy of notice.

I believe, however, the most powerful of Williams's English experiences in this sphere was with *Capitalism and Slavery*. One of his examiners for his Doctorate was Professor Coupland, an Oxford professor and the admitted authority on the history of slavery in England. Williams's thesis made mincemeat of

Coupland's published books. Yet it was unanswerable. Coupland, I understand, said that if he had known what Williams had brought out he would have written his books differently. The book is dedicated to Professor Ragatz of America, the acknowledged master of this period, who encouraged Williams all the way for what he recognised was a highly significant revaluation of one of the most important historical events in world history. Another authority, an American, reading the book, said over and over again: "I would never have believed it."

SUPPORT OF PEOPLE

This then was the foundation of the education of the future politician and nationalist. He had absorbed the culture and attitudes of Britain as a part of European civilisation. But on political issues in general, particularly colonialism, he had seen the anti-colonial case completely triumphant in exposition and discussion. In his own particular field of history, he had overthrown the traditional view, fortified by English university studies that the main cause of the abolition of British slavery was British good-will and repentance for evil. While paying full tribute to the work of the abolitionists (Clarkson is one of his heroes), he demonstrated that slavery had been abolished because it was advantageous to the rising British industrialists who wanted no more of this backward mode of production. Since *Capitalism and Slavery*, not a squeak has been heard in serious opposition. The champion of West Indian nationalism today is merely carrying out politically what was firmly established in his own mind against all comers by his studies and experience in 1933-1939. Given such a background it will be seen why the idea of a Colonial Office official telling him to do this and not to do that is intolerable to Williams. As long as he was solitary he had to take it. But the moment he was sure that he had a majority of the people behind him, his present drive to independence was on the order of the day. He has recently stated that all constitutional questions on the West Indies and all reserve powers should be in the hands of the Federal Government. It is perhaps the most revealing of all his statements; yet it has passed almost unnoticed. People continue to probe into his "psychology" and his "ambition" and all sorts of personality refuse, and make no serious attempt to grapple with one of the most profoundly based and sharply organised political personalities of our time. The first time that an attempt is made in the West Indies to understand the political personality of Williams West Indian politics will make a long stride forward.

A LUCKY MAN

Williams is a lucky man. Nothing better for his future development could have happened than going to lecture at Howard, the Negro university in the United States. I spent 15 years in the United States beginning about the same time. I saw great deal of Williams there, I observed him, and I observed myself both then and now. These are some of the conclusions I have drawn.

1) As can be seen from the careers of Nkrumah and Azikiwe, years in the U.S.A. develop in you a dynamism and readiness "to do things and go places" which is characteristic of that extraordinary people. They learn by doing. Only Americans could have embarked upon the gallant but inherently futile attempt to enforce teetotalism by law. An American company would come to Trinidad tomorrow, and having made its plans would forthwith pull down the Salvatori building and put up another bigger one without the slightest hesitation. Furthermore Williams worked in a Negro university. The Negroes in the U.S. are a people on the move restlessly seeking openings to advance themselves to equality. In this they are the most American of Americans. Live there for years and if you have energy and perspectives you absorb this spirit. Over and over again I see the clash between this readiness to move, to go ahead, in Williams, and the traditional pawky, little by little, thus far and no further conceptions and procedures of the Colonial Office, even when they have good intentions. What

makes it worse is the fact that behind his American sense of rapid movement, and the urgency of the local situation, Williams has his past experience of British traditionalism which I have described above. The Colonial Office is to him not merely imperialism. It is all that he saw stripped bare and turned inside out in 1933-1939.

Secondly, in America, a West Indian learns for the first time what the race question really is. You see the thing in its nakedness and its deep historical roots, its effect on racialists and anti-racialists. There is nothing personal about this. It should be known that after reviewing *Capitalism and Slavery,* an American professor of Columbia University wrote that he wished Dr. Williams would devote his method and power of analysis and research to the study of the abolition of slavery in the United States. The compliment is remarkable. But more remarkable is the recognition of the need for the best brains, not to try to push the horrrible thing in a corner but to probe as deeply as possible into it, to study it, where and how it began, to see how it has developed, where it is going. The American professor of History detected not only the intellectual power but what was more important, the attitude which would take one side but yet never lose its balanced objectivity before the facts. This deep American appreciation of capacity to deal with so thorny a subject as American slavery puts in their place all charges of racialism and anti-Americanism.

Williams could not find time to do this work but West Indians, I hope, can feel some pride in the fact and better still learn something from it.

OUR SPECIAL ROLE

Let me give a personal experience here. When *The Black Jacobins* was published in French, it was read and deeply admired in Haiti. I unreservedly took the side of the slaves. Yet it was years before they discovered that the book was written by a Negro and a West Indian. That testifies to the historical objectivity. I have myself written Marxist papers on The Negro Question in the United States which have been stated by critics to be the best ever done in that mode on this question in the United States. Unable to work on the history myself, I have initiated studies among my American colleagues which I know will result in the publication of some of the finest historical work ever done on the Civil War and the Negro Question in the United States. More of that another time. I go into this because I believe that the West Indian intellectual has a role to play in world history on this and many other questions. He is a part, organically a part, of Western civilization, that is the framework of his mind. But he is in a sense outside of it, and can see much that escapes general notice. In that there is much of the confidence and power with which Williams deals with the Colonial Office and the State Department. He knows the civilizations they represent (or misrepresent) from the inside. On the race question in particular, the West Indian Negro can feel and be indignant but it has not shaped every moment of his life for generations as it has shaped the life of Americans. Our peculiar historical development is a handicap—our intellectuals lack political spirit—but it gives certain advantages which can be of use to ourselves when free and to others far larger and more important than we are. Time and independence will show this. *Capitalism and Slavery* is not only West Indian history. It cleared up a lot of rubbish in English history. It is a pity that Williams never had the chance to assist in the clearing up of what, despite the work of men like Carter Woodson and Dr. Dubois, is still the greatest rubbish heap in American history (and it is constantly and copiously being added to, for example, by Professor Nevins).

Williams, then, saw the true race question, in the United States and knows it to be one of the most pernicious cancers of civilization, to be struck at in whatever shape it appears. This is not anti-Americanism. It is pro-humanity. His approach to the number of races who constitute the Trinidad community bears the stamp of his long historical discipline in examining these questions objectively in their origin and development. A new generation is being trained in this approach. It will take time but racial arrogance and racial obscurantism in Trinidad are doomed.

THE U.C.W.I.

In America too Williams learnt the essentials of education as developed by a people without the long European tradition. He mastered the American approach and was very conscious of it in his book on education in the West Indies. The preparation of this book was typical and gives as good an insight into Williams's character as anything else. He was willing to go to UCWI to teach. But before he went he wanted to let everyone know what kind of university he thought the West Indies needed. Oxford he loved and still loves but Oxford suits England, not the West Indies. And the University the West Indians need most is a university which is the result of examining first the idea of a university, then all universities, particularly these in undeveloped countries, and adapting all this to West Indian needs. And he is sure he can do this better than any Englishman. He is ready to consult with them but they must discuss what he or other West Indians propose. They are not to propose for us to discuss, as happened with Federation. That is Williams all over.

He began from Aristotle. He read everything he could find out about universities, particulary in undeveloped countries. He interviewed U.S. and foreign professors. Then he wrote his book and, as with Ragatz, he submitted it to the highest authority he knew, John Dewey. Dewey warmly approved and wrote an introduction. Williams is accused of arrogance. If you know something he will listen and take complete notes, consider it carefully and if need be change completely his previous ideas. He listens with great patience to the ordinary uninstructed citizen. But he takes incredible pains to find out all that he can about his subject and if people come around talking big or talking carelessly, he is extremely impatient, and as he sees very quickly where an argument or idea is weak or ill-based, he is not prepared to make allowances. Thus he is in constant conflict with what he uncompromisingly calls "fools who waste my time." Time is very precious to him. He smokes cigarettes in order not to spend time cleaning and filling a pipe.

I saw his manuscript on education often and learnt a great deal from it. A valuable memory of it, which will explain much of Dr. Williams's political career is my frequent admonition to him: "I wouldn't say that if I were you."

"But why?"

"I can say that, I am a free man, I can say what I please. You had better not."

If I have said that to Dr. Williams once, I have said it fifty times over the years. He would argue. I would be quite firm: I did not want to see him get into unnecessary trouble. He was always chafing at the restraint his official positions imposed upon him. 1956 released a long-coiled spring.

He was influenced but not fundamentally changed by his stay in America. For his classes at Howard he embarked upon a project into which he roped me, and to this day I wonder at it. It was a three volume collection of extracts from world literature and world history illustrating the development of civilzation from primitive man to the present day. I believe the volumes should be published and used in the schools of the West indies. The thing had to be stencilled and mimeographed and bound at Howard where for all I know it is still in use.

I am insisting that Williams is a lucky man. I can't go into exactly what that signifies now, but his next job was research for the Anglo-American Caribbean Commission. His perpetual conflicts with his employers he has himself made public. I shall not therefore spend any time on that aspect except to say that it was one long piece of unremitting infighting with the British Government and the American Government. It was always a losing battle. The wonder is that Williams held on for so long. He had little to fight with except ideas. But by this time he had written *The Negro in the Caribbean,* and *Capitalism and Slavery* had been published. He could not be thrown out easily. By nationalist lectures and writings he made getting rid of him a question which could have political repercussions (and didn't it have them?). When the end came he was as I have said trained for his present job as few men have been.

PREPARATION FOR PREMIERSHIP

He had had a long and arduous conflict with the British and American Governments on precisely the future of the West Indian economy and society. People who talk about Williams's inexperience of politics are merely shooting off. That conflict lasted for years, with Williams using every device to hold up his end, advance his ideas and get his way. When he became Chief Minister the conflict that started all over again was on the same issues, with the same opponents. He was therefore perfectly at home, only now he had control of a government and had the people behind him. I know much of that story and the method used then is still the same. Do good work which had to be accepted as marking process. Meanwhile fight inside. But at the same time write articles, give lectures, etc., building public opinion so that any plan to dismiss him abruptly would have to take into consideration the force of nationalist public feeling. The method today is the same, only in a more propitious environment, with the real power the power of mass support, on Williams's side.

The work at the Anglo-American Commission filled one great gap in Williams's equipment. It made him acquainted in the most comprehensive and intimate manner with the West Indian economy as a whole. That was his daily work for years. To us who grew up in the thirties, a strong central government and national economic development as the indispensable basis of a successful Federation is second nature. We cannot think otherwise. But to these general ideas and his knowledge of West Indian history through the centuries, Williams now had an opportunity as no other West Indian politician ever had of constant study and coordination of the West Indian, in fact the Caribbean economy, taken as a whole. When he says West Indian nationalism he speaks from deep down. When he says a strong Federation and a West Indian national economy, he speaks from roots almost as deep. He cannot think otherwise. For him to depart substantially from these principles would be to make a wreck of all his studies and the experience of a lifetime. To establish the truth about the central fact of our history, slavery and its abolition, he had to challenge ideas which had been accepted and taught in British universities and schools for a hundred years. This was the seminal experience by which he passed from youth to manhood. As I have tried to show, by accident and instinct his whole career fortified and amplified this early orientation. The whole has culminated in the struggle over Chaguaramas. When he says that he will break the Chaguaramas issue or it will break him, it is not a phrase. It expresses the whole life-experience of a man, exceptionally gifted in ability, character and power of will. The speech at Arima, *From Slavery to Chaguaramas*, should be read and re-read by all who, for whatever purpose, wish to understand Dr. Williams.

DR. WILLIAMS: WEST INDIAN

Williams is above all a West Indian. His work at Howard had included the teaching of Latin-American relations. In particular the Negro students at Howard University always wanted to learn from their professor all that he could tell them about Cuba, Mexico and Venezuela. Williams covered the ground very thoroughly. He was made a member of the staff of a foundation in the United States devoted to research (The Foundation for Foreign Affairs). His sphere of research was the British Empire. Working for this foundation, he was able to study the rising nationalist movement in Africa in great detail. But as usual he concentrated on the Caribbean. The only difficulty was that when he wrote his papers and monographs more often than not the foundation refused to publish them.

Somewhere about 1944 Williams met Manley for the first time and from the very beginning they got on famously. Manley came to Howard University to receive his Honorary Doctorate while Williams was there. Later Manley became a member of the Caribbean Commission. Many of the projects introduced into the Commission by Williams were discussed in advance with Manley. That Williams was able to stay so long there was because of the support given to him by Manley and the Puerto Ricans. And if Manley had won the 1950 elections in Jamaica, either the whole Caribbean Commission would have been reorganized or Williams would have left the Commission to go to work with Manley in his planning department.

He had better luck with Puerto Rico and Cuba. Munoz Marin, the celebrated Governor of Puerto Rico, was and remains a firm friend. Williams, Manley and Munoz Marin had long discussions together on the conditions and development of the West Indies and it is no accident that Manley in Jamaica and Williams in Trinidad have modelled so much of their Development Programmes on the Puerto Rican experience.

But Williams is first a scholar. At a great conference in Puerto Rico he outlined his conception of a syllabus for West Indian studies. This aroused such enthusiasm that when the conference was over he was asked to stay at the University and carry through the programme. This, however, he was unable to do. He had better luck with the Cuban dictatorship than with the foundation in democratic America. He spent a whole summer in Cuba studying Cuban history. When the Cuban people honoured perhaps the greatest scholar that the West Indies have ever produced, Fernando Ortiz, with the publication of three large volumes of essays by different hands to commemorate the 60th Anniversary of the publication of Ortiz's first work, Williams contributed a masssive essay on Race Relations in the West Indies. I have it among my papers and I read it again quite recently. It is fully worth publishing not only for Cubans but for other West Indians as well. But that it remains unpublished is only another of the many crying examples of our need for an independent publishing house.

Williams has been tireless in his pursuit of original material and information about West Indian history. He has spent vacations travelling over Europe, in Holland, in Copenhagen, in Spain, digging out original material on the West Indies that has been buried for centuries. When I was preparing *The Black Jacobins,* I had to leave Paris and spend some days in Bordeaux and in Nantes. I was interested to hear from Williams that he also, in pursuit of material on the slave trade and the West Indies, had also had to visit those two cities.

He has written and I also have a copy to which I regularly refer, an absolutely magnificent manuscript which deals with the history of all the West Indian islands from Cuba to Trinidad. I am certain that no such history of the West exists anywhere else. But when there will be time to prepare that M.S.S. for publication God only knows. Too much time has to be wasted on the Colonial Office and the State Department.

A word or two more about Williams's West Indian contacts to throw more light on his political personality.

Along with Manley and Munoz Marin must be mentioned Cesaire of Martinique, one of the most brilliant scholars and politicians that the West Indies have ever produced. Cesaire was a Stalinist and he had accepted the French colonial doctrine of assimilation, that is to say that all French colonials, Chinese, Indians, Africans, should ultimately become good Frenchmen. In 1955 Cesaire was breaking with Stalinism and along with many other French colonials, was breaking also with the doctrine of assimilation. Williams was in Brussels, doing a spell with the I.F.C.T.V. as consultant on plantation workers. Daniel Guerin, a friend of ours who has visited the West Indies and written a very fine book on his impressions, asked Williams to come over to Paris to meet Cesaire and some of the others. It was a strategic move. There was a meeting for Williams which was attended by Cesaire and nearly 100 intellectuals and students. Williams spoke on his faith as a West Indian. The speech made a profound impression and had just the effect hoped for by Guerin who knew the ferment that was going on in the minds of Cesaire and others. The details will have to wait for another time. But it was not long after that Cesaire led the breakaway which today is almost complete among French colonials from the theory of assimilation. This is not to say that Williams was responsible for the collapse of assimilation on which many French colonials, particularly Africans, had been working for years. But Williams as a West Indian, who had such wide experience of Europe and yet was so completely devoted to the idea of West Indian nationalism, undoubtedly had a great effect on Cesaire. If you listen carefully to Williams in ordinary conversation you will note that he always speaks of Cuba, Puerto Rico, Martinique, etc., as if they were one with us.

I hope I have said enough to show why Williams is in every sense as complete a West Indian citizen as it it possible to be today. I hope that this will explain and help people to understand why he thinks and speaks as he does on Federation.

To have arrived at so completely a nationalist outlook carries with it certain dangers, certain not merely inevitable but necessary dangers, necessary because you have to arm yourself at all points to resist the encroachments of powerful enemies of the as yet immature national personality. Dr. Williams's education and general knowledge and understanding of Western culture stand him in good stead. One of his most cherished projects is the calling of a great conference in the West Indies of Writers and Artists in which he will bring together West Indian writers and artists, English, French and Spanish and the greatest figures in modern literature and art, Jean Paul Sartre, Francois Maurice, Stephen Spender, Edmund Wilson, Brazilian artichects, Indian and Japanese film producers.... The idea is to project the West Indies into the very centre of Western culture where, it can judge and be judged, learn and perhaps even teach a bit. This whole question of West Indian nationalism is not an easy one. First it has a life of its own, that is to say the forces that control and direct it are and must be to a substantial degree unknown, not easily seen far less measured. Secondly, crude or violent attempts to manipulate it, even with the best intentions can do more harm than good. Any government has enormous power to do harm and less power to do good, though it can do much good. Williams's whole past leads him to concentrate on the political aspect on which he will not concede an inch; elsewhere he is more circumspect, ready to welcome, to stimulate, to include and not to exclude. As I say this is a very difficult question. I tremble to think of the mess that would most certainly be made were the influence and power of government in other hands. The insensitivity of State Department, Colonial Office, and certain West Indian public figures is a model of what ought to be avoided. More of this another time.

PARTY ORGANIZATION

As will be obvious, I have not gone into such matters as his power of work, his day-to-day political technique, the sharpness of his tongue. These and similar matters, as I have said, have their place. But they can matter only if the man as he is, is understood and accepted, and I have tried to show what he is and how he became that way. He can be broken, he cannot be changed.

This is the Convention appraisal, and to complete the picture, I want to point out one great gap, the only one in Dr. Williams's preministerial preparation, the only serious one. He had no experience of party organization. And before he and his colleagues could learn he and his Party were pitchforked into power. Five years in opposition, the experience of most new political parties, would have made a world of difference here. The theoretical foundations of PNM were well laid. But no human being can at the same time run a government and direct the organization of a party. If I can venture upon some advice to the Party at this Convention, it is to take this task upon itself and concentrate all its force and attention upon the organization of the Party. I have been for over twenty years a party functionary of one kind or another. For almost as many years I was a member of an international committee before which the affairs and fortunes of parties all over the world would periodically come up for review. The present secretary has many qualifications for his task. But the party must think in party terms. Indifferent organization is a weakness and politics has an uncanny instinct for finding out the weakness of a party and making it pay heavily for it. The comic opera DLP is not the proper comparison. The British Labour Party, the Conservative Party (very well organized), Nkrumah's CPP, the PNP of Jamaica, these have much to teach.

The Party so far has every reason to be proud of itself but only with a clear consciousness of what still remains to be done. So far it has followed the course of nationalist parties, making up for lost time. It has done and is doing what needs to be done. The Women's League shows signs of a great future. The NATION can become one of the great journalistic voices of the underdeveloped countries. But these are so far mere possibilities which can be realised only by the full development of the Party as an organization. Except in one respect it has broken no new ground. Struggle for independence, Development Programme, etc. here the Party is only catching up with the rest of the world. Its distinctive contribution to nationalist and even world politics is political education. I have never seen or heard of any political forum (in non-revolutionary periods) where addresses of the level of Dr. Williams's speeches have been consistently listened to by popular audiences. The credit has to be divided equally between the confidence and courage of the speaker and the receptivity of the audience. That in the last analysis is the secret of Dr. Williams's politics. Everything he has ever learnt, and he has learnt a great deal, he is able to stand and say and his popular audience listens for three, four, five hours at a time. This is the West Indies at its best. There is the promise that we shall achieve equality with other peoples and have the immense satisfaction and stimulus (very important to people with our history) that we do not only receive but are giving to the common stock of culture. This is Dr.

Williams's own special contribution, the impact of his individual personality, the historical accident. And yet in the Hegelian dialectic the organic movement proceeds by way of accidents and the sum of accidents constitutes the organic movement.

It is a truly great achievement. The long scholarly training and rigorous intellectual discipline seemed to have been nurtured to find fulfilment in the untutored but eager Trinidad masses. The accident turns out to be no accident after all. It is the genius of the people, following streams widely diverse with apparently no connection, to coalese in the end and gather strength for wider and further advances. It is a phenomenon often noticed at great moments in history and is a tested guarantee of ultimate success. Dr. Williams is of the people, even though some who listen can neither read nor write. A people is finding itself. The jackals and the mongrels are snarling and yapping, but the caravan is crossing the desert and will reach its goals.

I find it impossible, in fact it is impossible, to separate a convention of a mass party from the general public. I hope this appraisal will be considered by others beside the party. The Colonial Office and the State Department in their frantic desire to bend to their purposes, to humiliate and to exploit a small people in their long overdue effort to stand on their own feet and express themselves as an independent nationalist community, are guilty of one of the most wilful, unnecessary, cruel and sordid pieces of bullying in all the wretched history of imperialism. Instead of recognising what Dr. Williams represents, and he represents the future of the West Indies, they descend to the meanest and most contemptible tricks and dodges, ready to ally themselves with self-seeking, discredited and even grossly dishonoured and dishonourable elements in the population. There is no excuse whatever for it. All this will be made clear in good time. They can read or not read, that is their business, these teachers of how to govern, who fail in the first principle of government, to understand what and whom you are dealing with, a people suppressed for centuries who are fighting to be free and have found a leader who represents their best hopes. Where the whole history of the passing of colonialism should prompt them to say: "We welcome your determination and your sense of principle. It augurs well for your future," we find instead that humanity, generosity, even the formal courtesies of civilized intercourse, seem to shrivel in them as they meet someone who knows his mind and speaks it. They have blundered enough before. To them one more blunder does not matter. It is life and death to us.

That is why there are two elements in our population to whom I hope what I have written will contribute something new. The former ruling classes have to decide; political power is now out of their hands; if they do not want the national community that Dr. Williams is working for, what do they want? and how will they get it? The alternative to a Williams is a Trujillo. Look round the Caribbean Sea and think over what you see there. It is this which makes the attitude and policy of Colonial Office and State Department the shocking and evil thing that it is.

The second is the Federal Government. Its conflicts with Dr. Williams seem endless. I am convinced that for this the Colonial Office is responsible. But when two sides find themselves unable to get together,—exasperate each other at every turn, while professing adherence to the same principles, it is often the sign of deep and irreconcilable political divergences which have not yet appeared but which each side instinctively feels. The angularities of Dr. Williams's personality occupy too much attention. Lloyd George, Franklin Roosevelt, Winston Churchill frequently said the most wounding things, but people looked at what they stood for and shrugged or smiled away the rest. The conflict is the more confusing because, as everyone who knows Dr. Williams at all well knows, he has no inclination whatever to supplant the present Federal Government, being fully occupied with his present work, plans and perspectives. Here all of us suffer terribly from the lack of political journalism of an honest and serious kind. *The Trinidad Guardian* deals in slanders, scandals, suppression of facts, and analysis always on the level of the lowest attributes of human character. Thus there is no high level clarification such as politicians in more advanced countries enjoy. It is possible that this attempt to show the experiences and forces that make Dr. Williams what he is can assist to a more helpful appreciation of his politics and procedures. I hope so. The recent article in *The Times* was a fair and just appraisal. But while we welcome such, we should do these things for ourselves.

That is what independence means.

C. L. R. James with his son Nobby and his third wife, Selma James.

ADDRESS TO THE PNM WOMEN'S LEAGUE

by
Erica Williams-Connell

Erica Williams-Connell as she prepares to address the 33rd Annual Women's League Convention in 1990.

This lecture was delivered at the Thirty-third Anniversary of the PNM Women's League at the St. John's Ambulance Centre, Port of Spain, October 1990.

ADDRESS TO THE PNM WOMEN'S LEAGUE

Mr. Political Leader, Chairwoman of the Women's League, distinguished guests—When I was invited by the Chairwoman of the Women's League, Marilyn Gordon, to speak to you I was somewhat alarmed at the alacrity with which I accepted her invitation. After all, I've spent well-nigh on 39 years attempting not to attract attention to myself and would probably have continued quite blissfully to do so had not my blood been set to boiling recently by the scurrilous attacks, a great deal muted now, I notice, as a result of the coup attempt, on the memory of my father and that of the nation, your founder Eric Williams.

My father, as several of you know, was guilty of many things — no one is more acutely aware of this than I—of arrogance, a blind and trusting faith, yes, I can tell you this now, sometimes in the wrong people, stubbornness and I could go on. These very human failings were far outweighed by his love for Trinidad and Tobago and his people, which manifested itself in a selflessness and devotion that few can commit to today. But a more honest man I have yet to encounter, and if I have a choice—to believe the unfortunate politicking of the current regime, or in the integrity of Eric Williams—do I need to go on?

Some of you may understandably query my right in speaking here today. After all, I don't reside here and I share none of your daily frustrations. I quote from some revolutionary turned reporter, "More than half her life has been lived away from these shores, leaving a big question as to her 'Trinidadian-ness!' " Well I do have that right—as the daughter of the man who led this nation for almost a quarter of a century and more important, I have the right of a Trinidadian's love for her country. A Trinidadian who has never ceased to feel that these islands, this Trinidad and Tobago, is home. I live abroad, but my heart is here.

There are many issues I'd like to touch on today, and you'll forgive me for jumping about, but after so many years of mainly

Address to the PNM Women's League

self-imposed silence, I must squeeze into a few minutes an accumulation of comments and observances.

I suppose it would be too much to ask that I be quoted correctly, if at all, by certain members of the press, and by the "political analysts", to whom, by my appearance here today, I am giving much reason to speculate. But that is really one aspect I find so unseemly in our national psyche. This propensity we have to exaggerate, to attribute motives, and in fact deeds, to people who have absolutely no knowledge of same. Whose utterances are grossly and deliberately taken out of context, not once, but time and time again, and worse, in many instances, with the acquisescence and complicity of the said members of the press.

In one sample, my father, at the airport to welcome Hasley Crawford after his incredible Olympic feat, was congratulating him on his ability and perseverance, notwithstanding our then lack of facilities. He was explaining that although the Government had not been able, due to the unavailability of funds, to provide the infrastructure to actively inspire our numerous athletes—as he put it, "that is not now the problem." Because of our oil revenue the Government now had the wherewithal to offer such encouragement as was necessary. Translation? Money is no problem.

In a second famous misquotation, a former minister, nettled by accusations of PNM corruption, attempted to put such charges into an entirely proper perspective by likening the very venal practices the PNM was being blamed for to the fact that many in our society, and this is still true to an extent today, although much less so now, many in our society expected to be paid for a full day's work while giving only half a day's effort. Thus, "all ah we tief!" Translation? PNM professes crooked habits. But I'll expand on this later.

Just how much longer are we going to willfully mamaguy ourselves by repeating this nonsense, and, even more insulting, tolerating people who, having a forum to correct these misinterpretations, fail to do so.[1] It is surely good to poke fun at oneself, and nowhere is this more self-evident than in Trinidad and Tobago. But humour has its place, and we must learn to be serious.

None of us was laughing on July 27, 1990, and all of us were afraid, or should have been, for our beloved country and its democratic institutions.[2] But already I see, both here and abroad, a kind of lackadaisical, nine-days-wonder-type attitude, and while the jokes may be a welcome release valve for pent-up emotions, still, I cannot help but bemoan the general lack of concern about the episode as a whole that I seem to be confronting.

What is even more astonishing is the fact that one senses little sympathy among the population for those Government Ministers who were held hostage—and one even hears regret that the Prime Minister was not killed. In truth, I cannot subscribe to such sentiments. While my father was alive, my daily hell was to imagine just that sort of occurrence befalling him. I don't know how I would have faced life, or Trinidad and Tobago, if it had. And so, having gone through my own baptism of fire in 1970, I wouldn't have wished that even on my worst enemy.[3]

I think the present administration has had the great misfortune of presiding over Trinidad and Tobago's affairs at a time when the economy is obviously in a shambles, although I understand there are some tentative signs being shown of an upswing. And they have obviously made their mistakes. Pettiness and bickering continue to be a feature of partisan politics in Trinidad and Tobago, as is opposition for opposing's sake. The Government's well-documented obsession with the PNM still

---

[1] "Mamaguy" is a Trinidadian expression that means "to deceive." [SRC]

[2] On July 27, 1990, a group of Muslims under the leadership of Abu Bakr stormed the Red House, the seat of Government, and held the NAR and other members of government hostage for a few days. They were subsequently cleared of all charges when it was ruled that they received an official pardon from the acting President at the time. [SRC]

[3] In February 1970, while Eric Williams was prime minister, members of the Trinidad and TobagoRegiment also attempted a coup d'etat that was unsuccessful. [SRC]

Address to the PNM Women's League

reigns supreme. For what else would you call their objective to further demoralize the party, and I say demoralize decidedly.

They have used every cheap and tawdry trick in the book to attempt to tar us all with the same brush, and what is worse, as far as I can see, we have let them do it unchecked. Whether or not they have succeeded is another matter.

Since 1986 it has become popular to attribute all of the various negatives in the country either to the excesses of the PNM or to its inadequacies. When you repeat the fashionable slogan that the PNM did nothing for the country in 30 years, you are being downright unfair, and what's more, ungrateful—a common enough trait, I suppose, but certainly one of the more unsavoury ones. Moreover, one sees attempts to deliberately fan the fires of ingratitude by taking a perfectly worthwhile and laudatory policy and twisting its rationale to suit anti-PNM goals. I quote from a *Guardian* article: "We were being pampered by a Government whose major strategies were to appease the electorate in order to maintain popular support."

Well, now everybody feels free to give their own definition of the policies of the previous Government. What is it they say? Hindsight is the only kind of sight? So I'm going to put in my two cents. I'm not going to make any apologies for PNM management. I'll simply say that while the policies were mostly visionary, some of the managers—and there were many—just didn't implement them satisfactorily.

Further, and I speak from personal knowledge of the convictions of the man at the top, I know, no matter what anyone else may think they know, that the intention was to pass on the wealth of Trinidad and Tobago to the population where it rightly belongs. This is what the state of Alaska does with its oil revenue. In 1990, for example, every man, woman and child received US $ 952 of its oil dividends. You can be sure there is no one there griping about "patronage."

If, in Trinidad and Tobago, the unfortunate result of such PNM largesse was the creation of a generation who looked for handouts rather than to themselves in order to fulfill their own destiny, as another opinion has it, then this needs to be rectified. But let me ask you, What do you imagine the critics would have said if the profits from our oil windfall had not been passed on to the population in the form of improvements in the infrastructure, and in other initiatives, such as school feeding, book grants, free bus passes for students and senior citizens—to mention a few? I can just hear the baying and howling of the wolves.

Now when they talk about the revamping of such programmes—make no mistake about it—they are merely continuing those originating with the PNM.

And let me pose another question. What do you suppose the Government is going to do, in an election year, with any oil profits garnered from the Iraq/Kuwait crisis. I wonder if, in passing the benefits on to a needy population as they will surely be morally obligated to do, I wonder if they will call it something else? My guess is we will just have to wait and see.

But to get back to the oft-heard refrain—regurgitation, really—it is the PNM's fault that the looting was so widespread and destructive - what was the phrase? Oh yes! "As a result of the political culture the people had been given over the past 30 years" - or some such verbiage!

And Abu Bakr was the PNM's fault! Most heinous of all, they even seek now to link the coup with the corruption debate in Parliament. Just what are they trying to say? That the PNM had to resort to such measures in order to keep the Government from spilling the beans? What rubbish! Better to read Shakespeare's *Macbeth*—"unnatural deeds do breed unnatural troubles." And if the sun don't shine tomorrow, I suppose that will be the PNM's fault too! In fact, anybody's but theirs. No possibility of this Government shouldering the blame for attempting to forcefeed a restive population the stringent economic measures of the international lending community. No possibility of acknowledging their insensitivity to the plight of the people and lack of basic human understanding as to how far the population could be pushed, how many erosions of income they could take. Even allowing for the fact that governments often have to make difficult and sometimes unpopular decisions, as this one has had to do on many occasions, still, they have acted with an extraordinary absence of compassion.

No possibility, even, of admitting to the gross breach of national security that led to the aborted coup. Now, suddenly, and as result, we hear of pay raises for the nurses, freedom from the I.M.F., improvements in the minimum wage bill, and the urgent need to attend to the requirements of the Protective Services, those guardians of our democracy! Talk about shutting the coop after the fowl get away.

It was these same Protective Services who, a short time ago, were completely emasculated, both in terms of manpower, in equipment and in morale. What else would you call the Presidential pardon, no less, of a convicted cop killer and the shortage of even the most elementary tools of the trade, such as cars. What message do you suppose that state of affairs sent to the Protective Services and the criminal element?

But have they succeeded in their planned annihilation of the Party? I think not. Some may believe we are at the bottom of the well, but I say we must climb out. We must break from this mould that they have crafted for us. The plot has backfired, it is clear, and I think I speak for many when I say they enormously miscalculated the focus of their attention. While people were having their salaries cut and in many cases losing their livelihood, they were talking about O'Halloran and his alleged millions.

So compulsive was their fixation, they even set up a commission to investigate past PNM contracts. Perhaps they forgot it was a PNM Government who issued a warrant for O'Halloran's arrest? Perhaps they could not quite comprehend that they had actually routed the PNM in free and fair elections.

Perhaps they didn't understand that the people put them there to get on with the business of running the country—not to dig graves or dredge up the past. Which is not to say, ladies and gentlemen, that I do not fully endorse the indictment of those who flout the law of the land. But having said that, it was merely a matter of handing over prosecutable evidence to the Ministry of Justice and letting the law take its course and even that they did not do. What did they do? They continued to kick the PNM when we were down—one of the most fundamental principles in child rearing and one that most parents teach their children not to do. They showed respect neither for a past President nor a former Prime Minister, and Ministers of Government, who had already been unceremiously booted out of public office, were further humiliated in a forum where no recourse to law is permitted.

In short, their "one love," and various and sundry mouthings about "healing of the wounds brought about by the political process," had already turned into "one hate" early in their administration—to coin a phrase. But you know what they say? When you spit in the air it must come down! And I think it is beginning to fall. Just as an aside here, it is interesting to note that some recognition was paid to my father lately at Los Bajos. For what? For his conception of one youth centre! Not for his wisdom in dealing with our youth or their education, mind you! Do I get a picture of a drowning man desperately clutching at straws?

As a footnote to all this, though, let me briefly review just a few of the more questionable practices that the Government has never adequately been able to explain. There is the sale and lease-back of BWIA aircraft, the Mount Hope engineering and maintenance agreement, the inability to account, in Parliament, with any kind of assurance, for the expenditure vis-à-vis the "Football Massive" facilities during the World Cup match. Possible political interference in the now defunct Hospital Management Company, and suspected improprieties surrounding procedures employed in the awarding of certain contracts.

I enumerate these simply to set the record straight, and to affirm that money and power are breeding grounds for corruption—no matter who holds the reins of office. It has been so throughout the ages, and, regrettably, will always be. To believe

Address to the PNM Women's League

otherwise is to be naive about human frailty. Which is not to say that corruption should be condoned either within or without the PNM Simply and succinctly put as in John, Chapter 8, verses 1 – 11 "Let he who is without sin cast the first stone." Corruption in Trinidad and Tobago is rampant throughout the society. The Government would have you believe that this designation is reserved solely for card-carrying members of the PNM who, reportedly, steal millions. But I say that if you have to pay a WASA truck driver extra to bring water to your house on a hill, he is tainted. So, too, is the subcontractor you may have to bribe with liquor to get a job completed with a minimum of delay. Think back to the wanton wastefulness and devastation that was a hallmark of the recent uprising—people who filched TVs and had no electricity and stole excessive amounts of food that had to be trashed due to lack of refrigeration facilities.

On an equally important note, I am chagrined to hear, even among members of my own family to boot, this most insidious of phrases—"there is no one to vote for". It baffles the mind that this degree of nonchalance and pure misguided logic, if such it could be called, could still exist in sectors of the population—even after Abu Bakr almost took that right away from us. How many more lessons must we be taught? What is it going to take for us to realize that the right to vote for the government of one's choice—no matter how uninspiring you may think the choices appear to be—is one that must be cherished and guarded zealously, never willingly relinquished.

I do not concur with the view that one should be persecuted or be denied an opportunity to serve because one's political views differ from my own. This country is large and varied enough to accommodate everyone who wishes to exercise their constitutional right, whichever party one may support, for we have a common ground—Mother Trinidad and Tobago. So I cannot tell you who to vote for—that is a matter for the individual conscience, but I can tell you to vote. If you feel that the current regime has lived up to your realistic expectations, if you feel that you are substantially better off today than you were before—vote for them. But let me make a few significant points in order to assist you in your deliberations.

In the 46 months during which the N.A.R. has shielded power, how many housing lots have been completed? They promised to develop 10,000 units a year.

The IADB loans, which enabled them to extend work on the dual carriage-way at the Churchill Roosevelt Highway and to erect a number of schools, had already been negotiated during the PNM's tenure—and one can only pray that their boast of building more schools for the same money does not sacrifice quality for quantity. In addition, the ratio of teachers to students per class has decreased.

Unemployment is at an all-time high—some 22% and rising. The N.A.R. pledged to eliminate joblessness. And, perhaps as disgraceful as anything else, for all the world to see, long lines of "refugees" daily humble themselves at the gates of the U.S. and Canadian embassies.

Public servants, the same ones who rejected a government offer of 6% in the 1980's and insisted on some 28%, have seen the removal of their cost of living allowances, not to mention a cut in salary of 10%.

Our nurses and medical professionals are migrating to greener pastures. Patients, who can ill-afford to, have to pay for their own medications, when they are available, and old men beg their doctors not to send them to the hospital "to die!"

And do I even need to mention VAT? There's a good joke about what the acronym stands for, but I won't go into that here. But seriously, it is a scandal that VAT should be levied on school books and on drugs. An unhealthy citizen cannot possibly be a productive one and will simply cost the State more money in the long term.

And the University cess! We again appear to have forgotten another Eric Williams exhortation—we carry the future of Trinidad and Tobago in our school bags. Well, what use is a school bag if you can't manage to purchase the books, or to go to college, if you should so desire? I respectfully submit, ladies and gentlemen, that we are regressing to where we used to be in 1956, at least in this case, when access to education was usually denied to those who could command neither wealth nor status.

This is the economic expansion plan we heard so much about in 1986? And these are the "positives we must count," or so we are told?

Of course they will say that they did not know the extent of the financial troubles when they took over. Well, I say phooey to that! Only a fool would have been unaware of where the country was heading at the time. The trend was crystal clear, and once you viewed our petroleum economy in any sort of world context, the situation became even more obvious.

What you have here is a former government who attempted to let the country down gently, who strove to bridge the gap between being oil rich and oil poor, without destroying the society in the process. What you have there, is a government who duped the population into believing that they could heal all wounds, right all wrongs, and put the country back on the road to economic prosperity.

Another cause for great anxiety is the fact that the issue of race has again reared its ugly head in our polyglot society, and, of course, our "class system" has never really been abolished. Perhaps I need to recall to you the words of my father on the occasion of our Independence in 1962. "There is no mother Africa, no mother India, and no mother China. There is only mother Trinidad and Tobago, and a mother must never distinguish between her children."

This "dream," for such it was, at least to him, is more relevant today, perhaps, than even he imagined it could be. Are we never going to accept that no man is better than another? That the differences become only a question of education, exposure and opportunity?

I see latent racism and blatant class discrimination everywhere in Trinidad and Tobago, and I confess to be shocked by it. I vow to do the very best by my beloved child in this regard, so that, hopefully, by my example, and that of her father, she may also grow up to understand this vital tenet of human equality—adherence to which will enable her to live in peace and harmony among her peers, a standard that students at UWI in this country would do well to emulate!

All this talk of children brings me to a new subject very close to my heart—the total disintegration of family life and structure. Nowhere was it more well-demonstrated than during the July plundering, where one heard of families participating in that unlawful event—parents and children side by side, head to head in their nefarious doings. In the last twenty or so years, vast amounts of knowledge in child development theory have been gleaned by various authorities in the field. It has been proven that, mostly, children learn by example. Just look at what we have been teaching them.

My own sense of parental responsibility has come to me late in life, and, like all those newly converted to the cause, I am absolutely appalled at the kind of influences under which our young must mature. The violence and generally loose morals which characterize much of what kids watch on TV today, the very fact of television itself, a passive, non-imaginative activity that does nothing to bring families closer together and creates generations of gawk-eyed children. The heavy metal music with its suggestions of suicide, drugs and rape. The lack of any kind of social conscience, not to mention absence of manners, that is a feature of adolescence in the '90's. The sense of futility among our own youth, of going nowhere fast—the adult supervision and discipline that is missing in the lives of many children in today's nuclear families. The families themselves—many of them single-parent—with the only parent working and scraping to make ends meet. These trends trouble me greatly, as they should each one of us who belongs to the society of motherhood, and I yearn for days past, for simpler pleasures and less complex problems. Even taking cognizance of the extravagances of youth when all of us are guilty, at one time or another, of a multitude of transgressions, there is no question but that our babies are floundering—dropping out of school, smoking crack, getting pregnant—children having children—and so the cycle begins again, with prospects for a decent future looking grimmer day by day.

These men who run governments—they haven't got a clue. They are not mothers—by and large they don't wipe the bottoms, kiss the knees and sap the heads. They don't work the two shifts that most Moms do. What is it they say? The hand that rocks the cradle is the hand that rules the world? Well I say our children need us, and we'd better start doing both and with far more effectiveness than has previously been the case. Thus, the theme of today's conference—"If it is to be, it is up to me" — is particularly meaningful.

And this brings me, really, to the final point I would like to make here today—that of the role of the PNM, as I see it anyway, in these, certainly different, circumstances in which we find ourselves.

The new PNM must rise, like the phoenix, from the ashes of the old and must renew its commitment to this precious land. The new PNM must recognize and admit its mistakes and vow to do better if given another chance. We must, once again, assume the mantle of political power and continue to advance the cause of human dignity. The new PNM must not shunt aside the experience and knowledge of its original members but must involve them, perhaps in a different capacity, in its affairs, all the while heeding the views of the electorate. These "old-timers," as it were, in keeping with the natural order of things, must step aside and allow the "new blood" to take a shot at leadership. But they still, undoubtedly, have much to contribute—no one likes to be made to feel redundant, and I find the trend of thoughtlessly discarding that which is no longer of any use to us, personally distasteful. As a mentor has it—a society that does not respect or honour its elders is one without hope of fulfilling its potential. But above all, the new PNM must not hang its tail between its legs like a beaten dog taking its licks. It must rise up and take the offensive, even in the face of the bitterest criticism, and better it will be. We must not get into the habit of acknowledging anti-PNM personal perspectives as truth. We know what we did, and why, and by and large, though we must accept responsibility for the areas in which we fell down, we are proud of our achievements.

You only have to look at the Trinidad and Tobago of 1986 and compare it, if you can, with 1956, and while one must allow for some spontaneous progression, which, by the very nature of things, would have taken place anyway—it is as plain as day—a large proportion of our growth has been as a direct consequences of PNM and PNM freedom. We don't want gratitude, don't get it anyway. But we should insist on fair play.

For the country, we need to start, at least in my view, giving credit where it is due, and supporting any Government when they enact laws or institute programs that will be beneficial to our people. On balance, one would have to say that there are a couple of areas in which the NAR has moved the country forward—notably, in the field of self-reliance and non-dependence on the Government as a solution to all problems. In this, perhaps, they had no choice given the straitened condition of the country. Nonetheless, some strides have been made in this regard.

Trinidad and Tobago has been able too, because of the NAR, to experience another Government where this had not been possible before, and this has merely served to enhance the contributions of the PNM, and to imbue them with a greater sense of value.

They also showed us that it was possible, however briefly, to bring together all of the various elements in the society, even though they were unable, finally, to take advantage of this opportunity.

As for the politicos, I trust that attempts will be made, at least in the near future, to bring the level of political life in Trinidad and Tobago to an acceptable standard, so that the vulgar and inappropriate attacks on personalities, and even on their families, might cease, except where their personal behaviour impacts upon their performance in office. The Government of the day will always provide us with enough ammunition with which to tackle their policies, without having to resort to the sort of smut that is a regular feature, both in our press, and on the lips of the population at large.

I hope too, that we, as a Party, will seek the widest possible consensus in decision-making. After all two heads are always better than one, and we have a lot of good heads here. If we have disagreements within the Party, we must keep them "en famile," vision, PNM execution, and rigorously object to members hanging their dirty laundry out to dry. That is playing right into opposition hands. Above all, we must give no section of the population the notion that there is any rift to be healed by a marriage of convenience, such as has been tried before, and has long since failed. And after all the thrashing out of diverse views and opinions, we must then come together, the leader and the led, solidly behind the majority, understanding that one does not have to appreciate all of the policies all of the time, but being a loyal Party man or woman nevertheless.

The die is cast ladies and gentlemen. We can either squabble and sit out the 1991 elections, or we can unite ... fight ... and win!

Thank you for your attention.

BOURNES ROAD ADDRESS

by
Erica Williams-Connell

Williams with his daughter, Erica in 1956.

This address was delivered at Bournes Road, St. James, at a PNM political rally on December 4, 1991.

BOURNES ROAD ADDRESS

Mr. Party Chairman, Deputy Political Leader, PNM candidates, friends and well-wishers.

It has been one year since I made my first political speech, and although I now find myself in the uncomfortable position of having to best my own achievement, it feels good to be home.

I am well aware of the criticism that I shall attract by being here, speaking now. Let me preempt some of the inevitable comments from the kitchen cabinet—"PNM plays final card," "PNM pulls rabbit out of hat," "PNM, insecure, needs Erica to help win," "The Roman pro-consul comes to town." Oh I forgot, they used that one already and they are going to say that I am defending the indefensible, and so on. You know, I have no quarrel with a kitchen cabinet, but oh Lord, at least let them be able to cook-even if they are, to quote the Prime Minister, "getting prettier and prettier." Well, we do not think good looks are a qualification for running the government, and I do not believe you think so either—remember Ivan Perot? Some political analyst, who might better serve us in the kitchen, might even let me in on the many instances of lack of patriotism that he claims I could be charged with.

But seriously, ladies and gentlemen, I am here because I want to be, because as a member of the party which my father founded, I could do no less than be here with you, in what is the prelude to either our victory or our defeat. As a Trinidadian living abroad, I do not consider that I have abdicated either my right to serve my country or my political party. And so I am here today to give you a broad overview of our previous record in government.

In its first plan, entitled *The People's Charter*, written in 1956 and amplified in *The Chaguaramas Declaration* of 1970, the PNM listed several political aims: immediate self-government, the political education of the people, and I quote, "the elimination of racial and other forms of discrimination from our society and promotion of interracial solidarity, inviting all sections of the community, irrespective of race, class, color or creed to work for the commonweal."

Ladies and gentleman, I respectfully submit that in our thirty years of government we more than amply fulfilled those aims. Who was it that instituted national holidays for our Muslim and Hindu brothers? I do not focus on the day of rest but on the fact that, in one fell swoop, the national importance of these religious festivals was placed on the same footing as our traditional Christian days of celebration. Those of our citizens who are of East Indian ancestry have organized cultural programs, radio and TV shows and installed retail stores to propagate their heritage, and we have encouraged that. In fact, and I say this without fear of contradiction, had it not been for an enlightened PNM government in those critical years of self-determination, I doubt you would now be seeing such integration of the cultures as expressed in chutney dancing and Drupatee, and let us not forget that it was a PNM government that sent Ashford Sinanan, a noted Opposition Parliamentarian of East Indian descent, to India in 1969 as Trinidad and Tobago's High Commissioner.

One so-called journalist claims that in his statement, "oil and sugar don't mix," my father used a classic euphemism to keep sugar and oil workers divided at the level of party politics, and he goes on to imply that this contradiction was a prime example of PNM politics with respect to race. Let me recall to you some of my father's own words on the occasion of his 1970 Convention Address in which he attempted to rationalize the causes for the Black Power revolution. While the African culture, he says, is "intellectually constructive and psychologically legitimate, it has its possible dangers if it is overplayed, if it seeks to dominate and denigrate other cultures which have contributed to Trinidad and Tobago." And again, in referring to the subject of race relations within the PNM, "PNM recognizes neither racial differences nor sectarian differences nor color differences nor class differences...... Reaction knows no color...... You members of the PNM must understand once and for all that you do a great disservice to your national cause if you think that every white person or every Indian is anti-PNM or that every black person is pro-PNM. You shall know them not by their color or their race, but by their fruit."

A typical example of how we learned our lessons, from, yes, a PNM government was in the aftermath of last year's coup. In many developing countries, our Muslim compatriots would have suffered a tremendously violent backlash, the likes of which we have never seen here and hope never to. While there were some reported and disturbing instances of retribution, no widespread organized vendetta ever materialized.

I have heard it said that the PNM deliberately contributed to the unhappy delineations that separate the various sectors of our society today. Let me not be misunderstood—at no time in our history, past or present, was the PNM ever a party to this type of plan, if such there was. Indeed, the very colors of our Party flag, white, brown, yellow, and black denote the unity and equality of all races under the PNM banner. No, ladies and gentlemen, the divisions in Trinidad and Tobago already existed when we came into power. We neither created nor fostered them, and I challenge anyone to prove otherwise. The fact that these splits may now have been exacerbated, as in a report earlier this year that cited black entrepreneurs as experiencing difficulties in obtaining seed capital from established financial institutions, or another report which claimed that private-sector employers were demanding from executive search firms professionals possessing certain racial characteristics that were clearly discriminatory against blacks — the fact, ladies and gentlemen, that these divisions may now be aggravated cannot be laid at the door of the PNM.

A little personal anecdote here. There are few who would realize that when Bhadase Maraj lay dying in Park's Nursing Home, it was a PNM government who, at the request of his family, cordoned off the area to overzealous well-wishers, the better to ease his passing.

And how was it possible for our East Indian comrades to

achieve such a measure of economic success were it not for the fact that the PNM had done exactly what it had promised?

In its original social aims, the PNM cited the adoption of the international standards worked out for all categories of workers. No one can quibble about our adherence to than tenet. In fact, while workers marched in all manner of processions during our thirty year tenure, and with much less provocation than they have recently encountered, today they face shrinking wage packets and retrenchment, foreign bosses, a complete violation of and disregard for their bargaining entitlement, yet still, the marching has not escalated. No doubt we should, ourselves, have devised the brilliantly strategic ploy of offering government jobs to self-styled trade union leaders!

Between 1960 and 1964, ladies and gentlemen, 230 trade disputes were recorded involving 74,574 workers with a loss of 803,899 man days. By 1965, however, it had become clear that we were witnessing a marked deterioration in the industrial relations system, which had previously been modeled on a voluntary concept. As a direct result of this then, and with the government's industrialization thrust hanging in the balance, the controversial Industrial Stabilization Act was introduced allowing for the compulsory recognition of trade unions by employers, the inauguration of the Industrial Court, and the regulation of prices and commodities. This act was replaced by the Industrial Relations Act of 1972, which better provided for the improvement and promotion of industrial relations conceding certain instances in which strikes and lockouts, virtually curtailed by the prior act, were permitted.

Another social agenda pledged by the PNM was the provision of more and better houses, schools, and social services for the population. Armed with the watchwords "To educate is to redeem," the PNM set forth to change forever the face of education in Trinidad and Tobago. In 1956, for example, when the PNM came to power, there was a total of 15 secondary schools nationwide. Those 15 secondary schools accounted for 14, 024 students with only 236 being eligible to attend on a nonpaying basis. By 1986 an additional 80 secondary schools and two new technical colleges had been constructed with a teacher/student ratio of 21:1, up from a high of 37:1 in 1956. We now had a total of approximately 150,000 students attending free secondary schools in Trinidad and Tobago. Libraries were introduced in all senior comprehensive, sixth form, junior secondary, and composite schools, and all primary schools built after 1972 were equipped with similar facilities.

Adult education, too, benefited under the PNM regime with, by 1983, a total of thirty-one such centers available in Trinidad and another nine in Tobago.

Before 1956 only four island scholarships a year were offered in Trinidad and Tobago. Between the period 1976 to 1986, 4,740 persons were awarded scholarships or full-pay study leave to pursue higher education in fields vital to Trinidad and Tobago's requirements. The cost of these scholarships was some TT$150,100,000. One may thus conclude, ladies and gentlemen, that the intelligentsia of this land owe their tertiary education and subsequent position to PNM vision.

UWI opened its St. Augustine campus in 1961 with 96 students, this figure jumping to 22,499 Trinidad and Tobago nationals enrolled at the three campuses between 1976 and 1985, all on a nonpaying basis. This situation, however, exists no more.

In 1986, our national literacy rate was a staggering 95 percent, among the highest in the developing world, and who should take the credit for that? In spite of this, in recent years we have seen a decline in the quality of education, for what other reason could there be for the botching of the Police Service entrance examination by a whopping 90% of applicants, some with university degrees? And now, most ludicrous of all is the current effort to link the PNM's free secondary education program with our flourishing crime rate!

Among the social schemes instituted were book and uniform grants for children, free bus passes for students and senior citizens, old age pensions, the public assistance program, food subsidies and food stamps, grants to nonprofit organizations, namely the Blind Welfare Association, Red Cross, Cancer Society, Servol and others, the Rent Restriction Bill, and the school feeding program. Despite what one hears, this program was never discontinued by the PNM. As in the normal course, the program came to an end during the Christmas break, with its assumption intended at the commencement of the new school term. When you decided to exercise your constitutional right and vote another government into office, it was that government which chose not to restart it. By the end of 1985, however, the government was supplying 2.8 million meals a year to primary schools in the more depressed areas. Free bus, medical, and dental services were also obtainable in schools during the PNM administration.

The youth in Trinidad and Tobago, too, have been abundantly provided for under a PNM government. In sport, the several playing fields, coaching programs, the National Stadium, assistance to national sporting organizations, and the refurbishing of swimming pools in outlying areas all point to the PNM's special interest in and emphasis on the youth of our nation. In 1986 we established a fund for stimulating self-employment among unemployed and under-employed young people. Of the TT$1,000,000 originally appropriated, some TT$700,000 had been disbursed by July of that year. Youth camps and youth centers too accounted for a percentage of the government's efforts at inspiring our young, and the training procurable at the camps, ladies and gentlemen, continued for a period of two years with a 70% employment placement as opposed to the current 200 hours of training.

Housing was provided through a diversity of plans, direct loans, isolated building lots, provision of developed lots, squatter organization and resettlement as in Shanty Town, and the construction of housing units. Between the years 1956 and 1969, government expenditure on housing was $54.1 million with new housing units not including sugar belt units, amounting to 7375.

Some $3.3 billion was spent in the years 1976 to 1986 with a yield of 29,382 housing units for low-income families; 3,122 lots were developed from Diego Martin to Point Fortin and Mayaro in Trinidad and from Buccoo to Charlotteville in Tobago. In the sugar areas, the Sugar Industry Labour Welfare Committee spent some $5.1 million of government funds on the development of housing sites and disbursed some TT$31.2 million in housing loans. Assistance was also given to the trade union movement's housing accommodation agenda in the supplying of infrastructure in such regions as Lopinot, Pleasantville, and Valsayn. As a consequence of all this, in ten short years from 1976 to 1986, the PNM was able to rehouse just under 10% of our population. Now tell me that we did nothing.

Although you have heard much about the present "economic miracle," one overzealous supporter even comparing it to the first heart transplant operation (there is only one problem with that - the patient died), on the economic side, it was the PNM that promised the reorganization of the economy to make the fullest use of all the resources of Trinidad and Tobago, both physical and human. If we did not accomplish this, then who initiated the IDC with small business loans available at 3% definite, encompassing all areas of industry from lawn mowers to drugstores, snocones to bakeries? In the last 20 years, the IDC has approved some four thousand loans applications worth $150 million. Who tried to turn what one expert terms "a nation of commission agents into manufacturers." In 1956 we inherited 66 industries in Trinidad and Tobago. By December 1986, 1,200 companies had been approved for duty-free concessions by the IDC. Who exhorted the nation to "buy local"? I see they have renamed it "Buy Trinidad and Tobago" and have adopted it as their own! It is true that we had some problems; you remember the light bulbs that would not light and the razors that cut everything but hair? But who was it that introduced the investment, initial and depreciation allowances available to pioneer industries in order to compete in overseas markets? I can tell you who! It was the PNM, let us not be confused about that! And we did not forget the disadvantaged either . They accuse us of "squandermania." I cite the Constitution which says in part that "the people of Trinidad and Tobago believe the operation of the economic system should result in the material resources of the community being so distributed as to subserve the common good." I argue that is exactly what the PNM attempted to do and did so. Just what would they have had us do? Having acquired the funds almost involuntarily, as it were, would you rather we had not met public requirements? Why do they not ask the beneficiaries—you the people. We made sure that, after being so long disenfranchised, control of the commanding heights of the economy, as one writer put it, were placed fairly and squarely where they rightfully belonged—in the hands of the population. This can no longer be said to obtain today, ladies and gentlemen, with monopolistic conglomerates virtually running the Government and setting economic policy, or so we are told, with, and I quote a former PNMite, "the dismantling of the State sector, privatizing and selling it to people who have the money to buy."

And the vendors, their place in the sun is a prime illustration of the PNM's regard for the disadvantaged. While there were difficulties in the way the situation was managed, the intention was never to kill the established storefront trade, but to give vendors a sense of self-sufficiency, of self-worth. We are a nation of vendors, after all, our families have always, at some time or other, sold eggs or flowers, cakes or jams, peanuts or toolum. They even said I was selling tamarind balls in Miami, as if I would ever be ashamed of any such honest work. This section of the community takes pride in being able to contribute to their family's well-being, in however small a fashion, and especially in these times of hardship, and if that takes the form of selling ice blocks or pholourie balls, then so be it. We must find a way to facilitate and encourage their enterprise, even while allowing for the legitimate concerns of the businessman.

We were responsible for the inception of the NIS, Mortgage

Bank, Central Bank, Development Finance Company, Unit Trust, the Productivity Centre, the nationalization of financial institutions which were then able to provide local investment, the National Gas Company, Metal Industries Company, Trintoc, the National Energy Corporation, the Shipping Company of Trinidad and Tobago, the National Commercial Bank, the Urea Company, Tringen, Fertrin, the National Flour Mills, the Stock Exchange—do you want me to go on? And then there was the enormous expansion of telephone and electricity facilities to accommodate the unprecedented industrialization of the nation.

Credit unions and cooperative societies were developed and encouraged under the PNM and some personal tax liability was deductible for shareholdings therein. Industrial estates were dispersed throughout the country so that no one zone could become more developed than the next—in areas such as Chase Village in Carapachaima, Diego Martin, Diamond Vale, Milford Road in Tobago, Trincity and Macoya, Biljah Road, Pt. Lisas, Pleasance Park, Morvant, O'Meara, Harmony Hall in Princes Town, Frederick Settlement in Caroni, East Dry River and Sea Lots. Moreover, ladies and gentlemen, since 1986 not one industrial estate has been initiated!

The Export Development Corporation commenced with us. We were cited as having done zero to encourage export earnings, but it is interesting to note that in a special report issued by the London-based Economic Intelligence Unit, export earnings in the 1980s, under a PNM government, were at one of the highest all-time levels.

We initiated ISCOTT and a number of other downstream industries that were planned to maximize our natural resources; yes, the same ISCOTT that is currently making money under new management. And the Methanol Company -another mistake as was the entire Pt. Lisas project according to some uninformed and unimaginative critics—the Methanol Company in 1990 registered a profit of TT$90 million. In fact, Pt. Lisas, directly or indirectly employing some four to five thousand workers as of

1984, was an idea that originated from the South Chamber of Commerce aimed at weaning the economy from its total reliance on oil. Although the cost of establishing these industries eventually proved to be too high and returns took somewhat longer than anticipated, we can now point proudly to the fact that, because of PNM foresight, Trinidad and Tobago is now the world's second largest producer of ammonia, and we expect other successes to follow. No true businessman in his right mind, however, will tell you he expects to make a profit within the first three to five years of an operation, and particularly one of the magnitude of Pt. Lisas. As an aside to all this, our welders had become so skilled by the time Pt. Lisas had been completed that several were in danger of being wooed by Bethlehem Steel of America to take up permanent jobs there.

Now, we are faced with the much-vaunted EPZs designed primarily to employ cheap labor but with nothing having so far materialized.

In terms of the much maligned negative list that the World Bank now claims was in effect for too long, as difficult and unpopular as it was to live under its restrictions, it was a necessary evil, affording would-be manufacturers the protection they needed to develop and sell their product.

And finally, when there was danger of a foreign buyout, who bought Angostura and arranged for the repurchasing of the company by its original owners, and on a most favorable basis? When Alstons, the new McAl Group, faced a takeover by a British entrepreneur, who introduced the amended Aliens Landholdings Act, specifically devised to protect them and others, at the request of two prominent businessmen.

In the areas of health, water, and electricity, following are some statistics. By 1986 WASA was producing 700% more water than it did in 1956 with water projects having been accomplished in a number of areas nationwide. T&TEC customers in 1956 amounted to 29,000 homes, primarily in urban areas; by 1986 this figure had leaped to 270,000—an increase of almost 830%, although the population had multiplied by a mere 33%. Street lighting in 1961 consisted of 5,500 lights; in 1986 we were up to 43,000.

Health expenditure amounted to TT$10,038,000 but by 1986 this figure had mushroomed to just over TT$566,000,000 with the development of primary health care providing the cornerstone for our national health policy. Also as of 1986 a total of 103 health centers existed in both Trinidad and Tobago, and strides had been made in the provision of vaccinations for newborns, the oral rehydration program, a decrease in the child mortality rate, blood screening, an improved mental health and dental program, food and drugs and substance abuse control, to mention just a few. In spite of all this, the management of and conditions in our major hospitals have long been a bone of contention, even in a PNM administration, and by all accounts the situation has worsened drastically within the past five years.

In agriculture also I have heard the critics-one, totally misrepresenting, and predictably so, what Eric Williams said about the populace no longer being required to be "hewers of wood and drawers of water"—of course he was speaking within the framework of being enslaved by these occupations, of course he did not mean that Trinidad and Tobago should import all its food.

It was a PNM government that, allowing for the exclusive importation of rice by the National Flour Mill, insisted that it commit to purchasing our total rice production on an annual basis. The result of this system has been a continual growth in the number of rice farmers throughout this land, to the extent that they now number some five thousand as opposed to three hundred in the mid-1980s.

By 1965 the government had embarked on a significant agricultural resettlement scheme whereby farms were expected to be involved in food import substitutions such as vegetable and root crops, fruit, pork, chicken, beef, and milk. In this particular project, the government provided most of the development cost and basic infrastructure, as well as the ten thousand acres that were distributed.

A similar program was in effect for the conversion of lands no longer needed for sugar cultivation in an attempt to meet our national objective, which was to expand the domestic food supply and to reduce current levels of imports. This proved to be the case during the first half of 1985, when food imports were TT$56 million less than in the comparable 1984 period.

In order to further provide an incentive to farm, tax deduction on holdings of one hundred acres or less was entertained, flood loans repayable at 25% of the original amount borrowed were offered, subsidies extended to include such items as fertilizers, provision of high-quality seedlings, planting material, and so on, and as important, the Agricultural Development Bank made 95 percent loans available at a ridiculously low 3%.

Between 1976 and 1985, then, the government spent some TT$408.1 million to boost agricultural production as compared with TT$2.5 million in 1956. Yet still we are told we did nothing. The fact is, ladies and gentlemen, that the oil boom of the 1970s encouraged many to flee the traditional rural areas, and I believe the dramatic increase in agricultural production today has less to do with any institutionalized program enacted within the last five years than it has to do with a failing economy and the well-known theory that agriculture flourishes in times of adversity.

The fishing industry too has been the beneficiary of sound PNM planning. Duty-free concessions were given on fishing boats, gear, vehicles and equipment, and some TT$45.4 million was spent between 1970 and 1985 on incentives, loans and subsidized fuel. In addition, beach landing and marketing facilities were erected in areas such as Icacos, Erin, and Orange Valley with improvements made in Toco, Matelot, Cocorite, and Grand Chemin. Training was also made available at the Caribbean Fisheries Training and Development Institute. Unfortunately, though, the near collapse of the National Fisheries Company, set up to supply fish and shrimp for export and to the consumer at a reasonable price, has been a great disappointment. Much more therefore needs to be done.

In summary, ladies and gentleman, by the end of our thirty-year term, and as a direct result of our oil windfall, the PNM had provided Trinidad and Tobago with a sound infrastructure in the areas of water, electricity, telecommunications, major arterial roads, a highly literate and technically skilled population which was essential for our development drive, and a well-cultivated airline route structure making Trinidad and Tobago entirely accessible to other parts of the world. In this we were superior to most other developing countries in the Third World.

In the domain of culture the PNM's contribution has been outstanding-the Best Village program, now virtually defunct, was initiated as a result of the extensive Meet the People Tour of the 1960s undertaken by the then prime minister, who desired to see firsthand how the people lived and to get a personal feel for their many requirements. On such occasions, the villagers would display handicrafts, stage cultural shows, and insist that he sample their culinary delights. The outcome of this was that he conceived the idea that in addition to the basic amenities, the villages craved a tangible outlet for cultural expression. Always troubled by our propensity to look toward other developed cultures for entertainment at the expense of our own, my father came to realize that a program such as Best Village could provide the ideal vehicle for raising the consciousness of our own nation vis-a-vis our national heritage. It was therefore Best Village, with its emphasis on things quintessentially local, which popularized such indigenous dishes as "oil down" and "cook up rice" to the extent that these and others are now considered perfectly appropriate for the main dinner table. And just look at what has come out of Best Village-Daisy Voisin, Sugar Aloes, United Sisters, and a host of others!

Few would be aware of this, but the social implications of the program were so impressive that we had visits from officials at Ryerson University in Canada and a Chicago-based nonprofit organization with a view to setting up cultural exchange programs for college credit where our villagers would have had the benefit of their technical expertise, and we would pass on to them aspects of our culture as experienced in the villages. This agenda, too, as an added benefit, involved the youth of our nation by keeping them off the street and employed in a more productive capacity. Arts and crafts flourished as a direct result of the Best Village program which tapped a previously hidden and largely unexplored wealth of talent latent in our society.

By our policies and plans, who was able to imbue both steelbands and calypsonians with a unique sense of significance and stature that had hitherto not been the case, if not the PNM-no matter how many trips to Nigeria they have been promised?

While I am of the view that Tobago, like Trinidad, has benefited under PNM rule, I confess to being appalled at the lack of certain of the most basic facilities in our sister island, as reported some time ago in the press, such as transport and reservations, where at one juncture one had to dial to Trinidad to made a booking on BWIA; electricity, which is too closely linked to that of Trinidad; banking, with Tobago branches being less than autonomous and continually having to relay requests to Trinidad. Even the Central Bank has only one visiting representative there per week, and the delay in due process leaves much to be desired. It is apparent that Tobago's development has not kept pace with that of Trinidad, and although I do not favor any breakup of our union, more must be done by which ever party that wins the election to ensure that Tobagonians regain a measure of the respect they perceive has been denied them all these years.

But in all these triumphs, ladies and gentlemen, for which we should be justifiably gratified, I would be doing you a disservice were I not to mention some spheres in which I personally feel we fell down, which is not to say that there were not also some in which we could have done better. Most notably, our roads have long been in a sorry state of affairs. Coincidentally, I do see some improvement lately!

Toursism, too, has not been made the most of, though you could hardly categorize the establishment of most of our major hotels under a PNM government as lacking in progress. The fact is that we were always wary of creating a force that we were unable to contend with, having tangible examples of this right in our backyard, so to speak. And that, it seems to me, is the ever-present tourism specter-the danger of becoming dependent on the tourist dollar with its vagaries and unsavory connotations was always a consideration, the temptation ever near of submitting to a Club Med situation, which one's own residents would have been unable to patronize. We must now move quickly and expeditiously in this field to forestall our neighbors from completely annexing our reputation in staging what some dub "The Greatest Show on Earth." I am not one who subscribes to the view that other Caribbean Carnivals can only serve to enhance ours. If one knew anything at all about the North American tourist market, one could not help but recognize this fallacy for what it is.

Tourism does not just mean spending $2.5 million on a facelift for Maracas Beach. It means behavior modification, an acceptance and comprehension by the general public of the fact that service does not signify servitude, and it means the institutionalization of the most elementary of standards. An interesting thing happened to me in Tobago last year. I had just finished eating some of Miss Jean's mouth-watering crab and dumplings and wanted to wash my hands, so I went into one of the facilities and asked to do so. The attendant said I would have to pay and I did. When I asked for soap, he laughed!

And of course there is corruption, complacency, and arrogance. We did not acquit ourselves well in either of these fields, even though our party policy is morality in public affairs. Without in any way wishing to exonerate such behavior, I stubbornly maintain that much of it stemmed from the very fact of our longevity and our "humanness."

You have heard ad nauseam how we failed to implement the Integrity Commission. Let me again quote the words of my late father in a speech he made in Woodford Square in 1955. Yes, thirty-six years ago!

"The party is of the opinion that every legislator, every Minister, every councillor, every top civil servant even, must be required by law to divulge annually all the sources of his income. In recommending similar legislation to Congress in 1951, former President Truman of America said: 'As a general rule, I do not like to see public officials, or any particular group, subjected to rules and requirements which do not apply to the rest of the population. But at the same time public office is a privilege, not a right. And people who accept the privilege of holding office in the government must of necessity expect that their entire conduct should be open to inspection by the people they are serving.'

'With all the questions that are being raised today about the probity and honesty of public officials, I think all of us should be prepared to place the facts about our income on the public record. We should be willing to do this in the public interest....

'I know of no other single step that will do so much good, so quickly, in protecting the reputations of our public servants and, at the same time, in producing concrete indications of any really questionable practices.'"

My father goes on to say "my colleagues and I are of the opinion that this legal provision for the annual disclosure of income must be required not only of the individual concerned but also of the members of his immediate family. Only by such a drastic step will the people of Trinidad and Tobago be convinced beyond a shadow of doubt that public office is not sought for personal gain."

In effect, ladies and gentlemen, integrity legislation in Trinidad and Tobago was never passed by a PNM government because, as a result of the wide cross-section of personnel it embraced, it caused no end of a stir and was shelved for further consultation. We refused to compromise PNM principles in the passage of a bill that had no teeth, and I would simply ask you to recall who it was that religiously declared his assets-and publicly-and actually requested that the auditor general take an inventory, which was scrupulously adhered to at the time of his death, both of his personal effects and those belonging to the State.

Let us for a moment try to put this in perspective without resorting to the histrionics of the kitchen cabinet. We formed a government for thirty years. During that time, we raised Trinidad and Tobago's standing in the international community and our own here at home. The period also saw, unfortunately, certain of those in high positions abuse the confidence of the electorate and involve themselves in corrupt practices. There was also some degree of mismanagement. We acknowledge that. But as the campaign has progressed, various and sundry ravings have categorized us as "evil," "a force to be exorcised," "Godless"-we have even been accused of dabbling in obeah and other such bizarre "quasi-religious" inferences which have become less and less credible.

I contend that during this thirty-year interval, we did no worse and certainly much better than any other Party either could or would have done. If you seek saints, ladies and gentlemen, look elsewhere, for you will never find them in any government composed of people like you and I with all our strengths and shortcomings-some of us are competent, others are not, some truthful, some not, some with scruples, others without. You will always get your fair share of tyrants, brigands, and well-meaning individuals. We have some of them, and so do others, but by and large, we strive to be a party that cares about the people it serves.

Have we learned our lesson? I think so. Looking at the entire picture retrospectively, my feeling is that 1986 and our massive electoral defeat was a long time in coming. This is just a personal view, understand. We were overdue for our "comeuppance," as it were. Some of us had forgotten that election to public office does not mean increased opportunity for self-aggrandizement, does not mean that we can forget the people who put us there for four and a half years only to take up their problems six months before an election. It does not mean that we are any better situated than anyone else. What it does and should mean, to me at any rate, is that the people have seen fit to put us in a position of sacred trust- a trust that should be discharged with humility and integrity. To betray that trust by a sense of self-importance, shirking responsibility, only indulging in the cocktail circuit-in short, to squander that privilege of serving one's country is deserving of nothing less than public scorn and ridicule at the very least! A politician, like Caesar's wife, as my father used to say to me so often, must be above reproach, and the vast majority of persons, not unnaturally, still expect those elected to public office to dance to the beat of a different drummer-to uphold a higher ideal.

I am here tonight to tell you that you can teach an old dog new tricks. I maintain that we have learned from that failure and that the invaluable lessons we have been taught as a party by you, the population, will be put to good practical use in the years to come. I consider that an important ingredient for the next government of Trinidad and Tobago is the ability to weather any storm-to keep the ship of State on an even keel throughout, and to rise above the whims and fancies of life in a developing republic. I hold that our abilities have been more than adequately put to the test and have not been found wanting, for in few other Third World countries, ladies and gentlemen, has there been a party which, having been in power for thirty consecutive years, did not resort to election fraud, violence, detention of political prisoners-all in an attempt to nullify its electoral overthrow. The PNM complied gracefully with the will of the electorate. We were humiliated, disrespected, publicly vilified, privately shunned, and former ministers had a difficult time making ends meet.

And so, ladies and gentlemen, the outcome of the 1991 elections is in your qualified and capable hands. It goes against the grain for me to urge anyone to vote for one political party as opposed to another. For me to do so would be to relinquish the very principles of freedom of choice and democracy that I was brought up to affirm and that the PNM has so long espoused. No, you must follow the dictates of your own conscience, vote for substance rather than showmanship, and in the final analysis, you can only pray that you have made a decision that will ultimately prove to be in the best interests of our State, our family, and our children's future. For that is what I judge needs to be emphasized-our children, the shining hope of our Republic, their health, the inculcation of moral values, discipline, so that we shall never again have to read about inexcusable incidents like the Mucurapo attack on Tranquillity, vocational training and education. In short, we need a return to the old family values where a child who steps out of line could count on being chastised, not just by his parents but by his friends' parents and by any other adult who might be nearby. In the United States of America it has been estimated that eighth graders—that would be students around age fourteen-spend an average of 21.7 hours per week watching TV, 5.6 hours doing homework, and 1.8 hours on extracurricular reading. This is an astonishing statistic that we never wish to have applied here in Trinidad and Tobago. As an extension of all this, our children need jobs. As one opinion has it, "desperate people do desperate things"—hence our burgeoning crime rate, and for those who can conceive of no future—why say no to drugs?

And so I leave you to your very crucial deliberations as to who should govern our country over the next five years. Judging from the views of the electorate, there is a section of the population that takes the disquieting approach—"same callaloo, different crabs"—politicians are getting a bad name, and the result could be voter indifference, particularly among the young. It is patently clear that the citizenry is fed up with the politico whose sole aim is to stamp on his opponent simply to elevate himself. If you cannot stand on your own merits, it is fruitless to expect that you can have any sustained success in winning votes merely because of the shortcomings of an antagonist. The very ones who claim that we are, and I quote, "thieves and crooks who come to you in sheep's clothing," or who characterize us as "Ali Baba and his 40 theives" refuse to recognize the good points of a competitor and claim they wish to represent you with "honor ... and dignity." It is just not cricket! How honorable or dignified is it, I ask you, to distort and misstate simply to raise your own standing—what do they take you for, fools? I suggest that this kind of deception illustrates the most fundamental contempt for your powers of discernment and of reason. Fellow citizens, I sound a note of warning-the outstanding element in voter feedback is one of utter disillusionment and apathy. No longer do we feel, as in my father's words, that politics is the art of the possible. The general consensus is that all politicians are the same, greedy, inept, corrupt, loud-mouthed, and incompetent—with no real answers to the problems of today, far less those of tomorrow. If we do not, at least in the PNM—I cannot presume to advise others—concentrate on the issues affecting our population, instead of tearing each other to pieces in animal-like fashion, then we shall have to accept the consequences and all that implies for the future of this party and our own future as natives of this well-loved land.

It is said that a nation almost always gets the government it deserves, and if that is so, then we must vote. It is an inalienable right that we cannot, should not, surrender for only by voting can we truly express our belief and faith in the democracy we all cherish. Only by voting can we ever obtain a government of the people, by the people, for the people. To do less would be to make a mockery of the fact that other members of the universal brotherhood of man are dying at his very minute for that privilege.

If you do decide to vote for the PNM, do so because you trust that we can provide honorable, proficient government and a decent legacy for your children-at least as far as is humanly possible. Do not fall into the 1986 trap of voting one party in merely as a means of booting the other out. Not one party can be all things to all men, and every party, indeed every leader, will make mistakes, as do we all in our daily lives. Beware of raising your level of expectation to impossibly high standards, seeking to impose behavioral precepts on others that you would, at the very least, not exact from yourself. Even the PNM cannot work miracles and will need to balance the oft-times unrealistic demands of workers against the imperatives of a global economy, with ours being buffeted by all types of superpower policies and restrictions. There are no painless ways forward. In the words of Poland's first non-communist prime minister on the subject of his own country's economic malaise, "There are no abracadabras. There are no shortcuts. We need energy and stubbornness and courage."

In essence, we need a government that is effectively able to communicate the need to be patient, we need a government willing to tighten its belt along with our suffering people, even while acknowledging and continuing such sound measures recently enacted and proposed as the expanded anti-dumping legislation, the setting up of a community college, the augmentation of self-help programs, the Citizen's Advisory Bureau, the deregulation of the communications media, and the social legislation passed with specific reference to women and children. We need a government that will treat, as a matter of urgency, the need to reach out to all farflung areas in our twin-island nation, furnishing them with the most fundamental of infrastructural necessities-roads, electricity, water, bridges, health, education. L'Anse Fourmi has as much right to expect these as St. James. We need a government that will actively encourage, and more than just verbally, the reconstruction of areas of Port of Spain devastated during the coup—and before its second anniversary! Most of all, we need a government that, however fiscally responsible, will not see itself as balancing a giant checkbook-for each entry in the debit column, ladies and gentlemen, represents a family complete with frustrations, needs and aspirations. In short, we need a government that will recognize that a country's greatest asset is its inhabitants and will introduce an open-door policy so that their grievances can be aired. Ministers must no longer be inaccessible to the public as was sometimes the case in the previous PNM administration.

I maintain that the PNM today is such a government and that we remain as committed to the principles and ideals of our founding father as we ever were. Of course things have changed, styles, personalities, faces are different. But this is as it should be-not to change would be to remain stagnant. If we ever hope to govern this nation again, we cannot succumb to that stance.

There has been some furor over the resignation of prior party stalwarts. I should remind you that in my own father's day we suffered some of these, and at the time they elicited the same public speculation as to internal malaise etc. I do not mean to trivialize the loss of these individuals to the party. We wish them well, whatever their future status. We are sorry to see them go. We regret that that oft-repeated adage about politics and compromise was not adhered to by all concerned. But, ladies and gentlemen, this is all part and parcel of preelection tension and I see nothing unusual in the recent wrangling. This is a given, particularly during such high-pressure stakes as a general election, and in this, neither the PNM nor Trinidad and Tobago is singular. This view, however, is in no way to be taken as a condemnation of the distressingly undignified and public arena in which the whole process occurred. If we have party cares or dissatisfactions, it is one thing to let one's voice be heard. It becomes quite another to broadcast these in public. Party affiliation and involvement I liken to a marriage. It is not irrevocable, by any means, but while we are in it we owe it loyalty and allegiance. If we are unhappy and must speak out, let us do so in the appropriate forum, at the appropriate time, and in the appropriate manner. Bickering and generally providing grist to feed the mills of the national press and with which to titillate the community are irreconcilable with what I consider should be our party's ideals. A caveat to our detractors- as President Bush so succinctly put it in a warning to Iraq's Saddam Hussein, and I have taken the liberty to apply this to a PNM context.

You may be tempted to find solace in the diversity of opinion that is PNM democracy. You should resist any such temptation. Diversity ought not to be confused with division. Nor should you underestimate, as others have before you, PNM's will.

But the party must move on from such shenanigans. Now, we have an opportunity to woo others who may not have been affiliated with either the PNM or its objectives in the past-no matter-it is time for them to be associated with our future. A political party must always solicit newcomers. By so doing, we can only become more vibrant, more relevant vis-a-vis the concerns of the day. One of the main reasons why we lost in 1986 was because of the very perception that, in local parlance, "it was the same ole khaki pants!" But let this endorsement of "new blood" not be mistaken as approval for any attempt to set aside our experienced party activists. These supporters have earned their place in our party hierarchy. It remains to be seen whether the newcomers can do so as zealously and as diligently as their longtime counterparts.

I have talked at length about what type of government I should like to see manage Trinidad and Tobago's affairs over the next five years, but something needs to be said about our equally vital obligation as a people, for we can never again fall victim to the "dependency syndrome"—to coin a popular phrase-that we are constantly being told we were responsible for encouraging. One conveniently forgets that it was a PNM government that in 1981 warned that the fete was over, it was time to go back to work. Aware of the prevailing economic conditions and the need to cushion the inevitable blow to a people grown spoiled on oil riches, the government of the day decided to draw down on our reserves, which had been created especially for the purpose of promoting our social and economic development over the long term when it was assumed that oil revenues would have tapered off. The government also began to divest itself of its prior commitment to subsidies, to name just a few of the steps that were taken to cope with a contracting economy.

But to get back to the so-called dependency syndrome, we should be quick to admit and to applaud the strides made and fostered by the present government in this regard, although how much of this tactic was determined by choice remains debatable. We cannot continue to look to the government, even in times of plenty, to solve all our country's ills, but rather, we must work together as a community to launch and execute self-help projects, provide assistance to the needy, become involved in Big Brother programs for children in single-parent families, be activists in our school system, to name just a few. Under the watchful eye of our trade unions, we must ensure that not one worker's rights are trampled upon. Workers and unions, however, at least in my view, must give up the adversarial posture they often assume in negotiations, and both company and union membership must develop a symbiotic relationship, for in truth, the company cannot exist without the worker, the worker cannot survive without the company—the demise of one signals the termination of the other. We must play hard and work hard.

As important as all of the foregoing, ladies and gentlemen, is the graciousness with which we conduct ourselves either in victory or in defeat. If the nationals of Trinidad and Tobago wish to return the PNM to the heights of political power in this country, so be it. I, for one, will not argue with that, but I can conceive, personally, of no more awesome responsibility. Let me be perfectly clear on this next point, however. In our understandably enthusiastic response should such an event occur, there must be no question, no tolerance of victimization, retaliation, or revenge. There can be no room in this party for such conduct. It cannot and must not be sanctioned either within the higher echelons or in the rank and file. All those persons who cast their vote elsewhere followed the decrees of their own principles-no more, no less. They must not, repeat not be made to suffer for their choice, however misguided. It is their right. Such is the stuff of which civil war is made. No—they must be shown the error of their ways by our proffering an olive branch, by our tireless efforts at their representation. They must not be made to feel excluded, left out in the cold—they are our brothers, sisters, husbands, children. We must prove to them that we can rise to the occasion, address their concerns. We must behave with decorum. We must not seek to emulate the mistakes of others, wasting time ferreting out misdeeds—real and imagined—we must get on with the business of running the state, employing innovative methods to alleviate spiraling unemployment, improve the economy, and educate our children in a safe and sanitary environment, with a view to ever-advancing technologies. As an aside, one leading party reportedly promises schools toilets for Christmas—we intend for them to be accessible year-round. Our teachers, those sometimes unappreciated professionals who can have such an enormous influence on our children's lives, need to be recognized for the invaluable work they do. When we, as parents, send our children to school each morning, we depend on teachers to take up where we leave off, and far too many parents either cannot or will not retrieve this obligation at the end of the school day. The disgraceful rate at which crime rises on an annual basis needs to be checked.

On the subject of health, there needs to be a beefing up of the three major hospitals in Trinidad and the one in Tobago and the imbalance corrected in the expenditure on Mt. Hope to the detriment of the aforementioned. In many cases, the most rudimentary equipment such as ECG machines is unavailable, and the need to attract and maintain the level of qualified, compassionate staff working under proper management conditions is of paramount importance. For some time now, it has been theorized that Mt. Hope has become, in effect, a white elephant. I believe that we need a government that will undertake creative measures to ensure its complete integration into the national health system and will assure that its facilities are not underutilized.

We need to encourage potential "refugees" to see these pastures as green. According to a recent report, in 1989 some thirteen thousand Trinidad and Tobago nationals had applied for refugee status in Canada alone, and I could go on. But all this must be done while still attempting to maintain our credit rating by repaying our recently increased, despite hysterical protestations to the contrary, massive foreign debt which has risen from TT$8.6 billion in 1986 to well over TT$16 billion today. When you read about this in the press, ladies and gentlemen, make sure they identify that it is TT dollars we are talking about.

Actually we need, in this instance, to start from scratch, as in 1956, desperately moving to assuage the distress of our growing dispossessed. Where there is legal cause for concern, both within the party and outside, the law must take its course. But let us ever be mindful that we shall have only five short years in which to make a difference before the people are called upon once again to exercise their constitutional right. Let us therefore make every day count.

And if we should lose.... I know you cannot conceive of this eventuality, but all things are possible, after all. Well, we have lost once before-and how! But for heaven's sake let us not cry on television.... or resort to violence—we had enough of that to last a lifetime in 1990! More to the point, I am here to tell you that this time around it will not be winners take all and losers forfeit everything, for we have demonstrated our mettle, have been down and were able to rise, have been kicked and stood tall, and for one simple reason, ladies and gentlemen—we have come to understand that success is not how many times adversity can be said to have passed one by. Rather, success depends on how many times we have been able to begin again—even in the face of the greatest misfortune-and 1986 was that—for us. As the saying goes, when life deals you a lemon, make lemonade. We have come from three seats in 1986 and will, with your help, good faith and trust, go to how many on December 16?.... Maybe, but let us not be disheartened if we should fall short of that number, for we shall have given them a run for their money. Let me remind you that this party, the PNM, is in this for the long haul. We are not one of these fly-by-night marriages of convenience, one of these hastily assembled groups calling themselves political parties, disintegrating entirely after they lose their deposits—or win their elections! We are here to stay, as a force to contend with-win or lose, and stay we will.

And so, ladies and gentlemen, I stand before you tonight to state publicly that I am proud of the PNM, proud of what we have attained, both in our successes and in our setbacks. We stand on our record. We have made mistakes, who has not? Some of our own members have let us down, and badly. But we have paid your price, have given you your pound of flesh, and when the dust is settled and you and I are long gone from this earth, I affirm that history will be kind to the PNM, and fair.

I leave you with a passage from the conclusion of *The People's Charter*, as pertinent today as ever it was in 1956 when it was written, although I have adapted it slightly to today's context:

The People's National Movement promises no paradise, offers no millennium. It makes no idiotic promise to you that you will not have to work any more or that pennies will drop from heaven; it pledges, to the best of our ability and given the many factors that need to be considered, that you will have jobs and decent conditions of labor, decent wages, a just share of what you produce, and social security for yourselves and your children. It does not hold out the ridiculous economics that you will pay no taxes; it pledges that your taxes will be spent on the social services you need. A vote for the People's National Movement is a vote for your own education, a vote for government that "vows" to be honest and decisive, a vote for the dignity of labor, social justice, racial fraternity, economic expansion, a sensitive constitution, and a chance for you to hold your head high and for your children to hold theirs higher among the peoples of the world.

Carl Sagan, the distinguished American scientist, in an article on the effects of global warming that I have likened to the issues involved in this upcoming election, refers to a quotation in the Book of Proverbs-"They set an ambush for their own lives." He says and I quote, " The ambush we are setting is for the next generation, for our children. Escaping it will require what is perhaps our most seriously depleted resource: intelligent, unselfish, farseeing and courageous leadership."

Ladies and gentlemen of South Port of Spain—I assert that the People's National Movement continues to provide such. You must know the difference. Thank you.

APPENDIX: THE PNM AND THE UNIVERSITY OF WOODFORD SQUARE: A HISTORICAL RECORD

PNM Weekly, June 18, 1956, pp. 2–3.

APPENDIX:
THE PNM AND THE UNIVERSITY OF WOODFORD SQUARE :
A HISTORICAL RECORD

The People's National Movement will go down in history as the only political party in the world which has given its community its own University.

In Trinidad and Tobago where education is not compulsory, school buildings leave much to be desired, certificates are the principal goal, and the wealth of parents or the winning of a college exhibition or island scholarship by the child determines who gets advanced education. The free, open-air University of Woodford Square and its colleges throughout the length and breadth of the country, where attendance is voluntary, where knowledge is not equated with examination successes, has caused a profound revolution in the political and cultural life of the community. The parking problem on University night, the sight of people in their thousands carrying stools, chairs and benches, the rapt attention of the audiences sustained over long periods in uncomfortable positions, the wide range of colours, classes, races and creeds from which the student body is drawn—all combine to make the University of Woodford Square a unique educational institution and cultural agency in cosmopolitan Trinidad and Tobago.

The University is today the nerve centre of the P.N.M. But it antedated by several months the public emergence of the P.N.M. Christened on July 19, 1955, it was born on June 21, when Dr. Eric Williams, on the night of his separation from the Caribbean Commission, lectured on "My Reations with the Caribbean Commission" to the first large audiences which have since become familiar. The first lecture, like the majority of those which followed up to January 24, 1956, when the P.N.M. was publicly launched, was given under the auspices of the People's Education Movement, an agency of the Teachers' Economic and Cultural

Appendix: The PNM and the University of Woodford Square

Association, whose moving spirits were prominent in the small band of individuals who helped to organise the P.N.M.

In four months after June 21, 19 lectures were given in different parts of the country including one in British Guiana when Dr. Williams attended as an adviser at a Caribbean Conference of Plantation Workers convened by CADORIT, the Caribbean Area Division of the International Confederation of Free Trade Unions. The details of this phase of the programme follow:

1955

1. June 21, Woodford Square, "My Relations with the Caribbean Commission, 1943–1955"
2. June 28, San Fernando   "
3. July 5, Woodford Square, "Some Economic Problems of Trinidad and Tobago"
4. July 10, Point Fortin   "
5. July 12, San Fernando   "
6. July 15, Tunapuna   "
7. July 18, Port of Spain, "Lands and Peoples of the Caribbean: Jamaica"
8. July 19, University of Woodford Square, "Constitution Reform in Trinidad and Tobago"
9. July 21, Tunapuna   "
10. July 22, Couva   "
11. July 23, Point Fortin   "
12. July 24, Fyzabad   "
13. July 25, Arouca   "
14. July 26, San Fernando   "
15. July 29, San Juan, "The Need for Racial Understanding"
16. July 31, Port of Spain, Tailors' Convention, "The Credit Union Movement"
17. August 1, San Fernando, "The Significance of Emancipation Day"

18 August 2, Sangre Grande, "Constitution Reform in Trinidad and Tobago"
19 August 11, Georgetown, B.G., "The Implications of Federation"
20 August 15, Princes Town, "Constitution Reform in Trinidad and Tobago"
21 August 16, University of Woodford Square, "The Historical Background of Race Relations in the Caribbean"
22 August 18, Macaras, Caribbean Training College, "The Meaning of Federation"
23 August 19, Charlotteville, Tobago, "Constitution Reform in Trinidad and Tobago"
24 August 20, Scarborough, "The Historical Background of Race Relations in the Caribbean"
25 August 21, Scarborough, "The Historical Background of Race Relations in the Caribbean"
26 August 22, Gasparillo, "Constitution Reform in Trinidad and Tobago"
27 August 23, San Fernando, "The Historical Background of Race Relations in the Caribbean"
28 September 13, University of Woodford Square, "The Case for Party Politics in Trinidad and Tobago"
29 September 14, Barataria   "
30 September 15, Cantaro   "
31 September 16, Princes Town   "
32 September 20, San Fernando   "
33 September 22, Chaguanas "
34 September 23, Point Fortin "
35 September 24, Fyzabad   "
36 September 25, Couva, "Labour in the Sugar Industry"
37 September 25, Palo Seco, "The Case for Party Politics in Trinidad and Tobago"
38 September 26, Arouca   "
39 September 28, Gasparillo   "

Appendix: The PNM and the University of Woodford Square

The Political Education programme was suspended during Dr. Williams' absence, from October 9 to December 18, 1955, as a result of an invitation from the International Confederation of Free Trade Unions in Brussels to attend as its adviser to an international conference on plantation workers in Geneva and to assist with research work on that subject. During his mission abroad, however Dr. Williams was invited to deliver a number of lectures on West Indian subjects, as follows:

40 November 26, Paris, "My Faith as a West Indian" (to French West Indian students)
41 December 6, House of Commons, "The Federation of the British Caribbean"
42 December 8, British West Indian Students Centre, "The Federation of the British Caribbean"
43 December 15, Trade Union Course, Kingston, Jamaica, "Research as an Aid in Wage Negotiations"
44 December 15, Kingston, "The Federation of the British Caribbean"
45 December 16, University College of the West Indies, Jamaica, "The Future of the West Indies"
46 December 16, Spanish Town, Jamaica, "International Standards for Plantation Workers"

On his return to Trinidad the public lectures of the People's Education Movement were resumed. Prior to the launching of the P.N.M. the following lectures were delivered:

47 December 29, University of Woodford Square, "Report on My Mission to Europe and Jamaica"

1956

48 January 5, Univerisity of Woodford Square, "The Pros and Cons of Federation"

49 January 6, Arouca   "
50 January 8, Usine St. Madeleine, "International Standards for Plantation Workers"
51 January 9, Point Fortin, "The Pros and Cons of Federation"
52 January 10, San Fernando   "
53 January 11, Princes Town   "
54 January 13, Tunapuna   "
55 January 14, Rio Claro   "
56 January 17, University of Woodford Square, "Further Thoughts on Federation"
57 January 18, Gasparillo, "Federation"
58 January 19, Chaguanas, "International Standards for Plantation Workers"
59 January 20, San Fernando, "Further Thoughts on Federation"

On January 24, 1956, the P.N.M. was launched in the University of Woodford Square. The Political Education Programme was thereafter taken over by the P.N.M. It was devoted to the launching of the Movement in various parts of the country and to the discussion of a wide variety of subjects of topical interest. Lectures were also given in Barbados and Grenada which Dr. Williams visited in his capacity as adviser to CADORIT, thereby strengthening the growing federal influence of the P.N.M.

The programme of lectures from January 24 to June 14, 95 in all, bringing the grand total to 154, is as follows:

60 January 24, University of Woodford Square, Launching of the P.N.M.
61 January 26, Tunapuna   "
62 January 27, Point Fortin   "
63 February 1, Princes Town   "
64 February 2, San Fernando   "
65 February 6, Sangre Grande   "
66 February 17, Bon Accord Junction, Tobago "

Appendix: The PNM and the University of Woodford Square

67 February 17, Moriah, Tobago   "
68 February 18, Scarborough   "
69 February 18, Belle Garden   "
70 February 19, Speside   "
71 February 19, Roxborough   "
72 February 19, Charlotteville   "
73 February 23, University of Woodford Square,
      "The Bandung Conference"
74 February 24, Siparia, Launching of the P.N.M.
75 February 25, Cedros   "
76 February 26, La Brea   "
77 February 26, Icacos, "The P.N.M.'s Economic Programme"
78 February 26, Point Fortin, "The Bandung Conference"
79 February 27, Arima, Launching of the P.N.M.
80 February 28, San Fernando, "The Bandung Conference"
81 March 1, Barataria, Launching of the P.N.M.
82 March 2, Diego Martin   "
83 March 5, Morvant   "
84 March 7, Sangre Grande, "The Bandung Conference"
85 March 8, Belmont, Launching of the P.N.M.
86 March 9, Barrackpore   "
87 March 10, Rio Claro   "
88 March 11, Guayaguayare   "
89 March 11, Mayaro   "
90 March 12, San Juan   "
91 March 13, Tunapuna, "The Bandung Conference"
92 March 15, Chaguanas, Launching of the P.N.M.
93 March 16, Carenage   "
94 March 17, Maracas Valley   "
95 March 19, Laventille   "
96 March 20, Gasparillo   "
97 March 22, University of Woodford Square,
      "The Plantation Workers of Trinidad and Tobago"
98 March 23, Arouca, Launching of the P.N.M.
99 March 25, La Lune, Moruga   "

100 March 25, Basseterre, Moruga   "
101 March 26, Barbados Workers' Union, Bridgetown, "The Place of the Trade Unions in Caribbean Society"
102 March 27, Barbados Workers' Union, Bridgetown, "The Place of the Trade Unions in Caribbean Society"
103 March 28, Women's Group, Petit Bourg, "The Place of Women in Caribbean Society"
104 April 4, St. James, Launching of the P.N.M.
105 April 5, Cantaro, Launching of the P.N.M.
106 April 8, Siparia, "Self-Help Friendly Society Movement in the Caribbean"
107 April 9, Women's Group, Belmont, "The Place of Women in Caribbean Society"
108 April 10, Marabella, Launching of the P.N.M.
109 April 12, University of Woodford Square, "Political Trends in 1956"
110 April 13, Debe, Launching of the P.N.M.
111 April 15, Port of Spain, Seamen and Waterfront Workers' Union, "The Place of the Trade Unions in Caribbean Society"
112 April 16, Port of Spain, Caribbean Women's Conference, "The Place of Women in the Caribbean Society"
113 April 18, Sangre Grande, "Political Trends in 1956"
114 April 19, Barbados Workers' Union, Caribbean Trade Union Rally, Bridgetown, "The Report of the Board of Enquiry on the Dispute in the Printing Industry"
115 April 26, University of Woodford Square, "Political Trends in 1956" (2)
116 April 28, St. James, St. James Star Friendly Society, "The Friendly Society Movement in the Caribbean"
117 May 2, Grenada National Party, St. George's, "The Future of the Caribbean"
118 May 3, Grenada Trade Union Council, May Day Address, "The Place of the Trade Unions in Caribbean Society"

Appendix: The PNM and the University of Woodford Square

119 May 3, Y.M.C.A., Grenada, "The Place of Women in Caribbean Society"
120 May 3, Grenada Trade Union Council, Gouyave, "The Future of the Caribbean"
121 May 4, Council of Friendly Societies, Grenada, "The Friendly Society Movement in the Caribbean"
122 May 4, Anglican Girls' Secondary School, Grenada, "The Responsibility of Young Women in the Caribbean"
123 May 7, Sangre Grande, "Political Trends in 1956" (2)
124 May 10, University of Woodford Square, "Background to Enlightenment"
125 May 11, Tacarigua, Launching of the P.N.M.
126 May 14, Jackson Square, Port of Spain, "Europe, America and the Caribbean"
127 May 15, Mount Lambert, "The Development of Caribbean Nationalism"
128 May 16, Laventille, "Political Trends in 1956"
129 May 17, University of Woodford Square, "The Voter and the Vote"
130 May 18, New Grant, Launching of the P.N.M.
131 May 19, Port of Spain, P.N.M.'s Women's League, "The Place of Women in the P.N.M."
132 May 20, Morne Diablo, Launching of the P.N.M.
133 May 20, Penal   "
134 May 22, San Fernando, "The Voter and the Vote"
135 May 24, Coal Mine, Eastern Counties, "Caribbean Agriculture in Historical Perspective"
136 May 25, Cedros, "The Voter and the Vote"
137 May 26, Point Fortin   "
138 May 28, Icacos, Launching of the P.N.M.
139 May 27, Irios Forest   "
140 May 27, La Brea, "The Voter and the Vote"
141 May 28, Arima   "

405

142 May 29, Curepe "
143 May 31, La Lune, Moruga "
144 May 31, Grand Chemin "
145 May 31, Basse Terre "
146 June 3, Toco, Launching of the P.N.M.
147 June 4, San Fernando, P.N.M.'s Women's League, "The Place of Women in the P.N.M."
148 June 5, Port of Spain, Nursing Association, "The Place of Women in Caribbean Society"
149 June 10, Gran Couva, Caroni South, Launching of the P.N.M.
150 June 10, Tortuga "
151 June 10, California "
152 June 10, Couva "
153 June 12, Fyzabad, Launching of the P,N.M.
154 June 14, University of Woodford Square, Restatement of the Fundamental Principles of the P.N.M.

The Political Education Programme of the P.N.M. has become the decisive force in the political life of Trinidad and Tobago. Political thinking has been raised to heights hitherto not attained. Forgotten centres and neglected men and women have been brought into the cultural stream. The beauty of the tropical night has assumed a new meaning for the thousands who storm the gates of the University. The record of the past year proves that the P.N.M. made no idle boast when, adopting the phraseology of unemployed seamen, it took as its motto: "The P.N.M. stands for Knowledgism."

SELECTED BIBLIOGRAPHY

WORKS BY WILLIAMS *(CHRONOLOGICALLY)*

"The Golden Age of the Slave System in Britain." *Journal of Negro History* 25 (1940).

"British West Indian Slave Trade After Its Abolition in 1807." *Journal of Negro History* 27 (1942).

The Negro in the Caribbean. Washington, D.C.: Associates in Negro Folk Education, 1942.

"Laissez Faire, Sugar and Slavery." *Political Science Quarterly* 58 (March 1943).

Capitalism and Slavery. Chapel Hill: University of North Carolina Press, 1944.

"Race Relations in Puerto Rico and the Virgin Islands." *Foreign Affairs* 23 (January 1945).

"Historical Background of British Guiana's Problems." *Journal of Negro History* 30 (1945).

"Proposed British West Indian University." *School and Society* 63 (April 1946).

"Education in Dependent Territories in America." *Journal of Negro Education* 15 (Summer 1946).

Ed. *Documents Illustrating the Development of Civilization.* 3 vols. Washington, D.C.: Kaufman Press, 1947.

Education in the British West Indies. Port of Spain: Guardian Commercial Printery, 1950.

Ed. *Documents on British West Indian History, 1807–1833.* Port of Spain: Trinidad Publishing Company, 1952.

Ed. *The British West Indies at Westminster: Extracts from the Debates in Parliament.* Port of Spain: Historical Society of Trinidad and Tobago, 1954.

Constitution Reform in Trinidad and Tobago. Port of Spain: Teachers Economic and Cultural Association, Public Affairs Pamphlet, no. 2, 1955.

Historical Background of Race Relations in the Caribbean. Port of Spain: Teachers' Economic and Cultural Association, Public Affairs Pamphlet, no. 3, 1955.

Economic Problems of Trinidad and Tobago. Port of Spain: Teachers' Economic and Cultural Association, Public Affairs Pamphlet, no. 1, 1955.

The Case for Party Politics in Trinidad and Tobago. Port of Spain: Teachers' Economic and Cultural Association, Public Affairs Pamphlet, no. 4, 1955.

My Relations with the Caribbean Commission. Port of Spain: Teachers Economic and Cultural Association, 1955.

Federation: Two Public Lectures. Port of Spain: PNM Publishing, 1956.

Perspectives for Our Party. Port of Spain: PNM Publishing, 1958.

From Slavery to Chaguaramas. Port of Spain: PNM Publishing, 1959.

Economics of Nationhood. Port of Spain: Government Printing Office, 1959.

People's National Movement: Major Party Documents, Vol. 1. Port of Spain: PNM Publishing, n.d.

Selected Bibliography

Massa Day Done: A Masterpiece of Political and Sociological Analysis. Port of Spain: PNM Publishing, 1960.

Perspectives for the West Indies. Port of Spain: PNM Publishing, 1960.

Our Fourth Anniversary. Port of Spain: PNM Publishing, 1960.

History of the People of Trinidad and Tobago. Port of Spain: PNM Publishing, 1962.

"Speech on Independence." *Nation,* August 31, 1962.

Documents of West Indian History. Port of Spain: PNM Publishing, 1963.

Reflections on the Caribbean Economic Community: A Series of Seven Articles. Port of Spain: PNM Publishing, 1965.

British Historians and the West Indies. London: Andre Deutsch, 1966.

Britain and the West Indies. London: Longmans for the University of Essex, 1969.

Inward Hunger: The Education of a Prime Minister. London: Andre Deutsch, 1969.

PNM Perspectives in the World of the Seventies: An Address. Port of Spain: PNM Publishing, 1970.

From Columbus to Castro: The History of the Caribbean, 1492–1969. London: Andre Deutsch, 1970.

Nationwide Broadcast. Port of Spain: Government Printery, 1970.

Some Historical Reflections on the Church in the Caribbean: An Address. Port of Spain: Public Relations Division, Office of the Prime Minister, 1970.

The Chaguaramas Declaration. Port of Spain: PNM Publishing, 1970.

"The Blackest Thing in Slavery Was Not the Black Man." *Revista Interamericana* (Puerto Rico) 3, no. 1 (1973).

"The Case Against Proportional Representation." *Round Table* (Great Britain) 249 (1973).

"A New Federation for the Commonwealth Caribbean." *Political Quarterly* (Great Britain) 44, no. 3 (1973).

PR: To Dissolve Present PNM Majorities. Port of Spain: PNM Publishing, 1973.

"The Threat to the Caribbean Community." Port of Spain, 1977.

The Political Leader's Address. Port of Spain: PNM Publishing, 1977.

Political Leader's Address to a Special Convention of the PNM. Twentieth Anniversary, 1981.

Forged from the Love of Liberty: Selected Speeches of Dr. Eric Williams. Edited by Paul Sutton. London: Andre Deutsch, 1981.

ANNOTATED WORKS ON WILLIAMS

Azeez, Malik A. "The Legacy of Eric Williams: A Selected Bibliography." *Current Bibliography on African Affairs* 21, no. 3 (1989): 267–73.

    References are provided for the analysis of the intellectual, historical, and political legacy of Eric Williams.

Beckles, Hilary. "*Capitalism and Slavery:* The Debate over Eric Williams." *Social and Economic Studies* (Jamaica) 33, no. 4 (1984): 171–89.

    Reviews the criticism of *Capitalism and Slavery* and argues that while Euro-American historians and economic historians have been critical of the work, West Indian scholars have found inspiration in it.

Selected Bibliography

Boodoo, Ken I., ed. *Eric Williams: The Man and the Leader.* Lanham: University Press of America, 1986.

    Essays on the life of Eric Williams. The book attempts to unravel the enigma of the man and analyzes Williams's contribution to Trinidad and Tobago and Caribbean society.

Carrington, Selwyn H. H. "British West Indian Economic Decline and Abolition, 1775–1807: Revisiting Econocide." *Canadian Journal of Latin American and Caribbean Studies* 14, no. 7 (1989): 33–49.

    Reviews recent critiques of *Capitalism and Slavery* and takes issue with the thesis presented by Seymour Drescher's *Econocide: British Slavery in the Era of Abolition* (1977).

Cudjoe, Selwyn R. "Eric E. Williams: His Intellectual-Political Legacy." In *Movement of the People.* Ithaca: Calaloux Publications, 1983, pp. 6–60.

    Reviews Williams's intellectual work and argues for his empirical-pragmatic approach to scholarship. It also analyzes his political contributions to Trinidad and Tobago.

Darity, William, Jr. "The Williams Abolition Thesis before Williams." *Slavery and Abolition* 9, no. 1, 29–41.

    Cites British scholars writing prior to Williams's *Capitalism and Slavery* who had arrived at conclusions similar to Williams's. He questions whether Williams did not know about them or simply ignored them.

Deosaran, Ramesh. *Eric Williams: The Man, His Ideas and His Politics (A Study of Political Power).* Port of Spain: Signum Publishing, 1981.

    Reviews the social and political forces that shaped the personality of Williams and attempts a systematic psychological study of Williams as a political leader.

Drescher, Seymour. "British Capitalism and British Slavery." *History and Theory* 9, no. 1 (1988): 29–41.

    Assesses the influence of *Capitalism and Slavery* on the historiography of British slavery.

Ifill, Max B. *The Politics of Dr. Eric Williams and the P.N.M.* Port of Spain: People's Democratic Society, 1986.

    Argues that Williams was a reactionary and conservative thinker with political notions rooted in the nineteenth century and that the PNM, a nonsocialist party and government, is a racist organization.

James, C. L. R. *A Convention Appraisal.* Port of Spain: PNM Publishing, 1960.

    A discussion of Williams's politics and his strength as a leader.

John, George. *Williams: His Life and His Politics.* Port of Spain: Trinidad Express, 1991.

    Pictorial essays that reflect on the life and times of Williams.

Jones, Anthony Mark. *Eric Eustace Williams, His Publics.* Barataria: Educo Press, 1983.

    Examines the social and historical forces that conduced toward the shaping of Williams. Emphasis is placed on his Trinidad environment. It is the closest to a biography on Williams that has been written.

London, Clement B. G. "Forging Cultural Identity: Leadership and Development in Mass Education in a Developing Caribbean Country." *Journal of Black Studies* 21, no. 3 (March 1991): 251–67.

    Examines Williams's attempt to preserve Trinidad and Tobago's culture through the development of local talent and the establishment of the Better Village Program.

Mahabir, Winston. *In and Out of Politics.* Port of Spain: Imprint Caribbean, 1978.

>Discusses Mahabir's five-year association (1956–61) with Williams and the PNM. It gives a balanced appraisal of Williams's achievements, alludes to his political intellectual strengths, and describes his tendency to be vindictive.

Parris, Carl D. "Personalization of Power in an Elected Government: Eric Williams and Trinidad and Tobago." *Journal of Inter-American Studies and World Affairs* 25, no. 2 (May 1983): 171–91.

>Examines the strategies employed by the political leadership to restore popular confidence, focusing on the period 1973–81 and Williams's tenure as prime minister.

Richardson, Elton C. *Revolution or Evolution and other Writings including The Scholarship of Dr Eric Williams.* San Juan: Imprint Caribbean, 1984.

>Outlines the author's close association with Williams during the formation of the PNM and subjects the policies of the latter organization to a sustained criticism. He accuses Williams of "intellectual dishonesty," claims that Williams had "no standing among scholars," but argues that Williams was "a political genius suited to his epoch."

Robinson, Cedric J. "Capitalism, Slavery and British Historiography." *History Workshop Journal* (Great Britain) 23 (1987): 120–40.

>Reviews misconceptions of *Capitalism and Slavery* and demonstrates that such interpretations have been imprisoned by false conceptualizations of the economic aspects of the British abolitionist and humanitarian movements. He also concerns himself with the relationship between the profitability of slavery and the financing of the industrial revolution.

Rogers, De Wilton. *The Rise of the People's National Movement.* Port of Spain: De Wilton Rogers, n.d.

> Examines the rise of the People's National Movement, the party of which Williams was the leader, and its deterioration from a democratic to an autocratic organization.

Rohlehr, Gordon. "History as Absurdity." In Orde Coombs, *Is Massa Day Dead? Black Moods in the Caribbean.* Garden City, N.Y.: Anchor, 1974.

> Criticizes Williams's excessive reliance on facts in *From Columbus to Castro* and argues for a more creative, humanitarian approach to historiography with greater concern for people's lives than for facts and figures. Condemns obvious historical omission and repetitions from past works that are included in the text *(From Columbus to Castro).*

Seukeran, Lionel. "Eric Williams in Retrospect." *Caribbean Affairs* 4, no. 2 (April–June 1991), 103–23.

> Examines the career of Williams and argues that his work constituted a continuation of an economic and political scene. Williams's genius, he argues, consisted in "coalesc[ing] and congeal[ing]" these forces and leading them in a new direction. He sees Williams as one of the most important leaders of the Caribbean and places him on par with leaders such as Winston Churchill, Jawahalal Nehru, and Kwame Nkrumah.

Sebastien, Raphael. "State Sector Development in Trinidad and Tobago." *Contemporary Marxism* 10 (1985): 110–27.

> Discusses the development strategy of the PNM and argues that Williams's economic policy failed the country.

Solow, Barbara. "Caribbean Slavery and British Growth: The Eric Williams Hypothesis." *Journal of Development Economics* 17, nos. 1–2 (1985): 99–115.

> Supports Williams's thesis in *Capitalism and Slavery* that slavery in the British West Indies contributed significantly to English industrial growth in the second half of the

eighteenth century, refutes objections raised to criticisms of Williams's hypothesis, and concludes that colonial slavery increased British national income which allowed it to industrialize.

Solow, Barbara L., and Stanley L. Engerman. *British Capitalism and Caribbean Slavery: The Legacy of Eric Williams.* New York: Cambridge University Press, 1987.

Argues for the centrality of *Capitalism and Slavery* in the writing of Caribbean history and reexamines the ideas advanced by Williams in this original work.

Sutton, Paul. "The Historian as Politician: Eric Williams and Walter Rodney." In Alistair Hennessy, *Intellectuals in the Twentieth-Century Caribbean.* London: Macmillian, 1992, pp. 98–114.

A comparison of the careers of Williams and Walter Rodney, scholar-politicians, each acting in the cause of freedom and each uniquely qualified by intellect and temperament to play a leadership role in the social-political debates of his time. Although the author argues that Williams's political priorities were driven by the interest of the petty bourgeoisie and those of Rodney by that of the working class, he concludes that each was shaped by and so ought to be understood as responding to the demands of his generation.

CONTRIBUTORS

ERIC E. WILLIAMS

Born on September 25, 1911, to Henry and Elisa Williams, Eric E. Williams was educated at Queen's Royal College and Oxford University, where he received a Doctor of Philosophy degree in December 1938. His doctoral dissertation, "The Economic Aspect of the Abolition of the West Indian Slave Trade and Slavery," was considered "an important contribution to research on the subject," Williams noted in *Inward Hunger: The Education of a Prime Minister* (1969). In 1944, the dissertation was published as *Capitalism and Slavery*. In 1939, Williams migrated to the United States, where he became an assistant professor of social and political sciences at Howard University. There he organized several courses, especially a humanities course for which he developed a three-volume work called *Documents Illustrating the Development of Civilization* (1947), a work of which he was most proud. In 1946 he was offered a full professorship at Howard even though his commitment to the Anglo-American Caribbean Commission, where he began to work as a consultant in 1943, prevented him from accepting the position. Leaving Howard in 1948, Williams became the head of the Research Branch of the Anglo-American Caribbean Commission and deputy chairman of the Caribbean Research Council. When he was denied the chairmanship of the Caribbean Research Council in 1955, he resigned and subsequently became involved in the politics of Trinidad and Tobago. Although Williams was somewhat active on the political scene before his formal departure from the Caribbean Commission, his first major political speech, "My Relations with the Caribbean Commission" (1955), signaled his formal entrance into Trinidad and Tobago politics.

One year later, working with the People's Education Movement (PEM), which sponsored a number of his speeches throughout the country, Williams formed the People's National

Movement (PNM) of which he became the leader. In September of that year the PNM was successful in the national elections (his party won thirteen of the twenty-four seats), and Williams became the chief minister of the country from 1956 to 1959, premier from 1959 to 1962, and prime minister from 1962 to 1981. He died in office on March 29, 1981. On the day of his death there was great mourning in the society. Often called "the Father of the Nation," Williams remains one of the most (perhaps the most) significant leaders in the history of modern Trinidad and Tobago.

GEORGE LAMMING

George Lamming, one of the foremost intellectuals of the Caribbean, is the author of *In the Castle of My Skin, The Emigrants, Season of Adventure, Of Age and Innocence, The Pleasures of Exile, Natives of My Person*, and *Water with Berries*. He has been widely honored for his writings, receiving a Guggenheim Fellowship, a Canadian Council Fellowship, and an Honorary Doctorate from the University of the West Indies. For the past fifteen years he has been involved actively in the political and cultural activities of the Caribbean region.

C. L. R. JAMES

C. L. R. James (1901–88) has emerged as one of the most important thinkers in the world today. Born in Trinidad, West Indies, James is the author of *The Black Jacobins, Beyond a Boundary, Notes on Dialectics*, and many other important works. A political organizer and prolific lecturer, James taught at Harvard University, Northwestern University, and the University of the District of Columbia. An activist in the Pan Africanist Movement, he became friendly with many of the leaders of the Third World.

ERICA WILLIAMS-CONNELL

Erica Williams-Connell is the daughter of Eric Williams. She works actively to keep the memory of her father alive and continues to participate in the affairs of Trinidad and Tobago. Her two addresses in this collection are her first political speeches.

SELWYN R. CUDJOE

Selwyn R. Cudjoe, professor and chairman of the Africana Studies Department, Wellesly College, has written extensively about other Trinidadian figures. His books include *V. S. Naipaul: A Materialist Reading, Movement of the People,* and *A Just and Moral Society.* A visiting scholar at the Afro-American Studies Department, Harvard University (1992–93), Professor Cudjoe is the editor of the *CLR James Journal.*

INDEX

General headings are provided under Williams, Eric E.: AUTHOR; AT THE CARIBBEAN COMMISSION; EDUCATIONAL THEORY; ORATOR; PAMPHLETEER; POLITICAL THEORY ON; RELATIONS WITH; HIS SCHOOLING; SPEECHES MODELED ON. Page entries in bold type indicate chapter and chapter sub-headings. The word *"passim"* following page references indicates scattered references throughout those pages. The letter "n" following a page references indicates footnote. The word "mentioned" in parenthesis indicates a passing reference to the person, and the word "quoted" following a person's name or heading indicates a direct quotation. Prepositions at the beginning of subheadings have been ignored in determining the alphabetical order.

abolition of slavery, 339
absentee landlords, 79
"Address to the PNM Women's League," **354-367**
adult education, 374. See also People's National Movement; and Williams, Eric E. POLITICAL THEORY ON
Africans, 30, 31, 241
African slaves, 95, 96n
Agricultural Credit Bank, 256
    loans to
        large scale planters, 257
        Dr. Richardson, 258-259
        small farmers, 257-259
        under People's National Movement, 258
Agricultural Development Bank, 381
agricultural resettlement scheme, 380
Alaska, oil revenues of, 357
Alcazars, Sir Henry, 247, 307
Alexander, C. W., 47
Alexander, W. J., 47
Alexis, Jack, 30
Alice in Wonderland, quoted 97
Alien Land Holdings Act, 9-10, 379
Ambakaila, 101
American naval base, 273
American Slavery as It Is: Testimony of a Thousand Witnesses, 15,
    quoted 18
Amerindians, 30, 31
ammonia, 379
Anglo-American Caribbean Commission. *See* Caribbean Commission
Angola, Portuguese, 252
Antigua. *See* sugar, economics of
Antokol, Dr. Norman, 6
Appendix, 412-413
Aristotle, 105, 340
assimilation theory of the French, 345-346
Azeez, Malik A., 404
Azikiwe, Nnambi, 334, 337

Babb, John, 8n
Bachelard, Gaston, 98n

Bailey, Victor
    on acquiring English, 44
Bakr, Abu, 356n, 358, 359, 361
Bandung Conference, 21, 236, 308
Barbados, 190, 244
Basdeo Panday: An Enigma Answered, 44n, 101n
Beckford, George, 6
Beckles, Hilary, 404
"Behind the Bridge," linguistic culture of, 46
Benjamin, Walter, quoted 57
Best, Lloyd, 3n
Best Preparation, **331-333**
Best Village programme, 382-383. *See also* Williams-Connell, Erica
Beyond a Boundary, quoted 104
Bird, V. C., 132-133
Bishop, Maurice, (mentioned) 104
Blackburn, Robin, 14
Black Jacobins, The, 14, 15, 333, 338-339
    quoted, 17
Black Power, 92-95, 103
Black Reconstruction in America, 14
Blind Welfare Association, 375
Bogle, Paul, 14
Bolshevik Party, 215
Bomb, 3
Boodoo, Ken I., 405
Book of Proverbs, quoted 396
Books Cited, **108-110**
Bourdieu, Pierre, quoted 47n
"Bourne Road Address," **370-396**
Bradshaw, Robert, 133, 201
    quoted, 152-153
British Guiana, 331
British Labour Party, 117, 149-150, 195, 210, 217, 229
British Parliament petitioned, 50
British parliamentary democracy, 334
British Tory Party, 174
British trade unions, 210, 251
British West Indies, 138, 200. *See* Caribbean Commission
"British West Indies in World History, The" 131
Brother Boynes, 39

Index

Bryan, Victor, Minister of Agriculture, 258-259
Buhle, Paul, 104n
Burke, Edmund, 54, 66, 68-69, 90, 91, 92, 105, quoted 186-187. *See also* Williams, Eric E. SPEECHES MODELED ON
Burnham, Forbes, (mentioned) 104, 331
Burnley, William, a slaveholder, 20-21, 36
Bush, George, 391
Butler, Uriah "Buzz," 56, 98, 179, 311, 333
BWIA, sale and leaseback of, 360, 383. *See also* Williams-Connell, Erica

Caballero, Luzy, 246
Cabral, Amilcar, 80
CADORIT, 413, 416
calypso, 75, 100, 102, 105, 383.
Calypso and Society, 75n
Campos, Albizu, 14-15
Canada, 244, 249-250, 288, 382
Canada-West Indies Agreement of 1926, 260
Cancer Society, 375
Capitalism and Slavery, 14
    dedication of, 70, 72
    government views of, 115, 126-128, 131-132
    press views of, 114-115
Caribbean Affairs, 33n
Caribbean Commission, 51, 73, **112-165,** 200, 202
    bureaucracy of, 124
    function of, 135-140
    opposition to Williams's appointment, 121-122, 143-146, 398
    views, 145-149
    work, 155-158
    writing and speaking, 115-132 *passim*
    organization of, 135-140, 162
    propaganda of, 123
    Research Council, 136, 121, 398
    Secretariat, 150-160
    working environment at 123-132, 138-144, 162

X, Mr. 61-62, 115-122, 129, 131, 164.
See also Williams, Eric E. AT THE CARIBBEAN COMMISSION; Williams, Eric E. *My Relations with the Caribbean Commission*
Caribbean Discourse: Selected Essays, 37
Caribbean Economic Community, 273
Caribbean Fisheries Training and Development Institute, 381
Caribbean Women's National Assembly, 53
Caribbean Women Writers, quoted 42
Carifta, 272
Carmichael, Mrs., 95, 96n
carnival, 309. *See also* People's National Movement
Caroll, Lewis, 97
Carr, Andrew, 37-38, quoted 38
Carrington, Selwyn, 55n, 405
Casas, Bartholome de las, quoted 15-16
Case for Party Politics, 1955, The, **65-70**
Case for Party Politics in Trinidad and Tobago, 66, **168-205**
Case for West Indian Self-Government, 333
Castoriadis, Cornelius, quoted, 65, 67n
Castro, Fidel, 261 (mentioned), 104
Central Bank, 378
Central Office, Reorganized, **218-219.** *See also* People's National Movement; Williams, Eric E. POLITICAL THEORY
Cesaire, Aime, 311, 345-346
Chaguaramas, 261, 262
Chaguaramas Declaration, The, 88, 92-97, **272-316,** 370
    I. Introduction, **272-276**
    II. Task of Reconstruction, **276-279**
    III. Guidelines for the New Society, **279-310**
    IV. Trinidad and Tobago, the Caribbean and the Third World, **310-312**
    V. The New Society, **312-314**
    VI. The Role of the Party, **314-316**

423

Chamber of Commerce, 197
Chamber of Industry and Commerce,
　　14, 15, 17-22 *passim*, 30-31
　　supporter of Manning, 13
　　responds to Maxie Cuffie, 4n
Churchill, Sir Winston, 125, 262, 350
Cipriani, Arthur, 14, 98n, 179, 245, 307, 311
Clarkson, Thomas, 246
C. L. R. James's Caribbean, 104n
C. L. R. James Reader, 91n
Cobo Jaw Bones, 101
Cole, G. D. H., 335
Collens, J. H., quoted 37
colonial legacy, 9-10, 19, 31, 275, 280, 292, 299, 302-305, 308
　　on Amerindians, 31
　　on East Indians, 31, 241
　　on education, 303
　　on illegitimacy, 304
　　on land ownership, 292
　　on land tenure, 304
　　on the Negro family, 292
　　of slavery, 31, 241-245
　　on values and ideologies, 302
Colonial Office, 168, 197, 216, 336, 337-338
　　on constitutional reform, 190
　　on election postponement, 188-190
　　on proposed university, 127-128
　　on Williams's contract, 149-150.
　　See also James, C. L. R.; Williams, Eric E. AT THE CARIBBEAN COMMISSION
Colonial Review, The, quoted 128-129
Columbia University, 338
Commission of the Government of India on Indian indentured immigrants, 250
Commission of Inquiry into disturbances in Trinidad in 1937, 250
Committee of Legislative Counsel
　　on child labor and education, 250
Commonwealth of Nations, 266, 272
Commonwealth Prime Minsters' Conference, the first, 73-74
　　communism, accusations of, 145-149. *See also*
Williams, Eric E. AT THE CARIBBEAN COMMISSION
Community Centres, 277
Conference of Independent African States, 236
Confidence in the People, **284-285**
Congo, The, 252
Congress Party of India, 215, 236
Constantine, Learie, 54n
Constitution, The, 268
Constitution Reform of Trinidad and Tobago, 183, 189-190, 194-195, 282-283. *See also* Colonial Office; Williams, Eric E. POLITICAL THEORY
Convention, Third Annual, 208, 213, 236. *See also* People's National Movement
"Convention Appraisal, A", 32, 98n, 99n, **329-351,** 406
　　Best Preparation, **331-333**
　　Colonial at Oxford, **335-336**
　　Highly Literate But..., **333-335**
　　A Lucky Man, **337-338**
　　Party Organization, **347-351**
　　Preparation for Premiership, **342-343**
　　Role of Personality, **330-331**
　　Support of the People, **336-337**
　　Our Special Role, **338-340**
　　The U.C.W.I., **340-342**
　　Dr. Williams: West Indian, **343-347**
Coombs, Orde, 95n
cooperative societies, 291, 378
coupe d'etat, attempted, 356n
"Coup in the PNM," 29n
Coupland, Professor, 335-336
Cowal, Sally, U.S. ambassador, (mentioned) 6
Crawford, Hasley, 355
Creative Arts, the Mass Media and Sports, **308-310.** *See also* People's National Movement
credit unions, 378
Creole, 38, 42, 98n
Crowley, Daniel J., quoted 38-39
Crown Lands Programme. *See* People's National Movement

Index

Cuba, 311, 344
Cudjoe, Selwyn R., 21n, 73n, 78, 400, 405
   introduction to *Four Caribbean Slave Narratives*, 37
Cuffie, Maxie, 3n
   responds to Morgan Job, 4

Dagga, Macandal, 98n, 103
Darity, William, Jr., 405
Davidson, Basil (mentioned), 73
Democracy, definition of, 266-268. *See also* Williams, Eric E. POLITICAL THEORY ON
Democratic Labour Party, 79, 238, 348
   and daily press, 214
   and domination of big business, 233
   and Massa Day speech, 252, 254, 256, 259, 260
   and PNM, 82, 84-85, 232-234
   and racialism, 234
Demosthenes, 91. *See also* Williams, Eric E. SPEECHES MODELED ON
Deosaran, Ramesh, 405
Devastation of the Indies: A Brief Account, The, 15-16, 31n
Development Finance Trust, 378
Development Programme, achievements of, 211-213, 217. *See also* People's National Movement
Dewey, John, 31, 128, 340. *See also* Williams, Eric E. SPEECHES MODELED ON
Documents in British West Indian History, 73
Domestic Manners and Social Conditions of the White, Coloured, and Negro Population of the West Indies, Vol.2, 96n
Donaldson, John, 47
Donaldson, John, Sr., 2. *See also* People's Education Movement
Donovan, Bill, quoted 30
Dr. Williams: West Indian, 343
Drescher, Seymour, 406
Du Bois, W. E. B., 14, 339

Economic Aspects, **287-302**
Economic Intelligence Unit, London-based special report of, 378
Education in the British West Indies, 53, 73, 124, 127-128
Eisenhower, President, 213
Elections, **235**
   1950, 168-183
   1955, postponement of, 176, 188-190, 199, 202-203. *See also* Colonial Office; People's National Movement; Williams, Eric E. POLITICAL THEORY
Elizabeth II, 263
emancipation of slaves
   in Grenada, 247
   in Puerto Rico, 246
   in St. Croix, 246
   in St. Vincent, 247
Emigrants, The, quoted 320-322
Emmett, Robert (mentioned), 39
emigration, 394
Encouragement of the National Private Sector, **290-291**
Engerman, Stanley L., and Barbara L. Solow, 409
English history on abolition of slavery, 339
Enriquillo, 311
EPZ, 379
"Eric E. Williams and the Politics of Language," 24, 32, **36-106**. *See also* Williams, Eric E. AS ORATOR; Williams, Eric E. SPEECHES MODELED ON
"Eric Williams in Retrospect," 33n
Evening News, 260
Export Development Corporation, 378
Express, 4n, 6n, 7n, 14n
   on Walter Rodney, 13-14

Facing Reality, 73
Farquhar, Peter, 238, 254, 260
Fascist Party, 215
Federalist, The, 228
Federation, 77, 190, 200, 201, **230,** 272-273, 350. *See also* Williams, Eric E. POLITICAL THEORY ON

425

Fertrin, 378
"field slaves," 96n
fishing industry, 381
Five-Year Plan, Third, 277, 288
Foreign Affairs, Williams's article for, 125-126
Foreign Domination of the Economy, Ending of, **287-290**
Foreign Subjection, **233**. *See also* Williams, Eric E. POLITICAL THEORY ON
Forged from the Love of Liberty, 32
Forty Years in the Steelbands, 57n
Foucault, Michel, 98n
Foundation for Foreign Affairs, 343
Four Caribbean Slave Narratives, 37
"Four Freedoms for Jamaica, The" conference on, 124
French colonial theory of assimilation, 345-346
French Patois, 38
From Columbus to Castro, 95n
Froudacity, 50
Freyre, Gilberto, 241
Full Utilization of our National Resources, **299-300**

Gandhi, Mahatma (mentioned), 130
Garvey, Marcus, 14
GATT, London conference on, 133, 149, 201
Geneva Conference, 249-251
Gettysburg Address, 91
Ghana, 210
    Convention People's Party of, 215, 236
    Constitution of, 334
Glissant, Edouard, on slave language, 36-37
Goddard, George, 56-57
Gomes, Albert, 67, 260
    party manifesto, 173-183
    regime of, 173-183, 185
    quoted, 51
    on Williams, 52
Gordon, Marilyn, 23, 354 (mentioned), 26
Government by the People, **213**

Government for the People, **211-213**
Granado, Donald, 47
Greaves, Hal, quoted 24-28
Grimké, Sarah M., quoted 17-18
Grounding with My Brothers, 80
Guide to Trinidad, A, quoted 37
Guidelines for the New Society, **279-281**
Guillen, Nicolas, 311
Guppy, Mr. Lechmere, Mayor of San Fernando, 307
    on immigrant conditions, 248

Haiti, 311, 338
Haitian despotism, 247
Hamilton, Alexander, 228
handicrafts, 277
Haracksingh, Kusha, 26
Harris, Wilson, 50n
Hart, Eddie, 64n
Harvey, George, 8-9
Hatuey, 311
Henry, Paget, 104n
Highly Literate But..., **333-335**
History, Fable and Myth, 50n
History of Mary Prince, A West Indian Slave, The, 15n
History of the People of Trinidad and Tobago, 50n
Hodge, Merle, 3n
    on creole, 104
    quoted, 29, 42n
Hospital Management Company, 360
house slaves, treatment of, 247
Howard University, 31, 73, 144, 337, 341, 343
    faculty summoned to Dept. of Justice, 145
    Norman Manley honoured, 148, 344
    Williams leave of absence granted, 117-118
    Williams offered a professorship, 113-114. *See also* Williams, Eric E. My Relations with the Caribbean Commission
How Europe Underdeveloped Africa, 13-14

Index

IADB loans, 362
Ideal Party Member, 227
IFC, 8
Ifill, Max, quoted 98-99, 406
Illuminations, quoted 57
IMF, 8, 13, 22
In and Out of Politics, 58n
Income Distribution and Unemployment, **295-296**
Independence Day Address, **89-92, 266-269** quoted, 89. *See also* Williams, Eric E. POLITICAL THEORY ON; Williams, Eric E. AS ORATOR
India, Congress Party of, 215
Indo-Caribbean peoples, 30
Industrial estates, 378
Industrial Relations Act of 1972, 373
Industrial Stabilization Act, 373
International Conference of Free Trade Unions, 249-251, 415. *See also* sugar, economics of
International Relations, **226-227**. *See also* People's National Movement; Williams, Eric E. POLITICAL THEORY ON
international sport, 309-310
Inward Hunger: The Education of a Prime Minister, 43n, 74, quoted, 44, 49, 77, 102n
Irish Free State, 233
Irish Nationalist Movement, 233
ISCOTT, 378
Is Massa Day Dead?, 95n

Jagan, Dr. Cheddi, 331
Jamaica
  its constitution, 190, 244
  election of 1949, 169-172
  model for PNM, 192, 205. *See also* Manley, Norman; People's National Party in Jamaica
Jamaicans, conference of, 124
Jamaican Sugar Manufacturers, 133
James, C. L. R., 6, 14, 22, 32, 46n, 50n, 52, 57n, 75n, 88n, 98n, 99, 399, 406
  Black Jacobins, The, 14, 15, quoted 17, 333, 338-339, 399
  Capitalism and Slavery, 333-341 *passim*
  on the Caribbean Commission, 341, 342
  on the constitution, 336-337
  on Development Programmes, 344
  and the DLP, 348
  in Marxist debate, 73
  on *Massa Day Done,* 83
  on "Negro Question in the United States," 339
  on People's National Movement, 329
  on political parties, 330
  quoted, 17, 104, 105-106
  relationship with Williams, and his, 71-72, 73
  on slavery, 339
  on *Trinidad Guardian,* 329-330
  Williams, and his appraisal of, 329-351
James, Selma, (mentioned) 74
James, William, 31. *See also* Williams, Eric E. SPEECH MODELED ON
"Jean and Dinah," 75n
Jillian, Teresa, 48n, quoted 47-48
Job, Dr. Morgan, 3-10, 13, 15, 19, 20, 22, 30-31
  quoted, 3
John, George, 406
Johnson, Kim, 6n
Jones, Mr. Creech, 149
Jones, Anthony Mark, 406
Juppy, Mr., and 1889 Franchise Commission, 50

Knibb, Rev. William, 246

labour migration, 243, 262
Lacan, Jacques, 103
Lamming, George, 6, 88, **318-325,** 399
  quoted, 106
Language and the Colonial Subject, **83-88**
Language and the Trinidad and Tobago Experience, **41-51**
Las Casas, Bartolome, Roman Catholic Bishop, 246

427

Laski, Harold, 229
Lee, Grace, collaborator of James
  recollections on Williams, 73-74
Legal System, The, **304-305**
Legislative Council, 190
Levitt, Kari, quoted 10-13
Lewis, Arthur, 73, 138, 205
Lewis, Matthew, absentee landlord, 239
Lincoln, Abraham, 91, 104, 105
  quoted, 264
Lincoln at Gettysburg, 91n, 104n
literacy rate, 374
literary and debating clubs, 43, 44, 47
Little Rock, 252
Lloyd George, David, (mentioned) 130, 350
Locke, John, 31. *See also* Williams, Eric E. SPEECHES MODELED ON
London, Clement B. G., 406
Lopez, Consuelo, thesis "C. L. R. James: Rhetoric of a Defiant Warrior," 69n, 82n
Los Bajos, 360
Loss of El Dorado, The, 20
L'Ouverture, Toussaint, 14, 311
Loyalists in Northern Ireland, 233
Lucky Man, A, **337-338**

MacCabe, Colin, quoted, 80n, 83-88 *passim* on writing history, 64-65
McCloud, Erol, president of OWTU, 13
Magna Carta, 130
Magnum, 21-23, 29
  editorial quoted, 23-24
Mahabir, Winston, 58n, (mentioned) 104, 407
Maharaj, Stephen, 258-259
Maka Fouchette, 101
manifestos
  of 1945 British Tory Party, 174
  of 1949 People's National Party, 169-172
    quoted, 170, 172
  of 1950 regime of Gomes, 67, 172-180 quoted, 173-175
  of 1956 PNM election, 209
  keeping promises of, 181-183. *See also* Gomes, Albert; People's National Party (in Jamaica)

Manley, Michael, (mentioned) 104
Manley, Norman, (mentioned) 104, 132-133, 147-150, 189, 344. *See also* Howard University; My Relations with the Caribbean Commission
Manning, Patrick, 13, 23-26 *passim*
  and divestment, 8-9
  and the PNM, 7-10, 21, 30
  quoted, 7
Maraj, Bhadase, 330, 372
Marin, Munoz, governor of Puerto Rico, 130, 132, 133, 344
Marti, Jos_, 14, 246, 311
Martinique, 311
Massa
  anti-intellectual outlook of
  in Barbados, 244
  and the Canadian Federation, 244
  colonial legacy of, 241-242
  definition of, 239-246, 253
  and economic development, 241-242, 250, 252, 254
  and immigrant workers, 240-243
  in Jamaica, 244
  and power to punish, 241
  and West Indian policies, 242-244, 253, 254, 257
  and workers' wages and lives, 243, 248, 249, 253, 254, 256
Massa Day Done, 5, 64, **77-83, 238-264**
  language of, 84-88
  reception of, 86
Matthews, Dom Basil, 49, 199
Mboya, Tom, (mentioned) 73
medical and dental services, 375
Meet the People Tour, 382
Merquior, J. G., 98n
Metal Industries Company, 378
Methanol Company, 378
metropolitan rule, 322
midnight robber, 38, 105
"Midnight Robber, The," quoted, 38-39
"Mighty Sparrow, The," 88n
Mighty Sparrow, The, "Outcast," 56n
Mighty Sparrow and the PNM, 75
migration of labour, 243, 262
Mill, John Stuart, 125
Milne, Anthony, quoted 6

Index

Milne-Home, Josephine Mary
   quoted, 40n
Mitchell, Nello, (mentioned) 26
Moonilal, Roodal, 44n, 101n
Mortgage Bank, 378
Motivation of the People towards
   Self-Reliance, **291-293**
Mount Hope, 360. See also
   Williams-Connell, Erica
Movement of the People, 21, 73n, 78n
Mudie Commission on Federal Capital
   Site, 209
*My Relations with the Caribbean
   Commission*, 46n, 51, 53, 55,
   57-65, 59 78-79, **112-165**
   audience at, 58. *See also Williams,
   E.: My Relations with the
   Caribbean Commission*
Myalism, 19

Naipaul, V. S.
   Loss of Eldorado, The,
      (mentioned) 95
      quoted 20
   The Middle Passage, 56n
   The Mystic Masseur, 42
Napoleon Bonaparte, 191
*Narrative of Events, since the First of
   August, 1834*, 15
Nation, The, 74, 82, 348
   important role of, 260
   quoted, 91
National Alliance for Reconstruction, 8,
   366 (mentioned), 26
National Anthem, 93n
National Bird, 267
National Coat of Arms, 266, 267
National Commercial Bank, 378
National Energy Corporation, 378
National Fisheries Company, 381
National Flag, 266, 372
National Flour Mills, 378, 380
National Flower, 266
National Gas Company, 378
National Guard, 266
National Slogan, 267
Negro in the Caribbean, The,112-132
   passim, 144

Antigua Star, review of, 116
Colonial Review, The, quoted
   128-129
   sugar planters to, reaction of,
   120-122
West India Committee Circular,
   review of, 116
   Mr. X's reaction to, 115-116, 120
Negro Question in the United States,
   339
*Negro Slavery Described by a Negro,
   Being the Narrative of Ashton
   Warner, a Native of St. Vincent's*,
   15n
Nehru, Jawaharlal, training and
   experience of, 335
Nevins, Professor, 339
New Society, The, 284-285, 292, 293,
   308, 309, **312-316**
New York Herald Tribune,
   review, 114
New York Times, 4n
NIS, 377
Nkrumah, Kwame, (mentioned) 73, 337
   training and experience of, 334
Notes on Dialectics, 73

Observer, quoted 252
O'Halloran, John, 359
Oilfield Workers Trade Union, 13
Olivier's, Lord Sydney Haldane,
   governor of Jamaica
   *White Capital and Coloured
   Labour*, 126
One World, 251
Order of Precedence, 268
Organization of American States, 273
Ortiz, Fernando, 344
Our Special Role, **338-340**
Outline of a Theory of Practice, 47n
Overthrow of Colonial Slavery, 14
Oxaal, Ivar, 75n
Oxford and Cambridge, 251-252
Oxford University, 31, 131
   Magliss, attended meetings of,
   146. *See also* Williams's, Eric E.
   HIS SCHOOLING

429

Padmore, George (mentioned), 73, 74, 104
  training and experience of, 334-335
Paine, Thomas, 99
Panday, Basdeo,
  quoted, 44n, 101
Parris, Carl D., 407
Party and Legislature, **220-221**. *See also* People's National Movement; Williams, Eric E. POLITICAL THEORY ON
Party Development Programme, **231-232**. *See also* People's National Movement; Williams, Eric E. POLITICAL THEORY ON
Party Education, **222-223**. *See also* People's National Movement; Williams, Eric E. POLITICAL THEORY ON
Party Finances, **230-231**. *See also* People's National Movement; Williams, Eric E. POLITICAL THEORY ON
Party Headquarters, **217-218, 324**. *See also* People's National Movement; Williams, Eric E. POLITICAL THEORY ON
Party Member, The Ideal, **227**. *See also* People's National Movement; Williams, Eric E. POLITICAL THEORY ON
party newspaper, 22-23. *See also* Williams, Eric E. POLITICAL THEORY ON
party politics. *See* Williams, Eric E. POLITICAL THEORY
Party Politics in the West Indies, 22, 71n, 74, 88n
  quoted, 83n
PEM. *See* People's Education Movement
People's Charter, The, 73, 93, 272-273, 312, 316, 370, 396. *See also* People's National Movement
People's Education Movement, 47n, 52-53, 412-413, 415, 416, 420
  under Rogers and Donaldson, 2
  words to action, 44-46

People's National Movement, 19, 21, 22, 33, 39, 47n, 73, 74, 75-76, 252, 324-325, 396, 398-399
  and accusations of mismanagement, 355-359
  and the Agriculture Credit Bank, 258
  and Black Power rebellion, 92-95
  on broadcasting, 213
  candidates of, 23
  and the carnival, 309
  and Central Office, 218-221
  and Community Centres, 277
  constitution of, 29
  conventions, 208, 213, 236, 273
  and creative arts center, 306-307, 309
  Crown Lands Programme, 277
  decline of, 83
  development programme, 211-213, 217, 231, 263
  development of Tobago, 278
  DLP contrasted to, 82, 84-85
  and educational reforms, 276-277
  and finance of election campaign, 263-264
  and fundamental law reform, 305
  general secretary, selection of, 29
  Hal Greaves quoted, 24-27
  and handicrafts, 277
  history of, 71-76 *passim*
  and housing programme, 277
  on infrastructure, 278
  on legislature, 220-221
  under Manning, 7-10, 21, 30
  on mass media, 309
  on model for party, 192, 205
  and national culture, 277
  and participatory democracy, 23
  on party newspaper, 208-209, 221-222, 223
  The People's Charter, 272-273, 316
  and planned development, 214-215
  pledge to trade unions, 297-298
  political decline of, 3-10
  on political education, 208, 222-226, 412, 415, 416,, 420

Index

on private enterprise, 212
on public works, 211-212
on religious holidays, 306
and sports, 309-310
and Village Council Movement, 277
and Youth Camps, 277
and Youth Centres, 277. *See also* Williams, Eric E. POLITICAL THEORY ON
People's National Movement Draft Report of the Constitution Review Committee, 29n
People's National Party (in Jamaica), 169-172, 192-194
  manifesto of, 169-172
  quoted, 170, 172. *See also* Jamaica; Manley, Norman
People's National Party of Jamaica, 147
  organization of, 192-193
Pericles, 69, 90, 91, 92, 105
  quoted, 205. *See also* Williams, Eric E. SPEECHES MODELED ON
Perot, Ivan, 370
Persad, Kamal, 4n, quoted 6
Personality of PNM, The **236.** *See also* People's National Movement; Williams, Eric E. POLITICAL THEORY ON
"Perspectives for Our Party," 22, **70-77,** 81, **208-236**
Petroleum and Petrochemicals, 279, 294, 392
Philip, Marlene Nourbese, quoted 36
Phillips, Rev. James, 246
Philosophy, Politics, Autonomy
  quoted, 65, 67
Pierre, Donald, 47
Pierrot, Grenade, 37, 38
"Pierrot Grande," 37, 38n, 105
Pioneer Industries Ordinance, Aid to, 176
Plato's philosophy, 49. *See also* Williams Eric E. SPEECHES MODELED ON
"PNM and the University of Woodford Square: a Historical Record," **412-421**

PNM Go Forth, 22
"PNM miracles," **208-209**
PNM Record, **225.**
PNM Weekly, 30, 74, 82, 208
  quoted, 51
Political Aspects, **281-286**
Political Leader, **228-230.** *See also* People's National Movement; Williams, Eric E. POLITICAL THEORY ON
politics defined, 25-27
Politics of Dr. Eric Williams and the PNM, The, 98-99
Politics of Language, The, quoted, 54, 99-100
"Poly-Tricks vs Politics," quoted 24-27 *passim*
Popular Participation and Totalitarianism, **286**
Populares Party of Puerto Rico, 147
Port-of-Spain Gazette, quoted 131
Portuguese Angola, 252
Preparation for Premiership, **342-343**
presidential pardon, 356n
Princess Margaret, 263
Princess Royal, 266
Priority to the Party, **215.**
private enterprise. *See* People's National Movement
Private Sector, Encouragement of the National, **290-291**
Privileges Bill, 268
Productivity Centre, 378
Promotion of the People's Sector, **293-294**
Pt. Lisas project, 378-379
Puerto Rico, 129, 129-138 passim, 197, 205
Public Sector, The Role of the, **290-291**

Queens Royal College, 71
Question de sociologie, 47

Race and Colour, 305-308. *See also* Williams-Connell, Erica
Racialism, **234.** *See also* Williams-Connell, Erica
radio and television programmes, 299

431

Ragatz, Professor, 336, 340
Rance, Sir Hubert, 200-201
Rance constitution, 200
Rance Report, 201
Rastafarism, 19, 247
Reading Circle, The, 47
Reconstruction, The Task of, 276-279
Red Cross, 375
Regional Economic Committee: Williams's appointment, 201-202. *See also* GATT, London conference on
Regional Public Policy Symposium, 10n
Rent Restriction Bill, 375
Reorganized Central Office, **218-219**. *See also* People's National Movement
Return to the Source, 80
"revolution," connotation of, 273-274
revolutionary song, 96
rice farmers, 380
Richardson, Dr. Elton, 258-259, 407
Rienzi, Cola, 14
Rise of the People's National Movement, 2n, 39, 41, 44-58 passim, 70, 75n, 83. *See also* Rogers, De Wilton
Roberts, Cecil (Churran), 30
Robinson, Cedric J., 407
Rodney, Walter, 6, 13-15, 21, 31, 80, 104, 409
Rogers, De Wilton, 2, 70, 75n, 408
   on decline of People's National Movement, 83
   quoted, 39, 41, 44-58 *passim*
   repudiates Williams, 71-72. *See also Rise of the People's National Movement*
Rohlehr, Gordon, 75n, 95n, 408
Role of Personality, **330-331**
Role of the Party, **314-316**
Role of the People, **283-284**
Role of the Public Sector, The, 290
Roosevelt, Franklin D., 213, 350
Roumain, Jacques, 311
Royal Commission of 1897, 247
   on subsistence wages of sugar workers, 247, 249

Royal Commission of 1910 on commercial relations between Canada and BWI, 249-250
Royal Commission of Inquiry of 1896, 249
rural areas, 211, 279
Rural Development, Urbanization and Unemployment, **300-302**
Ryan, Selwyn, 3n, 5
Ryerson University in Canada, 382

Sagan, Carl, 396
St. Paul, quoted 269
Santa Domingo, 311
Schoelcher, Victor, 246
school feeding programme, 375
School libraries, 374
Schools, Week-end, **225-226.** *See also* People's National Movement; Williams, Eric E. POLITICAL THEORY ON
Sebastien, Raphael, 408
Secretary of State for the Colonies, 190, 195-196, 262. *See also* Colonial Office
Seepaul, Occah, (mentioned) 26
Senate, composition of, 283
Servol, 375
Seukeran, Lionel, quoted 33, 408
Shango, 19
She Tries Her Tongue, 36
Shipping Company of Trinidad and Tobago, 378
Siewah, Samaroo, 44n, 101n
Sininan, Ashford, 252, 256, 258-259, 260
slavery in St Croix, 246
Smith, Olivia, quoted, 54, 99-100
Social and Cultural Aspects, The, 302-310
Solow, Barbara, 408-409
Soulbury Commission, The, 132-133
South Chamber of Commerce, 379
Speaker, The, 268
Stanley, Colonel, Secretary of State for the Colonies, 163-164
   praises *Capitalism and Slavery*, 115
   quoted, 163
Steelband Association, 56-57, 309

Index

steelbands, 383. *See also* People's National Movement
Stock Exchange, 378
Stollmeyers, 247
Subordination of the Party, **214-215**
suffrage, universal adult, 68, 91, 282
suffrage, universal male, 50
sugar, economics of, 121-133 *passim*, 240-241
Sugar Industry Welfare Committee, 376
sugarcane farmers, 255
sugarcane workers
    housing, 255-256
    wages and salaries, 279
Sunday Express, 4n, 6
Sunday Guardian, 9n
Sunday Mirror, 29
Support of People, 336-337
"sweet talk," 40
Sutton, Paul, 409

Tacarigua, 30, 36, 44, 79n
Teachers' Economic and Cultural Association, The forerunner of PEM, 44
T.E.C.A., (mentioned) 47
T&TEC, 379-380
Theory and Practice, **285-286**
Theory and Practice of Creole Grammar, The, 42n
Think Again book-launching of, 5-6
Third Five Year Plan, 277, 288
Third-World countries, meeting of, 272
"This Prophet Deserves Honour," 4n, 6
Thistle Debating Society, 47
Thomas, J. J., 42n, 50
Thomasos, Arnold, 47
Through a Maze of Color, 51, 52n
Times, The, 351
Times Literary Supplement
    review, 114-115
Tobago, development of, 278
Tracking the Signifier, 80n, 83-88 *passim*
trade "liberalisation" policy, 7-14
Trade Unionism and Popular Participation in the Economy, **296-298**

Transformation of Party Press, **221-222**. *See also* People's National Movement; Williams, Eric E.
POLITICAL THEORY
Tringen, 378
"Trinidad and the Revolution in Political Intelligence," 88, 318-325
Trinidad and Tobago Constitution Reform, 183, 189-190, 194-195, 282-283. *See also* Colonial Office; Williams, Eric E. *political theory on*
Trinidad and Tobago, the Caribbean and the Third World, **310-312**
Trinidad and Tobago Chamber of Industry and Commerce. *See* Chamber of Industry and Commerce
Trinidad Country Club, 5-6, 19
Trinidad Guardian, 4n, quoted 8, 80, 329-330, 350-351, 357
    biased reporting of PNM, 259-260
    Canadian ownership, 259, 263
    commitment of, 29
    on Massa Day speech, 238
    on People's National Movement, 21
Trinidad Legislatve Council of 1925, 245
Trinitopec, 8
Trintoc, 8, 378
Truman, Harry S., quoted 191, 213, 385
    quoted, 191
"Two Worlds in Conflict," 80, quoted 50-51

U.C.W.I, The, 340-342
UNESCO, 154
United National Congress, (mentioned) 26
United Nations, 272
United States, 93, 210
United States history on abolition of slavery, 339
Unit Trust, 378
University College in Jamaica, proposed, 246

433

University Commission. *See* University of West Indies
University Council. *See* University of West Indies
University of the West Indies, 127-128, 303-304, 364, 374
Upper House, composition of, 283
Urbanization and Rural Development, **300-302**
Urea Company, 378

Valley, Ken, 8
values and ideologies, **302**. *See also* colonial legacy
VAT, 362-363
Village Council Movement, 277

Wallace, Henry, 126
WASA, 379
Washington, Booker, T., 105, 165, 204. *See also* Williams Eric E. SPEECHES MODELED ON
Washington, George, 228
"We Must Face the Facts, change the Culture". *See* Job, Dr. Morgan
"We Need New Heroes," 14
Week-end Schools, **225-226**. *See also* People's National Movement; Williams, Eric E. POLITICAL THEORY ON
Weld, Theodore, 15
"West Indian, The," 239-240
West Indian Conference, 151-162. *See also* Caribbean Commission; My Relations with the Caribbean Commission
West Indian Federation, 77, 190, 200, 230, 272, 273, 350
West Indian migration, 245, 262
What Kind of Party? **215-217**. *See also* People's National Movement; Williams, Eric E. POLITICAL THEORY ON
What the DLP offers, **232-233**. *See also* Democratic Labour Party; Williams, Eric E. POLITICAL THEORY ON

White Capital and Coloured Labour, 126
WIFLP, 230
Wight, Sir Gerald, 81, 238, (mentioned) 79
Wilkie, Wendell, quoted 251
Williams's Entrance into Trinidad and Tobago's Politics, **51-57**
Williams, Eric E. AUTHOR
  "British West Indies in World History, The," 131
  Capitalism and Slavery, 14, 126-132 *passim*, 333-341 *passim*
  "Colonial at Oxford, A," 335
  Documents Illustrating the Development of Civilization, 398
  Documents in the British West Indies, 73
  "Economic Aspect of the Abolition of the West Indian Slave Trade and Slavery" (thesis), 72, 398
  Education in the British West Indies, 73
  From Columbus to Castro, 95n
  "From Slavery to Chaguaramas," 343
  History of the People of Trinidad and Tobago, 50n
  Inward Hunger: The Education of a Prime Minister, 43n, 74, 398
    quoted, 44, 49, 77, 102n
  Massa Day Done, 5, 64, **77-83, 238-264**
  My Relations with the Caribbean Commission, 46 n, 51, 53, 55, **57-65,** 59, 66, 78-79, **112-165,** 412
  Negro in the Caribbean, The, 112-132 *passim*, 144
  Perspectives of Our Party, 22, 74, 81
  "Two Worlds in Conflict," 50-51. *See also* Selected Bibliography, **401-404**
  AT THE CARIBBEAN COMMISSION
    accused of communism, 145-149
    declined post as Agricultural Economist, 144

Index

headed Research Branch in Trinidad, 137, 398
lacked freedom to write and speak, 115-132, 200-202
opposed by Dutch, 144-145
proposed trade mission vetoed, 140-141
protested against extravagance, 142
Mr. X, 61-62, 115-122, 129, 147, 164

EDUCATIONAL THEORY, 322
abolitionist scholarship, 339
teaching of world literature and history, 341

ORATOR, 41, 54-55, 322, 348
use of cultural symbols, 75, 105
use of language of his people, 40-41, 48
rhetorical style, 48, 59-65, 66-70, 73, 75, 78-82, 84-88, 89-92, 105

PAMPHLETEER, 48, 53-54, 64

POLITICAL THEORY ON,
autonomy, 8-9
the constitution, 194-195, 282
co-operatives, 291, 293
democracy, 89-90, 266-268
demonstrations, 256
diplomacy, 312
elections, 192, 235
employment, 279
federation, 190, 200
honesty in government, 190-191
illegitimacy, 304
independence for the Caribbean, 281-282
international relations, 226-227
international sports, 309-310
land tenure, 304
language and class, 50
liberal capitalism, 280
manifestos, 181-183
Marxism, 280-281
mass media, 299, 300
national identity, 307
national party
for capital and labour, 196
for educational system, 198, 302-304, 311
for industrial and social legislation, 197
for race relations, 198
for religious questions, 198
the *New Society*, 284-285, 292, 293, 308, 309, 312-316
opposition parties, 67-70, 168
paternalism, 292-293
party
discipline, 194
education, 223-226
funds, 193-194
journalists and orators, 222-223, 228
member, the ideal, 227
politics, 183-184
programme, 194-196
records, 225
political education, 186-188, 199
of the people, 199
the political leader, 228
power of a president, 282-283
profit-sharing, 197
protection of textiles, 202
public opinion, 185
public service broadcasting, 187, 213
race relations, 255, 264, 305-310
revolutionary change, 273-276
role of the University, 303-304
sources of income, 191
taxation, 298
technical and vocational education, 278, 301
tourism, 188, 203
Upper House, 283

RELATIONSHIP WITH
audience, 100-102
Caribbean Commission, 112-165
DLP, 82
father, 43
James, C. L. R., 22, 32, 70-75 *passim*, 102-103, 261
Manley, Mr. Norman, 147-150
Mr. X, 61-62, 115-122, 129, 131, 164

435

HIS SCHOOLING
  at Oxford University, 31, 48, 72, 164
  at primary and secondary schools, 43-44, 63, 164, 398
SPEECHES MODELED ON
  Bible, 75-76
  Black Power, 93-95
  Burke, Edmund, 68-70, 91, 105
  Demosthenes, 91
  Dewey, John, 31
  James, William, 31
  Lincoln, Abraham, 91, 105
  Locke, John, 31
  Pericles, 69-70, 105
  Plato, 49
  Washington, Booker T., 105
Williams and the History of Politics, **97-104**
Williams-Connell, Erica, 5, 33, 399
  on accomplishments of PNM, 371-383
  on benefits of arts and crafts, 382-383
  on Citizen's Advisory Bureau, 390
  on commerce, 377-379
  on the Constitution, 377
  on the "dependency syndrome," 392
  on father's legacy, 21
  on foreign buy-outs, 379
  on government practices, 360-364
  on health, 394
  on housing, 375-376
  on influence of television on children, 364-365, 388
  on infrastructure, 383
  on loans to small businesses, 376
  on National Association for Reconstruction, 366
  and oil profits, 358
  on presidential pardon, 359
  on programmes for youth, 375
  on race relations, 363-364, 372
  on role of new for PNM, 365-367
  on self-help programmes, 390
  on standards at the University of West Indies, 364
  on tourism, 383-384

Williams: West Indian, Dr., **343**
Williams's Entrance into Trinidad and Tobago Politics, **51-57**
"William the Conqueror," 88
Williams, James, 15
Wills, Garry, 91n, 104n
women slaves, 36
Women's League, 254, 348
Woodford Square, 5, 46, 53, 67, 263, 323, 384
Woodford Square, University of, 208, 331, 412
Woodson, Carter, 339
"Working Women's Words and the Condition of Their Production(s)," 48
World Bank, 379. *See also* IMF
World Cup Match, facilities for, 360. *See also* Williams-Connell, Erica
World War II and the movement of the masses, 251

X, Mr. of the Caribbean Commission, 61-62, 115-122, 129, 147, 164
  attacks *Negro in the Caribbean, The*, 115-116, 120

"Yankees gone, PNM take over now, The," 75n
Youth Camps, 277
Youth Centres, 277

Zandolee, 101